# The DOWN SYNDROME Transition Handbook

# The DOWN SYNDROME Transition Handbook

## Charting Your Child's Course to Adulthood

*Jo Ann Simons, M.S.W.*

Woodbine House ◆ 2010

All rights reserved under international and Pan American Copyright Conventions. Published in the United States of America by Woodbine House, Inc., 6510 Bells Mill Road, Bethesda, MD 20817, 800-843-7323. www.woodbinehouse.com

**Library of Congress Cataloging-in-Publication Data**

Simons, Jo Ann.
 The down syndrome transition handbook : charting your child's course to adulthood / by Jo Ann Simons. -- 1st ed.
     p. cm.
 Includes bibliographical references and index.
 ISBN 978-1-890627-87-4
 1. Down syndrome--Patients. 2. Children with mental disabilities. 3. Social adjustment. I. Title.
 RJ506.D68S56 2010
 618.92'858842--dc22

2009047424

Manufactured in the United States of America

10  9  8  7  6  5  4  3  2  1

*To my husband, Chet, for your support*

*To my parents, Elaine and Shep, for believing in me*

*To my children, Jon and Emily, for your inspiration*

# Table of Contents

## Acknowledgements

Books do not get written without lots of help. I had lots of help and I want to thank some people. First, I want to thank Woodbine House for accepting my proposal and Susan Stokes, my editor, for providing me with valuable comments and assistance.

I want to give much thanks to both the national organizations for Down syndrome—the National Down Syndrome Society and the National Down Syndrome Congress. Both of these important groups helped me collect some of the pictures of the teens and young adults you see in this book. Rita and Tom O'Neill, Carol Bird, Roberta Wilfand, Carol Bird, Bill Corbett, and scores of other families shared their stories with me so that I could share them with all of you.

Attorney Ken Shulman of Boston and one of the authors of *Special Needs Trust Administration Manual: A Guide for Trustees* reviewed and made valuable suggestions to the chapter on legal issues. Attorney and parent Kathleen Marafino of Syracuse, New York, provided assistance in the chapter on Getting the Most Out of High School.

Stephanie Smith Lee, Senior Policy Advisor of the National Down Syndrome Society's National Policy Center, together with Madeleine Will, Director, provided extensive and current information and edits to the chapter on Postsecondary Education. Stephanie's work contribution made this chapter the most current information yet written.

I could not have even thought of accomplishing the task of writing this book without the encouragement of my employer, at the time I started this book, The Arc of East Middlesex, Inc. The Board of Directors and our staff at the time, especially Paula Vrattos, Susan Ring Brown, Kerry Mahoney, and Michael Berardo, supported my efforts and made sure all was well during my "writing Fridays," vacation days I took that made it possible for me to both work and write.

My current employer, the Cardinal Cushing Centers, Inc., shares with me the passion and vision to create innovative opportunities for individuals with disabilities and their families for meaningful and productive lives. They provide me a place to continue my own professional journey.

Writing this book was a little like taking a vacation. I took many Fridays off from my job to be able to write for two or three days at a stretch. Not that writing is easy, but it was a change in my routine. In the summer, I sat overlooking the ocean from my computer; in the winter I sometimes didn't leave the house after I had come back from my early morning visit to the gym. Come baseball season, I had to fit writing in with Red Sox games. All vacations are good. Even the ones where you don't go anywhere. They give you an opportunity to sleep, replenish, or even write a book.

Last winter, I had a true vacation that provided me with the opportunity for some wonderful travel. But, as I am about to share with you, the issues around transition and disability were never very far away. We spent a few days in Acapulco, Mexico, before boarding a cruise ship for a trip through the Panama Canal. While we were in Mexico, we walked a lot and I often noticed people looking at our son, Jonathan. Maybe I am sensitive, but it seemed like he was a curiosity. Maybe he was, since I didn't notice anybody else with a disability on the crowded boardwalks. On the mobbed beaches, I expected the stares. Jonathan has had open heart surgery three times and has an implanted defibrillator. His chest looks like someone did a poor job of laying railroad tracks down.

The other noteworthy thing about Mexico was that we were constantly barraged by people selling time shares. We learned to look away and say "no, gracias." So, when we went to see the famed cliff divers, I avoided an aggressive timeshare saleswoman. As I walked away, she said, "No timeshare" and she pointed to Jonathan and said, "I have a daughter. She has the same face." She was no longer a pushy timeshare salesperson; she was me. She was you. She was the devoted mother of an eighteen-year-old daughter with Down syndrome. She shared with me that she had raised her daughter by herself and that her daughter went to school and she was worried about the future. She shared with me her love and pride. I gave her my business card and she gave me a life lesson when I least expected it.

As we boarded our cruise ship, I noticed a couple in their seventies pushing a man with significant disabilities in a wheelchair. I presumed he was their son. Seeing this family reminded me of the lifelong commitments that our brave and wonderful families make everyday. It also reminded me of my lifelong and never-ending commitment to Jonathan and that for us, transitions are a journey.

This book would never have been written if it were not for my family. First and foremost, I would like to acknowledge Jonathan, who has been and continues to be my inspiration. I thank my parents, whose unconditional love for me and my family has been demonstrated in so many ways. Throughout the writing of this book, they regularly suggested that I finish early and not to count on getting an extension. Thanks also to my husband, Chet Derr, who really does love pizza and store-bought food; maybe more than my cooking? He let me use his computer to write this book at home, with a big screen and the view of the ocean from his office—even after I wiped out his hard drive a few years ago. Finally, and never least, my thanks go to my daughter, Emily, who, through no choice of her own, became part of this universe of exceptionality, and who really does understand why I do what I do.

# Introduction

*Transition is about planning for the next phase in your child's life. The more informed a family of a transition-aged student with Down syndrome, the more likely that their child will have a successful transition. While transition can take place over a number of years and can begin at various ages, most families begin to think about transition when their child is in high school. Some families start earlier and some start later. Some individuals and their families know instinctively what they want, but most people find the transition period stressful and full of uncertainty.*

*This is a time for natural growth and discovery and a time to try new things and even make some mistakes. Families and those who care about students with Down syndrome will learn that the decisions and choices that are made can be changed or even abandoned. During this period, change is inevitable. Growth, however, is optional.*

This book will help to make the transition from school to adult life easier and perhaps even fun for your child or student with Down syndrome or a related disability. While the term Down syndrome will be used primarily throughout this book, the information will be helpful to families and professionals who are concerned with the transition of students with any intellectual or developmental disability. You will learn a lot about yourself and your child during this journey. Unlike other books, this one was written by a parent-professional. I have lived through my son's transition and survived to write this book. I have also guided hundreds of other families as they sailed through the new waters of transition.

Life is filled with transitions and they bring both worry and rewards. I really believe in the cliché that "when one door closes, another opens." Maybe it is the optimist in me that sees the opportunities and the possibility of growth that come with change. I do, however, recognize that some degree of sadness often accompanies change. I am sure that you can remember a high school graduation, whether your own or a child's. Even though it was a joyous time, there was lots of crying, as kids realized they were leaving familiar friends, teachers, and even communities to strike out on new adventures. As sad as people are at high school graduations, few would want to spend extra time in high school, however. Students are ready to move along the path of independence toward postsecondary education, employment, or military service.

Even if you are feeling sad about your child's school days ending, I want you to be excited about the prospects for his or her future. This is the time to plan for the next part of your child's life. That means you have to recognize your worries and address them. This book will give you tools and information to address your worries about the future, including employment, housing, funding, friendship, family relationships, and having fun.

Unlike other transitions, the transition from school to adult life does not take place on a specific day. It is not like graduation day or the day you got your driver's license. You don't have to make decisions on a specific schedule. It doesn't matter if your child is 8, 18, 29, or even 38. This book is designed for any family who is looking to guide their child on the road to adulthood. It does not matter where on that road you or your child might be.

Professors and parents Rud and Ann Turnbull, cofounders and co-directors of the Beach Center on Family and Disability and two of my personal heroes, once said that "parenting a child with a disability is a marathon and not a sprint." I am often reminded of their wise words whenever I want a quick resolution to an issue about my son, Jonathan. I want to borrow their words and alter them to tell you that the "transition from school to adult life for a student with Down syndrome is like an Ironman Triathlon." It takes gathering information, training, endurance, perseverance, resolve, and resources. This book will give you the information, but the rest will be up to you.

My interest in the subject began when I began considering my son Jonathan's adult future. It was hard to imagine him as an adult and it was even harder to imagine me letting him become an adult.

> One "snow day" when Jon was 14, I wanted him to come to work with me instead of staying home alone. He did not want to come with me and said, "I am growing up." Then he placed his hands on my shoulders and said, "I know this is hard for you, but I am not your little boy anymore." So, I had to take the big step and let him stay alone.

I realized when my son was very young that he was going to be an adult for a lot longer than he was going to be a child and I needed to pay attention to that. I was still concerned with his education, but I became consumed by his long-term future. I did lots of research and began to share my experiences with other families.

There are many books, resources, and websites that offer information about the transition from school to adult life for individuals with disabilities. I am not aware of one that specifically addresses Down syndrome and related disabilities, however. Most transition guides are written by professionals and individuals with many university degrees. I wanted to write one that was real, down-to-earth, and friendly and that incorporates what I have learned through guiding individual families and groups of families through the transition process.

As I began to address audiences of families and professionals throughout the United States and in several foreign countries, I was continually told that my frankness and honesty was refreshing. I often received notes and emails from families who had attended my workshops and they reported on the positive steps they had taken as a result of listening to me. I continued to tell families real stories of real people and share important strategies and suggestions with them. They, in turn, shared their stories with me. My husband, Chet Derr, often told me I should write a book so I could help even more families. I did not think I could possibly find the time to write a book, so I let the suggestion pass until I realized that there would never be enough time. Now seemed as good a time as any to make the time.

You have been told many times that you are the expert when it comes to your child and it is still true. You have been your child's best teacher and most knowledgeable guide. Your role doesn't change now; there are just new areas to explore. You will always be the parent, but now you may have the opportunity to become a guide, mentor, teacher, advocate, and advisor. At the same time, your child will be increasing his or her levels of independence and competency. You will learn to begin letting go.

You can use this book in several ways. You may want to read it cover to cover or you may find it more useful to just read the chapters that you have a current interest in. Perhaps you are the kind of person who is engaged by stories and anecdotes and finds long stretches of text boring. I included lots of interesting (I hope) examples of real families and real individuals with Down syndrome for readers like you. If you like, you can just read the stories in the boxes and you will still get a lot out of the book. In some cases, names and other identifying characteristics have been changed.

# What Is Transition All About?

When most typical students are finishing high school, they are asked "What are you doing next year?" There are basically only three options—work, the military, or college. Students who choose work or the military either visit a military recruiter or pick up the help wanted section of the newspaper. There are not many roles for parents whose children choose these options.

If college is the next step, there are many potential roles for parents to play. Or not. While some parents play an active role in the college process, many other families leave the whole process to the student. These families are either not able to provide support or believe that this process is a good opportunity for the student to begin her journey to independence.

For the active family or student, there is much to consider. Often the college process begins way before high school. Children may be pushed to excel at sports or in the arts in order to be attractive to college admission officers. Later they are encouraged to take as many advanced courses as possible, do well on admission tests, have unusual summer experiences, and provide needed community service. Families often describe the college process as overwhelming.

I have been through the college admission process. It is long, expensive, and often disappointing. You wonder: Should my child repeat the SAT? How many colleges should she apply to? Do we need to visit them all? Do we hire a writing coach for the admission essay? Who do we know at her first choice school who can put in a good word? Should she apply early decision? What will happen if she doesn't get into her dream school? The truth is, our children often do not get into their first choice of a college and they survive. It takes a bit longer for parents to get over the disappointment.

Many families report that despite the stress of having a child apply to college, there were some very positive aspects of the process. For some families, poring over college catalogs or taking virtual university tours are purposeful activities to do together. Others speak fondly about the new bonds with their children that are created taking trips to visit colleges. I enjoyed this activity so much that my daughter and I visited colleges whenever I could combine a business trip with a college trip. We visited way more colleges than were necessary, but the opportunity to spend time with my daughter at this point in her life was something I knew I wanted to do. I knew that soon she would be gone and I would never have this time again.

The college process can create chaos in families. It is also different for every family.

You will experience many of the same stresses and ups and downs with the transition of your child with Down syndrome. The biggest difference is that we have built an industry around some common events and given it special names. We have made it more confusing for families than it should be. Rather than just asking, "what are you doing next year?" we call it transition.

The most important thing you can do is be involved in your child's transition. You will have to understand the adult service system and take an active role in transition planning. The more you know, the more likely there will be a positive outcome for your child.

# Common Hurdles

Families of transition-aged students with Down syndrome have shared many of their stories and concerns with me. What I have heard is that families want more information and they want it in time to be useful. They often do not understand the difference between services that they are *entitled* to receive—like special education—and services for which there are no entitlements—like adult services. ("Adult services" is the catch-all term used to describe supports such as job coaching, specialized transportation, housing and residential supports, day services, and other services that most adults with developmental disabilities need to have successful and purposeful lives.)

Many families are aware of the need to create a meaningful life and may have participated in some sort of exercise that creates a vision for their child. They are not, however, prepared for a system that does not have the financial resources to assist them in making the vision a reality. Families are further frustrated about the inequities that exist within states and between states and struggle to understand why some students get services and supports and others do not.

Families recognize that there is a priority system and waiting lists for services, but want a systemized and transparent approach to the allocation of resources. For far too many families, it seems that "the squeaky wheel" family gets the services. Families want providers who will be creative and provide innovative, quality supports. Far too many providers, when asked by families to do something different or try something new, are told: "It's not how we do things" or "You are not realistic." Families also want service providers and governmental agencies to be respectful of their culture and provided in their native language. Families want to see that "partnerships" can be real and built on mutual respect.

Many families are frustrated by the success stories of individuals with Down syndrome who can easily work, live independently, drive, and marry that are featured at our conferences and in our media. They want a system that will provide innovative services to individuals who require more intensive supports to achieve their vision.

This book won't create better systems for providing transition services or change fiscal realities. It will, however, make you more informed and put you in a better position to change the transition experience for your child or student. It is also my hope that you will feel empowered to work to change policy decisions and budget allocations in your state. It is important to understand that you have the power to make changes and to get what you want.

# My Personal Learning Curve

I am not a college professor sitting in an ivory tower and this is not a textbook. I graduated from Wheaton College in Massachusetts, and, rather than spend a year abroad, I spent my junior year in Connecticut at Trinity College. I went right to graduate school and received my Master's degree in Social Work from the University of Connecticut. I was interested in organizations and policy and could see myself working on any number of issues. I got married right out of graduate school and a year later, we were expecting our first child. Since up until that point, my life seemed to be going according to my plan, I figured this baby would do the same. The baby would be born, I would continue to work, and the baby would grow up to go to an Ivy League school and perhaps be a Rhodes Scholar. Maybe an Olympic athlete. Like most expectant parents, I had big dreams.

As it turned out, Jonathan did not go to an Ivy League college and he is not a Rhodes Scholar. He, as I've already mentioned, was born with Down syndrome, and, like 40 percent of our children, he also was born with a heart defect. He actually was born with four of them (Tetrology of Fallot). I was so stunned and hurt when he was born that I never put any Ivy League or any other college shirts on him. In the beginning, I was mourning all the things I thought I had lost.

Jonathan had his heart corrected and assorted other medical conditions addressed, went to school and summer camps, played in Little League and other youth sports, and graduated high school. He received a postsecondary education at the Riverview School and Cape Cod Community College, where he bought his own college shirt. Along the way, he was third in the world in Special Olympics Golf and was inducted into the National Jewish Sports Hall of Fame. He moved into a house with a roommate, moved out and into his own house with a roommate, and then decided he didn't want a roommate. He has worked at some jobs just for the friends he made there or for the paycheck. He has also worked at some jobs he loved.

Jon has had girlfriends, but has never had his heart broken. His passion is sports. He is a lucky man; he has already seen eight world championships in his Boston lifetime—three for the Celtics, three for the New England Patriots, and two for the Boston Red Sox. He has never missed watching Wrestlemania and can tell you the match-ups of every one of them. He has a rich social life that includes friends and family. He loves to travel and is currently trying to taste every beer of the world. He keeps track of this feat in one of his several beer books. He is making more progress than I might want.

This did not all just happen. It took lots of planning and coordination. Lots of my own kind of research and perseverance. You see, after Jonathan was born, I figured that the life I planned was not actually going to happen. I had to plan another life and I decided to take what appeared to be my life's greatest challenge and make it into an opportunity. As I found out later, there is even a term for that. It is called "reframing" and it has served me well. I take a challenging situation and reframe it and make it into something more positive. It is a coping strategy that sometimes drives my family crazy. I was so passionate about making Jon's life meaningful, after an initial period of negativity, that, I realized, Jon's life would be meaningful if my life was meaningful.

Jon's birth launched my career. Within twelve weeks of his birth, he was the first infant with Down syndrome in day care at the North Shore Jewish Community Center in Marblehead, MA, and I was working. After a few months, I managed to talk my way into a position with the Massachusetts Department of Mental Retardation. Not long after, I changed jobs and I helped to establish a comprehensive family support program at the North Shore Arc. After two more stints in state government, I become the Executive Director of the Arc of East Middlesex, a position I held from 1993 until 2008. I am now the President/CEO of the Cardinal Cushing Centers of Massachusetts, where I finally have the opportunity to create a campus-based transition program that is ideal for students with Down syndrome. (It includes attendance at a local community college.)

At every one of these positions, I have had supervisors and Board members who have supported every path I took. I served the National Down Syndrome Congress as President, helped establish the Massachusetts Down Syndrome Congress, and I serve on the Board of the National Down Syndrome Society. I have been on the Board of Special Olympics, Inc, and served as an advisor to their Healthy Athlete Program, a program I helped envision. I have consulted to the State of Hawaii and I have spoken in Ireland, Northern Ireland, Japan, Canada, and Guatemala, and in many states about issues of concerns to families of people with Down syndrome.

Every parent of older children I have spoken to, no matter where, has the same questions and concerns. Most of them fall into two categories. What happens when my child with Down syndrome leaves school? And, what happens when I am no longer here?

To address the latter concern, staff from The Arc of East Middlesex and I created a form called "Footprints for the Future." This easy-to-use document, which can be freely downloaded at www.theemarc.org, is a special form that enables you to record information about your child and your expectations and directions for both today and in the future. You do not have to lie awake at night wondering how you will convey all that you know about your child to caregivers. They will know everything you know. This form is not protected by copyright, so you can copy it to your hard drive, a CD, or save it on a flash drive. In the future, when you need to make a change, you can easily make the change.

To address the issue of what would happen when my child finished school, I gathered lots of information. I began thinking about it years before Jonathan would finish school. I summarized some of this information in a brief article for the Arc of Massachusetts and then in an article for *Disability Solutions*. At about the same time, I began giving workshops on the topic, which have become increasingly well attended. At the conclusion of one of those workshops, Dr. Dennis McGuire of the Adult Down

Syndrome Clinic at Advocate General Hospital in Illinois told me that I ought to consider writing a book based on my workshop. Fortunately for me, the good people at Woodbine House agreed.

I do what I do for Jon, but I wrote this book for you. Like your child does for you, my son brings me more joy and happiness than I could ever have hoped to receive. I summed up my feelings one May in a column I wrote for the newsletter of the Arc of East Middlesex. (See box below.)

## Mother's Day Musings

If you are a mother, you probably remember your first Mother's Day. The one when you were actually a mother. You were no longer just a daughter or wife. You might not remember the actual day. I don't. I do remember the circumstances that made me a mother. I become a mother just a few days after Mother's Day in 1979 when my first child, Jonathan, was born. It wasn't what I anticipated. He was born with Down syndrome and 4 heart defects. Every year, he reminds me with this affirmation, "I made you a mother." He continues with "I made you a mother and I made Nana and Pa grandparents." And something else.

He made me much more than that. He made me strong so I could stand tall next to the physicians and surgeons whose life his hands were in. He made me trust those same doctors. He made me strong so I could refuse to take him home from Children's Hospital upon his birth until someone from their Down syndrome program came to speak to me.

He made me persistent so I could spend countless hours prodding and cajoling a day care center to accept him at 12 weeks and a summer camp when he was three. He made sure I was still persistent in convincing an overnight camp to let him be the only camper with a disability.

He made me an advocate so I could articulate the needs of persons with developmental disabilities to legislators, members of Congress, and even Presidents.

He made me hopeful for a society where every member has value and worth.

He made me proud when he stole home on a wild pitch in Little League and was third in the world in golf in Special Olympics. He made me proud when he graduated from high school and went on to community college.

He made me strong so I could be there for him during 4 heart operations, endless other hospitalizations, and when I had to tell him he had to wear hearing aids and not go on carnival rides. He amazed me when he accepted all the curve balls life has thrown him.

When he was 13, he went with me to a bowling banquet for some of our residents from the Arc's group home. When I came back to the table where he and his sister were sitting, he said something that stunned me. He said, "You do this work because of me, don't you?" It was a moment of great honesty because he would now be able to relate himself to a group of adults with developmental disabilities. So, I told him, "Yes, I do this because of you."

So, now for that something else. On every Mother's Day, he reminds me that he made me a mother *and he gave me my career.* I couldn't ask for better Mother's Day gifts.

\*\*\*

Recently someone gave me a bumper sticker. I think it was meant to mock all those bumper stickers that brag about kids making the honor roll. This one says, "My kid has more chromosomes than yours." I couldn't be prouder.

I wish someone had told me when Jonathan was born, as he did when he was 19, to just "get over it." I wish I had known that I would worry about college, drinking and driving, sexual relationships, and sibling rivalry. I wish I had known that crossing the midline and mean length of utterances would not be good predictors of his ability to become a successful adult.

Jon began seizing every opportunity to be independent when he was in high school. He resented my meddling; and his sister's bossiness and his father's silliness were sometimes embarrassing. He was a teenager on the brink of leaving home and he began emotionally trying to separate. One day, he walked out of the door and into the car of a classmate for a ride to school at 7:30 a.m. He told us that he planned to study in the cafeteria after school and that he would be going by bus to the boys' basketball game at 4:30, as he was the manager. He said he would need a ride home from school at 10 p.m. For those of you not good at math, it was going to be over 14 hours from my telling him to "have a good day" to the time when I would see him again. (This was before the age when kids had cell phones.) To be sure, he had done this before, but it did not stop me from wondering all day if he would make it to the bus, if he would have money for a drink, if he would get something to eat, and, most importantly, if he would be on the bus when it returned. That day went off without a hitch.

The next day presented Jon with another opportunity to show me how capable he was of managing his own activities. It was the first day of mid-term exams, so the buses weren't operating on their usual schedule. I called home from work to see if he had arrived. I listened to the messages and heard Jon say, "Well, I guess nobody is home. I am going to walk." I called home an hour later and Jon answered the phone. I asked him how he got home and he said, "Sawyer's dad." "You mean Sawyer from the basketball team?" I asked. "Yeah," was his reply.

That's when I told him how proud I was of his independence, but that it was hard for me to watch him grow up and let him go. In typical teenager fashion, he told me: "You need to get over it."

You know that Ivy League shirt I was afraid to put on Jonathan? He has about a dozen of them now, along with jackets and hats. He proudly wears the Big Red colors of Cornell, where his sister received both her undergraduate and law degrees. Looking at college T-shirts does not make me sad any longer. And it makes Jon swell with pride over his sister's accomplishments.

# Keep Following the Cheese

While I was writing this book, I read a popular book that held some important lessons for me related to the business of transition. It may be helpful to you in establishing a framework for how you will look at all the changes that will be occurring in the years ahead. You may have already read the book *Who Moved My Cheese?* by Spencer Johnson, MD, since it has been a bestseller on many book lists and has more than 100 million copies in print.

The book uses a short and simple story to illustrate some basic principles regarding change. Two pairs of mice are used to represent two different ways that we humans respond to change. The mouse pairs are named "Hem and Haw" and "Sniff and Scurry." One pair refuses to recognize that things have changed (in this case, their cheese has moved), and, rather than adapting, just waits for things to get back to normal. The other pair, recognizing that the cheese has moved, goes looking for new cheese. There are many other valuable lessons in the book, but that is it in a nutshell.

You need to decide now whether you are going to fight the changes ahead or embrace them. The point you need to come back to often during the transition from school to adult life is that all the cheese has moved. Nothing is going to stay the same. Just like the mice, the sooner you understand, adjust, and celebrate the opportunities that change can bring, the more successful these times will be.

You are going to become an expert in the transition process—I promise. It is not as overwhelming as all the books and professionals want you to believe. It just involves new language and new concepts. Much like when you began the journey into the world of Down syndrome and disability, you will probably hit some rough spots, but you will definitely rise to meet the challenges.

# CHAPTER 1

# Transition—What's It All About?

*How do you actually begin to think about transition for individuals with Down syndrome? We will examine what it means for typical students to transition and even think of our own transitions. This is a period for natural growth and discovery and a time to try new things and even make some mistakes. You will learn that while these decisions seem so very important, the decisions and choices can be changed, altered, and even abandoned. Nothing about the transition from school to adult life is irreversible.*

*Transition takes a lot of planning and there are many ways to start. The family of a transition-age student with Down syndrome (beginning at about age 14 and continuing throughout adulthood) needs to take an inventory of their knowledge level of available opportunities and possibilities early in the process. While some individuals and their families know instinctively what they want, most people find this time to be confusing and stressful.*

*Various planning tools and options are presented in a simple format and discussed. The planning tools have different names (Person Centered Planning, Whole Life Planning, Future Planning, etc.), but they all share the common element of assisting families and individuals to identify their goals and dreams.*

The transition to adult life can start as early as you want. For some families, it began in the first months after the birth of our child with Down syndrome, when we began to worry about his or her future. Some people say transition ends when your child, as an adult, takes control over his own life and decisions. I do not believe it ever ends. My sweet 85-year-old father still expects me to call and report to him about every take-off and landing of every plane flight of every member of our family. He worries when I am out late at night and driving home alone. His worries about my son Jonathan could fill volumes, and it is only recently that he can imagine Jonathan growing older and being safe and loved, when he might not be around to ensure it. It means he finally trusts my husband and me to properly watch over Jonathan.

I just this moment got off the phone with my son, who, in taking control over his life, drank six beers this week and had just returned from the liquor store with another six-pack. Sometimes taking control means making decisions that might not be healthy. I am sure that some of you reading this paragraph smoke cigarettes, even though you know it might kill you and take you away from your children, or worse, require your children to care for you. We all need support and tools to make better decisions.

I suggested to Jon that he take the six-pack out of the refrigerator and put it out of sight and save the two beers that are left in his refrigerator for the New England Patriots game on Sunday. I know he listened to me. I do not know if he took my suggestion. That is the hardest part of transition. Letting go. It means letting your child make some bad decisions. The alternative is to maintain such control over your adult child's life that he misses the joys and disappointments of his own successes and failures.

## Steps in Transition

Webster's dictionary defines transition as: "a passing from one condition, form, stage, activity, place, etc. to another." During transition, the vast majority of students with Down syndrome are passing *out of* high school. The activities and places that they are passing *into* are more varied. That is, there is no one set destination point for young adults with Down syndrome.

Part of the transition process involves choosing the activities and places that are most appropriate for an individual student to transition to. Chapter 2 explains in detail what must be planned for during the transition period under the Individuals with Disabilities Education Act (IDEA). In general, however, the goal of the transition planning process is to determine: 1) where the person will live, 2) what he will do after he leaves high school, 3) what types of skills he can learn, and 4) what assistance he will need to be as independent as possible.

## A Year-by-Year Overview of Crucial Steps

The Arc of East Middlesex and The Arc of Massachusetts put together a Fact Sheet on Transition which contains a brief overview of what to do at the various stages of your child's transition. It is a basic guide to much of what is contained in more detail in the rest of the book. I have made some additions and modifications to it based on my experiences and the experiences of others.

## Steps in Transition

**Age 13, 14, and 15**

- Talk about the value of work and teach behaviors that develop employment potential.
- Provide opportunities to see people at work in different settings.
- Allow as much independence as possible; assign responsibility for certain chores to help instill a positive work ethic.
- Promote appropriate behavior at home and in social situations.
- Provide opportunities to make choices and decisions, to explore and take risks, and to learn from experiences of success and failure.
- Assist in good grooming skills and emphasize the importance of physical fitness.
- Think about volunteer job opportunities in the community, paper routes, or other ways to develop job skills.
- Continue the above activities throughout the teen years.
- Consult a lawyer and financial advisor with expertise in individuals with disabilities about a special needs trust.
- Ensure that functional math and reading skills that will lead to more independence are being taught.
- Make sure that communication continues to be emphasized at home and at school, and that speech therapy or assistive devices are provided, if necessary.

**Age 16**

- Encourage self-advocacy skills in your child.
- Develop a long-term plan (5 years) to cover educational, vocational, and independent living skills.
- Be sure your child's IEP addresses all the areas where skills are needed.
- Have your child attend IEP meetings.
- Consider a first job experience for your child if he is not already working.

**Age 17**

- If you are planning to apply for Social Security Insurance (SSI), get information about eligibility from your local Social Security office. (You can find your local office at www.ssa.gov.) Students who have assets exceeding $2,000 are not eligible for SSI benefits (see Chapter 6). Consult an attorney or financial planner about a special needs trust or other arrangement that will protect eligibility for benefits.
- Investigate the possible need for guardianship and other options for legal protection. In the United States, all people are presumed to be legally competent to make all life decisions once they reach the Age of Majority. The Age of Majority is currently 18 in all states, except in Alabama and Nebraska, where it is 19, and in Colorado, Mississippi, and Pennsylvania, where it is 21. Guardianship is a legal procedure requiring a clinical evaluation and a petition to the probate court. Not all individuals need to have a guardian, and less intrusive alternatives are preferable. These include power of attorney, health care proxy, and conservatorship (see Chapter 3). **Responsible party: family/student.**

(continued on next page)

## Steps in Transition *(continued from previous page)*

### Age 18

- Apply for SSI and/or SSDI and Medicaid. If your child is eligible for SSI, he will automatically be eligible for Medicaid. If not eligible for SSI, apply separately for Medicaid. **Responsible party: student/family.**
- Register to vote. **Responsible party: student/family.**
- Apply for an extension of your private health insurance to continue child's coverage, if available.
- Determine your child's eligibility for adult services through the appropriate state agency that is responsible for adult services for people with mental retardation or developmental or intellectual disabilities. **Responsible party: state agency.**
- Obtain an official picture identification card for your child from the appropriate state licensing agency, usually the motor vehicle department. The importance of this step cannot be overstated. No individual over the age of 18 can board a commercial airline flight without a government-issued picture ID. **Responsible party: family/student.**
- Males must register for Selective Service. **Responsible party: family/student.**

### Age 20

- By age 20 (or 2 years prior to terminating special education, and this will vary by state and by personal circumstances) make sure a referral for adult services is made. The school special education administrator should initiate a referral to the appropriate human service agency that will support your child as an adult. Your child may have to go through an eligibility determination. **Responsible party: human service agency(s)/student/family/school.**
- Begin to visit adult service providers in your area.
- Create a resume or portfolio of your child's work (writing samples, drawings, list of positive attributes, etc.) and a list of references. **Responsible party: school/family/student.**

### Age 21

- Begin the process to identify a new primary care physician who cares for adults to replace your adult child's pediatrician.
- Submit an application to Section 8 waiting lists for a federally funded affordable housing voucher 1-2 years before you anticipate your child will need a voucher.

It is your responsibility as parents to make sure that your child progresses through all the steps in the transition process. Do not make the mistake of waiting for the school or some state or local agency to guide you through this process. While the school has legal responsibilities to provide transition services under IDEA, as discussed in Chapter 2, you must be ready and willing to take the initiative.

*Unless otherwise noted, it is the family's responsibility to make sure these steps are accomplished at home or school.*

# Having a Vision

Having a vision is different from having a plan. A plan is a series of clear and identified steps. This book will help you with developing many different kinds of plans that may be helpful in making transitions. A vision is a statement of what you (and your child) want. The plan helps you get there.

You probably had a vision for your own life. This vision might or might not have been shared by your parents. My aunt has a saying when she talks about her adult children. When asked about her boys and their accomplishments, she says, "It's not  what I would have written in their baby books." So it is for most of us. My parents are very proud of me and I know that. But, I also know that they had a different vision for my life. Most importantly, they supported my version of the vision.

It can be very helpful to begin the process of transition planning for your child with Down syndrome by having a vision for him. It is important, however, that your child actually drive the development of his vision.

My vision for Jonathan began really broadly: I wanted him to have a full life. I wanted him to be safe from exploitation and I wanted him to have meaningful days. I wanted him to be healthy and surrounded by people who respected him.

But, after I involved Jonathan in the process, the vision became more meaningful. A vision is not stagnate. It must grow and change as the individual grows and changes.

As the years have passed with Jonathan, we have learned that *our* vision is for him to work year-round. *His* current vision is that he is quite satisfied and pleased with his seasonal career in golf operations on a golf course in a New England state.

While the vision for your child can be broad, as in "I want Sara to have a meaningful life," it is more helpful if you involve your son or daughter in developing a series of short and specific sentence that complement your broad vision. Ideally, you should end up with statements that cover:

1. how your child would like to spend his days once he leaves high school;
2. where he would like to live;
3. who he wants to live with; and
4. other broad areas.

The box below lists some possible vision statements to get your child thinking. You may use these to start a conversation with your child or use some of your own to create a vision statement.

If your child has difficulty expressing himself or is not verbal, make sure that he has the opportunity to express his desires in other ways, such as by pointing to pictures that show his preferences. You might want to make a list of the situations where he was most happy or expressed the most joy. For example, if your son is most happy when he is swimming, you might want to make sure that swimming becomes a high priority activity and it is part of his daily life. Although swimming might not

## Vision Statements

- I want to work with animals or children.
- I want to work in an office, on a golf course, etc.
- I want to have friends to hang out with.
- I want to live in an apartment.
- I want to be part of my religious community.
- I want to learn to get around my community (bus, cab, family, staff).
- I want to be healthy.
- I want a boyfriend/girlfriend.
- I want to learn to cook.
- I want to spend time with my family.
- I want to move out of my parents' house.
- I want to go on vacations every year.
- I want to learn to drive.
- I want competent staff to assist me.
- I want to be safe.
- I want a pet.
- I want to go to college.

seem like it's that important, it provides exercise, the use of community resources, an opportunity to practice dressing skills and showering, and it brings him joy and gives meaning to his life.

The Person-Centered Planning process described below can also help ensure that the individual with Down syndrome is able to contribute to developing his own vision.

**WHAT IS REALLY IMPORTANT**

There are some things that may be so important to the future of your child that you and he will not be not willing to compromise on them. Some people call these "nonnegotiable." Do not worry if you and your child don't have a long list of nonnegotiable things, as some people are just more flexible than others. While some people have rather strong feelings, others do not.

If you are getting stuck with this exercise, skip ahead to Chapter 12 and the section on "The Family's Role in Ensuring Quality" for more ideas about what to include in your vision statement.

## Really Important Things

- I need to be part of my religious community.
- I do not want to live where there is lots of traffic.
- I want to pick my roommate or live alone.
- I want to be near public transportation.
- I have to live with my family.
- I must be treated with respect.
- My support staff and family must respect my decisions.

# Who Can Help You Plan for Transition?

**HELP WHILE YOUR CHILD IS IN SCHOOL**

While your child is in school, IDEA requires that the school help you with the transition process in certain specified ways. Under the law, this assistance must begin the year your child turns 16, but some states require that it begin earlier, often at age 14.

Chapter 3 goes into detail about the transition services schools are required to provide. In general, however, you should know that these services will be based on your child's transition goals. As in the past, your child will be entitled to related services based on the goals that are chosen for him. Some of the people who provide these related services will be school system employees with specialties that are already familiar to you. For example, your child might need the services of a speech-language pathologist to help him improve his speech intelligibility on the phone—if that is one of his transition goals.

You might want to invite individuals who work outside the school system to be part of your child's transition team, depending on his needs and goals. For example, someone from the state or county department of vocational rehabilitation might be part of the team if they have job training your child could benefit from, or a representative from an adult service agency might be invited if the team is discussing skills your child needs to work on to live in a certain type of setting they offer.

A case manager/service coordinator from the adult service agency may be assigned to oversee your child's transition plan. If someone is not assigned, you should request it. This individual should assist in making your child's transition from high school into the adult service system easier.

## HELP AFTER YOUR CHILD LEAVES SCHOOL

While your child is still in school, he will be *entitled* to transition services and guidance from the IEP team. Once your child ages out of school or graduates, he is no longer automatically entitled to any services. (See Chapters 2 and 6 on legal and financial issues.) Most young adults with Down syndrome, however, do qualify for services and supports from adult service agencies, based on their level of disability.

Unfortunately, being eligible is not the same as receiving services. It doesn't mean that the services are necessarily available when you need or want them in the transition process. There are long waiting lists for adult services in many parts of the country. Waiting lists get longer and services scarcer in challenging economic times.

There can also be vast differences between what you think your adult child needs and what the funding agency thinks he needs. A good example is in the area of supervision. You may be unwilling to leave your son alone, but during interviews, observations, and testing, it is determined that your son, with some training, can stay alone for a few hours a day. You may not like the idea, but unless you can back your objections up with something more than your "mother's instinct" (e.g., he set the house on fire or let a stranger into the house), you may not get what you want. Instead, your son may receive what he needs.

When adult services/supports are available, they can include:

- service coordination, including arranging, coordinating, and monitoring the services your child receives;
- individual supports (e.g., assistance with food shopping, cooking, money management, household skills);
- day supports, include assistance with communication and self-help skills, community involvement, and relationship building;
- employment supports (e.g., job development, job coaching, job training, transportation);
- community residential supports, include supervision or assistance with community living skills and daily living skills;

- facility supports (assistance for those placed in residential care in the large, institutional settings which do still exist in many states);
- family supports, including education, training, or cash subsidies for parents;
- Respite care for families.

## Services and Supports

While it might seem like semantics, there is an important philosophical difference between the words "services" and "supports." The word "services" conveys the message that the individual is in need of services, whether they be academic, vocational, or any other service. It also includes the idea that there is an agency that determines and dictates those services. At its core, that agency has a belief in the role of the agency as important to the success of the individual.

The word "supports," on the other hand, implies that the individual is at its core. It presumes that the individual and his or her family know what they need, rather than the agency, or other provider, knowing what the individual needs. Supports are then offered.

If you have not thought about these differences before, think about your own use of services vs. supports. If you are receiving services, you are getting what is offered. Even in the most positive situation, like a day spa, you must pick from a predetermined menu of services that others think you should want or need. On the other hand, suppose the same day spa (if they were not really only interested in making money) asked you how they could support your needs. You might get a very different array of opportunities.

That is our goal for individuals with Down syndrome—for each person to be seen separately and distinctly from anyone else and to get the supports he wants.

# The Role of State Agencies in Providing Adult Services

Most providers of adult services are not state agencies. Instead, state agencies in most states provide the funding and sometimes the service coordination. They contract out the actual delivery of services. Again, some of these agencies may be involved in your child's transition plan while he is still in school, or you may not have any dealings with them until after your child graduates.

State agencies are public agencies. They are complex and seem to have many layers of bureaucracy. Each state has a mental retardation or developmental disability agency (MR/DD), which will be the primary state agency that provides funding for your adult child. (Note that these agencies may also be referred to as intellectual/developmental disability agencies—I/DD.) In some but not all states, this agency also serves families of younger children. For example, it may provide family support services or some service coordination. As an adult, your child may also receive services

## The Importance of Language

In most cases, if it is yellow and quacks, it is a duck—unless, that is, you are speaking about the importance and power of language that describes people with disabilities. If you have a child with Down syndrome, you could use that label, Down syndrome, and not have to be involved in the larger discussion of intellectual disability. However, the term Down syndrome is unlikely to serve you completely since our children are involved in school, work, and community life with people of various ability levels and various diagnoses.

Although there are valuable national organizations, such as the National Down Syndrome Society and the National Down Syndrome Congress and their affiliated parent groups, there is no state agency in any state that is devoted solely to individuals with Down syndrome. We are part of the larger community of intellectual disability. So this section on language is intended to get you up to speed on the language you will encounter, if you aren't already.

I am sure that most of you have used the terms "idiot" or "moron." You might have even called yourself an idiot after taking a wrong turn or leaving the oven on when you left the house. You probably never gave it a second thought. However, at the beginning of the last century, the terms "feeble-minded," "idiot," "moron," and "imbecile" were actual medical terms that were used to describe people with a below average IQ. Each term was associated with an IQ range.

As those terms became offensive, the terms "educable" and "trainable" were developed by educators to differentiate between students who they thought were capable of being taught basic academic skills and those who could only be trained to complete simple tasks. Children with Down syndrome, because of their identifiable facial features, were routinely trotted off to the trainable classrooms. There, regardless of their potential, they were taught to dress and feed themselves, while more typically appearing peers were given the opportunity to learn to read and do simple math.

Then there was the age of labeling people by the skills they might be able to acquire, and we used "vocational," "prevocational," "basic skills," and "sensory stimulation." In reality, they were IQ classifications in different clothes.

Still with us are the "retarded" terms: mildly retarded, moderately retarded, severely retarded, and profoundly retarded. In the 1980s, the Chicago-area Down syndrome parent group, the National Association for Down Syndrome, had buttons made and distributed that read "mildly normal," "moderately normal," "severely normal," and "profoundly normal." It made all of us who saw them and wore them think about what labels can do to people. I certainly wondered what my life would be like if I were labeled "mildly normal."

To complicate everything, in the 1970s the federal government adopted the term "developmental disabilities." This is a general term that involves a disability that occurs before age 18, during the developmental years (hence the "developmental" part of the term) and results in substantial loss of functioning in several areas of life (hence the "disability" part of the term).

Then, in the latter part of the last century, came the self-advocacy movement. Self-advocates agree on one thing—they hate the term "mental retardation." Like "idiot" and "moron" before, the

(continued on next page)

## The Importance of Language *(continued from previous page)*

word "retardation" or its shorter versions of "retard" or "tard" had left lasting and unpleasant memories on many individuals and families. Not too many years ago, a popular group released a song, "Let's Get Retarded." So large was the outcry that the group rereleased the song with changed lyrics and the revised title, "Let's Get it Started." In fact, whenever the term is used in a negative light in the media, you can count on a quick and public response by self-advocates and family members.

There is now a movement under way to get rid of the term "mental retardation." Many states have discontinued the use of the term and adopted the term developmental disabilities or intellectual disabilities instead. The former President's Commission on Mental Retardation has become the President's Commission of Persons with Intellectual Disabilities. The leading professional organization, the former American Association on Mental Deficiency, became the American Association on Mental Retardation, and has now gone on to become the American Association on Intellectual and Developmental Disabilities—all within my son's lifetime.

Back to my duck. You have probably long ago noticed that your child's peers may have disabilities other than Down syndrome. The same laws that protect him protect individuals with other disabilities as well. We are part of the universe of exceptionality. While this book is written from the perspective of Down syndrome, in many cases, much of the information is valuable for people with other kinds of intellectual disabilities.

---

from other state agencies, like the one responsible for vocational rehabilitation. The MR/DD agencies usually receive large amounts of state funding.

The MR/DD agencies are criticized by some and scrutinized by many—legislators, politicians, families, individuals, policy makers, and advocates. They are also essential for our adult children with Down syndrome. Most of our kids could not have any kind of meaningful life without these agencies and the people who make them work. These agencies seem to have unnecessary regulations and burdensome policies. The truth is that they are annually expending millions—and, in some cases, billions—of dollars of taxpayer money in every state. Most of these taxpayers do not care one bit about people with Down syndrome or related disabilities. They would just as soon see this money used to lower taxes, reduce a state deficit, or repair bridges and highways. Many taxpayers see our children as an unnecessary tax drain. That is a reality and another reason why you must be effective advocates, not just for your child, but for the system as well.

These agencies are also accountable for the expenditure of money and for the safety of the individuals that the money is used to support. Regulations ensure accountability.

To locate your state MR/DD or I/DD agency, contact or visit the website of the National Association of State Directors of Developmental Disabilities Services (NAS-DDDS). (See the Resource Guide.)

A small number of readers, because of wealth and influence, may think they do not need the resources of a state agency. This may be true. However, even if you are able to pay for adult services yourself, be aware that almost all providers of services receive state and/or federal funding and will be required to meet state regulations. Being familiar with state agency policy may be helpful to you.

# Service Delivery Models

Different states have different methods of parceling out services to the adults with disabilities in their communities who qualify. You will hear these different methods referred to as "service delivery models." The following descriptions of how adult services are generally delivered might have names that are different in your state.

**AGENCY-DIRECTED SUPPORTS**

The most common way that adults with Down syndrome receive services is through private agencies that receive funding from the state MR/DD or I/DD agency. While the majority of these agencies are not-for-profit corporations, there are some for-profit companies that provide services for individuals with disabilities.

In some states, families may choose from a number of agencies that provide the same or similar service—employment supports, for example. In other states, you may be directed to a specific agency and have only limited or no other alternatives. In states where there is choice, competition develops among agencies and quality usually improves. Look at it this way. If there is only one agency that provides employment supports in a community, there is little incentive to be innovative or creative or to respond to individual needs. On the other hand, if several agencies in a community all provide employment supports, they are more likely to be continually improving in order to grow and prosper.

You may already be familiar with these kinds of agencies, since some of them may be the same agencies where you received early intervention, family support, or recreation services. Or they could be agencies solely devoted to providing services for adults.

When not-for-profit companies provide services, the companies are established as charitable organizations and have many public reporting requirements. For example, you can go to www.guidestar.org and search its database on millions of nonprofits. You can view a nonprofit's tax return, called a "990," and even see the salaries of their highest paid employees. Their financial statements and annual reports are open to the public. More importantly, a nonprofit has a Board of Directors that governs the organization. Board members typically represent the community and the interests of the organization.

I hold a strong bias in support of not-for-profit organizations because of their Board governance. I especially favor not-for-profit organizations where a majority of the Board members have a strong personal interest in the organization, as in family members of individuals who receive services from the agency. I also believe that a Board should have members who can assist the organization in ensuring quality, innovation, and fiscal integrity.

In contrast, a for-profit company does not have to be "transparent" in its operations. The salary of its top executives does not have to be disclosed and there is no requirement for other kinds of reporting. Nor are family members given a voice in the governance of the organization. That being said, for-profit companies can and do provide good services.

## The Importance of Choice and Quality

While there has been a dramatic increase in the number of opportunities for families and individuals with Down syndrome to determine what supports they receive and who delivers services to them, it only works if there is choice and quality. In some areas, there is a vast array of service providers to choose from. In other areas, there may be only one provider of services. It's like saying to an individual, "You can have any color shirt you want, as long as it is the blue one." Quality is almost always linked to some level of healthy competition.

There is wide variation among agencies between states and even between communities. Corporate culture differences account for some of the differences, as do the quality of the staff, roles for families, and the ability of an agency to individually tailor their services.

**CONSUMER-DIRECTED SUPPORTS**

In some communities, adults with disabilities and/or their families are allowed more freedom in determining what services they will receive than in the agency-directed model. When an individual is given the right to control a specific amount of federal or state money, several terms may be used to describe it: consumer control, self-directed funding, self-determined funding, individual or family control, direct funding, and individualized budgets. In some states, the money is given directly to the adult with disabilities or the person who is handling his finances. In other states, the money may be given to an agency to be disbursed upon your instructions or in accordance with a mutually agreed-upon plan.

In the consumer-directed model, the individual is at the heart of the services or supports. I think it is easy to think about this model in the context of making a major purchase such as a car. You have to consider price, quality, and service. You might like one dealer because they will do the running around for you and get the car registered and insured. You might prefer spending less and doing the running around yourself. You might not like a particular dealer so much, but decide to buy from them anyway because the business is located close to your office and getting repairs will be easy. In other words, buying a car involves more decisions than just finding a model you like.

In the consumer-directed model, you and/or your child decide what specific services he should receive with the money allotted to him—for example, a job coach and assistance with housekeeping. You then find the supports from an agency or you and your child may hire your own staff. If you hire your own staff, you might be responsible for the business side of being an employer. That might mean conducting background checks, recruiting and supervising staff, and processing a payroll. You might be able to contract the business side out to a "broker" (see below), but you would have to pay for that service.

You will be responsible for coordinating the supports. If you hire someone to be your son's job coach and he gets sick or goes on vacation, ensuring back-up will be your responsibility. You will also provide training and make sure that you are getting what you are paying for. On the other hand, if you do not like what you are getting, you are free to change staff and start over. With the responsibility of hiring staff comes the opportunity of terminating staff as well.

**PRIVATE PAY**

Using the private pay model, you pay for all the services your child needs out of your own pocket. This gives you the ultimate in control and flexibility. It is also the least used model, for obvious reasons. Most people cannot afford to pay for the supports that their child needs, over the long term.

Families are often surprised at how much services and supports can cost. For example, if you purchase job coaching through an agency, in addition to paying for the job coach's salary, you will be paying for your fair share of payroll and unemployment taxes, health insurance and other benefits, and an overhead cost that covers such things as insurance, printing, and postage.

A few families are wealthy enough that they do not need to deal with the requirements for government support and eligibility. However, even if you have the resources and can pay out of pocket for services, you still have to find what you want to buy.

**BROKER MODEL**

The Broker Model can be an option for families who have consumer-directed supports or who are paying for services themselves. Brokers have experience in assisting families through the maze of available services and supports. They serve as a middle person between the individual and the needed supports and services. Some work for agencies and others are independent from service providers. You have lots of control in the broker model and less of the bureaucratic responsibility. You will have to pay for the broker's expertise and for any services you wish to purchase.

The broker model has been embraced by some families and advocates as excellent, innovative policy. On the surface, it is. Individuals and families have great control, but there are some drawbacks to consider. For example, the cost of doing business, the cost of living, goes up every year. With each succeeding year, you have to pay more than you did the previous year for the same things. When this happens to families, they simply must do with less, unless they have had a corresponding increase in family income or salary. In many states, there is no mechanism to adjust for this increase in costs. (This problem can also crop up with consumer directed supports.) The bottom line is that with the broker model, usually your money will not go as far from year to year and that will translate into a reduction of supports for your child. You will also have to consider whether you have the time or stamina to participate in this way in the delivery of supports to your child.

I am a little cynical about this concept. I wonder if, in addition to being creative, it is a way to shift burden and responsibility, and introduce cost-savings to families? However, if you don't like your choices, you can always start your own agency. Many agencies began just that way.

On the other hand, I have worked with many happy, if weary families, who know that their children are receiving the highest quality of supports through the broker model. They are willing to take on the additional case management and deal with the bumps in the road, knowing that they have the fullest flexibility in the service delivery system.

**FISCAL INTERMEDIARY**

A fiscal intermediary is someone who is hired by an adult with disabilities or his family to receive consumer-directed funds and then disperse them for services as directed by the adult and/or his family. It is another way for an individual and/or his family to handle individual consumer-directed funds. A fiscal intermediary is required in most states because most states have a law or policy that prevents families or individuals from directly receiving funds.

Typically, the fiscal intermediary disperses the funds according to an approved plan and takes care of any associated payroll issues—for instance, paying the salaries and payroll taxes of whoever works with your child. The fiscal intermediary takes a percentage of the funds in exchange for doing this.

# Self-Determination and Families

This book is written on the assumption that it will be read by a family member or a trusted professional. While I attempt to make the individual the center of all decision, I recognize that my readers, by and large, will be family members. The position that the family is the driving force in transition planning, however, is at odds with the concept of self-determination.

The term self-determination means just what it sounds like. The person with disabilities himself determines where he will live, what kind of job or education he will pursue, what relationships to be involved in, and what he will do with his leisure time, just like any other adult does. That is, he is empowered to take charge of and responsibility for his own life.

Transition is the time for us to begin to share and then shift power and decisions to our children. That is what the self-determination gurus are teaching us. They believe, correctly, that adults with disabilities ought to be the conductors of the train, so to speak. Families, they believe, may have similar interests, but they could be competing. Take, for example, Sylvia, a young woman with Down syndrome, who wants to walk to work, but would need to cross a street with lots of traffic to do so. Sylvia and her adult service providers believe that she can learn to safely use the traffic signals to cross the street. Her mother is steadfastly opposed to the suggestion. Who is the winner? In this case, the mother wins. The bigger question is who the loser is. That would be Sylvia, who does not have the opportunity to learn a new skill, take a risk, and, more importantly, know that she really has a voice in her future. There has to be a process where your child's interests come out just slightly ahead of yours.

In truth, I believe that most of us have unconsciously made self-determination a cornerstone of our children's lives. We have openly encouraged choice-making by our children and we have let them take risks. Every day they went to school to be included in their community, or took swimming lessons, or participated in the neighborhood Scout troop, they were learning how to make their voices heard—to make their own decisions.

Letting your child play in traffic is just stupid; teaching him to cross the street is brilliant. In other words, although I believe that you, as a parent, need to be involved in transition planning for your son or daughter with Down syndrome, your role needs to diminish over time. You need to learn to listen to your child and let him make decisions to the extent practical and possible.

# Person-Centered Planning

Up until this point, this chapter has focused mainly on the roles of parents, schools, and agencies in transition planning for young people with Down syndrome. Clearly, those of us who believe in self-determination believe that the most important role in transition planning belongs to the person with disabilities himself. That is why the concept of person-centered planning has developed.

Person-centered planning has become so common a term in the intellectual disability world that it is almost like a cell phone—everyone has a version. It is important to understand what being person-centered is and is not. It is a simple enough concept. The person with the disability is the center of the planning. His or her dreams and desires come first and they drive the planning. We are not discouraged by unrealistic goals and we are willing to be flexible and creative in reaching them.

There are formal "models" for developing a person-centered plan, but not everyone has to use one of these models to end up with a transition plan that is person-centered. Some of us are list makers and others of us keep most of our planning and tasks in our head. Some of us lead with our head and others lead with our heart. Some of us analyze everything in a situation and make a list of pros and cons before making an important decision. Others rely heavily on intuition. These are the people who are more apt to "know it when they see it."

If you are more comfortable with making decisions and trust your instincts, the different planning tools that follow may not be of interest to you. You may feel comfortable with establishing a vision for and with your child without having to participate in a formal planning process. You do not have to participate in a "person-centered planning" process to be able to guide and support an individual towards a rich and inclusive life.

**PERSON-CENTERED PLANNING TOOLS**

In addition to being a concept, person-centered planning in also a real process. During the past thirty years, beginning with Jack Yates in 1980, several different individuals have developed their own person-centered planning tools. They all share common beliefs that include listening, recognizing the gifts and talents of the individual, giving the individual control over his life, and sharing power between the individual and those who are in service to him.

At the core of any person-centered planning process is a series of questions. Typically, a group of people, who are close to and chosen by the individual, gathers together to try to answer these questions. Among the questions may be:

- Who am I?
- How do I learn best?
- What kind of supports do I need?
- What do I like?
- What do I dislike?
- Who are my friends?
- What is important to me?
- What are my dreams?
- Who can help me?

The people selected to help answer these questions usually meet together at the person's home or another convenient location one or more times to help the individual and his family clarify a vision for his future. Sometimes group members are asked to commit to doing things to help that vision become a reality. For example, one person might volunteer to gather information about specific types of supports available in the community, while another might agree to use his or her contacts to locate jobs or other opportunities. A group may be formed to come up with a broad vision for the person or to solve a very specific problem, such as where to find a job for him.

If you are interested, stuck, confused, or just want some additional input and support, consider using one of the following person-centered tools. See the References to find out how you can get additional information about the methods described below.

### ESSENTIAL LIFESTYLE PLANNING (ELP)

Michael Smull developed this process to help individuals develop a plan to identify how a person wants to live. Using a "Learning Wheel" and a process that includes listening and asking, a snapshot develops of an individual's present day and how he wants to live. Regardless of the level of the person's disability, this process allows for the development of an essential lifestyle plan that balances the competing interests of "desires, needs, choice, and safety." This process is especially well suited for teens and adults who are less verbal or nonverbal.

### MAKING ACTION PLANS (MAPS)

The MAPS process is one of the best-known and most widely used person-centered planning processes. Listening to what the person wants is at the core of this process developed first by Marsha Forest and Evelyn Lusthaus and then expanded upon by Forest, John O'Brien, and Jack Pearpoint.

It uses seven questions to facilitate and "map" the planning process. The questions are:

- What is a MAP?
- What is the person's history or story?
- What are your dreams for the person?
- What are your nightmares?
- Who is the person?
- What does the person need?
- What is the plan of action?

This process may be used while the student is still in public school to help ensure that his IEP is meeting his personal needs and that he is fully included in his school and community.

### PLANNING ALTERNATIVE TOMORROWS WITH HOPE (PATH)

This process, also developed by Forest, O'Brien, and Pierpoint, can be used by both individuals and organizations who want to become driven by the service needs of an individual. That is, it may be appropriate if it is clear that someone needs particular services to have a good quality of life as an adult. It is particularly useful in complex situations that require the sustained involvement of resources and people over a long period of time.

Generally, a parent, guardian, or other family member of the person with disabilities will be the "pathfinder." This person identifies a problem or problems related to the future of the individual with disabilities for a group of interested people to solve. Another person writes down what is decided at the meeting.

The seven steps of the process are:
- the dream (what the parent/pathfinder would like to see happen);
- sensing the goal (envisioning what changes would need to occur for the goal to be met and setting a timeframe for accomplishing those changes);
- now (the reality for the person with disabilities at present);
- who is on board (which people can help realize the dream and what they can do to help make it a reality);
- how are we going to build strength;
- three/six month goals;
- first steps.

## Jared's Experiences with Person-Centered Planning

During one of Jared's IEP meetings in high school, we learned about a service being provided by a local agency, the Nemasket Group. It was a facilitated group process, where Jared's friends, family, and support people from the high school were invited to our house in an effort to help better connect him to the social and recreational opportunities in our community. We set up a group of about 12 to15 people and referred to it as Jared's Circle of Friends.

The group met every six weeks or so for about a year. Members did a lot of personal networking to find community activities for Jared, and we had homework assignments between meetings. The group members were committed to helping Jared and really did some nice things for him.

The group was reconstituted about a year ago to help Jared find a job. Most of the same members attended in addition to some new ones, most notably the minister from our church and his wife. It was this group that made the connection for Jared's job at the supermarket. An offshoot of this group was also formed to help Jared with his business.

About three months ago, we once again assembled a group with a different set of players to help Jared find an apartment. The group members have a lot of energy and Jared is pleased with having everyone trying to help him get a place of his own.

### CIRCLES OF SUPPORT

Some of you are probably already familiar with the phrase "Circle of Support" or "Circle of Friends." Circles can be used in many contexts to support different people, but they are also a popular tool for people with disabilities who want more inclusion in school or everyday life. A Circle can also be used to help someone with Down syndrome or another disability achieve their goals for transition.

To help an individual with Down syndrome achieve his goals and dreams, a group of people is formed. Members of the group include family, friends, community members, and anyone who is interested in the individual and who is willing to help the person become part of his community. Membership is really loose and anyone can be invited to join.

The most successful groups have a leader or facilitator and meet regularly. The leader understands the objective of the group, which is to be a support to the individual, and ensures that the meetings of the circle serve that purpose. While regular meetings are usually desirable, some circle groups only meet when necessary to address a specific situation. For example, how will Carlos get to work now that he has his ideal job? The circle would brainstorm ideas and hopefully identify an acceptable solution.

## Jason's Circle of Support

In elementary school, Jason was surrounded by the same group of neighborhood friends who really knew him. School was predictable. As he approached middle school, we were very nervous about the changes in store for him. We weren't sure how he would do with changing classes and with all the new students he would need to get to know.

Someone suggested that we start a Circle of Support. I was the leader and maybe that wasn't ideal, but I wanted to give it a try and we didn't have lots of time. We invited Jason's friends, teachers from his present school, his Little League coach, a neighbor, and teachers and an administrator from the middle school. We developed plans for some of the challenges we knew we would face—like making sure Jason had friends to eat with in the cafeteria and responding to any teasing that might occur. We also talked about some of his quirky behaviors.

The group was invaluable and the transition went better than I expected. Over time, the need for the circle diminished and it was hard to get people together regularly. I can see the Circle coming together when there are future challenges to discuss—like finding Jason a job or keeping him safe at the Senior Prom all-night party!

A Circle of Support can benefit all the members of the group, as all the support need not be directed to the individual with the disability. To be really successful, all group members must benefit and that comes when the group reaches beyond the purpose for which it was originally designed.

For many families, they are their own "Circle of Friends."

### DECIDING WHETHER TO TRY PERSON-CENTERED PLANNING

There are a couple of situations in which I think that a person-centered plan can be particularly useful. The first is when you are really stuck in thinking about your child's transition from school to adult life. Bringing other fresh and creative voices into the room can help to generate new ideas and opportunities.

The second situation is when you are working with a school system that is not responsive or creative. Developing a well-defined plan with a thoughtful group of people can help you better identify goals and ways to achieve them. It is like that mobile phone advertisement where they are out testing coverage areas and there are hundreds of people behind the technician supporting the network. Although your school doesn't have to agree to do anything that was decided upon outside of school during your person-centered planning process, they may agree to provide services to support the plan if you can explain how they support transition goals. It may also be helpful to ask people from the group to attend the IEP meeting to assist you in presenting the ideas to school staff.

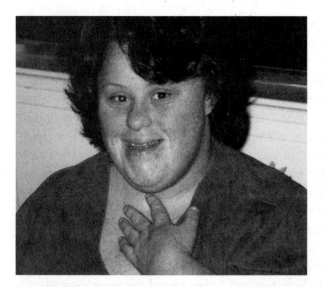

If you are now totally confused by person-centered planning, take heart. I still do not completely understand the subtle differences between all the processes. Comparing person-centered planning to cell phones again, all cell phones do what they are supposed to do and that is to make telephone calls. Some place the call with a send button, some are voice-activated, and some use the call button. All of them are confusing until you get used to them. There are also many other ways to communicate—with land phones, email, letters, faxes, and personal visits. So too are there many ways to plan for your child's future. You can use one of the planning processes above, you can use your own process, or you don't have to do anything at all. After all, some people still don't have a cell phone.

## A WORD ABOUT AGENCIES AND PERSON-CENTERED PLANNING

Many agencies will claim in their promotional materials and in speaking with you that they are "person-centered" and that everyone they serve has a "person-centered plan." I might question these claims because they are difficult for most agencies to achieve. I have also seen an agency that claimed that everyone it served had a person-centered plan, but when I looked at one of the plans, the major goal was for the individual to take a vacation—and she just happened to want to vacation at a condominium owned by the agency.

Another issue worth pointing out is that agencies usually operate, consciously or unconsciously, in the best interest of the agency. That can sometimes be in conflict with the best interests of the individual. You might want to ask an agency that claims to be person-centered to give you a couple of examples of decisions the agency made that favored an individual at a cost to the agency.

I am not suggesting that these "person-centered" agencies are not good agencies; they are probably among the best in your area. They are undoubtedly thinking about important issues. They just might not be honest with themselves, however. For example, Maria might need 15 hours of job coaching a week and the agency might be only getting reimbursed for 10 hours. Chances are that Maria will only get 10 hours because the agency may go out of business if it makes unsound financial decisions and gives Maria what she needs. On the other hand, if Maria only needs the extra 5 hours for one week and the agency is unwilling to figure out how to make that happen, it may not be in business very long since individuals and their families will find more flexible providers.

It has been my experience that agencies are usually "agency-centered," and while it does not have to be mutually exclusive, it is difficult to be "person- centered" at the same time. It takes a commitment by an agency to be "person-centered" and it must start at the top, with the chief executive officer.

## Transition Planning Is Ongoing

Jonathan had been happily living in his own home in another part of the state for almost six years when our next-door neighbor told us he was selling his home. My husband, Chet, told me he was considering buying it because he thought that maybe

Jonathan would want to live there. That same weekend, my daughter, Jonathan's only sibling, informed me that she planned on having a guest house on her property for Jon to live in.

Missing from these conversations was Jonathan. I decided to include him and I told him about Chet's and Emily's ideas. He didn't think much of Chet's idea, because, as he said, "I already have my own house." Emily's idea sort of interested him and he wondered if the cottage would have an extra room and if his father could live there, too. I was noticeably absent from his plan, so I seized the moment to explore the future a bit. I told him that he might want to consider living with Emily when both his father and I were no longer living. He replied, "That will be okay."

So, on a weekend that I discovered that the various members of our family had different visions for Jonathan's future, I was able to begin the most difficult transition planning discussion of them all. That, of course, is discussing with your child with Down syndrome the plans for him when you are no longer here. I am sure that Jonathan had wondered about it before, but had never raised the issue. Sometimes the planning happens when you least expect it, but our discussion went easier than I thought it would.

If you haven't already realized it, the transition process never really ends. Visions change. People change. There are always new transitions.

# CHAPTER 2

# Pomp and Circumstances:
## Getting the Most Out of High School

*Getting the most out of high school can be summed up in three letters—IEP. In the U.S., this legal and enforceable document, the Individualized Education Program, is the foundation piece for transition planning. During the transition years, families need to take a new look at the provisions of IDEA, since there are specific requirements related to transition. Understanding the law will assist you in making sure your child is learning skills to prepare her for adult life. The transition checklist included in this chapter can help families identify useful life skills. This checklist can then be used to identify goals and implementation strategies to consider for the IEP and to build into home routines during the transition years.*

*Many states have adopted high stakes achievement testing for high school students, and this creates both opportunities and challenges for students with Down syndrome. Students with Down syndrome can expect access to the general education curriculum, although families must often make tradeoffs when meeting the various educational needs of their children. Some families find it difficult to decide among the available educational options while trying to balance present desires and future needs. This chapter will make it easier.*

No law has done more to help individuals with Down syndrome and other disabilities in the United States than the law that guarantees your child's right to an education—the Individuals with Disabilities Education Act (IDEA). While you may be very familiar with the law, the following overview will help you understand the regulations as they pertain to the transition from school to adult life.

Ideally, you should familiarize yourself with the regulations related to transitioning before your child reaches transition age. That age may be 14, 15, or 16, depending on where you live. Under IDEA, transition planning must be incorporated into a student's Individualized Education program (IEP) beginning with the first IEP to be in effect when the child turns 16, or younger if determined appropriate by the IEP Team or required by state law. Ask your child's IEP team if you are unsure when transition planning begins in your state.

# IDEA Regulations and Transition

When your child is in elementary and middle school, the focus of her educational program is supposed to be on academics. That is because under the Individuals with Disabilities Education Act (IDEA), special education is intended to help students access and make progress in the general education curriculum. Your child is also entitled to receive the related services, such as physical therapy or speech-language therapy, that she needs to succeed in learning. Once your child reaches transition age, the fo-

cus broadens. While still working on relevant academic skills, your child is also supposed to begin preparing for life after high school. This involves setting goals for your child related to job skills, independent living skills, or other skills important to her future success, as well as providing her with special "transition services" to help her reach those goals.

When IDEA was reauthorized in 2004, language was added to the law clarifying the role that special education is to play in preparing students with disabilities for adult life. Specifically, the words "further education" were added to the statement of the purpose of IDEA:

"The purpose of IDEA includes ensuring that all children with disabilities have available to them a free appropriate education (FAPE) that emphasizes special education and related services designed to meet their unique needs and prepare them for further education, employment and independent living."

This means that your child's education should be helping her acquire the skills she will need after her public education ends. After graduation, will your child be ready for her next step? That next step could be further education, employment, and/or independent living.

Schools are generally in the business of preparing students for further education. Typical high schools, vocational high schools not withstanding, do not prepare students for employment. While high schools may claim they can provide job training and employment supports, they are not always equipped for this task. Some high schools realize this challenge and enter into partnerships with adult service agencies who have the expertise. Some schools have developed the expertise on their own.

Some high schools may claim they were teaching special education students independent living skills even before IDEA required them. They might point to a kitchen, bank, or a laundry that is set up in their school as evidence. Although learning how to use the bank, cook, and wash clothes is important, there is more to independent living than these few skills.

The truth is, it is generally up to you, the parent, to ensure that your child's IEP focuses on the appropriate next steps for your child—whether that be further education, employment, or independent living. It is also up to you to make sure that the major skills your child needs to learn are addressed in her educational program. The next sections explore how to set appropriate transition goals for your child and then ensure that she receives the transition services that will help her achieve those goals.

# Required Elements of IEPs for Transition-Aged Students

When your child reaches transition age, her IEP will continue to include all the same elements you have become accustomed to, including statements of her present level of performance, goals, related services needed to help her meet those goals, needed accommodations or modifications, and a statement about the least restrictive environment where she will receive her services. In addition, IDEA requires that three new elements be added to her IEP:

- "Appropriate measurable postsecondary goals based upon age-appropriate transition assessments related to training, education, employment and where appropriate, independent living skills.
- The transition services (including courses of study) needed to assist the child in reaching those goals; and
- Beginning not later than one year before the child reaches the age of majority under State law, a statement that the child has been informed of the child's rights under Part B, if any, that will transfer to the child upon reaching the age of majority…"

Each of these required elements is discussed below.

**POSTSECONDARY GOALS**

As stated above, your child's IEP should include transition goals related to training, education, employment, and independent living skills, if appropriate. And these goals are supposed to be based upon age-appropriate transition assessments.

You are probably well acquainted with how *educational* goals are set by giving your child a standardized test, determining what she can and cannot do, and then choosing skills and concepts for her to work on, based on her identified strengths and needs. The teachers are very familiar with the sequence of skills that students need to master in order to progress in a particular academic subject and usually have a written curriculum to follow, so choosing appropriate educational goals is relatively straightforward. Once your child is in high school, the numbers and types of educational goals chosen for her may be affected by:

1. the need to fit in time to work on goals for social skills, employment, and independent living;
2. whether your child is capable of satisfying all academic requirements for a high school diploma (see the section called "Graduation Practices," below, for more about this);

3. whether your child is likely to attend a community college or other postsecondary program after high school that has specific academic prerequisites (see Chapter 3 for further information);
4. Whether your child can still benefit from speech, occupational, or physical therapy or from other specialized services.

When it comes to assessments for vocational skills, teachers often use several assessment activities to gather information for employment planning. These include:

- *Observation of your child:* Since observations can be subjective, you might want to provide your own observations to whomever is conducting the observation.
- *Interviews:* Interviews can be either open ended, with no specific set of questions, or there can be scripted questions. The interview can be informal and conducted by someone your daughter trusts or by someone unfamiliar to her. You might want to suggest that your daughter's teacher conduct the interview in a regular instruction period.
- *Review of your child's record:* This can include review of formal and informal assessments, reports from physicians and other professionals, previous IEPs, and especially information from families.
- *Interest Inventories:* There are many tools available that are sold commercially to help students identify their interests and jobs that match their interests; there are also many questionnaires about vocational interests available online.

There are many assessments available that evaluate independent living skills. They cover all the areas in the Transition Checklist that follows later in this chapter. Since preserving independence is increasingly being recognized as important for retired people, you will begin to see even more of these kinds of assessments. A good one is from the State of Washington and can be viewed at: www1.dshs.wa.gov/pdf/ms/forms/10_267.pdf.

Often postsecondary goals are based on your child's "vision" of life after high school, often referred to as the student's "Postsecondary Vision" and should correspond to the vision statement already in the IEP. Here are some examples of postsecondary vision statements that may typically appear:

- Jon wants to work on a golf course. He has learned a lot from being on the school golf team and his summer internship at the driving range.
- Carly wants to work in a law firm and help people with disabilities.
- Tori wants to study childcare at the community college. She has enjoyed the time she has spent in the school daycare reading to children.
- Rick wants to experience work and leisure opportunities that enable him to fully participate in his community.

## CHOOSING APPROPRIATE TRANSITION GOALS FOR YOUR CHILD

It is important to have a tangible idea of your child's skills related to the real world to help you identify what areas need to be addressed. You may want to refer to

the Transition Checklist below for an idea of the skills your child has and what areas of need you may have overlooked. You may find this checklist very helpful at IEP time when the team is trying to come up with goals and objectives and you want to make sure goals included are practical and useful. This checklist provides some general areas to consider and to get you thinking of others. It is not meant to be inclusive of everything because our children are all different.

Use the transition checklist to identify goals to build into your child's IEP and your home routines during the transition years (age 14-21). Keep in mind that the checklist is very broad. Your child may already have mastered some areas. Others will require some thought regarding the steps involved and which of those your child needs to work on. Some goals may not be appropriate for your child, as they are tasks and skills that others may assist her with. It is a good idea to familiarize yourself with the entire checklist because these are the types of questions others are likely to ask you and your child when considering life after public education.

> *My feelings of being overwhelmed began my daughter's freshman year in high school. It seemed that once she entered high school the sense of urgency escalated. I remember continually being asked what our plans were when I didn't even understand the options.*
>
> *I wish I would've had another parent in our district to talk with when my daughter was in high school. I was overwhelmed with how much information I needed to know and what I needed to do. I needed a coach!*

> *I keep having these useless discussions with the transition bunch about how James does not need to learn to ride the bus, as he will have a car at his disposal. The bus stop is one mile from our house and he'll always have a support person with him, so I don't see the huge benefit to spending/wasting a good deal of time on a skill that is not important to us or him at this point. The reason, of course, they want to work on bus riding, is that "it's what is done." If James could ride the bus alone or if the bus stop was within a reasonable walking distance (it's also an unsafe road to walk on that goes up and down a huge hill), maybe it would make sense. But for where we live, it makes no sense.*

### FIGURING OUT HOW AND WHEN TO WORK ON TRANSITION GOALS

Perhaps you find the long list of skills in the transition checklist overwhelming. You may wonder how your child can possibly find the time to work on all those skills while still enrolled in regular academic classes in high school. You may be especially concerned if your child is enrolled (or planning to enroll) in inclusive classes with college-bound students. You wonder how they will have time to work on budgeting skills in Algebra class and you know they won't be talking about how to use public

# The Transition Checklist

**Safety Skills**—Can your child:

- Recognize a stranger
- Identify "community helpers" like police, firefighters, shop keepers
- Summon help
- Use a cell phone to call for help
- Dial 9-1-1

**Vocational Skills**—Can your child:

- Get to/from work, on time—using whatever mode of transportation is necessary—and meet the time requirements of a workplace
- Perform work satisfactorily—do what is expected
- Work cooperatively with others—understand the social systems in a workplace; understand the local customs such as where people eat and with whom
- Take breaks and lunch appropriately—manage time and schedules
- Wear suitable clothing—follow dress code requirements or be prepared for weather changes that might occur during a shift
- Use appropriate safety procedures such as using safety glasses when operating a lawn mower, wearing gloves and a hairnet to prepare food, or following whatever safety procedures are in place
- Follow directions—accept authority when told what to do and do what is expected
- Accept supervision and handle feedback, even when it is not positive
- Understand and explain her resume

**Social/Personal Skills**—Can your child:

- Recognize when she needs assistance or medical attention
- Use a toilet appropriately—to include observing proper hygiene, not stuffing the toilet so it overflows, etc.
- Supply appropriate personal identification
- Greet people and respond to greetings appropriately
- Use contemporary style of dress, hair, make-up—while individuality is important, looking appropriate may be required
- Use good grooming and hygiene skills—keep teeth clean, breath fresh, hair combed and clean, clothes clean
- "Talk" with friends/coworkers—communicate about work issues as well as areas of interest to others such as current movies or local sports teams
- Be courteous—treat others considerately and politely; use "please," "thank you," and "excuse me"
- Be responsible, reliable, and trustworthy
- Act happy when appropriate—nobody can be expected to *be* happy all of the time, but there are times and places where it is necessary to either be happy or appear to be happy, such as at a friend's birthday party
- Know where and with whom it is appropriate to share unhappy or negative feelings and thoughts

**Community Skills**—Can your child:

- Use public transportation—safely use a bus or train or call a cab and arrange for special transportation
- Be safe in traffic, obey traffic signals, and cross streets safely
- Be safe among strangers; understand social distancing
- Follow directions to a new location (either by following spoken instructions, reading a map or bus schedule, or following written directions)
- Shop for groceries—make healthy choices from the many similar products (there may be 14 varieties of bagels in your supermarket and they range from 110 calories to 530 calories)
- Figure out how a supermarket or big box store is arranged and find the right product, size, and style
- Shop for clothes and toiletries, keeping to a budget and choosing appropriate items
- Make necessary appointments—scheduling medical appointments, ordering prescriptions
- Take medications—the right dosage at the right time
- Use the phone (land lines and cell phones) for communication and emergencies and stay within any plan limits (such as minutes per month)
- Make and follow a budget
- Use bank accounts—use ATMs and tellers, make and record deposits and withdrawals, balance checkbooks
- Know how to seek help—stay calm, follow a plan, and know community and emergency contacts
- Handle money—use cash or checks or handle credit and debit cards with responsibility
- Read important signs, warnings, directions
- Sign her name and fill out basic information on envelopes or forms

**Recreation/Leisure**—Can your child:

- Exercise regularly
- Use free time for pleasure—choose reasonable activities when given a block of time that is not scheduled
- Pursue a hobby—find some activities that are pleasurable and sustainable and can be done alone or with others
- Perform required activities—dress appropriately for different occasions; bring needed equipment or supplies
- Use community resources—use a community pool or YMCA or be appropriate and safe in a gym or locker room
- Call friends to make plans with them—identify an activity and someone to do it with and initiate a phone call to plan it
- Read social cues such as body language and facial expressions
- Initiate conversations and be a good listener

**Domestic Skills**—Can your child:

- Plan menus or meals—know what makes up a healthy meal that she will enjoy
- Make a shopping list from menus—purchase necessary items for meals or recipes

*(continued on next page)*

## The Transition Checklist *(continued from previous page)*

- Prepare a breakfast, lunch, supper, or snack, or pack a lunch—make simple meals from recipes or heat healthy frozen meals
- Recognize when food is spoiled—"when in doubt throw it out"
- Turn off appliances and shut off the stove
- Wash dishes, pots, and pans—make sure that utensils and cutting boards are cleaned so they are safe to use
- Clean up apartment (bathroom, living areas, kitchen, and so on)—know which cleaning supplies clean specific areas and divide up chores among roommates
- Clean her own room—change sheets, put away clothes, and maintain a healthy environment with personal preferences respected
- Do laundry: use a washer and dryer—ironing is optional, knowing when to use a dry cleaner may be important, but operating a washer and dryer according to instructions is essential
- Perform simple household maintenance like replacing the toilet paper roll and changing a light bulb
- Budget time—be on time and ready with whatever supplies are necessary for the task; use a watch, alarm, or other electronic reminders
- Handle the unexpected from a power outage to a bus that doesn't show up
- Take safety precautions at home and in the community—for example, unplugging appliances in an electrical storm; avoiding unsavory individuals

**Transportation Skills**—The area of transportation requires more attention during the transition years because transportation problems can be the single biggest barrier to employment and friendship. You must make sure that transportation skills are addressed while your child is still in school.

Some of the modes of transportation and some skills to consider teaching include:

- Walking—crossing the street, understanding traffic signals, asking for help, being safe around other pedestrians and strangers
- Biking—bike and helmet safety, locking a bike, traffic signals, road rules applicable to bicycles
- Special public transportation—ordering and canceling rides, reporting dangers, procedures to follow if the ride never arrives
- Regular public transportation—paying for rides, reading schedules, mapping routes, resolving schedule changes, handling detours or unexpected changes
- Riding with others—asking staff for transportation assistance, requesting rides from friends or coworkers, knowing who to accept a ride from

No matter what mode of transportation your child uses, she must be taught how to ensure her safety and to report anything that makes her uncomfortable.

transportation in World History class. I think that you have to think about what kind of life you expect your child to have and what she will need to be successful. In addition, you may want to consider the following:

1. How long will your child be in high school? Do you think she will be in high school until she "ages out" of special education or do you intend to have her leave high school after four years?
2. Can the general education curriculum be adapted to match your child's goals?
3. Which skills can you teach at home? Some skills may not be appropriate or necessary, as each child's level of skill varies.
4. Will there be opportunities for your child to learn these skills after high school? Your child will continue to learn and acquire new skills as an adult.
5. What are you willing to give up? Is travel training more important than occupational therapy? Is including your child in general education classes more important than speech therapy?

**How Many Years Will Your Child Attend High School?** As discussed in more detail in the section on "Graduation Practices" below, many students with Down syndrome attend high school until they "age out" of special education services—this is often age 21, but can vary by state. This means they may have an additional two to four years in high school, depending on whether they took any extra years in lower grades and when their birthday falls in the year. Some families choose for their children to take mostly academic classes for the first four years of high school. Then, after their child "graduates" with her peers, they focus mainly or exclusively on vocational or life skills at high school for another couple of years. Other families may ask for their child to be enrolled in less inclusive special education classes for some or all of the high school years so their child can work more intensely on more functional skills. (See the section on transitions services below for information on some of the nonacademic programs that may help your child while in high school.)

**How Can the General Education Curriculum Be Adapted?** It also depends on what classes your child is going to take and your ingenuity in writing goals that incorporate transition goals. For example, if the school offers Family and Community Skills as an elective, can your child take it multiple times to learn cooking and menu planning skills? Is Health class an appropriate place for her to learn about good grooming and nutrition, or is the focus more on drugs and sex education? Can she work on cooperation and communication skills needed for employment in an academic class that has a lot of small group work?

**What Skills Can Be Taught at Home?** Which skills do you know how to teach? How much time and energy are you willing to spend at home in teaching your child these skills after school hours and in the summer? Is it realistic to think you'll be able to fit this teaching into your schedule when you haven't before? If you do decide to teach some skills at home, what strategies make it more likely you will follow through? For example, if you write down your goals or formally inform the school which skills you will teach your child, are you more likely to schedule time for teaching skills at home?

**What Will Your Child Do after High School?** As the vision for your child's life after high school becomes clearer, it may be easier to determine which skills can be worked on after high school graduation. For example, if your child is planning to go to a postsecondary program that teaches independent living or job skills, it may reasonable to put off teaching some skills until then. Or if it seems likely that your child will continue to live at home for several years after high school graduation, you may want to plan to teach some cooking, housekeeping, and shopping skills then.

## Ensuring Goals are Realistic and Appropriate

The IEP must have both realistic and appropriate goals. I think it helps to consider whether you would want or need the objective that is being considered. One day, after taking an overseas flight to deliver a speech on transition, I noticed ink all over my hands. Once again, I had forgotten that those rolling ink pens explode at high altitudes. My reward for forgetting was a handful of ink and a few ink stains on my clothes. I realized that if I had been a person with Down syndrome, this mistake, made repeatedly, could possibly have become the basis for an educational objective. I might even be forbidden to use those kinds of pens. Not everything has to be fixed. Sometimes, we just forget things.

### TRANSITION SERVICES

As you may recall from above, your child's IEP needs to include a statement about the transition services (including courses of study) needed to help her reach her postsecondary goals. But what exactly are transition services? According to IDEA, they are a "coordinated set of activities for a child with a disability that:

- Is designed to be within a results-oriented process, that is focused on improving the academic and functional achievement of the child with a disability to facilitate the child's movement from high school to post-school activities, including postsecondary education, vocational education, integrated employment (including supported employment); continuing and adult education, adult services, independent living, or community participation;
- Is based on the individual child's needs, taking into account the child's strengths, preferences and interests; and
- Includes instruction, related services, community experiences, the development of employment and other post-school adult living objectives, and, if appropriate, acquisition of daily living skills and functional vocational evaluation."

Your child must also be invited to attend her IEP meeting if postsecondary goals and the transition services related to those goals will be considered at the meeting.

Let's look at each of the parts of this definition to see what the law really requires:

## A RESULTS-ORIENTED PROCESS

The terminology calling for a "results-oriented process" is new with the 2004 revisions of IDEA. The wording is meant to emphasize that the focus should be on the student actually achieving her goals, rather than just on the process of providing him or her with transition services that meet the bureaucratic requirements of the law. Using a "results-oriented process," you should expect that your child's transition goals will be measurable, that she will receive instruction and services that will enable her to reach those goals, and that progress toward those goals will be tracked and reported.

## INCORPORATING YOUR CHILD'S NEEDS, STRENGTHS, AND INTERESTS INTO THE IEP

This part of the definition means that the IEP team must make a good faith effort to find out what your child wants to do after high school and must complete assessments and observe your child to determine what her strengths and needs are related to transition. In addition, your child must be given an opportunity to participate in any IEP meeting in which her transition goals and services will be discussed. Despite this requirement, it may be up to you, the parent, to ensure that your child participates in a meaningful way. Some school systems try very hard to get useful input from the student; others see student participation as just another box to check off during the IEP meeting. The following is an example of how *not* to include a student in the transition process:

> In our school system, this is the way they make sure they've fulfilled the requirement to take the student's interests into account: They pull the student out of class a few days before her IEP meeting and help her fill out a written form with a few questions such as "What jobs have you tried before? What kind of job would you like after high school?" The first time they asked our daughter, she said she'd raked leaves and picked up trash before and didn't want a job doing those things. She said she wanted to write children's books, so they wrote that into her IEP and then said that since she was taking English class, she didn't need any other transition services to help her meet her goals.

*None* of the planning should be done exclusively with the school district personnel and the student. It should all be an IEP team process.

## TRANSITION SERVICES THAT CAN BE PROVIDED

Let's look at each of the services that IDEA says can be provided as a transition service:

- Instruction—This can include classroom instruction from general education or special education teachers, as well as community-based instruction (e.g., lessons in taking the bus or shopping).
- Related services—This may be the time to make the case for reinstatement of therapies that may have been taken away when your child was younger because she didn't need them to make

progress in the general education curriculum or because you didn't want her pulled out for services. During transition years, goals may be identified that may best be supervised by an occupational therapist (grooming skills) or a physical therapist (bike riding) or a speech-language pathologist (phone skills).

- Community experiences—This can include any experience that will help a student achieve a transition goal, including learning how to order healthy and satisfying fast food, how to get help, or what to do if she is lost.
- The development of employment and other post-school adult living objectives (see Chapter 7).
- Acquisition of daily living skills such as cooking, cleaning, grooming—experiences and instruction may be provided in a special education class or general education class or through community experiences.

- Functional vocational evaluation—This is an assessment process aimed at determining the student's job interests, abilities, and skills. It involves observing the student's performance on a variety of tasks that are part of jobs or actually performing different jobs, as well as giving her formal vocational assessments.

In the past, when families asked for education and services that would assist their child in areas outside of what was considered "education," school officials often declined to offer these needed services. Often the excuse given was that employment and especially independent living were not educationally related. Fortunately, thanks to the most recent changes to IDEA, your school must consider providing services that can help your child achieve important skills in these areas. It does not mean, however, that every student with Down syndrome will want or need to learn these skills at school.

### PROFESSIONALS WHO CAN PROVIDE INPUT ABOUT GOALS AND SERVICES

Fortunately or unfortunately, it is not up to you alone to decide what transition goals and services belong in your child's IEP. Just as when your student was younger, teachers, therapists, and school administrators will have input into your child's IEP. But you and the school can also invite people from agencies outside of school who are knowledgeable about adult supports and the reality of life for adults with disabilities. These might include counselors from a vocational rehabilitation agency or representatives of adult service agencies. Their attendance is voluntary.

It is important to include representatives from the state agency that is likely to pay for adult services for your daughter after her public education ends. These representatives will generally be able to tell you if the services you are requesting for your child are available, if there is a waiting list, and if they have the funds to help you obtain them.

IDEA now requires your school to get your consent prior to inviting any representatives to the IEP. While I am sure that there might be a reason not to consent to their participation, I would not recommend withholding consent.

If representative(s) do not attend the IEP, the local education authority is not required to take any steps to get them to participate. Many times, these representatives do not attend because they are busy planning and providing services for individuals who they are currently responsible for. They may not have the resources to participate in planning for someone they will not be supporting for several years. If this occurs, make sure that these individuals and agencies are kept informed and responsible even if they are not able to send a representative to the IEP. You can do this by sending regular progress reports, copies of your child's IEP, and meeting minutes to them. It may also help to call the agencies yearly until the year before your child's education is going to end. Then those calls should become regular and more frequent.

Other new members of your child's IEP team during the transition years will include anyone whose contributions will add to the information being discussed. For example, some schools have transition teachers or specialists who can provide input about community resources or vocational assessment and training opportunities. Classroom aides, sponsors of after-school activities, or coaches might also have useful information to add.

> *One of the most frustrating things for me was being told what agencies were "supposed to do" and then being assigned staff from these agencies who never did what they were "supposed to do." Advocacy continues to be important even in the transition process.*

## WHERE ARE SERVICES PROVIDED?

As in past years, students who are transitioning are required to be educated in the least restrictive environment (LRE) in which they can achieve their goals. Depending on your child's goals, the LRE might be full inclusion in general education classes, or she might need to leave the general education setting for some or all of her classes.

In deciding about the setting where your child should receive services during the transition years, you have to consider the knowledge and skills that you want her to acquire and where those skills are best taught and learned. For example, if your daughter needs to learn typing skills for a future job in an office, an inclusive keyboarding class might be the best setting. If she wants to work on her clerical skills, working in the high school administration office might be the best setting. On the other hand, if she needs to work on developing age-appropriate language for social situations, a separate life skills class might be the best setting. Or, if travel training is a priority, the best setting might be with other special education students learning the same skill with a teacher taking the students into the community

## TRANSFER OF RIGHTS TO YOUR CHILD

Under IDEA, once a student with disabilities reaches the age of majority, she can legally exercise the rights to oversee her own education. That is, she can make her own decisions about goals, placement, and even whether to remain in school—unless: 1) a guardian has been appointed for the student; or 2) the student has formally delegated educational decisions to her parents, in writing, or has reached an informal agreement with her parents to allow them to continue to be involved in educational decision making. (Each state must establish procedures for appointing the parent of a child with a disability, or another appropriate individual, to continue to represent the child's educational interests, if the child still needs assistance in making sound educational decisions.)

Because some students are not ready to take on the responsibility for their own educational decisions at the age of 18 (or 19 or 21, depending on your state), IDEA requires that parents be notified one year before rights will transfer to their child. That gives parents and IEP team members an opportunity to discuss whether transferring rights is in the student's best interests. If so, they can prepare her for the transfer of rights. If not, they can work out how best to enable the parents to continue to participate in educational decisions.

# Graduation Practices

In most communities, a child with Down syndrome will complete her free, appropriate public education either: 1) when her entitlement ends (usually when she turns 21 or 22), or 2) the moment she receives her high school diploma. Families are caught in a dilemma.

We have been fighting for as much inclusion for our children as possible and many of them have gone to school in their communities and developed meaningful

and important relationships with other students. We need to remember, however, that when we were in high school we believed the friendships we had would never be severed. They were essential for our development—at that time. Judging by the number of people who do not attend their high school reunions, I would surmise that many of us learned they were not as important in the long run as we thought. But, at that moment, they were important. Can you imagine if we were given a choice that went something like this?

*You have a choice. You can graduate with your friends and receive your diploma or you can receive a scholarship for the next 2-4 years of your education.*

This is what is being played out in communities all across the United States. Students with disabilities are being asked to choose between graduating on time with their friends or staying in high school until their special education eligibility runs out—which is until age 21, under IDEA—and can be longer, depending on your state law and local practice.

While there are laws about age limits in place, in truth, local practices vary considerably. Some school districts allow a student to finish the academic year, even after the student is no longer eligible for special education services because she has "aged out." Other school districts may allow this to occur if the student's birthday is close to the end of the school year, and others will not consider the practice at all. You might be able to exercise some leverage over your district if they allow seniors to finish the school year, within the district, even if their family moves out of the district. In this case, you might argue that allowing your daughter to finish the school year is similar. However, from the district's perspective, requiring your daughter to leave school once she is no longer eligible might be an actual, direct savings to the district, whereas having a "typical" student leave would not result in any such savings.

Another dilemma facing some families is whether to encourage their child with Down syndrome to work toward achieving a regular high school diploma, or to allow her to receive a certificate of attendance or special education diploma instead. This decision can have far-reaching impacts on the benefits and opportunities available to your child after graduation.

### DILEMMA #1: HOW LONG SHOULD YOUR CHILD REMAIN IN HIGH SCHOOL?

Remember, under IDEA, your child is *entitled* to all the transition services described in this chapter. Once she graduates from school, she is not entitled to adult services. Although she may qualify for various adult services, there could be a waiting list to receive them or funding may not be available to her. Although our children are entitled to a free education under IDEA, that is the only entitlement for services that exists.

State agencies attempt to plan carefully for their new customers. That is why it is so important to include representatives of adult service agencies in the transition process. Agencies track the number of eligible students by the year they will become eligible. They expect that students will take advantage of their full entitlement to special education until that entitlement ends.

If a student with Down syndrome will achieve all the requirements for high school graduation before she ages out of IDEA eligibility, it is essential to let the appropriate state adult agency know as soon as it becomes apparent that this is going to occur. Although some state agencies may begin providing services upon graduation to an eligible individual, many do not expect to provide any supports to individuals with Down syndrome until after they "age out" of special education services. Many adult service agencies will not provide necessary supports at a time when they believe the local school district should.

It is important to understand that eligibility for adult services is almost 180 degrees apart from the IEP planning you have experienced. While the IEP is built upon your child's strengths, eligibility for adult services is decided upon deficiencies. You might want to celebrate your child's increase in IQ scores in high school, only to learn later that the score could be used to deny her services. More information on qualifying for adult services is in Chapter 4.

The majority of parents opt to for their children to remain the responsibility of the local school district for as long as possible, as there are generally more services available.

### DILEMMA #2: SHOULD YOUR CHILD WORK TOWARD A HIGH SCHOOL DIPLOMA?

Some students with Down syndrome are fairly passing the classes required to graduate with a diploma. Some may also be capable of passing any "high stakes" tests necessary for graduation. There is another group of students who are also passing these tests, but only with a little "help" from well-meaning but misguided teachers.

*Maria Perez was so proud of her son Carlos for having passed the required test for high school graduation, even if it was on his third try. She was jubilant and so was the rest of the family. While she and her husband were somewhat surprised that their son had actually passed, they were so caught up in their excitement that they let these feelings pass. Maria started looking at options for Carlos for after high school. She discovered that the state agency for developmental services wouldn't provide funding since Carlos had passed the high school exit exam, which meant his level of disability did not meet their eligibility guidelines. The Perez family later learned that one of their son's teachers might have "coached" him on the test. Since the school district would not be financially responsible for him any longer if he passed, nobody seemed to mind—until it was too late.*

If your child can't really meet the graduation requirements on her own, but she enjoys and benefits from the general education curriculum, you just need to make sure that she does not actually receive the diploma. You would be doing her a disservice by having her receive a regular diploma only to lose her eligibility for needed transition services as soon as she receives it.

On the other hand, if your child is truly capable of taking and passing all required courses, as well as any "high stakes" test, she should graduate because she has actually met the requirements for graduation and has demonstrated her competencies. She is also probably ready to go on to a postsecondary educational setting. These students with Down syndrome are the exception.

If your child is capable of satisfying all high school graduation requirements, the second consideration is whether the advantages of getting a diploma will outweigh the disadvantages.

A young adult with Down syndrome who graduates with a diploma will probably be eligible for:

- jobs that require a high school diploma, which may be higher paying than jobs for nongraduates;
- college and other postsecondary education programs, if admitted;
- vocational rehabilitation services, including job training and assistance finding a job;
- certain federal benefits (such as SSI and Medicaid), if her income is low enough to qualify.

A student with DS who graduates with a diploma may not be eligible for:
- additional special education or transition services after graduation
- some adult services, such as employment, housing, and family supports, because agencies use eligibility guidelines that consider an individual's past performance.

# Documenting Your Child's High School Achievements

More than likely, your student with Down syndrome will not be taking the regular high school exit test (if required in your state), although she will have been exposed to the general curriculum and has likely benefited from the high expectations that you and others have placed on her. Instead, her IEP team will come up with an alternative method of assessing her competencies.

**PORTFOLIOS**

Portfolios are one alternative method for evaluating and documenting a student's abilities and achievements. Think of a portfolio as a scrapbook updated for the 21st century. A typical scrapbook, perhaps created for an individual as a place to remember events, might have photographs, used tickets, and other mementos such as invitations and letters. A portfolio that is used to demonstrate the competencies of a student with Down syndrome must contain items that relate to the student's individual goals and objectives. This portfolio may contain pictures, videos, homework or schoolwork, formal test results and observations, reports, or audio recordings. For example, if the student had a goal to be able to make small purchases, a video of the successful transaction might be contained in the portfolio.

The contents of the portfolio may also be useful beyond high school. While I am not sure that a prospective employer will be willing to go through a portfolio to determine whether an applicant has the skills necessary for a job, it could be very helpful to a postsecondary program as additional admissions materials. It could also be useful to an adult service agency if your child is not able to adequately present her strengths in a face-to-face meeting.

**SUMMARY OF PERFORMANCE**

IDEA 2004 requires that a Summary of Performance (SOP) be developed for every student with a disability who graduates or ages out of special education. The language reads: "...*the local education agency shall provide the child with a summary of the child's academic achievement and functional performance, which shall include recommendations on how to assist the child in meeting the child's postsecondary goals.*" This summary should help your child as she makes the transition from school to postsecondary education or employment. This document may be used to determine eligibility for adult services, so you will want to be involved in its development.

The document is prepared during the last year of your child's eligibility for services and should condense and summarize all the pertinent information the school system has accumulated about your child. Think of it like a medical record except it is a school history. It should be complete so that the next provider of services will have the knowledge to be successful working with your child.

**TESTING AND THE NO CHILD LEFT BEHIND ACT (NCLB)**

This federal law, a law distinct from IDEA, has areas of interest and concern to families with a child with Down syndrome. The aim of this law is to make sure that all students can read and do math at grade level by 2014. Science proficiency is also tested. Testing occurs annually in grades 3 to 8 and once in high school. There are ramifications for underperforming schools, so some schools with many special education students are feeling pressure to have special education students exempted from testing.

The IEP team for a student with Down syndrome determines, on a yearly basis, how the student will participate in each subject test scheduled for assessment. This information is then documented in the IEP. There are several options for students with Down syndrome.

Some students with Down syndrome may take the standard test without modifications (changes in the content of what is tested). If so, they may take it with or without accommodations such as additional testing time, frequent breaks for rest, use of a calculator, or having someone read the test aloud. Other children take a modified assessment that still assesses the child against the grade level material but may have fewer test items to choose from, more illustrations in the test booklet, or perhaps allow students to use objects to demonstrate their knowledge of math concepts.

However, especially when our children reach transition age and the educational gap widens between them and their typically developing peers, many of our kids will be considered so cognitively impaired that they will qualify for alternative assessments based on alternative achievement models. They should still be expected to demonstrate progress toward their educational goals which are based on their access to the regular curriculum, but their assessments will be different. They may be able to present a portfolio for their assessment. The goal of NCLB is critical for special education students, who are often left behind. The simple solution may appear to be exempting special education students from standardized testing, and NCLB allows for alternative testing for some special education students. The risks of exempting our children from the test may be reduced access to the general curriculum and lower educational standards. While the government and Down syndrome advocates in Washington monitor and develop acceptable solutions, families need to make sure that their child is not automatically excluded from the standard tests and offered alternative testing. Since all of our children have different abilities, you want to make sure that the bar is set at the right height for your child.

# How Should Your Child Spend Her School Day?

The answer to this question is both personal and practical. It is also complicated and it can change over time. What might work in ninth grade might not work as well in tenth grade. To begin to answer this question, you should start with your child. Do you have a child who likes classes, homework, and assignments? Does she thrive on the pressure of tests and assessments or does it create anxiety? Does she want to carry books?

Next, you might consider what outcome you anticipate from high school. Will your child be working toward meeting graduation requirements? Will high school be the conclusion of her formal education or do you anticipate her continuing on to some kind of postsecondary education? Does she hope to get out of school and get a job as soon as possible?

Those are some of the practical questions.

The personal questions are harder to answer because every family is different. Although it may seem that everyone is marching toward inclusion or postsecondary education, you may not believe that this is the right direction for your child. Likewise, you might not believe that working is the best option. You might see your child as a volunteer, helping in a family business, or spending her day in leisure pursuits. Each family is different and our children are different.

*Jon liked the rhythm of school, he loved classes and having textbooks, put up with exams, and aligned himself completely with the Class of 1998. He made it easy for us to plan. He was going to spend four years in high school and it was going to be in an academic program.*

*Miranda, on the other hand, used high school to strengthen her daily living skills and "sample" various jobs. She got used to using her communication device and when she graduated found a part-time job shredding documents and a volunteer job at her church passing our hymnals.*

After considering the unique personal and practical issues affecting your child, you may have a better context for deciding how much of your child's time at school should be spent learning academics, acquiring job skills and experiences, and learning life skills. See the sections below.

## TAKING ACADEMIC CLASSES

Obviously, our children should continue to have access to the general education curriculum in high school to the extent appropriate, and the curriculum should be modified as necessary. These modifications should include ensuring that the material is provided in a format appropriate to your child's reading and comprehension level, or providing recorded books for those who can't read. Alternative forms of tests should also be available, as discussed above.

*Michael was a student with significant challenges in addition to Down syndrome, but his family was committed to inclusive education for him. He took Shakespeare in high school. His mother would read the text aloud to him at night and he would listen to it on tape by himself. His class projects included dressing up as Macbeth, Romeo, and Hamlet.*

If additional personnel are necessary for successful inclusion, that should be provided as well. Many students with Down syndrome benefit from an aide or an inclusion specialist who is with them for part or all of their day.

Some students with Down syndrome may decide to take classes in a postsecondary program such as a community college while still in high school. See Chapter 5 for more about this dual enrollment option, which may or not be available in your school district.

How much inclusion is right for your child is something the IEP team, including you and your child, should revisit regularly. If your child is not achieving her academic goals in her current setting, the amount of inclusion is one element to consider changing. For example, if your child is not learning how to handle money or read essential signs in inclusive classes, less inclusion may be worth considering. Although my son benefited from inclusion for most of his day, he was tutored daily in math and reading and we considered that his math and English classes. Some students with Down syndrome are ready for algebra and Shakespeare, but Jon benefited from the intensive instruction in functional math and reading skills.

Again, the specific classes that your child signs up for will depend on a variety of factors, including her own interests, her postsecondary goals, your school system's requirements, and local practices. But there are two subjects that I believe are essential

## Jon's Views on Inclusion

The following was written by my son, after he began attending his neighborhood high school in the beginning of his sophomore year. He had spent the previous nine years at a school in a neighboring town.

I am Jon Derr. I go to Swampscott High School. I take history, biology, typing and child development. I help out in the preschool. I work hard in every class and outside of class too. I work at Star Market. I like it there. I manage the basketball and the lacrosse teams. I am on the golf team and I can hit a golf ball about 175 yards.

I used to be in a special class at my other school. The teachers I had did not give a lot of work. They also did not give a lot of attention to me but they spend more time with the other classmates.

What I do in class is meet different students in biology and child development and history and in typing. In biology we do gene cross over and I do labs with a group. I also work with a group of friends on group work. When I do my work I have friends to help me. When I take a test I have a different test.

In math and language I meet with Gayle. She is nice but tough when I write fluff. Sometimes we do checks with money. In language we read books to learn.

I think you should put your children in class with their friends in other classes. They should have the chance to do the work.

for all students with Down syndrome to study: sexuality education and health and nutrition. (See below.)

### SEXUALITY EDUCATION

Sexuality education involves more than learning about the biology of sex as in "the birds and the bees." The biology part is very important. Our children must be taught about their bodies and about reproduction. Children who are taught in inclusive settings will learn about these issues beginning in elementary school and continuing through high school. In high school, our children will have the opportunity to take courses such as biology, child development, and psychology. All of these courses teach some of the elements of sex education.

It is the practical, everyday concepts of sexuality education (listed below) that are so important for our children. Despite some intellectual deficits, people with Down syndrome develop fairly typically as sexual beings. Ignoring your child's formal sexuality education is a guarantee that she will receive her sexuality education solely from television, movies, and peers and other individuals. This is a guarantee that your child will receive inaccurate and perhaps dangerous information.

While there is debate over who should teach sexuality education—families or the schools—the fact remains that our children must receive sexuality education in a manner that reflects individual family values and religion as well as the norms of our culture. I believe that it takes a combined effort. Families and schools must both be involved so that this important learning can be reinforced in all parts of our children's life. Most importantly, our children should be taught in a way that reflects tolerance and understanding.

Some of the elements of sexuality education that should be part of your child's education may include:

- public displays of affection
- issues of gender and sexual orientation
- masturbation
- sexual thoughts and fantasies
- pregnancy
- sexually transmitted diseases
- abstinence education and birth control
- peer pressure
- dating
- harassment

If your child does not have access to a comprehensive sexuality education, she will be at risk for abuse and exploitation. Sexuality education must be paired with instruction in the concepts of self-determination and empowerment so our children can be as safe as possible. Even though many of us fear the stranger, it is more likely that other individuals with cognitive disabilities will abuse our children. Education is our children's best protection.

To ensure that your child is taught the concepts she needs to learn, make sure that her IEP includes very specific goals in sexuality education. For example, a goal for health class might be: she will be taught that masturbation is a behavior that should only be practiced in private. You might want to investigate whether there are community resources such as adult service agencies that offer sexuality training. Your local mental health agency might also have sexuality groups for adults with developmental disabilities.

## HEALTH, WELLNESS, AND NUTRITIONAL EDUCATION

It is critical that our children have the opportunity to be included in whatever health and wellness education is available to the other students. It is naïve to believe that our children will not be exposed to the dangers of underage drinking, recreational drug use, sexual activity, or even the nonuse of seat belts. The teen years are naturally filled with rebellion and if our children miss hearing the important lessons aimed at typical teens, they are in danger of being hurt.

It may be helpful for your child to have specific IEP goals related to saying "no" to things that other teens or young adults may pressure her to do. These goals could involve the speech therapist in addition to the health or special education teacher. For example, a speech therapy goal along these lines might be appropriate for some students: In role play with the speech therapist and peers, Dawn will demonstrate verbal and nonverbal methods to say no to offers of alcoholic beverages, drugs, and sex. Another goal may be to say "no" if asked to get into a car with someone who has been drinking.

These are also important years for your child to increase her understanding of the relationship between health, exercise, and diet. While the school can be an important partner in these areas, it is also family members' responsibilities to be good role models. See Chapter 9 for more information on teaching your child about healthy choices.

> *Unfortunately, our school system only requires one year of physical education in high school. My daughter took the class in ninth grade and then didn't have the space in her schedule to take it as an elective in her other years of high school. So, it was up to us to figure out how to make sure she got enough exercise on a daily basis.*
>
> *Our major strategy was to have her start walking the mile home from school with her sister instead of getting a ride on the special education school bus. We figured she was learning important life skills—crossing streets independently, keeping an eye on traffic while walking—as well as getting good exercise. Our secondary strategy was to buy a Wii Fit. My daughter is not crazy about using it on her own, but if other family members are using it and we ask her to compete with us, she doesn't mind joining in—especially if we make sure she gets a better score than we do. She is also interested in seeing how many calories she has burned after each activity. This is helping her understand the connection between food eaten and the amount of work needed to burn off the calories.*

> *Samantha thoroughly enjoyed the required health education class she took in high school. Although she had always been resistant to our suggestions about what constituted a healthy snack or a reasonably-sized portion of food, she was more receptive to this information when she heard it from the Health teacher. She even started looking at food labels and noticing how many cookies, crackers, etc. were in one serving. She also started asking questions like "What's potassium? Why do I need it?"*
>
> *Unfortunately, like many of us, Samantha still has some problems with portion control. Even though she now understands the concept of a serving size, that doesn't keep her from wanting to eat more than one serving of something she likes. Lately, we've been buying prepackaged, 100-calorie snacks and emphasizing that that's about the right amount for a snack.*

## GETTING WORK-RELATED EXPERIENCES

Schools should also offer curricula that cover the skills that are required for success in employment. Progressive school districts work closely with area businesses and industries to provide trained and prepared entry-level workers. If you live in an area where, let's say, there are large manufacturing plants or pharmaceutical companies, your school ought to be collaborating with them so that students graduate with the skills that the industries are seeking. Part of that collaboration may include part-time employment during the high school years.

School districts treat employment for students with Down syndrome in different ways. Some school districts have ongoing and close relationships with one or more local companies and, every year, they place students in jobs in those companies. In this case, the school district basically "owns" the jobs because when the student graduates, she loses the job so it can become available to the next student. These "training jobs" are great for schools and lousy for students with disabilities. The advantage for the schools is that they can easily provide job placements and do not have to go out and develop jobs every year for their students. The disadvantage for students is that the jobs do not necessarily fit their interests or skills. Worse, they have to give up the job when they leave school.

If schools are going to be in the business of assisting students with disabilities in the area of employment, they must be committed to working with students individually. This means finding a job that is matched to the student and that belongs to the student, not to the school.

More and more school districts are beginning to understand that they are not good at employment services for students with disabilities. As a result, many of them have developed working relationships and contacts with adult service agencies that have expertise in employment practices. This has turned out to be a very positive practice. The schools continue to be involved in academic areas and the adult service agencies do job development and job coaching, operate job clubs, and work on skills that are work related. Families report a high level of satisfaction with these kinds of arrangements and also benefit from being introduced to agencies that serve adults. It often helps in ensuring a smooth transition from high school.

If you are not satisfied with the work experiences being offered to your child, bring it up to school officials, either at the IEP meeting or at another meeting. You might want to suggest that your school partner with an adult service agency that is successful in employment. You might want to do your own investigation with some local agencies and find out whether they have any interest in such an opportunity. Some families have been successful in bringing new ideas and new partnerships to their school districts.

## A Successful Employment Program

In Delaware, a program called "Early Start" works with high school students 18 months before they leave special education to help them find jobs that match their interests. Working with students before they leave school, in partnership with local service providers, this statewide program is designed to provide a seamless transition for students who would like to work as soon as they are out of school. Upon graduation, the student remains in his or her job—that is the intention of this initiative. The program gets high marks from both families and employers.

### WORK EXPERIENCES IN SCHOOL SETTINGS

The types of job education experiences available to students with Down syndrome vary a great deal from school to school and community to community. Here are some of the experiences that may be available to your child in high school.

**In-Class Work Experiences:** While it is often preferable for our students to gain work experience in the community, some students may not yet have the stamina, behavior, or skills to work in the community. These students may benefit from work experiences completed in the classroom with familiar staff. In some classrooms, the teacher may set up an area of the room as a production area to do either real or imaginary work. For example, students may do real work for the school, like getting a mailing ready for distribution. This kind of activity may include collating, stapling, folding, stuffing envelopes, and sorting. These same activities might be done as imaginary work, if there wasn't a real mailing to send out. Or, students might be put to work sorting and separating nuts from bolts. If your child is getting work experience in the classroom, you should make sure that it replicates as best it can a real work environment.

**In-School Work Experiences:** There may be opportunities for your child to have a variety of work experiences within the school. These could include working in the school store, selling snacks at lunchtime, shelving books in the library, participating in the recycling program, making copies for teachers, distributing the mail, shredding documents (especially good for nonreaders, who can shred confidential information), answering the school phone, or working in the cafeteria.

These experiences can be very helpful in exposing your child to a variety of jobs in the safety of the school setting. This might be a great opportunity for your child, especially if she does not enjoy academic demands and may need a daily break from them. On the other hand, if your child is highly motivated and enjoys classroom learning, these jobs may limit her access to the general education curriculum.

**Vocational Education Classes:** Vocational education refers to training in manual and practical jobs that are nonacademic. Some high schools have vocational education classes, for example, in the areas of office skills or auto mechanics. You may want to consider classes in the vocational services department of your high school for your child. My son took cooking, woodworking, and keyboarding from the offerings of the vocational department.

There are also separate vocational high schools that offer a wider range of vocational education programs. Students in these programs usually take classes from the regular high school curriculum as well as classes in job skills such as hair dressing, cosmetology, auto mechanics, information technology, and health-related fields.

**Internships:** Internships are work experiences in which the student performs some or all of the duties of a particular job for a period of time in order to try it out or gain work experience. Internships can offer important ways for your child to "sample" jobs. Internships are generally unpaid and can take place during the day in lieu of classes, after school, or during vacations or summer breaks. If your school has a strong internship program, staff can assist students in locating appropriate internships. If performing an internship is part of your child's IEP, the school should provide the support your child needs to be successful.

*The year that Jon's class graduated, he was considered a graduate, but actually had three more years of high school eligibility. There were three weeks between graduation day and the real end of the school year. I was anticipating that Jon would just stay home for those weeks before he went to summer camp. Since the school was obligated to educate him for those three weeks, however, they came up with the idea of using that time for internships. Each of those three weeks, they found him a different job and provided a job coach. It was a great opportunity for Jon to learn what he liked and didn't like, and one of the managers at one of his internships hired him a year later for a summer job.*

*Jared used high school to explore a variety of employment interests in his community through job sampling and volunteer activities. He worked at a dry cleaner, a discount retail outlet, and a landscaping company, and volunteered at the local animal shelter. Jared left high school with two part-time jobs. He worked at a local fitness center, and through the connections of his "Circle of Friends," landed a job at a supermarket. He left the fitness center when the supermarket offered him more hours. Jared recently celebrated his five-year anniversary with the company and now works just over 22 hours a week and more during the summer months.*

## LEARNING INDEPENDENT LIVING SKILLS

In addition to work-related skills, students need to learn the skills that will enable them to be as independent as possible. This is another area where schools sometimes fall short and lack expertise. Although some schools have set up laundry and cooking areas for special education students, you may prefer that these skills be taught away from the academic instructional environment of the local high school. For some families, that means a postsecondary program (see Chapter 6). For other families, it could mean working on the skills at home. Still other families may want to insist that the school use community resources to teach the skills—for instance, working on laundry skills at a community laundromat. Sometimes the local school district partners with a local adult service agency to develop and deliver these opportunities.

If you have decided you want your child to work on these skills at school, make sure they are included in the IEP as a goal or in the Coordinated Set of Activities. Some examples of activities are:

- Emily will continue to work on self-feeding skills.
- Brendan will continue toileting on schedule.
- Maria will develop a weekly budget.
- William will shop for his lunch daily in community stores.
- Taylor will learn to use the public transportation system to get to school.

*Our local Arc is very innovative. They developed a weekend program for students between the ages of 14-22, and it is kind of like a "real world" house for students with disabilities. It is not like the TV reality show with sex, drugs, and rock and roll. Instead, my daughter goes there once a month and learns to cook, shop, clean her room, make a bed, and get along with other students and work out real problems, not made-up ones in the classroom. She never unloaded the dishwasher before she went and I was afraid to let her use a stove at home. The staff taught her to use the stove safely. She would like to go more often but it is expensive. They have some grants to reduce the cost to families and some school districts pay for their students to go.*

**LEARNING SELF-ADVOCACY SKILLS**

There are not too many skills more important for your child to learn than self-advocacy skills. Just as you learned how to be an advocate for your child, your child must know how to advocate for herself. Your child probably has already learned some of these skills and you may have knowingly or unknowingly have taught them to her yourself. Maybe you began with decisions about food choices—for example, giving your daughter the opportunity to decide whether she wanted apple juice or orange

juice when she was small. Those early steps in self-advocacy have probably developed into larger decisions about clothing, activities, and friends. As your child continues to mature, it is important to continue to broaden the areas in which she can exercise decision making and control.

Self-advocacy can also be taught in a more traditional setting such as a class or in a club. It is most beneficial if it is a cornerstone of learning and woven into the fabric of all your daughter's lessons. Here are a couple of examples of self-advocacy goals. The first is for someone who is nonverbal and the second one is for someone who is shy and passive:

- Lauren will be provided with classroom support to improve her ability to use her electronic communications device to express her preferences.
- Margaret will express her preferences for movies when a choice is given to her and her peers.

Another way to work on self-advocacy skills is to ensure that your child attends her IEP meetings. At first, the goal might be for her to participate in the meetings, perhaps by answering questions about her own preferences or volunteering information about her abilities, interests, and goals. Later, she might work up to leading her own meeting.

We want our children to learn self-advocacy skills so they can be protected from harm, abuse, and exploitation. We also have to learn to respect our children when they use their self-advocacy skills to demonstrate their independence from us. Our children's skills must be respected if our children are to be safe.

Advocacy used to be the sole responsibility of families. However, the torch has been passed on to our children as the self-advocacy movement has strengthened and become better recognized. Many individuals with Down syndrome and other intellectual disabilities have found their voices. However, not everyone can assume this task without support. For those who find self-advocacy challenging, families and support staff must help them. This may mean allotting more time for meetings so your child can share her thoughts and information, and creating opportunities for your child to voice her opinion. The goal is for her to understand that her self-advocacy is expected and valued.

*At one of Jon's annual reviews, staff members suggested that he take a cash register course that was given regularly by the agency that provided him supports. Jon said he wasn't interested. He said he didn't work in a supermarket and had no plans to become a cashier. His dream job was working on a golf course. The staff were persistent and told him there was lots more to the course than just learning the skills associated with the cash register, like communication skills with customers, and those kind of skills were useful in many settings. I wanted to be seen as supporting the staff, so I joined in. Finally, Jon gave in and agreed to have taking a cash register course added to his annual list of goals.*

*I couldn't sleep that night because I realized that all of us, myself included, had disregarded Jon's opinions and voice. His opinions were logical and well thought out. Still, the room full of professionals and his mother ignored him and his self-advocacy. The next morning, filled with guilt, I called the team chairperson and told her what we had all done. The goal was removed and I was able to use this as a teaching example to the team that if Jon was going to be valued, he had to be heard.*

The self-advocacy movement is well established. It began in Sweden in the 1960s, then came to Canada and then the United States in the early 1970s. The first group, founded by some folks from Oregon, named the group "People First" because they disliked begin referred to as "retarded people." There are now local, state, national, and international self-advocacy groups, and conferences and conventions are regularly held. It is hard to determine just how many self-advocacy groups exist in the United States because the movement is growing so quickly. Some groups are sponsored by local Arcs and other adult agencies, and many receive funding from their state departments on disability. The national organization is now called "Self-Advocates Becoming Empowered." Individuals with Down syndrome are active in all levels of the self-advocacy movement.

Out of the self-advocacy movement came the realization that people who receive supports ought to be part of the system that makes the rules. As a result, self-advocates are on the boards of the National Down Syndrome Society, National Down Syndrome Congress, Special Olympics, The Arc of the United States, and virtually all their associated affiliates. Self-advocates are represented on most of the decision-making bodies of the adult service systems as well.

*The role of self-advocacy is so important in the transition process. Teaching and practicing self-advocacy skills and self-determination should start in middle school so teens are prepared to begin shaping their own lives. I didn't want to be the one steering the boat at the high school level, but my daughter was still learning and practicing-self advocacy. It took way more time than I thought it would. Take advantage of every opportunity you can (at home, school, and in the community) for helping your child develop skills in self-advocacy and decision making. High school is a time when they should be putting these skills into action.*

# Behavior

Students with disabilities are sometimes held to higher standards of behavior at school than typical children are. If you walk into almost any high school, you will witness kissing, hugging, and other sexualized behaviors in the hallways and cafeteria. Some teachers may notice and attempt to interfere, but in many cases it will be ignored. However, if your child with Down syndrome tried the same behavior, it would probably lead to lots of professional attention and a goal might even be developed to teach her "appropriate behavior."

In spite of this "double standard," it is important for our children to learn appropriate social skills. Many families will find that inclusion in general education classes will provide the environment and role models that will promote good social skills and behavior. Other families will want to make sure that IEP goals are developed to teach age-appropriate language and social skills.

Behavior is a way of communicating. If you have a child with Down syndrome who is verbal and well behaved, you might not be aware of the struggles of some families who have children with little verbal communication. What may appear as noncompliant behavior is actually a form of communication. It can be very challenging to figure out what a nonverbal student is trying to communicate, however.

If your middle school or high school child with Down syndrome struggles with appropriate behavior, it is essential to make that a focus during the transition years. Otherwise, her opportunities as an adult may be limited if her behaviors interfere with employment or her ability to participate in community activities.

*Carlos hated to have group home staff assist him in the shower. At least that's what we all thought. Every night, staff in his group home struggled as he fought and screamed. His family reported that he never behaved this way at home. After they were questioned about his shower routine, it developed that his family had always washed him beginning with his left arm, moving on the right, and down his body. Last was his shampoo and face. In contrast, the group home staff were beginning with a shampoo. As soon as the group home staff began to shower him the same way he was used to, he was fully cooperative and looked forward to showering. His struggle was his way of communicating that the staff were doing it all wrong.*

If your child has problem behaviors, it may be useful to have a "functional behavior analysis" (FBA) to determine the function that is being served by the behavior. The functional behavior assessment is a process for determining the cause or function of a behavior. It involves determining what happens before a problem behavior (the "antecedent"), as well as what the person receives as a consequence of her behavior. For example, does she get out of doing a task she does not enjoy? (If so, her behavior may be communicating: This is too hard for me, or this is boring, or I need a break, or I want to do what the other students are doing.) Does she get attention from the teacher or students? (If so, her behavior may be communicating: I need help, I want someone to talk to me, I like to make the other kids laugh, or I'm bored.)

The information obtained from an FBA is then used to plan interventions that could be used to teach the student how to get what she wants more appropriately. Once she can communicate her needs more appropriately, the problem behavior will be reduced or eliminated. "Positive Behavior Support" (PBS) strategies can then be used to encourage good behavior and to create a positive environment for the student where the factors (boredom, frustration, hunger, etc.) that set off inappropriate behavior are less likely to occur.

If your child has challenging or unsafe behaviors, you should insist on PBS. It is an evidence-based approach that school systems are required to use under IDEA. (IDEA refers to it as Positive Behavioral Interventions and Supports.) PBS shifts the focus from the noncompliant student to the behavior of others in the student's environment. For example, if your child runs out of the room every time a particular teacher asks her to do a particular task, an analysis needs to be done to determine whether it is the teacher or the task or something else that is causing your child to run away. The support she needs to be able to complete the task will be different depending on what is motivating her to run away.

If your child has already transitioned into adult services and she still has behaviors that prevent her from enjoying the quality life she envisions for herself, ask the funding agency and the supporting agency to address her behaviors through PBS.

# Extracurricular Activities

Extracurricular activities can offer an enjoyable way for your child to learn or practice skills. Your child can sign up to participate in an activity just like any other student, or you may need to get support and assistance from the school. If necessary, you can communicate directly with the coach or advisor about what you would like

your child to get from the activity, or you can discuss your child's needs more formally at an IEP meeting. The path you take will depend on the activity, your child's interests and skills, and her support needs.

Extracurricular activities range from competitive and intramural sports, art and drama clubs, and music and chorus activities, to social justice groups, writing and photography opportunities, and special interest groups. High schools usually have so many activities that it should not be difficult to find some that interest your child. Since our kids sometimes have difficulty in trying new things, your child may need some encouragement or convincing from you.

Regardless of the activity she chooses, your child may be able to learn or work on the following skills:

- time management—getting there on time;
- accountability—being where she is expected; doing what is expected;
- teamwork—working together to achieve a goal;
- belonging—being part of something;
- fundraising—participating in bake sales, car washes, holding a donation can;
- transportation—arranging rides to activities;
- dressing appropriately for the activity.

# The Use of Summer Vacations

Most of us like to think of summer as a time when the pace slows and there is a possibility of a vacation. Family vacations are wonderful opportunities to both strengthen family relationships and take a break from regular routines. For transition-age students, summers can also provide additional opportunities for your child to maintain skills and learn new ones. Below are some ways to enjoyably work learning opportunities into your child's summer.

**Summer Programs:** Many school districts offer summer programs or summer school for their students with disabilities who qualify. Since these programs are usually provided as part of your child's IEP, it is important that you discuss the necessity for year-round education during the annual IEP. Summer help is often used to staff summer programs, so they vary considerably in quality. If your child is offered a summer program, you will have to consider whether the program offered is a good option for your child, compared with other opportunities that may be available in your community.

**Community Recreation Programs:** Most communities offer year-round and summer recreation programs, and some community recreation departments also sponsor special recreation and leisure programs for individuals with special needs. Inclusion in regular recreation programs may be helpful for working on social skills with typically developing peers. Exposure to new activities may lead to the development of new skills. For example, a tennis class could help your child to strengthen eye-hand coordination.

**Camp Programs:** For many families, summer is all about camp. There are typical camps that are sponsored by YMCAs, Scouts, religious organizations, foundations, and private organizations. Typical day camps or overnight camps may not be required to offer special assistance to campers with disabilities, including assistance with self-care skills or extra supervision, if it would create an undue burden to the program, be very expensive, or fundamentally change the character of the program. Special needs camps can be a good option, especially if your child is lacking in self-care skills, needs additional support, or has never slept away from home before. The special needs camps have lower staff-to-camper ratios and are more accepting of the skill levels of our children.

*Camping is big in our community. When Jon was 3, he began attending a local day camp with the kids in the community. When he was 6, the children began going to a day camp that was a 40-minute bus ride away in a more rural setting. It just seemed natural that Jon would go, too. When the children began talking about going to overnight camp, it just seemed like we should join the discussion. So, I found a one-week YMCA camp that was designed for first-time campers. Jon was only 9 and we didn't know anyone since this camp was in another community. Jon had a great time and for the next two summers, he went for a month to the same overnight camp as his friends (a different camp from the one he tried the summer before), and the same one my brother and uncle had gone to before him. We made arrangements with the camp to have one of the counselors spend extra time with Jon and we compensated the counselor for that. Telephone calls were not allowed and neither were visits. Jon did fine. It was a long time for us.*

*When Jon was 12, he began going to camp for 8 weeks every summer. There was one visiting day. He rose through the ranks and spent 6 summers being ordinary. From there, Jon spent 4 summers at another overnight camp that included 30 campers with developmental disabilities among the 300 campers. At this camp, he lived in a house with other campers and had a job at camp in addition to typical camp activities. Jon learned at an early age how independent he could be.*

**Work:** For many of us, when we were teens, summer meant a break from school, but working can also be an extremely valuable summertime activity. Jobs for teens have several purposes—to earn a little money, learn some job skills, and keep busy and out of trouble. These same reasons are just as valid for teens with Down syndrome. See Chapter 7 for information on finding and keeping a job.

*When Jon had had 10 years of overnight camp and he was approaching 20 years of age, we began to think of summer as a time for him to try some jobs. He had a couple of internships in an office and at a country club. He found out that working in an office was boring and being in a kitchen hot, but being on a golf course rocked. He got to hit balls from the woods back onto the practice fairway. That led to a summer job at a different country club, where he helped run the driving range and assist in the bag room. Another summer, after a winter internship doing some maintenance activities, he worked at a summer day camp, on an island off the coast of Massachusetts, doing maintenance. Both of these jobs led him to future year-round jobs.*

**Volunteering:** In some states and in many communities, high school students are required to complete a specific number of community service hours to graduate. Some kids spend their summers volunteering. Others meet this obligation during the school year. There are one-time volunteer jobs such as picking up trash or weeding at a county park or helping to set up and run special events, as well as long-term volunteer jobs such as helping out at a retirement home or a daycare center. Some students design their own volunteer project. I know of a student with Down syndrome who spoke to school groups about having a disability for her community service project.

I think it is important to have our children participate in this requirement, so they can enjoy the benefits of "giving back." Too often, our children are seen only as recipients of community services, and providing a service can demonstrate their ability to contribute to their communities. Before Jon was old enough to work, he volunteered at our community center and at our synagogue. While he enjoyed the activities, I think what was most important was the community having the opportunity to see him making a difference.

**Family and Leisure Time:** For some families, the summer is about being together with no particular agendas and for others it means a summer of neatly laid plans. It may be time for family vacations, trips to the beach, and visits with relatives or hanging around in the neighborhood. Don't overlook the opportunities to teach and reinforce social and communication or other needed skills during leisure activities. I know families who have used this time to teach their son with Down syndrome to drive and others who have used it to enrich their family life.

# Balancing Work and Family

In both single-family households and in two-parent families, most families balance work and child responsibilities with great difficulty. In families where there is a child with Down syndrome, the lack of after school programs makes the balancing act much more difficult. The lack of childcare options for high school students in particular threatens the financial underpinnings of many families.

Some families reduce their hours of employment to ensure after school supervision for their children with Down syndrome, while others find a way to work at home. These are not realistic alternatives for most families. Most families are forced to piece together a patchwork of solutions—enrolling their child in after school activities, hiring "sitters," or seeking out after school programs for teens with disabilities at the local Arc.

You might also consider IEP goals for your child to learn the safety skills that will enable her to stay at home for some period of time. Here are some examples:

- Samantha will learn to identify and use her house key.
- Samantha will learn to enter her house, lock the door behind her, and call her mother at work to let her know she is home.
- Samantha will prepare a healthy after school snack.
- Samantha will learn to respond appropriately and safely to familiar and unfamiliar people at the door and on the phone.

*Jon had begun to stay at home for short periods of time. One afternoon, I had to take his sister to the dentist. As I was driving away from our home, I noticed several well-dressed, unfamiliar people going door-to-door in our neighborhood. I figured they were probably Jehovah's Witnesses. I hadn't yet taught Jon what to do if strangers came to the door when he was alone. So, as I drove by the strangers, I stopped and explained the situation and asked them not to ring our doorbell. They were understanding and skipped our house. I realized I had another lesson to teach Jon. You can't always think of everything ahead of time.*

# CHAPTER 3

# Movin' On:
## Postsecondary Options

*In the past, students with Down syndrome would usually stay in high school until they "aged-out" of special education, at age 21 or 22. While in high school, they may have been educated in general education, special education classes, or life-skill classes, with some training related to employment and transition issues. This may still be the case where you live. It may meet your child's needs.*

*Now, however, there are more options than ever for students with Down syndrome. This is true even for students who are not expected to earn a regular high school diploma. They can expect to experience something other than seven years of high school. From specialized programs to 4-year colleges, the opportunities are limited only by imagination and resourcefulness and resources.*

*Students with Down syndrome are attending two- and four-year colleges, vocational schools, special programs at colleges (both residential and nonresidential), and post-high school programs at special education schools, in addition to choosing to stay in high school until the loss of their special education entitlement.*

*Remember that under IDEA 2004, transition plans need to have measurable goals and outcomes that lead to postsecondary school and employment. Chapter 2 covered what your child should be learning in high school; this chapter will help you understand what can come after high school.*

Postsecondary education is a broad term that refers to education that comes after high school. Generally, it occurs after receiving a high school diploma. However, for students with disabilities who exit high school without a diploma, many postsecondary options may still be available. For students with Down syndrome, postsecondary options may include the traditional options of two- and four-year colleges, universities, community colleges, and vocational and career schools. They may also include special programs on college campuses, or programs operated by special education schools, your school district, or adult service agencies in your community. There are also post-secondary programs that may be operated collaboratively by two or more educational or other agencies in a community. They are often called "transition programs."

It is important to remember that there is no federal law comparable to IDEA that provides for a free and appropriate public education for students with disabilities after high school graduation. Nor are there laws that require programs to take your child's disability into account during the admission process (although Section 504 of the Rehabilitation Act of 1973 offers some protections once a student with disabilities is admitted to a program). The postsecondary school can apply the same admission standards to a person with Down syndrome as it does to any other student. It cannot, however, hold your child to a higher standard.

# Postsecondary Options for Students Still Covered by IDEA

In some states, students with Down syndrome may be able to attend free classes at community college, if this option is available to students with disabilities in general. Some school districts will pay the tuition costs for a community college under an agreement reached between the community college and a school district, some school districts have used grant awards to pay for the tuition, and some states actually offer this opportunity to their students. Students may also be able to attend other postsecondary programs at their school district's expense, if it has been agreed upon by the school district. These types of postsecondary opportunities generally only occur when the school district cannot offer a comparable program within the school district. IDEA does not *require* that school districts make postsecondary programs available to students with disabilities, free of charge.

If your child's IEP team agrees that the most appropriate setting for him to work on his goals is in a postsecondary program, and the school district cannot meet the IEP goals in a setting within the district, and they are willing to pay for postsecondary education, a family might expect that the school will pay for it. However, there are many localities where school districts are simply not willing to pay for postsecondary programs. For example, let's say that your twenty-year-old daughter has goals related to learning keyboarding and other office skills. The school doesn't have to send your child to business school to learn these skills if there are classes in the high school that cover the needed skills, even if the majority of the students in the classes are much younger than your daughter.

The sections below discuss types of postsecondary programs that may be available in your community. Make sure you thoroughly check out the options available to transition-aged students in your school district, since local practices vary considerably.

Also look into options that are available if your child chooses to leave school before his entitlement ends. In some areas, there may be Medicaid-funded programs that transition-aged students are eligible for. Or you may be in the financial position to pay for needed services or supports.

**POSTSECONDARY PROGRAMS IN THE SCHOOL DISTRICT**

Some school districts now offer "Transition Programs" for students with disabilities. These have been developed because families and students were not satisfied with seven years of high school and began demanding that schools do more for their child. Some families lobbied for expensive out-of-district placements at established postsecondary programs because there were no attractive services offered in their home communities. In response, school districts across the country have developed a variety of programs in an attempt to meet the needs of students with Down syndrome and other intellectual disabilities.

These programs can vary greatly, but may contain some common elements. These include vocational experiences, functional academics, and some independent living training. Some programs emphasize employment and transportation skills, while others include significant classroom time. Some programs may have ongoing relationships with community organizations such as the YMCA, adult service agencies or a local college, and offer some training or instruction through these organizations. In some places, several school districts have gotten together to develop a transition program to meet the needs of their students.

Some of these are stand-alone programs with classes that are just for transition-age students with disabilities who have "graduated" from high school, but still have several years of eligibility under IDEA. In other programs, however, students go to a college campus and take either credit or noncredit classes with other students, with and without modifications, as needed.

The benefits of these kinds of transition programs are that school districts can attempt to control the escalating cost of out-of-district placements, the student stays in a familiar environment, and there is often a seamless transition to adult supports and services after high school.

If your school district offers such a postsecondary program for students with disabilities, you should visit the program and speak to other families to determine whether this would be a good option for your child.

**DUAL ENROLLMENT**

A new practice that is usually referred to as dual (or concurrent) enrollment is beginning to emerge around the United States. It typically allows high school students to take college level courses at area community colleges or state schools. The students usually do not have to pay for the college credit but receive both high school and college credit. In the past, dual enrollment was usually offered to high school students who wanted to take higher level courses than available at high school or to engage students who were at risk for dropping out of high school. The practice is also popular for financially strapped families. In these situations, students can use the credits earned and reduce the number needed for a college degree.

In some communities, concurrent enrollment is now being used to offer students with Down syndrome and others the opportunity to take courses in a college environment with age appropriate peers. Like their typical peers, they do not have to pay for the courses, as long as they are enrolled in a participating high school. In these situations, the high school may provide the necessary educational supports, including, but not limited to, assistance with understanding the material, adapting it, note-taking, and social skills.

Students with Down syndrome who are able to take advantage of dual enrollment can experience a wider variety of courses than is usually found in high schools. They may be able to explore potential job interests, as well as their own interest in pursuing additional postsecondary education after their IDEA eligibility expires. Community colleges typically offer an array of vocational courses such as baking, medical technology, cosmetology, child care, etc. This arrangement also provides an opportunity for the student with Down syndrome to learn with age-appropriate peers, be a part of a college community, and receive good support in preparing for and obtaining employment.

Tom Sannicandro, a Massachusetts state representative and the father of a young man with Down syndrome, sponsored legislation that authorized an innovative program that gives high school students with cognitive disabilities access to regular college classes at state schools. While students are still receiving special education services, they are able to audit a course, either remedial, educational, or recreational, and receive the support of an educational coach from their high schools. What is unique about this initiative is that the local school district must provide academic supports, such as an aide to assist the student in the class.

## POSTSECONDARY AND TRANSITION PROGRAMS IN ADULT SERVICE AGENCIES

In some parts of the U.S., school districts, usually at the request of families, have reached out to adult service agencies to assist them in developing transition programs. Although these programs may not technically qualify as postsecondary programs, they can be very useful to students with Down syndrome. These agencies may be in a unique position to offer excellent employment and independent living skills training. Public schools have many educational obligations to students with disabilities, from those with mild learning or attention problems to those with very substantial disabilities; it is difficult for them to excel in all areas. Adult service agencies that specialize in supporting individuals with Down syndrome and related disabilities have developed an expertise in these areas. Consequently, more of them have developed school-to-work programs and work collaboratively with families and school districts.

If your school district has a transition program run by an adult service agency, your child might continue to take classes at the high school part time, and then leave the campus for part of the day or on certain days to take classes in work skills, do an internship, or work at a job. Or, he might leave the high school completely and might work on banking skills, travel training, and job exploration at the adult service agency, or perhaps even work fulltime, with support from the agency.

*Our local Arc has several programs for transition-age young people, including a unique weekend program that is a special needs version of the popular TV reality show Real World House. My son, Christopher, attends one or two weekends a month and he is taught many valuable skills there. They plan, shop, and prepare meals. They clean up the kitchen and bathrooms, and when the weekend is over, change and wash their linens. He is learning skills he could never learn in school and that he and I would fight over. In this environment, he is gaining confidence in his abilities. When he comes home, he is able to take the initiative and do some of the things he has learned—like empty a dishwasher. Unlike many programs, this one is not just for the higher functioning kids. It is a little pricey for the weekend, but we were able to get our school district to include it in his IEP and now they pay for some of the weekends and we are able to swing the others.*

POSTSECONDARY
PROGRAMS
IN SPECIAL
EDUCATION
SCHOOLS

Some students with Down syndrome attend privately run, substantially separate special education schools. These students are either supported by their school district or have private family funds to attend. Many of the schools are residential, meaning that students live at the school. In the past, these schools typically offered a course of studies through the 12th grade. In the last ten to twenty years, however, most of them have recognized their students' needs for postsecondary programs and have developed them. Some of these postsecondary programs are separate from their high school program, while others are an extension of the high school.

These schools and their postsecondary programs usually have specific entrance criteria. These can include intelligence testing and other educational measures. Some families have reported to me that they found the application process cold and unwelcoming. Some have even suggested that the schools are unwelcoming to students with Down syndrome because they fail to look beyond our children's appearance. These schools are not public institutions and they are allowed to set their own admissions criteria. This does not amount to discrimination.

In the past, many of these schools were geared toward students with learning disabilities, but now some schools have branched out to serve students with greater academic needs. More recently, students with Down syndrome are being "recruited" to these programs because they are often enthusiastic learners with minimal mental health issues.

Not all of these specialized schools are appropriate for students with Down syndrome. For example, a school that is geared to students who have a 4th grade reading level and who understand math concepts at a 3rd grade level is simply not a good fit for your child if he reads at a 2nd grade level and does not grasp mathematical concepts. No matter how good his social skills are, he will not be an appropriate candidate for that school because the materials will be presented in a format that will not be accessible to him. Private schools are allowed to determine their own admissions criteria, just as Cornell and Dartmouth can determine the type of student who has the potential to succeed. Additionally, if your child has a medical condition that requires more nursing than the school provides, your child may not be safe there, no matter how much you might wish for him to attend.

Programs based at special education schools sometimes offer postsecondary programs for students who have finished their high school studies at their school or elsewhere. Some of these programs enroll students who are in their mid- to late twenties, as well as transition-age students. Some postsecondary programs for students with disabilities require that the student have formally finished high school, and have either a diploma or a certificate of completion. Examples of these schools include Cardinal Cushing Centers ACHIEVE program, Riverview School's GROW program in Massachusetts, and Chapel Haven in Connecticut. The Berkshire Hills Music Academy in Massachusetts includes students with Down syndrome, although it was started as a program for musically gifted students with Williams syndrome.

The first step in considering these schools is to get a catalog or visit the school's website and try to talk to families who are familiar with the school. In spite of what I said earlier about entrance criteria, do not be intimidated by them if you believe your child will be a good fit with the school. Entrance criteria are guidelines and I have seen every school be flexible, especially if a student's family can pay the tuition.

Families and students are attracted to these programs for the quality of the educational programs and their staff, their emphasis on independent living skills, and the social opportunities they afford their students. Often, parents see a real social network for their children at these schools. Rather than being in the minority and trying to fit in, most students at these programs feel a sense of belonging and acceptance.

The cost to these programs can run upwards to $80,000 year, although some are less expensive. (If there is not a residential component, they are usually considerably cheaper.) Many families make great sacrifices to find the money to send their child, and some school districts pay the tuition.

A school district may consider paying or cost sharing with a family if they do not have a program in the district or if the family is successful in using advocacy efforts. Often, however, these advocacy efforts include hiring expensive legal representation.

## Universal Design for Learning

As a parent, you should be aware of the emerging innovation called Universal Design for Learning (UDL), which is rapidly transforming classroom instruction for special education students. UDL is an educational framework that provides flexibility in the ways information is presented, in the ways students respond or demonstrate knowledge and skills, and in the ways students are engaged in learning. It also reduces barriers in instruction, provides appropriate accommodations, supports, and challenges, and maintains high achievement expectations for all students. When UDL is properly implemented, goals, instructional materials, teaching methods, and assessments are designed from the outset to be accessible to all students.

UDL is making a difference in preschool through secondary school and shows great promise in postsecondary education, where more faculty are embracing universal design. When observing possible programs for your child, be sure to ask whether they are familiar with, and use, principles of UDL.

## THIRD TIER PROGRAMS

"Third tier programs" is a term used by some programs that provide residential, employment, and other support services for students who have finished their transition programs and are looking for something more long-term. They can also be called nontraditional postsecondary programs. Some of them grew out of special education schools and may be operated by or in collaboration with these schools or by groups of families of graduates. Others developed simply because families were looking for a place where their child might be able to live permanently in adulthood. Some of these programs may accept some government funding, but they are all private and generally attract families who can afford their fees. Fees are based on the level of need and generally begin at $25,000 for a low-level need, plus housing costs.

In these programs, individuals with Down syndrome have a life. They may work, go to college, volunteer, and take adult education classes or do a combination of activities. These programs are very attractive to families looking for both community and permanency for their child. Families who consider these programs are usually drawn to the social opportunities available for their children, perhaps because their children are experiencing social isolation, even though they might have had an inclusive public school education.

LIFE, Inc., on Cape Cod, Cardinal Cushing Centers, and Chapel Haven in Connecticut are examples of "third tier" programs. In these programs, participants reside in the community with support in their own homes and apartments. Many of the residents and their families find living in these communities to be satisfying even though they might have had an inclusive public school education.

# Postsecondary Education and College

The idea that students with Down syndrome can attend and benefit from postsecondary programs is not new. However, what it means to be included in postsecondary education is changing every year. Not long ago a postsecondary program for young adults with Down syndrome meant only a segregated program for people with disabilities. But today, families are constantly challenging their communities to include students with intellectual disabilities in a broad range of inclusive programs at community colleges and universities.

We have witnessed the remarkable educational and social achievements of our children when they were given the opportunity and exposure to the general curriculum and to their peers. Many students with Down syndrome have had the benefits of inclusion for all or most of their school careers, and when their peers leave high school, many of our kids are also ready for the "next step." The college campus and the community that it provides is a natural place for our kids to experience new opportunities and take new risks in the same environment as typical students their age.

There are now over 250 college programs for students with Down syndrome and related disabilities in the United States, and the number grows every year. There is great interest among families and a growing body of literature that is driving the development of these programs.

Taft College in California is considered one of the first colleges to offer students with Down syndrome the opportunity for postsecondary education and an opportunity to live on campus. Taft's Transition to Independent Living Program began in 1995 and has since spurred on many other institutions to see how they can play a role in educating students with Down syndrome and related disabilities. As word got out about Taft College's success, families around the country began efforts to duplicate Taft's model and develop new models. Colleges that had long ignored individuals with intellectual disabilities began to see the possibilities, often at the urging of families. Colleges had already experienced the success of students with learning disabilities and most had established "learning centers," note takers, and other supports for these students.

While there has been more hesitation by colleges to figure out how to include students with intellectual disabilities, they were often encouraged to try by their own education or allied health departments. In addition, some faith-based colleges or universities have recognized that serving a wider range of students is within their mission. For example, at the urging of a family, Misericordia University in Pennsylvania began a program that now includes a residential component. The program is called "Circle of Friends" and the young women in the program live with student mentors and learn employment and daily living skills. This college-like experience does not lead to a degree and costs families over $30,000 a year.

Expanding transition and postsecondary opportunities for people with Down syndrome and other intellectual disabilities has been of great interest to the National Down Syndrome Society (NDSS) for the past decade. Increased levels of interest from families, self-advocates, teachers, and parent associations across the country have reinforced the need and desire for these programs. NDSS has created and is implementing a strategic plan to promote postsecondary education for students with intellectual disabilities. See the NDSS website at www.ndss.org, click on "Policy," then "Legislative and Policy Agenda," and then "Transition and Postsecondary Initiative."

The interest of NDSS and its constituents has been driven by many factors. First, studies have shown that students with intellectual disabilities (including Down syndrome) who participate in postsecondary education are more likely to excel in academics, employment, and live more independently in the community. Second, many children with Down syndrome and other intellectual disabilities are now being included in public school and want to pursue postsecondary education like their peers and siblings.

Through a generous grant received from Laura and Steve Riggio, in 2004 the NDSS established a Steering Committee aimed at developing high quality, inclusive postsecondary model programs in New Jersey for students with intellectual disabilities based on the best practices of existing postsecondary programs. By learning from the excellent, though varied, programs that exist across the country, the Committee sought to expand on the successes of these other programs and develop a model to be replicated across the country. The Committee determined its four desired outcomes for the postsecondary program: academic enrichment, socialization, independent living skills, and competitive employment. Additionally, the Committee set its sights on creating a program that was affordable for all students.

Mercer County Community College (MCCC) and The College of New Jersey (TCNJ) received funding for three years from the NDSS to develop programs appropriate for students with Down syndrome and other intellectual disabilities. The first year of classes began in 2006 and both colleges now serve as successful models of postsecondary education.

Additionally, the NDSS and the College Transition Connection have developed a partnership project to create an inclusive model postsecondary program at Coastal Carolina University in South Carolina. The goal of this partnership project is to support the development of a program that will offer excellent postsecondary educational opportunities for students with intellectual disabilities to start in the Fall of 2009. The desired outcomes of the four-year Learning Is For Everyone (LIFE™) program are academic enrichment, socialization, independent living skills, and competitive or supported employment. LIFE™ programs are also being developed at USC Columbia and Clemson University.

Postsecondary education can occur in many different environments and at different points in a person's life. Postsecondary education can mean career or vocational schools and two- and four-year colleges and universities. Although many students go from high school into some kind of postsecondary education, other students take years and even decades before continuing their education. People with Down syndrome should have the same options and opportunities.

The sections below explore some of the types of postsecondary opportunities available to students with Down syndrome on college and university campuses.

## TYPES OF COLLEGE PROGRAMS

It is important to recognize that a postsecondary program is not essential for your child. However, if your child dreams of going to college like his brother or sister, this section describes some broad options to consider. To locate specific postsecondary programs that serve students with developmental disabilities, visit www.thinkcollege.net.

### FOUR-YEAR COLLEGES AND UNIVERSITIES

Four-year colleges and universities may be the last frontier as far as education for students with Down syndrome. While most families cannot imagine their child as a college student, other families have seen the possibility. A handful of young adults with Down syndrome have been admitted as degree-seeking students at four-year colleges and universities and a very small number have received an undergraduate degree. Others hoped to earn a degree and earn the required number of credits, but were never able to advance to higher level courses and were not able to receive a degree. Still others have attended college not to earn a degree, but to expand their horizons, learn skills that may help expand their employment opportunities, or for a variety of other reasons.

Some families are interested in real college opportunities in order to continue the inclusive educational opportunities that have proven to be successful for their child. Since college success is based largely on time management, good study habits, and increasing social confidence, some families see a real value in considering this option. Other families hope that the skills developed, contacts made, and internships and job experiences their child receives from attending college will lead to better employment options. Additionally, if the college has a residential option, students with Down syndrome can develop independent living skills. At this point, too few individuals with Down syndrome have attended four-year colleges to know what the long-term effects might be. However, preliminary research data are very positive and suggest that taking just one postsecondary course leads to improved employment, higher wages, and greater independence in the community

**Degree-Seeking Students.** Some of our children have the cognitive ability, reading levels, and other skills that may permit them to succeed in completing the requirements for a college degree. Bear in mind that students who matriculate at a college or university are expected to do the same work as other students, although they are eligible for reasonable accommodations such as extended time. Modifications that substantially alter the class content, assessments, required sequence of classes, etc. are typically not allowed. Each college has its own admission standards, although most require a high school diploma or its equivalent (GED). Many require standardized tests (SAT or ACT) as well, but there are increasing numbers that do not (see www.fairtest.org—under University Testing for a list).

If you truly think your child has the potential to handle typical college classes, the most important elements are a welcoming environment and the supports for your child's success. If the college has an outstanding Disability Support Office, that might provide a clue that they have the resources and motivation to work with your child. Classes with low teacher-to-student ratios are also important. See the section on "Supports and Accommodations in Postsecondary Programs" below for information on the types of accommodations that are available in college.

## Lee Jones, College Graduate

Lee Jones graduated in 2000 from Graceland University in Lamoni, Iowa, with a BA in Recreation and a minor in Theater. A personable and engaging self-advocate with Down syndrome, Lee uses his degree working at a YMCA and a community center as a fitness instructor, personal trainer, and in the membership department.

As with everything else with your child, you are in the best position to judge whether he has the motivation, determination, and academic potential to surmount the challenges of pursuing a bachelor's degree. You are also in the best position to judge whether your child has the social skills to succeed. In my experience, some, but not all, of the most academically capable students with Down syndrome have problems in this area. They may ask excessive questions, disturbing the class, have trouble differentiating between people being nice to them and people who are real friends, and may rely too heavily on teachers and professors.

**Nondegree-seeking Students.** Families are also approaching local colleges and universities seeking opportunities for their children with Down syndrome to attend classes without seeking a degree. Like other nondegree-seeking students, individuals

with Down syndrome can either take courses for credit (successfully complete all the work required of all students) or audit them for no credit (attend class but not complete any or all assignments at the level expected by the instructor). Remember that universities are not required to modify classes and assignments for your child because he has Down syndrome. They must offer accommodations such as extended time on tests and assignments, note takers, and preferential seating, however, for students with disabilities who can document the need for them. You may need to be creative when it comes to support in the classroom

A family may consider this option if there is a nearby college that might be welcoming and offers particular courses that are of interest to their child. Some families may want to offer their child the opportunity to experience "college life," however you may describe that, especially if there are opportunities for students to live on campus and increase their independent living skills.

# Testing for Postsecondary Programs

Some postsecondary programs specifically for students with disabilities are "open enrollment," meaning they allow anybody to enroll. Most of these programs, however, rely on IQ testing and school reports for admissions. Some require a writing sample and/or an interview as part of the application process.

Entrance to degree-granting colleges used to rely heavily on the SAT or ACT tests for admission, but recently these tests have come under heavy fire and every year there are more colleges that do not require these tests.

If the program that your child is applying to does require either the SAT or ACT, be sure that you ask for accommodations from the College Board or ACT company. Accommodations can include extended time, distraction-free testing environments, use of a calculator, recording answers in the test booklet rather than bubbling them in on an answer sheet, etc. If your child requires these or any other accommodations, be sure to apply for them many months before your child will take the test. The guidance counselor at your child's high school will probably be able to help in the application process, but you may need to help the counselor locate the documentation (to include copies of your child's IEPs and evaluations) that need to accompany the application.

For information on registering with accommodations for the ACT, go to: www.act.org/aap/disab/index.html.

For information on registering with accommodations for the SAT, go to: http://www.collegeboard.com/student/testing/sat/reg/ssd.html.

## TWO YEAR AND COMMUNITY COLLEGES AND TECHNICAL SCHOOLS

*Sara Wolfe really wanted to begin to audit college classes. Her mother contacted several local colleges, but was met with roadblocks at every turn. Meanwhile, Sara joined her local Arc Board of Directors. At her first board meeting, there was a discussion of the agency's annual audit. Sara, who was unfamiliar with the use of the word "audit" for anything except taking a course without credit, immediately spoke up and told the group she wanted to audit college classes. She discovered that there was another definition of audit, but in so doing, found out that another Board member was the president of a nearby college. He was so impressed with Sara that he quickly arranged for her to take classes at his college.*

*Sara's love for learning is almost insatiable. She began by auditing some college courses, but recently began taking them for credit. She has already amassed 12 credits without any modification or classroom assistance. For an assignment that required her to prepare a monologue from Shakespeare's* Richard IX, *she located a version of the play that was in English that she could understand. After reading that version, she was able to read and understand the original. She found this to be helpful in learning and memorizing her monologue. She got a B+ for the class.*

Community colleges and technical schools are excellent options for students with Down syndrome to consider for postsecondary education. They typically offer a wide variety of opportunities in both degrees and certificate programs. From Taft College in California, to Portland Community College in Oregon, to Cape Cod Community College in Massachusetts, to Owen Community College in Ohio, community colleges across the country are welcoming students into their classes.

Some of the advantages of community or technical colleges for students with disabilities are the following:

- They are readily available in most communities.
- They have flexible entrance requirements.
- Students can take as few as one class.
- They offer both degree and nondegree programs.
- They offer enrichment classes.
- They do not require students to live in campus housing.
- They are the most affordable postsecondary option

On the other hand, these colleges are not a great option for young people who do not like the academic requirements of school. If you have a child who can't wait to finish school, sitting in a classroom is not going to be an attractive option for him. They may also not be the right choice for students who require one-on-one assistance to pay attention in class, understand the teacher's lecture, and stay on task. Remember, colleges are not legally required to provide aides to enable students with disabilities to succeed.

## Associate's Degree vs. Certificate?

Since community and two-year colleges have less rigorous admissions requirements, getting into them is not as arduous as for a four-year college. In addition, students can choose whether they want to pursue a two-year associate's degree, or a certificate in a specialized area. As you will see in the following two examples, an associate's degree and a certificate can lead to the same result.

Many of us know Carrie Bergeron-Desai as an accomplished motivational speaker with Down syndrome and author of the heartwarming story, "The Special Tomato." She is also a graduate of Herkimer County Community College in New York, where she received an associate's degree as a teacher's assistant. While it took Carrie four years instead of the typical two years, she puts her degree to good use as a volunteer at a United Cerebral Palsy center, working with toddlers.

Melissa Silverman is another accomplished self-advocate who also performs alongside her magician father. A high school graduate who passed all the necessary exams for her diploma, she attended the Community College of Baltimore County and received a 90-hour certificate in childcare. She uses her certificate each day as a teacher's aide in a local preschool.

My son earned a certificate in Institutional Maintenance and Landscaping from Cape Cod Community College and has used his experiences in his jobs on golf courses and in maintenance positions.

## COLLEGE-BASED PROGRAMS

College-based programs are postsecondary programs for students with Down syndrome and similar disabilities that are located on college campuses and share some resources with the college. Their courses of study vary in length, from one to several years. The length of time is sometimes flexible so it can meet the individual needs of the participants. These programs are sometimes called "hybrid" programs because they have some elements of special programs while allowing and encouraging participation in inclusive opportunities.

In these programs, students usually have the option to audit regular college classes or take them for credit, and also to take classes specifically designed for students in their program. Some of the specially designed classes may be in basic math, time management, or understanding social situations, for example.

In most of these programs, employment opportunities are an essential part of the curriculum. Employment can be integrated into the program from the first year, or it may be deferred to the second or even third year of the program. It depends on the length and flexibility of the program. Employment opportunities may be on campus or in the community.

You can find many of these programs listed at www.thinkcollege.net.

## SUPPORTS AND ACCOMMODATIONS IN POSTSECONDARY PROGRAMS

As discussed in previous chapters, once your child graduates from high school or "ages out" of IDEA eligibility, there are no laws requiring that he receive a free, appropriate education (and the supports and modifications that would make that possible).

Colleges, universities, technical schools, and other programs that receive any federal funds, however, must abide by both the Americans with Disabilities Act and Section 504 of the Rehabilitation Act of 1973. The ADA requires the provision of "reasonable accommodations" to any qualified individual. Section 504 prohibits discrimination on the basis of disability, among other things. Practically speaking, these laws both require the same things of education programs:

During the admission process, students with disabilities must be considered for admission without regard to their disability. There cannot be an assumption that a student is not capable based on his disability.

After acceptance, schools are required to make reasonable accommodations to policies, settings, and procedures to avoid discriminating against students with disabilities. Examples of accommodations that may be useful for a student with Down syndrome include:

- large print texts or audio recordings
- extended time on tests
- providing a quieter, less distracting setting for test administration
- allowing the student to bring class assignments/tests home to complete
- preferential seating (e.g., at the front of the class)
- providing the class reading list before the semester begins
- allowing the student to tape record lectures or use a note taker
- allowing the student to respond orally to test questions
- use of a calculator
- use of spell check

Note that colleges are not required to make accommodations that change how much or what the student is expected to learn, nor are they required to provide any services that cost money—such as assistive technology devices or tutoring.

In a practical sense, the provisions of ADA and Section 504 related to postsecondary education are primarily used by students with disabilities other than intellectual disabilities. The laws were designed to prevent discrimination against "otherwise qualified individuals" (those who are capable of doing college work with relatively minor accommodations). Most students with Down syndrome will require modifications that are greater than what is required by these civil rights laws.

Although colleges and universities are not required to go beyond what ADA and Section 504 require of them, you should be aware that some programs do. In fact, some colleges and universities offer a full range of services through their Disability Support Center, to include:

- tutoring (often provided by undergraduate or graduate students)
- computer labs (where assistance in writing or planning papers may be available)
- regular meetings with a coach or disability coordinator to assist with organizational problems, scheduling, prioritizing, requesting accommodations
- study skills classes

In some colleges, these services may be available free; in others, students must pay for the assistance. You will have to determine whether your child will be successful with this level of support.

If your child takes a college level course and does not do well on his first attempt, it does not mean he needs to give up. Many college students without Down syndrome fail courses and repeat them, sometimes more than once, before they pass. Our children should also be allowed to fail.

# What Should Be Taught in a Postsecondary Environment?

There are many skills that are important for our children to work on during their postsecondary years. This is especially true for students who had wide access to the general education curriculum in high school. Sometimes when students with Down syndrome spend their high school years in general education classes, they do not receive education in the life skills that are important for their success in the adult world. The postsecondary years may be an ideal time to address these concerns.

Here is a checklist of specific skills that may be important to consider (over and above any specific job or academic skills that your child may be working on):

✔ Be able to complete a personal data form
✔ Be familiar with words found on an employment application

✔ Be able to complete an application for employment

✔ Assist in the preparation of a resume

✔ Develop interviewing skills

✔ Prepare for an interview, including using appropriate dress and personal grooming

✔ Understand employment paperwork such as W-4 forms, criminal background checks, and drug testing

✔ Understand the roles of boss and employee

✔ Learn workplace culture such as how to take a break and spend lunch time

✔ Learn what to do when you get lost

✔ Use public transportation and cabs

✔ Fill out a physician registration form

✔ Understand your medical history

✔ Wait for appointments or events (in a doctor's office, bus stop, etc.)

✔ Make appointments

✔ Understand computer and cell phone use and etiquette

This list may be longer for your child if he has still not mastered the majority of skills on the transition checklist provided in Chapter 2.

# Funding

When considering postsecondary program options, you must be prepared to foot a good portion of the bill. Just like college programs in general, these programs can be expensive. Some of the specialized schools or programs may be subsidized, but most are not. In addition, if you choose a program in a different state, your child may not be eligible for any financial assistance, and fees for out-of-state residents may be considerably higher.

Some families believe that their children can establish residency at some point and then be eligible for financial assistance or services from that state. Many states actively discourage this, however. In fact, public colleges and universities have very stringent requirements for residency that do not allow for a student to merely move to a state with the expectation of establishing residency for a couple of years in order to qualify for in-state tuition. You may be able to question and appeal this practice using an attorney who understands Medicaid regulations, funding, and how services are provided.

Although some postsecondary programs that are geared to students with intellectual disabilities may cost only the equivalent of a community college education, many are very expensive. Think college prices and then add up to fifty percent to account for the additional needs of students with disabilities. A mentioned earlier, costs can range up to $80,000 a year or more for a program that includes housing.

Most disability-specific programs do not offer financial assistance. This is because, unlike colleges and universities whose alumni contribute to scholarship funds, postsecondary programs are not able to tap into this resource. While they do fundraise, it is often for current building or program needs. Some students who attend postsecondary programs while they are still in public schools have succeeded in getting their school system to pay for the programs. In other situations, families have managed to work out a cost-sharing agreement with their school district. Most school districts, however, offer programs within the district so that they can control their costs, which makes it difficult for families to advocate successfully for these private programs.

> *Jon was the only student in his high school with an intellectual disability. While other students with disabilities were in the freshman class when he was a senior, he was a real pioneer. It gave us the opportunity to have Jon's needs and desires met.*
>
> *Jon had always expressed the desire to go to college. When Jon was accepted at a postsecondary program where he would live and be able to participate in a community college, our school district agreed to pay for three years, until he turned 22. We had worked with the school district for several years developing our vision for Jonathan, which included having him leave our community after 4 years of high school and continuing his education in a residential environment. Our community did not have an alternative transition program, and, since Jon had been the only student in his class with an intellectual disability, there was no cohort of students around which to develop an alternative program. Also in our favor, our community was not plagued by some of the fiscal challenges common today.*
>
> *Since Jon had spent four years in high school, included in the regular curriculum, we wanted his postsecondary education to emphasize the daily skills he had not had the opportunity to work on in high school—money management and banking, consumer skills, resume and interviewing techniques, job exploration, developing a leisure repertoire, household management, disability awareness, and, my favorite—what to do in an emergency.*

## FEDERAL LEGISLATION THAT MAY HELP WITH FUNDING

There are two important federal initiatives that would help families with children with Down syndrome and other disabilities with the cost of postsecondary education and other services.

### THE HIGHER EDUCATION ACT

The first is a recent change to the Higher Education Act, which covers financial aid for college students. The National Down Syndrome Society led a successful effort to amend the Higher Education Act to allow students who are enrolled in postsecondary programs for students with intellectual disabilities to be eligible for work study jobs, Federal Supplemental Educational Opportunity Grants, and Pell Grants. Prior to these changes, students with intellectual disabilities were typically not eligible for work study jobs or grants because they usually do not receive a regular high school diploma, pass a General Educational Development equivalency test (GED), or pass a college-administered "ability to benefit" test. In addition, a student with intellectual disabilities is typically not enrolled in a degree or accredited certificate program.

Regulations must be finalized before these new provisions take effect. It is anticipated that proposed regulations will be released by the U.S. Department of Education in summer 2009. There will then be a comment period before final regulations are published and students will be able to apply for financial assistance.

### THE ABLE ACT

NDSS is also playing a leading role in the introduction of a savings bill known as the Achieving a Better Life Experience Act (ABLE) of 2009. The ABLE Act will give individuals with disabilities and their families the ability to save for their child's future just like every other American family, and help people with disabilities live full, productive lives in their communities. The **ABLE Act** will allow individuals with disabilities and their families to create a disability savings account or "ABLE Account" of up to $500,000 that would accrue interest tax-free. The account could fund a variety of essential expenses for the individual, including medical and dental care, education, community based supports, employment training, assistive technology, housing, and transportation. The legislation prohibits amounts held by, or paid or distributed from any ABLE accounts from being treated as income or assets when determining eligibility for benefits provide by any federal benefits program such as SSI or Medicaid.

I mention these initiatives because it is important for you to be aware of what is happening on the federal level and in your state that may need your active advocacy. Once a bill idea is born or a change is contemplated to a regulation, there are questions that need to be addressed. Among them are how much money this will cost, whether there will be lost tax revenue, and whether there will be other policy requirements. It is often many years from the time a bill gets enough sponsors to be introduced into Congress before it gathers enough support to be passed. Along the way, families can play a critical role by sharing their stories with their elected representatives.

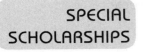
**HIGH SCHOOL SCHOLARSHIPS**

*When Jonathan was a senior in high school, he applied for two scholarships available to students in his high school. He met the criteria for both of the scholarships, which were based on overcoming personal challenges. While he was not going to a degree-granting college, he was continuing his education at a special program at a community college and at a residential transition program. The scholarship committee granted him both scholarships, based on his success in high school and his ability to rise above the challenges of his life.*

Most high schools offer college scholarships to students who meet the criteria of these awards. There are often scholarships that are established for students who have overcome some personal adversity, and these awards may be available to students with Down syndrome. There are also often scholarships based on need or membership in a particular high school club, sport, or activity, or scholarships funded by the PTA for children of PTA members. Since the criteria for these scholarships are established locally, they often do not require that a student be accepted into a degree-granting institution.

**SPECIAL SCHOLARSHIPS**

There are a few special scholarships that are available for students with Down syndrome and related disabilities. The Joshua O'Neill and Zeshan Tabani Enrichment Fund offers financial assistance to young adults with Down syndrome for postsecondary or enrichment studies. For more information, visit the website of the National

Down Syndrome Society, who administers the fund (go to www.ndss.org, click on "Self-Advocates," then "Self-Advocates Resources"). In addition, your local Down syndrome support group may fund small scholarships for local students who are attending a postsecondary education program. If your child has an additional disability, such as a visual impairment or hearing loss, you may also be able to locate financial aid specifically for students with those impairments.

### VOCATIONAL REHABILITATION FUNDS

It is important not to get discouraged by the high out-of-pocket costs of some programs. Some states may allow the use of Vocational Rehabilitation (VR) funds for tuition and fees for postsecondary education if you can show that the course of study will enable your child to reach his employment goals. For example, if your daughter is going to study child care and her study will meet whatever requirements your state has set forth for child care workers, then the vocational rehabilitation agency may agree to provide funds for her education. For more information on VR services, see Chapter 7.

### PASS PLANS (PLANS FOR ACHIEVING SELF-SUFFICIENCY)

A PASS plan may be worth considering if your adult child with Down syndrome is receiving SSI or SSDI and would like to be able to save up some of his own money to fund his postsecondary education. (Ordinarily, adults with disabilities can lose government benefits if they have too much money in savings.) Briefly, a PASS Plan can be used to fund a postsecondary program that will lead to reaching an employment goal. The plan, if approved, allows a SSI or SSDI recipient to save money without being penalized by the Social Security Administration. The multi-page application, available online or at your Social Security office, can be daunting, but efforts are underway to make the process easier. See Chapter 6 for more information about PASS Plans and other government benefits.

### COMMUNITY RESOURCES

Local civic and religious organizations may find supporting postsecondary education for students with disabilities a very appealing and worthwhile cause. They often take requests and applications from individuals in the community. Consider talking with your friends and relatives to see if they are associated with any organizations that provide individual awards or grants. The high school guidance counselor might also be aware of community organizations that sponsor scholarships In addition, you might want to check with your local Arc and Easter Seal chapters.

### AMERICORPS

AmeriCorps is our country's national service program, similar to a domestic Peace Corps. Through a network of partnerships with local and nonprofit organizations, it provides opportunities for adults to get job training and then use those skills to meet community needs. There are several different programs under the AmeriCorps umbrella, some of which provide housing or a small monthly living allowance. Participants volunteer for ten months to one year in areas of need in their communities. Upon completion of the program, volunteers receive a small educational stipend that can be used toward postsecondary education.

Some of the jobs that AmeriCorps members may perform include:
- tutoring and mentoring disadvantaged young people;
- building affordable housing;
- teaching computer skills;
- cleaning parks and streams;

- managing or operating after-school programs;
- helping communities respond to disasters.

Individuals must be at least 17 to participate, although some programs have a minimum age requirement of 18. One program has an upper age limit of 24, but others have no upper age limit. A high school diploma is not required for most programs.

Individuals with disabilities have successfully participated in this program. For more information and to apply go to www.americorps.org.

# What Kind of Postsecondary Program Is Right for Your Child?

*Ashley Wolfe, an articulate and motivated young woman with Down syndrome who has acted professionally, found at age 30 that she wasn't content with her job prospects. She had college experience and lived successfully on her own, but she wanted more than a job; she wanted a career. She thought that she would enjoy being a massage therapist since she liked getting massages herself. She applied and was accepted into a massage therapy program and looks forward to being able to offer high quality massages to other individuals with disabilities.*

Postsecondary education leads to increased job opportunities and higher income, even for people who do not have a high school diploma. It also provides some upward social mobility. Postsecondary education also helps students improve their reading, math, and critical thinking skills.

It is no surprise that students with Down syndrome and their families are also demanding the same access to these kinds of benefits. Our children could definitely benefit from better, higher-paying jobs. They need opportunities to improve their reading, math, and thinking skills. Our children also need more opportunities to acquire independent living skills, and their education should not arbitrarily end at some particular age.

When it comes to choosing the right postsecondary program for your child with Down syndrome, I think families sometimes make the decision too difficult for themselves. Often when families are faced with several forks in the road, going down almost any one of them will lead to a positive outcome for their child. In reality, the postsecondary program that is right for your child begins with what is affordable and available to you. Perhaps you and your child really want a residential program, but if you do not have the resources to pay for it, then it is not the right program.

My son was involved in the decision-making process when we were choosing a postsecondary program for him, and he visited various programs with us. He liked some programs and not others. In the end, however, it didn't really matter what we might have thought was right for him as he was not accepted everywhere. We had to choose among the options that were available. For some families, visiting programs might not be affordable and it may make sense to make virtual visits via the Internet.

As I have said, access to postsecondary education is our child's right, but it by no means is right for all our children. Our kids are all different. We all don't get to go to Ivy League schools or even college, but we can take different routes to attain a purposeful and meaningful life.

QUESTIONS FOR FAMILIES TO ASK

Jeanne Pacheco, Director of Admissions at the Riverview School on Cape Cod, prepared some questions for families to ask either prior to or during a visit to a prospective program. I have adapted her list so you can use it to evaluate any postsecondary program you are considering for your child:

*To gather information about admissions, find out:*
- What are the admission requirements?
- What kind of testing is required and how recent does it need to be?
- What is the cost of the program?
- Are there any additional fees or expenses?
- Is there any financial assistance available?
- When was the program established?
- Who are the members of the Board of Directors?
- How many students are enrolled?
- Are there any students with Down syndrome?

*To understand the nature of the program, consider the following:*
- Is this a short-term transitional program of 1 to 3 years or a long-term independent living program?
- How many months per year does the program run?
- If there is an academic component, what subjects are taught?
- What life skills, if any, are taught (money management, housekeeping, laundry, meal planning, fitness, etc.)?
- How are vocational and social skills taught?
- Is there an opportunity to attend a nearby college program? Does it require a separate application?
- Does the program accept public school funding or state funding?

*If this is a college-based program, consider:*
- What type of coursework is offered?
- What are the student/teacher ratios?
- What types of supports and accommodations are available?
- Are students assigned an advisor or case manager?
- What other activities are available to students (drama, athletics, music, etc.)?
- Is a degree or certificate awarded at the completion of the program?
- How do students take advantage of mainstream courses?

- What kind of marketable skills or jobs do students have upon completion?
- What specific supports are available (tutoring, counseling, peer tutoring, learning center)?

*For long-term programs:*
- What are the ages of the residents and what are the plans to ensure that the program does not "age" as the residents age? (You want to make sure that the program has sustainability. If all the residents are the same age and there is not enough "turnover" to ensure differences in the age of the residents, there is the risk that everyone will "age" at once and the program will not be viable.)

*For programs with a residential component:*
- What are the living options? Does everyone have a single room? Are the common areas adequate? Can your child personalize her room by painting it, hanging pictures, getting cable TV or Internet service?
- What are the expectations around meals? Do the students prepare them? Are there group meals or dining halls?
- How are special diets accommodated during mealtimes and when individuals might be away from the program?
- Do students have private bathrooms? If not, how many people share a bathroom?
- Who is responsible for cleaning bathroom and common areas?
- How are roommates chosen? How are roommate conflicts addressed?

*For any program:*
- Visit the program while it is in session. Consider its geographic location and the social and learning settings.
- Make sure you speak to families of current students and ask them to share their experiences and answer any concerns you have.
- Make sure your student speaks to current students.
- Are cars allowed?
- What are the policies regarding smoking, drug and alcohol use, and firearm possession?
- Are there any policies regarding sexual behavior and/or birth control?
- What types of employment-related services are available? Is there access to career counseling, job placement, and job coaches?
- What percentage of students are employed?
- What is the average number of hours worked per week and what is the average salary?
- What types of transportation are available?
- What community resources are there? Are there opportunities for individuals to use them outside of a group?

- How are health services provided?
- How is medication administered? What are the requirements for self-medication?
- What is the level of supervision provided during the day, evenings, and on weekends?
- What types of social and recreational programs are available and are there sufficient weekend activities?
- What kind of support is available to assist students in planning productive use of their leisure time?

# CHAPTER 4

## What's the Score?

*Everybody gets tested and not many people like it. For families with children with Down syndrome, testing began at birth and never let up. When our children were born, one of the first questions we asked was, "What's the Apgar score?" Maybe before we even knew our child had Down syndrome, we might have fallen right into the testing trap. While some of us may have had a prenatal diagnosis, most of us wanted a score and we wanted to compare that score with the perfect score of 10. It is the rare infant with Down syndrome who gets the perfect score.*

*The testing continued relentlessly, with many tests comparing our child's development with typically developing children: the Bayley Scales of Infant Development, The Differential Ability Scales, Wechsler Preschool and Primary Scale of Intelligence, Wechsler Intelligence Scale for Children, Stanford-Binet: Fourth Edition, Woodcock-Johnson, Kaufman Test of Educational Achievement, Peabody Picture Vocabulary Test, and other measures.*

*We don't have to like it, but we do have to live with it. Everybody gets measured—with weekly spelling tests, math quizzes, final exams. Some of our children are judged by the SAT or ACT. During the transition years, some new tests and assessment tools may be used to test our children with Down syndrome. These tests will be used to determine eligibility for adult services, and, perhaps, to determine what kind of services your son or daughter receives.*

## Why Test?

I personally never liked it when my son was tested. It always served as another reminder that he had Down syndrome and was behind in some measure. It could be his height, head circumference, mean length of utterance, or even his ability to pick up Cheerios.

I knew he was delayed, yet I hated the endless reminders that the tests brought to my attention.

The cynic in me also knows that testing is a business. People make a living producing, administering, and interpreting tests. There are many types of tests and sometimes there are only small differences among them. There are many professionals licensed to give these tests—among them are psychologists, neuropsychologists, school psychologists, developmental psychologists, social workers, and others. The tests themselves are considered proprietary. That means that the product is owned by an individual or a company and is protected by trademark or patent. What that actually means to a family, with few exceptions, is that unless you are qualified to administer the test, you are not allowed to see it.

In fairness, however, there are several very important purposes for testing transition-aged students with Down syndrome. They are to determine:

- eligibility for services;
- level of services needed;
- career interests and abilities;
- readiness for postsecondary education or college.

# Testing to Determine Eligibility for Services

As your child prepares to leave the school system, the state adult service agency will, in most instances, require her to undergo eligibility determination to see whether she qualifies for adult services. These services can include residential supports, employment supports, transportation, day programs, and service coordination. Even if your child received services as a child, from the very same agency (the Department of Developmental Disabilities, for example), she will most likely be required to undergo eligibility determination again.

For families of children with Down syndrome, this seems a little ridiculous. The extra chromosomes are still there, she still has Down syndrome, and many of you are thinking, "why can't I just send a picture?"

The reality is that each state has criteria to determine eligibility. While some states determine eligibility once, usually when the individual first requests services, many use different eligibility criteria for children than for adults. Some states are more lenient in determining childhood disability than they are for determining adult disability. This is due to the wider eligibility for services under IDEA, in some cases.

The other reality is that some students make enough gains and progress in school that they no longer need services as adults. This is the basic premise for providing special education in the first place—so students receive the help needed to master the skills necessary to be successful as adults.

Since there are no separate eligibility criteria for individuals with Down syndrome, you can expect that your child will undergo an eligibility determination for adult services. You should inquire with the appropriate state agency or with your school district as to the age this occurs in your state. In many states, it is at age 18. Test results from when your child was younger will not be considered in most situations, so don't bother getting your child tested at the earliest possible age in hopes you will somehow minimize the waiting for adult eligibility.

Although the overwhelming majority of people with Down syndrome will qualify for adult services, some of the most "high functioning" of our children may not be eligible. Eligibility usually is based on three factors:

1. Some states quantify it with an actual IQ score (usually below the 68-70 range), and other states use an "IQ score that is two standard deviations below the norm." Since the norm is 100, both definitions mean much the same.

2. The limitations in intellectual functioning must be accompanied by significant limitations in adaptive functioning in at least two of the following skill areas: communication, self-direction, functional academic skills, work, leisure, health, and safety.

3. The onset must have occurred before the individual's 22$^{nd}$ birthday.

This is meant as a general guide. Eligibility criteria may vary and you must check with your state.

## Denial of Eligibility

If your child is denied eligibility for adult services, you may want to appeal that decision. If so, you will want to make a written request for her file and any supporting materials that were used in reaching the decision. It will be important to understand the process and how the decision was reached. You can either manage the appeal yourself or hire an attorney who has experience with the adult service agency's regulations and policies.

There is usually only one reason why someone with Down syndrome would be deemed ineligible for adult services, and that is if she did not meet the disability criteria. If her IQ is over 70 and she has demonstrated that she does not have any significant deficits, she might not be eligible. While I have never personally seen an individual denied adult eligibility, I have seen many families who do not seek adult services.

Adults with Down syndrome might also be declared ineligible for adult services if they apply in a state other than the one where their parents live (whether or not their parents are their guardian). This sometimes occurs if the person with Down syndrome has attended a school or postsecondary program outside her home state. You and your child may decide that staying in the new state makes sense—she has friends, there are job opportunities, or some other reason. You figure that by making her a resident, she will them be eligible to apply for adult services in that state. This is like having a typical child try to establish residency in another state so she can be considered a resident and pay in-state tuition.

States that have many special education schools or programs that attract students from out of state have regulations that make it difficult or impossible for people from other states to receive adult services. In reaching a residency determination, the state will consider who paid for the student to attend the special education school or program The state will almost always be able to trace funding to an out-of-state source (either the family or school district). I have seen families spend over $80,000 to fight this decision. Some have been successful, but others still did not get services for their adult child with Down syndrome.

| TYPES OF ASSESSMENTS |
| :---: |

## INTELLIGENCE TESTS

*After the administration of IQ testing, the psychologist shared with me an exchange she had with Jon during the test. As I recall, she showed him the parts of an engine and asked him to put it together. He replied, "I guess if I knew how to build a car, I would know how to do it." Jon's answer demonstrated some thoughtfulness, but the strict scoring requirements of the IQ test meant that he received no credit for his answer. In the real world, this kind of strategy would be very helpful to Jon. But, IQ tests are not very real to me.*

Intelligence tests that determine an intelligence quotient (IQ) are considered norm referenced tests. This means that the scoring is determined by testing a very large sample of individuals and assigning scores based on the performance of the very large group who took the tests. Generally, a score of 100 is considered "normal" on these tests. These tests have tremendous implications for individuals with Down syndrome and related disabilities because intelligence testing is required in determining who is eligible for adult services and may also be used for admission to some postsecondary programs.

To qualify for adult services, an adult with Down syndrome generally needs to meet the criteria for intellectual disabilities (mental retardation), or whatever term is being used to refer to people whose cognitive limitations result in a score that is generally 70 or below. Some people with Down syndrome might also qualify for services from the state agency that supports people who are deaf, hard of hearing, or blind. However, the agency that supports individuals with intellectual disabilities generally has the expertise, service models, and resources to best assist people with Down syndrome.

The following are fairly standard ranges for scores on intelligence tests. Depending on the test, the ranges may differ slightly.

- 130 and above    Very Superior
- 120-129          Superior
- 110-119          High Average
- 90-109           Average
- 80-89            Low Average
- 70-79            Borderline
- 69 and below     Range of Mental Retardation

There are various assessment tools used to measure cognitive intelligence. Among them are:

- Wechsler Intelligence Scale for Children - Fourth Edition (WISC-IV)
- Wechsler Adult Intelligence Scale—Fourth Edition (WAIS–IV)
- Stanford-Binet Intelligence Scales—Fifth Edition (SBS)
- Kaufman Assessment Battery for Children—Second Edition (KABC-2)
- Woodcock-Johnson III Tests of Cognitive Abilities (WJ-III)
- Differential Abilities Scale (DAS)
- Naglieri Test of Nonverbal Intelligence
- Comprehensive Test of Nonverbal Intelligence (C-TONI)

## The Year Your Child Takes a Test Can Affect Her Score

A 2003 Cornell University study found that the year that an individual takes an IQ test can greatly affect the score she achieves. The variability is enough to have serious consequences. Since IQ scores tend to rise 5 to 25 points in a generation, the test is corrected and made more difficult every 15 to 20 years so the mean score can be reset to 100. According to The Cornell News, the researchers found that the number of children recommended for special education services with mild mental retardation tripled during the first five years after the new test was released compared with the final five years of an old test, even though there were no real changes in underlying intelligence.

Standard IQ tests measure verbal skills (such as the ability to define words or explain how two or more concepts are similar), nonverbal skills (such as the ability to copy patterns or predict what shape comes next in a sequence), short-term memory (such as the ability to repeat back a string of numbers, either forward or backwards), and processing speed (such as the ability to look at shapes that are keyed to numbers and write down the corresponding number).

In the past few decades there has been considerable attention to other forms of intelligence. The concept of emotional intelligence by Daniel Goleman and the multiple intelligence theory of Howard Gardner suggest that there are other parts of intelligence that matter that are not captured by standard intelligence tests. Although these ideas are fairly popular, they have had very little impact on the use of traditional intelligence testing.

### DRAWBACKS OF INTELLIGENCE TESTS

Most parents of children with Down syndrome believe that traditional intelligence tests have marginal use in their children's lives. Our children perform better than their test scores indicate, and the tests fail to capture their special talents. I think low scores on IQ test can also demonstrate lack of access to the education that typical children receive.

Most people agree that intelligence testing is flawed. While improvements have been made, the tests often fail to take into consideration cultural and racial differences, and they are not very good at determining learning disabilities. They can be valuable, however, in suggesting useful interventions and learning strategies.

Assigning an IQ number to an individual with Down syndrome often has the chilling effect of labeling the person so that others do not see the strengths she has. In addition, intelligence tests are often administered by people who have little or no experience with Down syndrome. These professionals need to (but often don't) consider:

- speech patterns of our children;
- potential for hearing loss;
- the need to develop a rapport with the examiner;
- the effects of an unfamiliar testing environment;
- the ability to sustain effort for the test.

The good news is that after your child leaves high school and eligibility has been determined, the adult service system will have little interest in her scores on the intelligence test. The system is more concerned with outcome measures. Intelligence testing ceased to matter for me a long time ago. Regardless of any test result, I still loved my son the same.

Currently, there is no getting around IQ scores to determine eligibility for some services and benefits—just like there is no way around some kind of measure for college admissions, be it grades, test scores, or some combination of both. This is a change from the school years, when parents can refuse IQ testing and still get special education services for their child.

*Jonathan was eight when I reluctantly agreed to IQ testing. I was totally opposed to it. I had long ago accepted his cognitive limitations and I did not see that there was anything to gain from intelligence testing. We knew he had Down syndrome and we knew how he learned best. What good could possibly come out of having a number assigned to him?*

*A few days after the test, the psychologist called me and shared with me some startling discoveries. During the subjective testing portion, where they looked at some emotional factors, Jon had provided some information that showed that he had seen or heard a sexually explicit event that he did not understand. The pieces all began to fall into place. Jon had been continually late getting to school even though he was picked up on time, his behavior had changed, he had experienced recent toileting accidents, and he had picked up new names for his private parts. Through the testing, we learned that the man driving Jon to school was sexually abusing him. After much therapy, Jon recovered and I had a new appreciation for IQ testing. I still hate the numbers, though.*

*Jon's first IQ score was pretty good. It was a high enough score for educators to see his potential, but just met the state cut-off for services. I think the testing people thought I was nuts because I actually said that it was the perfect score for those reasons. Two years later, the test was re-administered and his score was 10 points lower. I was not happy this time. I told the assembled professionals that if this trend continued, he would not have an IQ at all in another 10 years. They didn't think I was very funny.*

## GETTING THE "RIGHT" RESULTS

During the transition years, IQ testing can be used for two very different purposes: 1) as part of the admission process for a postsecondary program, and 2) as part of the determination process to qualify for Supplemental Security Income (SSI).

Here is where it gets a little tricky. If the IQ test is going to be used as part of the admissions process, you want your child to score as high as possible, since often a certain IQ level is required. In this situation, you want your child to be tested under the most favorable conditions. For example, you would want to make sure that your child is well rested, healthy, wearing comfortable clothes, and had a good meal and has snacks and a beverage available during the testing.

It may help to arrange a pre-meeting with the individual administering the test to go over the reason for the test (to get the highest score possible to gain admission to a postsecondary program) and to request breaks every 30 minutes if possible. You might stress that the written report reflect strengths that might not be apparent in the

test scores but would be helpful information to an admissions officer. You may also want to talk with the test administrator about the most appropriate test for your child. For example, would the WISC be more likely to show your child's strengths or the Stanford Binet? Would one of the nonverbal tests work better? In addition, you might consider paying for a private evaluation to make sure that testing conditions are optimal. You can also control who sees the results of the test when you pay for testing privately—which can be helpful if the results are not what you were expecting or hoping for.

If the purpose of the test, on the other hand, is to establish eligibility for SSI, it is not necessary to address the issues described above. You want to make sure that the Social Security Administration sees your child as having a clear disability as evidenced by her IQ score. Your child has to show evidence of disability, and the IQ test, along with medical support from her physician, is still considered the gold standard in determining disability. (See Chapter 6 for more on SSI.)

> When Jon was a senior in high school, the school psychologist administered an IQ test to him. Although the narrative was right on the mark, the score was surprising low. The psychologist shared with me that he had never given the test to someone with Down syndrome and the last time he had even seen Jon was 10 years earlier.
>
> Since Jon was applying to a postsecondary program that required an IQ score over a certain level, we privately paid for an independent evaluation. I found someone at a local pediatric hospital who had the experience I was looking for and I had an opportunity to share with her the reason for and importance of the test. The results of this test were much higher. Jon was admitted to the program of his choice, where he thrived and was very successful.
>
> That other test? The one with the lower score? I submitted it with his application for SSI, which was approved.

## SHOULD YOU ALLOW IQ TESTING BY THE SCHOOL?

Many parents prevent the school from doing IQ testing on their child, if at all possible, for fear that a low test score may lead to lowered expectations or fewer opportunities for inclusion. This is a personal decision. But as your child approaches the end of her high school career, it may be wise to consider IQ testing. If you don't have it done by the school, you will need to pay someone privately to do it to qualify your child for SSI and adult services. This can cost several thousands of dollars. While some of the expense may be covered by insurance, it can be expensive.

You will want to consider what you want to use the test score for and the experience of your school district in testing students with Down syndrome before going ahead with testing by your school. It may be prudent to consider having your school conduct IQ testing early in your child's high school career so you can determine your comfort level with using their testing to qualify your child for postsecondary education or adult services.

# Other Kinds of Information

Although the intelligence test, with all its flaws, remains a pillar for determining eligibility for adult services, there are other methods of getting good information that are important in developing a complete picture of an individual's abilities and needs to assist with planning during the transition process. These methods include interviews, observations, and other forms of assessments.

> **OTHER FORMS OF ASSESSMENTS**

Due to the acknowledged bias in intelligence testing for individuals with Down syndrome and other intellectual disabilities, other kinds of assessments have been developed that are more person-centered and positive. Two of these assessments are the Supports Intensity Scale (SIS) and the Inventory for Client and Agency Planning (ICAP). These tests are also norm based, but the norms were established using people with varying degrees of intellectual disability. These assessments were designed specifically to be used with persons with Down syndrome and related disabilities. They are both widely used and respected.

### SUPPORTS INTENSITY SCALE

The Supports Intensity Scale is especially useful for transition planning. It is an assessment that helps professionals evaluate the practical support requirements of a person with an intellectual disability, and plan services accordingly. The SIS provides a clear and comprehensive picture of what the individual wants and what supports it takes to fulfill his or her goals and aspirations. It has been adopted by the states of Colorado, Georgia, Louisiana, Utah, and Washington, and is in use by hundreds of private providers.

Its use for transition planning comes out of the IDEA requirement that all students receiving special education services receive a Statement of Performance (SOP) at the completion of high school. The SIS can identify the supports needs for a student with Down syndrome in the areas of postsecondary education, vocational education, integrated employment, adult services, independent living, and community participation.

The SIS was developed by ten disability experts and consists of an eight-page interview and profile form that tests the individual's needs for support in fifty-seven life activities and twenty-eight behavioral and medical areas. The Scale ranks each activity measured according to frequency of supports needed (none, at least once a month), amount (none, less than 30 minutes), and type of support (monitoring, verbal gesturing). The individual is not tested or observed for this test; rather trained staff answer questions about the individual.

**The key features and benefits of the SIS are that it:**
- Gives direct, reliable, and valid measurement of supports needed in 57 life activities in seven broad areas—home living, community living; life-long learning; employment; health and safety; social interaction; and protection and advocacy
- Provides a clear ranking of support needs in 15 medical and 13 behavioral conditions
- Identifies what practical supports are required to perform a task
- Presents an overall supports needs score and a percentile ranking of the person's needs based on national field test data

- Provides a graph of results so that you have a visual display of areas where the person has high vs. low needs for support
- Allows feedback from the individual and those closest to her so that a clear picture of the person's needs, preferences, and goals for life emerges
- Provides a solid knowledge base of information on the person to aid in developing an individualized, person-centered plan
- Is intended to lead to long-term independence and enhanced quality of life for people with intellectual disabilities.

Of practical use to parents are the specific supports that may be identified for your child. For example, the SIS might identify that your daughter needs support in preparing food at least once a week, for between 2 and 4 hours, and that the supports she needs are verbal or gestural prompts. Another example may be that your daughter needs full physical assistance with dressing at least once a day, for between 30 minutes and 2 hours.

The SIS is designed to be used by a wide range of school professionals and agency staff in the adult service system. Although it is protected by copyright laws, you do not have to have a specific license to use, administer, and interpret results.

## INVENTORY FOR CLIENT AND AGENCY PLANNING

The Inventory for Client and Agency Planning is a short, easy-to-use, standardized assessment that evaluates motor skills, personal living skills, community living skills, and overall independence. It is a valuable tool for determining an adult's eligibility for services, planning services, evaluation, and reporting progress. Inventory areas include diagnostic and health status, functional limitations, adaptive and problem behavior, residential placement, daytime program support services, and social and leisure activities. In addition, the frequency and severity of any challenging behaviors can be measured. There are eight categories of problem behaviors, including whether the individual hurts herself or others, destroys property, or exhibits socially offensive, uncooperative, or disruptive behaviors.

As with the SIS, the individual being evaluated is not tested or observed directly. Instead, people who are familiar with your child answer a series of questions about her.

The ICAP can be used to satisfy the requirements for secondary transition testing required under IDEA, to determine an individual's eligibility for adult services, and to determine eligibility for home and community-based services.

The ICAP is currently being used by several states for eligibility, planning, and resource allocation. It is not easily obtainable to purchase and can only be administered by personnel with the appropriate level of education and licensure.

**INTERVIEWS**

Interviews with family members, teachers, or others who know your child with Down syndrome should be part of any good review to determine whether she is eligible for adult services. Good interviews are especially important in conjunction with the SIS and ICAP. Both of these assessments are only as good as the information that is collected by the person conducting the assessment.

Sometimes, in a rush to complete an assessment, the examiner will not seek out the kind of information that will make the assessment as valid as it needs to be for your child. The ICAP, for example, was designed to be completed in twenty minutes. You should always ask to go over the questions and answers with the examiner. You have known your child for a lifetime; the examiner might have only met your child once and might only be using your child's IEP or progress notes to answer questions. These assessments are important to your child and you must know how they are being answered.

**OBSERVATIONS**

Assessments and interviews are very useful in determining who a person with Down syndrome is, but, it is also important for those who are doing the assessments to have the opportunity to observe your child in her natural environment, including at home, school, and in community settings. Sometimes observations are conducted by the same person responsible for the assessment.

Observations are especially helpful for individuals with Down syndrome who have more challenges. These individuals are more likely to demonstrate their strengths in the optimal environment—one which helps to demonstrate the high expectation their parents hold for them. Testing environments are artificial and your child may not be comfortable or at ease in them. You might suggest that interviews, testing, and any other assessments be done in a setting you choose.

*Jonathan's annual review (which is similar to an IEP meeting) to determine whether his services are meeting his needs is conducted in his home instead of in an office. He sits down first and the other members of his team take their seats afterwards. It is a natural environment and the one where he feels safe and in control. (More on adult annual reviews is covered in Chapter 7.)*

# Testing to Determine the Level of Services

Every state has developed some way to allocate resources to adults with disabilities who need services, regardless of whether they use the ICAP or SIS. If they don't use the ICAP or SIS or some other standardized assessment, there may be much subjectivity involved in determining what level of services your child needs.

It is important to point out that the ICAP and SIS are not meant to be used to determine eligibility. As discussed at the beginning of this chapter, eligibility for adult services is generally based on meeting the criteria of having intelligence in the range associated with intellectual disabilities. Instead, the ICAP and the SIS allow policy makers to use the results to allocate funding resources.

Generally speaking, the more needs an adult with disabilities has, the more supports she gets. The challenge for families and advocates is to make sure that there is funding available to meet *all* the needs that are identified rather than to use the results to prioritize limited resources.

Since assessment results can be used to allocate resources, and there are never enough resources, the examiner might feel pressure to give your child a more positive assessment. This may be especially true if he or she works for, or is under contract to, the agency that allocates resources. As a result, your child may not receive the supports she needs.

Massachusetts is using two components of the ICAP together with an assessment profile they created to determine what services a person needs. This approach has been specifically designed to clarify the difference between the preferences of the family and the individual and the person's actual need for supports. It involves looking at resources that are currently available to support the individual, as well as those that might be available in the future. The approach also considers special issues, such as medical and mental health concerns that might affect the need for support services. It also considers the family's capacity to provide care. For example, a family may want their child to live in a community residence where staff are present 24 hours a day. However, the assessment reveals that the individual can be supported safely in her family home with additional supports.

Through this combined approach, Massachusetts is attempting to reduce the subjectivity involved in determining how resources should be distributed. The tool is being used to meet the needs, not the wants, of the family and individual. It is supposed to create a level playing field so that each person with Down syndrome who has the same profile is treated the same, regardless of who they know or what they have.

Regardless of how assessments are being used in your state, it is up to you to make sure that the person assessing your child really knows your child. If you disagree with the assessment, its outcome, or its recommendations, investigate your options to appeal.

# Testing to Determine Career Interests and Aptitude

There are many types of assessments that may be used to identify your child's vocational interests. Even if you think you are quite sure of you child's interests, chances are that during her transition years in school, one or more standardized or informal vocational assessments may be done with her.

If your child has good reading skills, she might benefit from taking one of the "interest inventories" that are geared to typically developing students. Often these involve answering questions about what types of activities you enjoy (do you like to work with your hands? to talk with older people? to handle money?); what kind of setting you like to work in (would you like to work at a computer? outdoors? in a medical office?); and who you prefer to work with (would you like to work as part of a team? with just a few people you know well? with animals? with sick people?). There are many of these types of interest tests online, and the high school guidance counselor probably also has access to some that she can administer.

Some interest assessments are suitable for students with various levels of reading ability. For example, the "Envision Your Career Assessment" was developed for individuals with little or no English skills. By watching DVDs of various occupations, a student can indicate (or a teacher or parent can gauge) her interest in the various occupations. There are also various picture interest inventories designed for individuals with no reading skills. In addition to assessments, there are planning tools, presented like workbooks, where a student is guided through a series of exercises that examine work interests.

Regardless of what vocational interests these types of assessments might identify for your child, remember that she has the final say over what truly interests her. Even if test results show that your child might be potentially interested in doing particular types of activities, if she tries them and does not like them, that is the clearest indication of her interests.

# Making Sure You Get What You Need

Most of us describe our children in positive terms. We would not be parents or educators if we didn't. When our children were younger, if we wanted them on the swim team, we talked about how well they could swim. If we wanted them in the school chorus, we spoke of their love of music. This usually has served us pretty well in getting what our kids needed.

Projecting this positive attitude is not always the best strategy in the next phase of life, however. Going forward, our children's eligibility for services and supports will be based, primarily, on what they cannot do. This difference can be very hard for families and even teachers to understand.

You have probably been a cheerleader for your child for so long that when someone asks you about her, you instinctively talk about her gifts and talents. As your child enters the world of adult services, you are going to have to develop another response to use when talking with the gatekeepers of what your child needs.

To get you started, you might want to keep a small notepad around the house and in the car and jot down everything that you do or someone else does to help your child be independent or successful. For example, your daughter might take a shower by herself. However, you might set the temperature for her or have to remind her to rinse all the soap out. She may need prompting to take her medications. You may cut her toenails, make her appointments, clean her hearing aids, fill her humidifier, arrange her weekend activities, help her make purchases, change her sheets, cut her meat, fasten her seatbelt, etc. Until you write everything down, you may not realize how much assistance you actually give your child.

If you keep a list, when people come to judge your child and determine whether she needs supports and services, you can show them a complete picture instead of the one you are used to giving.

> Shortly after Jonathan moved into his own apartment, we applied for Personal Care Attendant (PCA) services for him. This would enable him to hire someone to come into his home and actually provide assistance to him. The number of hours he would receive, if he even qualified, would be based on the things he could not do.
>
> This process was hard for me. While I met with the nurse, I suggested to Jon that he watch TV. I did not want him to hear me describing all the things he could not do. It went against all I believed—I wanted everyone to see him for his strengths and gifts. He was living by himself in his own home and here I had to tell someone about all his deficits. But I got it. You don't get support unless you need it. It was just something I had to get used to after so many years of telling the world about what he had ac-

*complished and what he could do. It was a good wake-up call for me, as I began to see how much all of us helped Jon to be successful.*

*Jon got the PCA services that permit him to be as independent as he can be and get the support he needs. His PCA checks his defibrillator, cleans and maintains his CPAP machine, applies lotions, irrigates his ears, administers and orders medications, and provides household assistance, as well.*

# Pandora's Box

Testing, assessments, interviews, and observations are all important tools in making sure that a clear picture of your child emerges. But there is also something I like to call "Pandora's Box," and almost every single person I have ever been involved with in providing supports has one. It is the information that is left out—or, as I like to say—it is what is in "Pandora's Box." Most of the time, it is the unflattering information that families or teachers neglect to share. They feel that if they share the information, it may have a detrimental effect on how their son or daughter is perceived.

This strategy of withholding information is flawed because the contents of "Pandora's Box" are always revealed. Maybe not immediately, but eventually. Then it is your adult child who suffers because support people are not aware of a situation that they could have been prepared to handle.

The information you forget to share is the information you need to share. Several years ago, a teenage boy with Down syndrome inappropriately touched a younger boy with Down syndrome in the locker room during a tennis program sponsored by the agency I worked for. When I called the teenager's mother, she told me that he had displayed this kind of behavior before. This was important information to share, but she "forgot" to tell us. We would not have prohibited him from participating. We would, however, have made sure that he was supervised and never left alone with another individual, as he had been when they both went to the men's room together. A good service provider will not use any information you share to exclude your child, but to ensure that the correct level of staffing is present for her safety and enjoyment.

Nobody expects our children to be perfect, so open "Pandora's Box."

# A Personal Experience with Pandora's Box

This chapter was a difficult one for me to write. As a professional, I understand the need for assessments and that they have to be fair. After all, limited resources must be allocated in a rational manner. However, as a mother, any kind of evaluation, whether a formal test, assessment, or a doctor's visit, brings me back to a place I try to avoid, and that is a place where Jonathan's limitations are on display. It is probably the reason I reacted so emotionally in the following letter, which I wrote in response to a request for another assessment after applying for SSI benefits on his 18th birthday. While I never mailed the letter, I felt better after writing it:

Dear Jessica,

I am writing this as a response to your letter to my son, informing him of an appointment you have made for him because you cannot determine his eligibility for SSI from the materials submitted on his behalf.

I wish I could find some black humor in your letter and laugh it off, but instead it made me so very sad. Just over 18 years ago, while looking forward to the birth of my first child, I dreamed of all the things that mothers-to-be dream about. I dared to dream about a healthy child. But, it wasn't to be and on the day of Jon's birth, I learned that my first child had Down syndrome and 4 heart defects.

I was told about the many things he would never do. And in a single moment, my son became eligible for support from the Department of Mental Retardation and could look forward to things like the Special Olympics, special education, and early intervention.

What I didn't know then was that I could also look forward to doctors, doctors, and more doctors. Jonathan has endured open-heart surgery twice, cauterizations, echocardiograms, 6 ear surgeries, throat surgery, a head injury, multiple hospitalizations for pneumonia, and a broken leg. He has also been diagnosed with atlanto-axial instability and that means he is at higher risk to become a quadriplegic. If all this is not hard enough on his psyche, Jon is hearing impaired and wears hearing aids and has a phone that can be heard from anywhere in our house, regardless if we want to.

There is no child who is more loved than Jonathan. I've dedicated my professional life to the issues that affect him and his peers. Our family has celebrated each one of his achievements and applauded all of his efforts. He brings us much joy.

I have to admit I was taken back by my emotions on his 18th birthday, just a few month ago. I found myself grieving for everything he had missed. He missed getting his driver's license and he missed sneaking a cigarette and coughing from the carcinogens filling his lungs and deciding never to try it again. He missed riding aimlessly around town with the guys and he missed the sweet taste of his first kiss. He missed overnights with friends and he missed knowing more than his younger sister. He missed growing tall and he missed taking the SAT's.

So, on a day when I should have been worrying about what foolish teenage risk my son was going to take to celebrate his 18th birthday, I was making sure that I had adequately collected the medical documentation to establish his eligibility for SSI. I made an appointment with Social Security on his 18th birthday.

Today, upon returning from work, I opened your letter and cried. I wish my son were heading off to college instead to another appointment, which you arranged. You made an appointment for him to have a "consultative examination" to provide you with additional information because there is "insufficient evidence of a disability."

I know you are just doing your job, but so am I. I am Jon's mother and I have spent his entire life protecting him from unnecessary tests and examinations from a society that talks about his rights, but rarely respects them.

I cannot imagine what you are looking for. He cannot hear well, he does not speak clearly, he is restricted in his physical activities, he looks different, he learns slowly, and his IQ score certainly does not reflect the love in his heart or the happiness he brings to so many people.

Your letter gave him a Saturday appointment in August. Well, to begin, he is away at a residential summer camp then. How many parents of 18-year-olds do you know that pay for their child to go to camp? All the other 18-year-olds I know are working hard, saving their money, and partying these last few weeks before they head off to college. I will be picking our son up from a camp program for "special" campers.

Your letter goes on to instruct him to bring a driver's license. If he had a driver's license, I probably never would have applied to SSI on his behalf. I did not want a son who would become eligible for SSI on his 18th birthday. I wanted a son who would borrow the car.

I know that somewhere in the many records, tests, and assessments that have been submitted is the information you need. And Jonathan can avoid an unnecessary assessment.

# CHAPTER 5

# Legal Issues and Hurdles

*If you have put off planning for the future, the clock is ticking. You must have a will, at the absolute minimum. You will need to think about what will happen when you are not here and decide who will oversee the care of your child with Down syndrome and make the kind of decisions you would have made. You need to make sure that your estate plan is updated or do some estate planning, even if you do not think you have the level of assets that normally warrants an estate plan.*

*Some of the issues discussed in this chapter may be familiar to you, but there are new points to consider for families of older teens and adults. The biggest decision facing you will be to decide whether your child can rely on family and advisors to help him manage his life or will need a guardian to make those decisions. It is also important to understand the Americans with Disabilities Act (ADA) and how it prevents discrimination against people with disabilities, including Down syndrome, as well as the law that gives parents the right to take time off from their jobs to care for family members (including adult children with disabilities).*

*One of the major challenges facing our adult children is that they are rarely able to earn enough money to be self-sufficient. Unless you are in a position to support your child indefinitely, you must understand the relationship between disability and income. In the U.S., several government programs can provide assistance to low income individuals. These programs can help your child by supplementing income and by providing medical insurance. There are also housing, food, and fuel programs that can be useful and make it more affordable for your child to locate and maintain housing. Even when your child is an adult, there could still be some tax benefits to you, especially if you are considering how to finance housing for your child. These issues are discussed in Chapter 6.*

*While every effort has been made to ensure that the information contained in this chapter is accurate, this chapter is not intended to provide le-*

*gal, accounting, or estate planning advice. I hope that you will have enough background information to ask the right questions and know when to get professional advice when you need it. As in any situation with your child with Down syndrome, other parents will often have the best advice for you.*

# The Question of Guardianship

When your child was younger, you probably thought about who might make a good substitute parent for him in the event you and/or your spouse died. If you have a will, you named one or more people to act as guardian for all your children, in hopes that that person would raise them pretty much as you would have, giving them the emotional and financial support that all young children need. Usually when a guardian is appointed for a child who is under the age of majority (usually 18), the assumption is that once he reaches the age of majority, he will no longer need a guardian

Once your child with Down syndrome approaches transition age, though, you need to look at guardianship from another angle. Namely, you need to decide whether your child will need a guardian as an adult, whether or not you are still alive. The reason for this is that once a child reaches the age of majority, he is presumed to be competent to make his own decisions about everything, including:

- educational issues, such as whether to leave high school, agree to an IEP, or apply to college;
- medical issues, such as whether to start or discontinue a medication or agree to a specific treatment;
- consenting to behavior plans;
- financial issues, such as whether to enter into contracts or buy a house or a car;
- marriage, divorce, or other lifestyle issues

If there is reason to believe that your adult child would likely not make sound decisions about these things, or that he will not listen to advice from family members or others whom he trusts, then you may want to consider having a guardian appointed to make these decisions for him. There are also alternatives, however, which will be discussed below.

**IF YOUR CHILD IS UNDER EIGHTEEN**

You have probably already thought about what would happen in the unlikely event you, your spouse/partner, or the other parent were not able to care for your child.

Until your child is 18, you may use your will to name a guardian. If your child is under 18 and he is left without a named guardian, the court will appoint one. Anybody can petition the court to be named your child's guardian. More than one person can petition the court. This sets up the possibility of a family battle and the possibility that someone you would not have chosen will be named guardian.

In deciding who will be your child's guardian, you need to consider what is important to you. Consider each potential guardian and think about the qualities of that person and the home where he or she would raise your child. Many families naturally look at other family members as potential guardians. Parents often consider their children's aunts and uncles or their grandparents (if they are fairly young), but you may want to consider other relatives or close friends.

In choosing a guardian, you might want to consider some of these factors:

- Do we share values and morals?
- Would my child's religion be practiced?
- Is the home a place where my child would thrive?
- Are their children of similar age?
- Would there be enough resources to care for my child with Down syndrome?
- Does this person live in our community and, if not, are similar or better services available where the potential guardian lives?

*I have one sibling. We are not particularly close and he does not live in our community. My husband has siblings, too. But after much thought we decided that one of my first cousins, who shares our children's religion and has children the same age, would be the best choice for a guardian, even though she lived half way across the country.*

It is also important to name a successor guardian in the event that the guardian who is originally named is not able to serve as guardian. This eliminates the need to revise your will if the need for a successor guardian arises.

If your child is over 18 when you die, your will, even if it names a guardian, will not be controlling on this issue because the final authority rests with the court. It will, however, be introduced as evidence of who you wanted to nominate as your child's guardian if one needs to be appointed after you are deceased. Such a nomination is typically given considerable weight by the court.

## AS YOUR CHILD APPROACHES EIGHTEEN OR IF YOUR CHILD IS OVER EIGHTEEN

Few issues are as important or associated with so much emotion as the question of guardianship. In the eyes of the law, adults are considered competent to make all their own legal, financial, medical, and personal decisions once they turn 18, unless they are declared incompetent. So, when your child turns 18, he is presumed competent unless you take legal action to have him declared incompetent.

Guardianship is a serious issue. It is also a legal act. It requires a petition to the court requesting that the court determine that the person with Down syndrome is incompetent to make decisions and awarding that decision-making authority to another person—the guardian. In some states there are safeguards to ensure that people are not needlessly declared incompetent. For example, in some states individuals with disabilities have a right to a hearing, lawyers are required for the individual, or indepen-

dent evaluations are required. However, many unnecessary guardianships are still awarded because of old attitudes toward disabilities. This is because it is usually the parents who make the petition to the court. The judge sees the parents as having the best interests of their child at heart and awards the guardianship.

The bottom line is that an individual with Down syndrome has to be declared incompetent by the court in order for a guardian to be appointed. This is a matter of great significance.

Some professionals and service providers believe that it is easier to work with guardians than to teach self-advocacy and self-determination to individuals with Down syndrome. It often takes longer to help a person with Down syndrome understand some issues. For that reason, these professionals and service providers are often the people who suggest guardianship to families.

Most provider agencies see their relationship with families as a partnership and welcome family participation. Part of their mission is usually to respect the preferences of individuals they support. Sometimes, family members who serve as guardians use their power to overturn the choices and preferences of the individual with Down syndrome. For example, a 25-year-old adult with Down syndrome and a reputable friend might want to go to the local pub, have a beer, and watch a football game. Even though the individual has no problems handling alcohol, his parents don't think that people with Down syndrome should be permitted to drink. As his guardian, they can prevent him from drinking. By doing so, they can also take away his ability to make an adult decision.

Sometimes, families or others acting as guardians use their power in a way that may be harmful to an individual with Down syndrome. An example: an individual has seizures that interfere with his job, and he is having behavioral problems at home and in the community. A neurologist and psychologist suggest medication. His parents (who are also his guardians) refuse to allow him to have this medication. His condition worsens and the guardians still will not consent to any medical intervention. A petition could be introduced in court to have his parents removed as guardians. This will occur if it can be demonstrated that the parents did not act in their son's best interests.

Most families begin to think about guardianship as their child approaches 18, the age at which he is presumed competent. You do not have to have a guardianship in place by his 18th birthday, however. You may want to wait and see how your child manages in your community and with the service systems you use. Although guardianship can be revoked, you should not enter into guardianship proceedings if you think that there may only be a temporary need. There are alternatives that will be discussed later for these situations.

If your child with Down syndrome has limited or no communication skills and is dependent on you or others for the majority of his care, you should consider full guardianship. Make sure you understand exactly what rights your child will and will not have if you take this step, however. In some states, full guardianship strips an individual of the right to vote or marry. Even with full guardianship, however, some states do not permit guardians to make some decisions without specific authorization from the court. This may include sterilization, admission to a psychiatric hospital, or consenting to experimental medical treatment.

The laws of guardianship and the procedures for applying for guardianship are state specific. These laws are generally complicated and always require a hearing before a judge. It is almost always necessary to use an attorney for the guardianship process. Although anyone can petition the probate court for full or partial guardianship of an adult with disabilities, for this discussion, I will assume that you, the parent, will be petitioning on behalf of your child with Down syndrome.

Guardianship proceedings can cost several thousand dollars. There is the cost of the attorney and court and filing fees, and you may also have to pay medical or other professionals to file reports attesting to your child's competency. If the costs associated with seeking guardianship are a barrier, you may be able to receive free legal services from a pro bono attorney. Check with your local bar association or your state protection and advocacy agency.

The guardianship process will include some method of determining your child's competency. In some cases, this may involve an examination, evaluation, and testing of your child. In other cases, you may just need to have a medical professional complete a section of the guardianship petition. Regardless of the process your state uses, at least one professional will probably have to attest to the fact that your child is incompetent.

If you do not want to be your child's guardian and no other family member or trusted friend is willing to do it now or if you cannot find someone to act as a subsequent guardian after your death, there are what are called "corporate guardians." Corporate guardianship programs are often part of a human service agency and, for a fee, they are willing to perform the duties required of a guardian.

Your child's needs will change over time and the appropriateness of a particular guardian may change as well. It is important to periodically review your child's guardianship and his guardian. Guardians can be replaced if they are no longer willing to serve or if your child's interests would be better served by another guardian.

Guardianship laws have begun to change. Many states now offer limited or partial guardianships that can be tailor made to an individual so that decision-making power over the individual can be limited.

Let's say that your daughter has poor money management skills and you are afraid that she will sign up for credit cards and use them inappropriately. You might petition the court for a partial or limited guardianship that would limit her to managing small amounts of money and deny her the ability to enter into any financial contracts. She would, however, retain the right to make decisions about all other areas of life. Alternately, if your daughter only requires assistance with financial affairs, a conservator can be appointed by the court. A conservator may also be referred to as a "guardian of the estate" and is responsible only for overseeing the assets and finances of another person. Terms may vary among states.

For another example, let's say that your son has complex medical needs. You are not sure that he understands them or is able to make informed decisions about treatment options. In this case, you could petition the court to have a medical guardian appointed. This would leave your son competent to make all other decisions.

You can appoint different individuals to handle different tasks within a guardianship. For example, the medical guardian can be different from the financial guardian. Families often consider dividing up the responsibilities among siblings. I have seen situations where a sibling who lives out of state is the financial guardian and the local sibling is the medical guardian.

# Alternatives to Guardianship

Tom Nerney, Executive Director of the Center for Self-Determination, has said: "We have to reject the very idea of incompetence. We have to replace it with the idea of 'assisted competence.' This will include a range of supports that will enable individuals with cognitive disabilities to receive assistance in decision-making that will preserve their rights. . . ."

Thankfully, attitudes about individuals with Down syndrome and the need for guardianship have begun to change in many states. It is possible to obtain the same kind of guidance for adults with Down syndrome that they would receive from guardians without having them declared incompetent. Some of the alternatives, which may not be available in all states, are listed below.

Some of the documents that may help an adult with Down syndrome avoid having a guardian or conservator appointed include:

- **Advance Directives:** The name for written instructions your child with Down syndrome can sign, in advance, about his future medical treatment. Advance directives take effect if he becomes incapacitated and is unable to speak for himself or make decisions about his medical treatment. They are also called living wills. They can be easily prepared. There are state-specific forms readily available either online or in most hospitals.

- **Authorization to Advocate:** A document signed by the individual with a disability that appoints another person to be their personal representative or advocate and to assist in managing their affairs without limiting the individual's rights. These documents can be individualized to meet the needs of the person with Down syndrome. If your adult child has such a document, it can prevent the funding authority from using the lack of a guardian as an excuse not to talk to family members.

- **Living Will:** A document, signed while you are competent, that instructs doctors to withdraw or withhold artificial life support if you become medically "terminal." Living wills only apply to artificial life-sustaining procedures.

- **Power of Attorney:** A document, signed while you are competent, appointing someone you name as your "agent" to handle your affairs. There are "general" powers of attorney that convey a broad range of authority and "limited" powers of attorney that convey power over specific activities. A Power of Attorney should be drafted by a lawyer and it needs to be notarized.

- **Durable Power of Attorney:** A Power of Attorney becomes "durable" when the document indicates the agent's authority does not stop if you become incapacitated. Financial and medical Powers of Attorney can be made durable.

- **Medical (Durable) Power of Attorney or Health Care Proxy:** A type of Power of Attorney that appoints an agent to provide informed consent to surgery, medical treatment, personal care, and other medical or health-related matters. A Medical Durable Power of Attorney covers a broader spectrum of medical procedures than a Living Will can.

- **Financial (Durable) Power of Attorney:** A type of Power of Attorney that appoints an agent to make financial decisions and/or handle financial transactions for you.

- **Representative Payee:** A person designated by the Social Security Administration to receive monthly benefit checks on behalf of a beneficiary if this is determined to be in the beneficiary's best interest. A representative payee is appointed for an adult beneficiary when he is physically or mentally incapable of managing his own funds. Often, the Social Security Administration requires a Representative Payee (often called the "rep payee") to be named for a person with Down syndrome. See Chapter 6 for more information about government benefits that may require a representative payee.

Other planning options and techniques:

- **Special Needs Trust:** A trust used to provide supplemental funds for a person with a disability without jeopardizing access to government programs. See page 102.

- **Special Bank Accounts:** Bank accounts that require a co-signor to access funds, write checks, or transact business, or accounts that are in the name of another for the benefit of another person.

It is possible for a person with Down syndrome to use a combination of these planning strategies, with different people chosen to handle different responsibilities.

# Making the Decision about Guardianship

This issue of guardianship is so important that I thought it would be helpful for you to hear from two different families who each made a different decision around their son with Down syndrome. Both young men are very similar, live independently, and have jobs and loving and involved families.

**JOSHUA'S STORY—GUARDIANSHIP**

Rita and Tom O'Neill shared the following story about their decision-making process:

As our son, Joshua, was approaching majority, we began evaluating the issue of guardianship. In order to make the decision that was most comfortable for Joshua and us, we needed to ask and answer a number of questions for ourselves:

1. What is Joshua's skill level?
2. What level of independence would make Joshua most comfortable?
3. How did Joshua feel about being completely emancipated? (We asked him whether he was comfortable making decisions without family assistance.)
4. How did we feel about Joshua being completely emancipated?
5. What could we anticipate about Joshua's living situation as he was entering adulthood?
6. What supports would Joshua require?
7. What level of supports would maximize his opportunities for growth and for increased independence?

In addressing the above questions, we—the collective we—knew that Joshua would require some level of support throughout his life.

As we addressed the guardianship issue, we also needed to think about the situation with our immediate family. We have two sons: Joshua, who has Down syndrome, and his brother, Noah, who is two and a half years younger. As we considered our family as a whole, there were a couple of other questions related to guardianship that we needed to address:

1. What is the relationship between our two sons?
2. As best we could evaluate at the time, what level of involvement would best address our sons' relationship with each other as they were entering young adulthood and beyond?

To help you understand our thinking and ultimate decisions, we need to take a moment and discuss our family situation at the time we were making our guardianship decision. We went through the legal process when Joshua was 18 and Noah was 16. Joshua was 19 when he graduated from high school. Following high school, Joshua went to a postsecondary program and lived away from home. When he graduated from the program three years later, he chose to remain living in the community near that program. For the past six years, Joshua and his roommate have been living very independently halfway across the country from our home with support from an independent living program. Joshua might be best described as a fairly typical young man with Down syndrome. He has a great sense of humor and a very positive sense of self-esteem, he develops healthy relationships with people, and he has excellent social skills.

The collective goal we had—Joshua and us—was to assure Joshua as much independence as possible; as much independence as he wanted and could handle. We also wanted to ensure that he had an appreciation for the dignity of risk and that he had the opportunity to take risks, while knowing that there was a safety net when needed.

After much thought and deliberation about the above questions, our family chose to pursue guardianship. As a result of our collective discussions, we concluded that this option was the best choice. Throughout the process, Joshua was very involved.

It is now eleven years after we decided to pursue guardianship. We continue to view it as an important part of Joshua's growth and development. We do not feel that guardianship has in any way restricted him or his ability to make decisions. Today Joshua functions very independently and continues to grow and mature. While we are involved with his life, as we are also involved with the life of his younger brother, who is now 26. We respect both of our sons' maturity and independence. Joshua is a very goal-oriented young man and he takes great pride, as do we, in his many accomplishments.

We believe that the process families follow to make a decision about guardianship is very important, and that there are a number of questions that any family should ask as they work toward a decision. It would have been easier if there were some checklist, but it doesn't work that way. In the end, we went with our feelings. We wanted to assure ourselves that we would have maximum legal authority over Josh's affairs. We also knew that we would all protect his right to make his own decisions and live his life as if he were not under guardianship. It's a safety net for us. We continue to feel that the guardianship issue is an individual choice and that there is not one answer that "fits all."

**JONATHAN'S STORY—NO GUARDIANSHIP**

I never considered guardianship for Jonathan. Since I had spent his entire life fighting for him to be included and accepted, I could not personally ask a court to declare him incompetent. In our state, the guardianship petition requires independent evaluations by a social worker, a psychologist, and a physician, and each of them must check a box that says "incompetent." The whole process was offensive to me as Jon's mother. By the time he was 18, he had traveled independently, handled a credit card, and was well on his way to being a full adult citizen. Fortunately, we lived in a state that offers limited guardianships and alternatives to guardianship, so I knew that with good legal advice we could have safeguards in place for Jon without having to go the guardianship route.

I was able to be comfortable with this decision because Jon looks to trusted adults for guidance when confronted with important decisions. I was confident that he would continue to use this strategy in the future.

Prior to Jon's eighteenth birthday, we met with an attorney who specializes in disability law. At her suggestion, she prepared three documents for us:

- The Appointment of Advocate and Authorization for Jonathan, which gives his family the authority to be his advocate and authorize any services for him. It is recognized by the Commonwealth of Massachusetts.
- Health Care Proxy for Jonathan, which gives us the authority to authorize medical care and treatment.
- Durable Power of Attorney for Jonathan, which allows us to be his legal representative. When his identity was stolen and tens of thousands of debt was incurred under his name, having the Power of Attorney meant that I could resolve this problem for him.

Each of these documents had to be signed by Jonathan, notarized, and witnessed. I was named as the Advocate, Health Care Proxy, and the Durable Power of Attorney.

My husband (Jon's father) and his sister were named subsequently in that order if I became unavailable.

Had I ever doubted our decision to forgo guardianship, it was put to rest when he was 25 and facing a serious medical decision. After Jon underwent a cardiac MRI, we discovered that Jon needed to have a pulmonary valve replaced. While the surgery was inevitable, the doctor explained to us that it could be done now or it could be done in a year or two. I asked some questions about the progression of his condition, as Jonathan was symptom free and healthy. I also asked whether waiting would bring new technology or techniques. While the doctor left the room to get us a copy of a study of heart pressures, Jonathan turned to me and said, "I want to do the surgery while I am healthy." The surgery was scheduled immediately and was successful.

# Estate Planning

As the parent of an older child or young adult with Down syndrome, you have hopefully already done some estate planning. There are basically two parts that families of children with disabilities should be concerned with—a will and a special needs trust. Both are instruments that require the skills of a knowledgeable attorney to prepare. You may have already written a will and established a special needs trust. If you have them, you just need to make sure that they are regularly reviewed so that any changes to applicable laws or changes to your personal circumstances can be considered.

**WILLS**

Every adult who has children or assets should have a will, or Last Will and Testament, but many adults do not have one. It is difficult for many of us to have to plan for the distribution of our estate and the care for any minor children or adult dependents. That is exactly why you must have a will. You have a child with Down syndrome and you must make decisions that are in the best interest of your child and the other members of your family.

Some people think they can make their own will, perhaps with the free forms that can be downloaded from the Internet. However, there are special considerations when you have a child with Down syndrome that only an attorney familiar with the issues knows. This is not the time to call upon a family friend who happens to be a lawyer. I have seen many instances when smart and well-intentioned lawyers who were not aware of the special laws and situations that come into play when you have a child with Down syndrome unintentionally hurt the future of the child with Down syndrome.

In most cases, adults with Down syndrome do not need wills since they usually do not have any assets to distribute or children to consider. If, however, your child has assets to be distributed or children, he needs a will.

## HAVING A WILL TO NAME A GUARDIAN

As discussed above, guardianship is a complex issue when you have an adult child with Down syndrome. If your child is under 18, you can name a guardian in your will. This person would basically take over parental responsibilities for your child if you died before he was 18, though it is important to note once again that nomination has to be approved by the court. As previously discussed, nominating a guardian for an older (emancipated) child is also recommended because it sets forth your preference for who should act as a guardian if one is needed.

## HAVING A WILL TO DISTRIBUTE YOUR ASSETS

The other important reason for having a will is to distribute your assets. If you do not have a will, the court will distribute your assets according to the laws that govern your state. That is the last thing you want to happen if you have a child with Down syndrome because it could have far reaching and long-lasting negative effects on your child.

This brings us to one of the most difficult concepts for families to accept. In order for your child to be eligible for all of the various government benefits and many programs he will need as an adult, your child must not have too much money in his name. In fact, generally speaking, as of this writing, your child must not have resources of more than $1500 to qualify for Medicaid and $2000 for Supplemental Security Income (SSI). Resources include real estate, bank accounts, cash, and stocks and bonds. Some income is also counted. While there are some exceptions, if you leave your child money or other property outright in your will, that bequest will likely make him ineligible for needed benefits until those resources are spent. (See Chapter 6 for information about the crucial importance of Medicaid and SSI for most adults with Down syndrome.)

A good lawyer, familiar with the rules for government benefits, will make sure that your will contains the kind of language that will ensure your child's eligibility for all the benefits he may be entitled to receive. There are basically two ways to do this within a will. You can:

1. Decide not to leave any assets to your child with Down syndrome—this is called disinheriting your child and it requires you to state that you are not leaving any assets to him. Many families find this option unappealing.
2. You can have your attorney create a trust specifically worded to maintain government benefits and to provide for additional needs for your child. See "Special Needs Trusts," below. (If the ABLE Act described in Chapter 3 passes, you may also be able to have funds go to your child's ABLE account after your death.)

Unfortunately, our children must remain poor to be eligible for most of the programs that will be of benefit to them as adults. This is because the programs were established to assist individuals with financial needs. Some of the services your child will need will only be available if he qualifies financially for them.

A few families do not have to worry about these issues because they have adequate personal financial resources and they do not intend to rely on government benefits. Even if your family has vast wealth, however, it is wiser to preserve eligibility for your child with appropriate planning. One can never predict the future, and, in some cases, eligibility for government benefits is a prerequisite for services.

## A LETTER OF INTENT

Now that you understand the importance of making a will for naming a guardian, or other arrangements if you child is over 18, you can move on to another big worry for families—how do I convey my wishes and the needs of my child? Many families before you have also worried about this very thing. Several different organizations and individuals have developed templates to make it easy for you to put down everything from important medical information to preferred routines for your child.

These types of documents are generally referred to as a "Letter of Intent," but different authors may call them different things, including a Life Plan. I developed such a form called "Footprints for the Future." The document is intended to be like your footprints—you will leave them so others may follow them. You can download the form for free at www.theemarc.org or at www.cardinalcushingcenters.org.

## SPECIAL NEEDS TRUSTS

You might think, as I did, that only people with lots of money have trusts for their children, thinking of the stereotypical "trust-fund baby." I quickly learned that I needed to have a trust for my son with Down syndrome to provide for and protect him. Initially, as a new parent, I was able to accomplish this through our will, but it became obvious to me that I would have to have a "special needs trust" to fully protect him. You do not need to actually put any assets into to a special needs trust when you establish it, but it is there for the future when there might be funds to put in it.

A special needs trust, when properly designed by an attorney knowledgeable in this area, enables you to leave money to be used to benefit your child. It can be funded at any time. You can deposit money in it while you are alive, or fund it after your death.

A special needs trust permits you to provide funds to supplement your child's lifestyle. Your child will never be able to access the assets of the trust or make decisions about the distribution of the trust. Instead, a trustee will make these decisions in your child's behalf. This enables your child to still maintain eligibility for government benefits, if the trust is drawn up correctly, because your child will never have control of the assets. The government, therefore, does not consider it as an asset belonging to your child.

When you set up a special needs trust, you name a trustee. In most cases, the trustee would be you and your spouse, and you would also name a successor trustee. Many families consider naming a young grandparent and, later, the child's sibling, as a successor trustee. The trust also specifies how the remainder of the trust will be distributed upon the death of your child.

Remember that the person you name as trustee will be the gatekeeper of the trust. This means that the trustee decides if, when, and how money from the trust is distributed. You must think through this decision carefully.

I have seen a situation where the parents named the brother of their daughter with Down syndrome as the trustee, with the remainder of the trust to be given to the brother's children upon his sister's death. The parents were probably confident that their son would provide for all the unmet needs of their daughter. Unfortunately, it has not played out that way. The brother distributes very little of the trust to his sister. I believe he is thinking that if he keeps the bulk of the trust assets unspent, his own children will benefit. He probably thinks that his sister can get by with state and federal benefits. I am sure that it not what the parents had in mind. They probably wanted to ensure a higher quality of life for their daughter and figured that their son, who is successful, could provide for his own children. I am not saying that this will happen in every family, but you have to be aware of what kind of financial pressures the trustee may be under in the future. Even with this information, I have named our daughter as the successor trustee for our son's trust.

If your trust has significant assets, you might consider appointing a professional trust officer who will assist in making investments, filing the tax return for the trust, and making distributions from the trust. Many families appoint a family member and a professional trust officer as co-trustees.

When you establish a special needs trust, it is important to notify any of your relatives who might wish to make monetary gifts to your child with Down syndrome. They need to know that they should direct their gifts to your child's special needs trust, rather than to your child, unless they are sending him small sums, such as for a birthday present. I have met with my parents' attorney to make sure that any gifts they make to Jonathan go directly into his special needs trust.

To find a qualified attorney to establish a trust for you, call your local Arc, Down syndrome organization, or the local bar association. As we have learned from the time our children were born, other families can often be the best source of recommendations. Resist the temptation to use someone without experience in this area, no matter how close they are to your family or how well they might have served you in another legal situation.

## Pooled Trusts

Some families are concerned that they do not have enough assets in their special needs trust to afford to pay someone to manage it well. Or they may be concerned that there are no family members who can invest funds in the trust properly or appropriately designate the funds for use to benefit their child with Down syndrome after they die. Participating in a pooled trust can help families with these concerns.

In a **Pooled Trust,** an individual account is established within a larger trust, and it puts together, or "pools," the assets from many individuals to create a larger trust account that can be professionally managed both financially and programmatically. These "pooled trusts" are set up to maintain eligibility for Medicaid, Medicare, and other public benefits. The sponsoring agency may also provide individualized services to your child, from attending annual team meetings to ensuring that all his needs are met.

## LIFE INSURANCE

All parents need to consider purchasing life insurance once they have a family. Having a child with Down syndrome makes it even more important to think about your life insurance needs and your ability to afford it. There are several different life insurance products, and while they are generally not considered the best investment plan, life insurance may have a place in a total strategy for your family's future.

There are two basic types of life insurance:

1. Term life insurance, in which you choose the amount of insurance you want (e.g., $100,000, $200,000, $500,000) and then purchase a policy in that amount for a specified "term" of 10, 20, or more years at a set annual rate for that period of time. If you die during the term of the insurance, your survivors receive the face value of your policy, but if the term expires before you die,

your policy is worthless. (Generally, term life insurance can be renewed unless you have a life-threatening medical condition, but the older you are, the higher the annual rate.)

2. Whole life or universal life insurance is the other option. It is expensive because it has an investment component in addition to a life insurance component. If you stop paying for the policy, your contributions will still be available to your beneficiaries when you die. There are fees and commissions, so as a pure investment strategy, there may be better products to save for retirement. However, it may be a good savings and insurance tool for you.

There is another kind of life insurance product that families of children with disabilities sometimes consider. It is called a "second to die" policy. It insures two lives, such as a set of parents or grandparents. It is cheaper to purchase because it pays upon the death of the second insured individual.

*I bought a "second to die" life insurance policy on my parents' lives. I could afford this since they were able to "gift" me money to help with the annual dividend. Jon's future has been ensured and when my parents die, his special needs trust will be funded by the proceeds of this policy.*

Many parents, especially when they are young, consider inexpensive term insurance to be paid upon their death to help either the surviving spouse or the guardian to pay for their child's expenses. Since these policies can get expensive as the insured person gets older, some families prefer whole life products, which actually build cash value. If you do purchase a whole life policy, you need to be committed to it for the long haul, as these policies need to be held for a long time to see their investment value.

If you buy a life insurance policy, take care in designating the beneficiary. If you or other family members have life insurance and want to use this as a vehicle to provide for your child with Down syndrome, your child's special needs trust must be named as the beneficiary. This is very important to tell grandparents or other family members who may name your children as beneficiary.

Whatever path you take, make sure that nobody purchases life insurance for your child with Down syndrome. This will only complicate future benefits because life insurance, except for small burial accounts, is considered an asset for public benefits purposes. In addition, it is very unlikely that your child with Down syndrome will need the major benefit that life insurance provides—which is usually to compensate a family financially for the loss of a major wage earner.

# Financial Planners

**M**any financial services companies and independent professionals offer financial planning services specifically geared to families who have children with disabilities. These professionals can generally be divided into two groups: those who receive commissions for selling you products and those who charge a fee for their services. The advantage of consulting with a fee-only professional is that he or she is in a better position to offer objective opinions about products. However, if you are in the market to buy a particular product and don't need a great deal of guidance, seeing someone who works on commission might make sense.

Not everyone needs a personal financial planner. Just as some people prefer to do their own taxes, some people are comfortable doing their own financial planning. This is another area where you will want to become educated, though. It will be to your advantage to go to workshops conducted by financial planners.

If you decide to work with a financial planner, get references from other families or your local Down syndrome parent group or Arc. Check the credentials of any planner you are considering. This can be very confusing, however, since in the U.S. there are over 90 credentials for financial planners offered by 72 associations. Some credentials are pretty worthless, but others signify that the individual has passed exams and has a great deal of experience. Make sure that you have a personal comfort level with any advisor. You do not need to pick the first one you meet.

**A SPECIAL WORD FOR GRANDPARENTS AND OTHERS**

Your child with Down syndrome can receive all the love and attention from grandparents and other relatives and friends that they can give. When it comes to money and other assets, however, a child with Down syndrome cannot be treated the same as your other children. Some grandparents are in a position to buy savings bonds, establish a bank account or trust, or transfer stock to your child with Down syndrome. They might even want to establish an educational fund. They must not. This doesn't mean that grandparents can't give your child gifts. You just want to make sure that any monetary gift that would make your child ineligible for benefits are spent before your child turns 18.

As discussed in Chapter 3, there is much interest by Down syndrome organizations and family members in proposed legislation that would allow families to save for their children in a manner similar to the various college savings programs that exist. In the meantime, anybody who wants to provide for your child with Down syndrome must do so with an eye to preserving eligibility for future benefits. Grandparents are especially at risk for unknowingly making financial planning mistakes when it comes to their grandchild with Down syndrome. You will have to get involved and make sure that these wonderful and well-meaning relatives have wills that do not jeopardize your child's future. Even a little money in your child's name can wreck havoc on his eligibility for government benefits as an adult.

There is one financial advantage to being the grandparent of a child with Down syndrome or other disability. Under the Omnibus Reconciliation Act of 1993 (OBRA '93), this advantage is available to a grandparent or parent who requires nursing home care. Under OBRA '93, an adult who is entering a nursing home can transfer assets to an OBRA '93 trust and be exempt from Medicaid transfer penalties. For example, your parents need nursing home care, and they have assets such as a home or savings. Normally, to be eligible for nursing home Medicaid benefits, they must exhaust their assets before they can become eligible. However, if they transfer their assets to a special needs trust for the benefit of someone with disabilities aged 65 and younger, they are exempt from the "look back" period. The "look back" period prevents people from dispersing their assets in the five years previous to moving into a nursing home to become eligible for Medicaid.

In this scenario, upon the death of your child, any money left in the OBRA '93 trust must be used to pay back any Medicaid benefits paid on behalf of your child. It is important to note that an OBRA trust is different from a Special Needs Trust, which does not contain any payback provisions.

*I was recently invited to a Bat Mitzvah (a Jewish coming-of-age ceremony) for a young girl with Down syndrome. While it is customary to give monetary gifts for the occasion, the family included a tasteful note in the invitation that invited people to make a check to the special needs trust that had been established for her.*

## Beneficiary Designations

Be sure to regularly review your beneficiary designations on your retirement or life insurance accounts. If you die, the assets in these accounts will be distributed according to your beneficiary designations and not your will. So, whenever you update your will, or experience a major life event such as a birth, death, or adoption, review your beneficiary designations as well.

# Taxes

There are some important tax deductions and credits that you may be entitled to as the parent of a child with Down syndrome. The "Medical and Dental Deduction" is the one that parents are the most likely to qualify for.

To keep you on the right path, you should record all the medical and related appointments for every member of the family. Keep track of every medical, therapy, dental, and other appointment, whether or not your insurance covers it. Make sure you indicate the location of the visit, the amount you pay out of pocket, the mileage, tolls, and parking fees. Also record the costs of prescription drugs, eyeglasses, or other medically necessary equipment. This will become the cornerstone for determining whether you will be able to meet the threshold for taking advantage of the deduction. (Your records will also help you with benefits that will be discussed in Chapter 6.)

You may only deduct the amount of eligible deductions that exceed 7.5% of your adjusted gross income. For example, if you AGI is $50,000, you do not qualify for the deduction unless you have at least $3,750 in qualifying medical expenses for the year, since 7.5% of $50,000 is $3,750. In this case, you may only deduct the amount of medical expenses exceeding $3,750. (If your total medical expenses for the year were $6,000, you would have $2,250 in qualifying expenses.)

Some examples of qualifying expenses include:

- health insurance premiums;
- transportation to get medical and related care (using standard mileage rates);
- prescription drugs;
- eyeglasses and hearing aids;
- nursing care;
- therapy;
- cost of meals and lodging related to receiving hospital care;
- tutoring, under some circumstances;
- special education (including a postsecondary program) with a doctor's recommendation;
- psychological testing, such as might be required for entrance to a postsecondary program;
- Medical conferences related to your child with Down syndrome.

If your child is receiving Medicaid, many of these expenses will be covered, and it will become more difficult to meet the threshold for a tax deduction.

If you are a parent of low or moderate income, you may be eligible for the Earned Income Tax Credit. The age limitations are waived for our children. If you pay for child care so that you can work or look for work, like all parents, you may be eligible for the Child or Dependent Care Credit, depending on your income.

If you are employed, you can reduce your tax burden if you take advantage of an employer's 125 Plan or Flexible Spending Plan. These plans allow employees to pay for medical and child care expenses with pre-tax dollars under a payroll deduction plan. You should see your human resources department for information on plans available to you.

For a full discussion of tax topics, visit www.irs.gov and type any keyword you need information on into the search area. You may also want to consult with a tax advisor.

None of us likes to pay taxes. However, taxes take on a whole new meaning when you have a child with Down syndrome. That is because many essential programs for our children, from Medicaid to job training to SSI, are paid for with tax dollars. In addition, many medical breakthroughs that have improved the lives of our children and given them the opportunity to live healthy and productive lives have occurred thanks to government-funded research.

# Anti-Discrimination Laws

There are several important pieces of legislation that protect individuals with disabilities in the United States from discrimination. Although these laws are not specifically designed for people with Down syndrome, our children are covered by them because they have a disability. The most important anti-discrimination laws are the Americans with Disabilities Act and Section 504 of the Rehabilitation Act of 1973, discussed below.

## AMERICANS WITH DISABILITIES ACT

Not too long ago, people with disabilities were routinely discriminated against in many areas of life—employment, housing, transportation, and public places, to name a few. The Americans with Disabilities Act of 1990, or ADA, is the U.S.'s first comprehensive law for people with disabilities and is considered a landmark civil rights law. People with Down syndrome are protected under the ADA.

The ADA has four accessibility requirements. They are:

1. Title I—Employment;
2. Title II—Public Service;
3. Title III—Public Accommodations;
4. Title IV—Telecommunications.

### TITLE I—EMPLOYMENT

This section makes it illegal for employers with 15 or more employees to discriminate against individuals with disabilities, who are *otherwise qualified*. That is, if an applicant with disabilities is qualified to perform a job, employers may not deny him employment, refuse to promote him, or otherwise discriminate against him on

the basis of his disability. In addition, employers are required to make "reasonable accommodations" to qualified employees or applicants.

Reasonable accommodations can include assistance in the application process, including during the interview, and changes in the workplace that enable workers with disabilities to perform the job. For example, your daughter might need someone to read the job application and assistance in completing it. On the job, she may need extended time to finish training or may need visual supports to help her remember her job responsibilities. She may require the use of a job coach to train her to perform the job and to develop appropriate social relationships in the workplace. (See Chapter 7 for more information about job supports.)

This section of the ADA also provides you, as a parent, protection from an employer who might not hire or promote you for fear that you might miss too much work caring for your child (the association clause). It does not, however, give you special status. For example, if you need to leave work early every Wednesday because your daughter's program closes at 2 p.m., you must follow your employer's leave policy.

The important thing to know is that when your child enters the workforce, you can expect him to be treated without discrimination if he is otherwise qualified for the job. If you think your child is being discriminated against, you should contact your state's federally mandated Protection and Advocacy (P&A) Systems and Client Assistance Programs (CAP) for individuals with disabilities. Collectively, the P&A/CAP network is the largest provider of legally based advocacy services to people with disabilities in the United States.

*My son got his first job—working after school at the local supermarket—
when he was 14 years old. He was treated like any other applicant. However,
he was allowed to take the training video home for reinforcement and to
have a job coach assist him until he was ready to do the job by himself.*

### TITLE II—PUBLIC SERVICE

This section is fairly simple. Under ADA, all buildings that are open to the public
must be accessible. In addition, state and local governments may not discriminate
against individuals with disabilities. This means that people with disabilities must
have equal opportunity to benefit from all programs, services, and activities that are
run by state and local government agencies. This includes recreation activities, social
services, courts, voting, transportation, public education, and meetings. This section
also applies to state-funded schools such as universities, community colleges, and
vocational schools.

### TITLE III—PUBLIC ACCOMMODATIONS

Title III mandates that public accommodations cannot discriminate on the basis
of disability. A public accommodation is any building or activity open to the public,
and includes restaurants, hotels, theaters, shopping centers and malls, stores, libraries,
parks, private schools, day care centers, and other places. This section also applies to
private colleges and vocational schools.

The ADA provides individuals with Down syndrome access to adult day care
centers, camps, community swimming pools, and other recreational settings and guarantees your child the right to participate in these programs. However, your child still
must follow reasonable rules related to participating in the programs. For example,
if there is a rule that does not permit people with wounds in a swimming pool, your
child has to comply with the rule. In this case, everyone with wounds is being treated
the same, and the rule protects everyone's health. Likewise, if an amusement park
requires that riders be above a given height to ride a roller coaster, your teenaged or
adult child must abide by that rule if he is too short, even if other people his age are
tall enough to ride.

### TITLE IV—TELECOMMUNICATIONS

This section requires telephone companies to provide 24-hour-a day relay services
for people who have speech impairments or hearing loss. Since some people with
Down syndrome have a hearing loss, this section of the law may be of use to them if
they are able to type and use a TTY machine.

## SECTION 504 OF THE REHABILITATION ACT OF 1973

Section 504 of the Rehabilitation Act of 1973 was the first federal anti-discrimination law for people with disabilities in the United States. Today, the ADA provides
much broader anti-discrimination protection for individuals with disabilities. Section
504 is still useful, however, because it prohibits discrimination against individuals
with disabilities by any program receiving federal funding. These programs include
schools and most colleges, as well as activities sponsored by schools and colleges,
federal employers, and federal organizations.

If a child with disabilities does not qualify for special education services under
IDEA, this law ensures that he will still have equal access to school activities. Although

the law does not cover services such as therapies or assistive technology that cost the school money, it does require that schools make adaptations or modifications to the environment, instruction, or materials that enable the student to have an equal opportunity to learn.

Occasionally, children with Down syndrome are so "high functioning" that they do not qualify as having a disability under IDEA. In these cases, Section 504 ensures that the student's educational needs are met as well as the needs of students without disabilities. For example, if a student with Down syndrome only needs accommodations such as more time for assignments or seating at the front of the class, Section 504 would guarantee those accommodations.

Since most children with Down syndrome do qualify for special education under IDEA, Section 504 adds little to their rights and entitlements at school. It does, however, guarantee your child the equal opportunity to participate in extracurricular activities unless accommodations would be unreasonable and would require a "fundamental alteration of the program." Each school district might interpret this requirement a little differently, but here are some examples. If your child with Down syndrome wants to participate in the school chorus and needs assistance getting up and down the risers, that is a reasonable accommodation. Likewise, if there are no tryouts for an intramural basketball team, then your child with Down syndrome should be allowed on the team. The other team members may not like your child slowing them down, but they have to let him play anyway. However, if your son with Down syndrome wants to manage the varsity basketball team but requires supervision when traveling to away games, cannot keep a shot chart, and is not alert enough to get out of the way of play, and even with accommodations could not perform most of the duties of a manager, it would not be a violation of Section 504 to deny him the manager position.

If your child takes classes at community college, a technical school, or college, Section 504 provides important protections. The law requires that reasonable accommodations be provided to any otherwise qualified student with disabilities. These accommodations might include extra time on tests and assignments, use of a calculator, and assistance with note taking. However, the law does *not* require that assignments or the curriculum be modified. See Chapter 3 for more information about Section 504 and postsecondary education.

# Family and Medical Leave Act of 1993

This law addresses the needs of working parents and allows an employee to take unpaid leave from his job to care for a sick family member or due to his own illness. Among the protections, the law allows twelve work-weeks of unpaid leave every twelve weeks to care for a new baby, to handle adoption or foster care issues, or to care for a sick child, spouse, or parent. The leave can be taken a little bit at a time.

Thanks to this law, employees can take leave without fear of being fired or being moved to a lower job upon their return. However, only employers with 50 or more employees must comply with the law and you must have worked for the company for at least 12 months and 1250 hours during those 12 months to be covered by the law.

This law is especially useful for parents of transition-aged children or adult children who need to miss work to care for their children. The law specifically makes reference to adult children. To be considered an adult child under the law, the individual must be 18 years of age or older and incapable of self-care because of a mental or physical disability. Under the FMLA regulations, the term "incapable of self-care" means that the person needs daily assistance or supervision to provide daily self-care in three or more of the "activities of daily living" (ADLs) or "instrumental activities of daily living" (IADLs).

# The Health Insurance Portability and Accountability Act (HIPAA)

Most of us are familiar with the Health Insurance Portability and Accountability Act because we have to sign forms in medical offices stating that we understand how our personal medical information will be used and the lengths that are taken to protect our confidentiality. This law also protects the confidentiality of your adult child's medical information once he reaches the age of majority. If it is in your adult child's best interest for you to continue to have access to his medical information, you will need to take one of the steps described above under "Guardianship" or "Alternatives to Guardianship" in order to be able to communicate with his doctors, participate in decisions about medical treatments, or view his medical records.

You may not realize that this law also protects and improves American workers' health insurance coverage. The most important provision for families with a child with Down syndrome is that HIPAA severely limits the use of preexisting conditions to reduce or deny coverage when enrolling in health insurance plans.

There are two things for you to know. First, group health plans cannot exclude a preexisting medical condition from coverage for more than 12 months (18 months for later enrollees). (A preexisting condition is one that the person had before enrolling in the health plan.) Second, if the person with the preexisting medical condition had previous continuous health coverage lasting for 63 days or more, the 12-month (or 18-month) exclusion period must be reduced by the amount of time the coverage was in effect. This often reduces or eliminates the exclusion period for people with preexisting conditions.

# CHAPTER 6

# If I Were a Rich (Wo)Man, Or Money Makes the World Go 'Round

*Money does sometimes seem to make the world go 'round, but understanding how the various funding streams work will help you even if you are not rich. How do you pay for what you want? How do you begin to understand the complicated area of benefits? This chapter offers simple explanations and also discusses the risks and benefits of going it alone—without Medicaid. For example, some families would prefer to pay for healthcare through their private insurance, but did you know that most programs for adults with Down syndrome are actually paid through the states by Medicaid? If your child is not eligible for Medicaid, she may not have access to adult programs, which can include job coaching, supported living assistance, and more traditional supports like sheltered work.*

*This chapter covers all the possible funding sources a person with Down syndrome might be eligible for, including Section 8 rental subsidies, food stamps and food banks, SSI, SSDI, Medicare, Medicaid, transportation assistance, etc. An important new concept in funding, individual budgets that are directed and controlled by families, is also explored.*

*It is very important to consider the role your own private resources will play. If you are not paying or borrowing to send your child with Down syndrome to college, consider making the same monetary contribution to her future that you would to your other children. You might consider using the money you would have used or borrowed for college tuition to send your child with Down syndrome to a postsecondary program, use as a down payment on a house or condo, or pay for some other investment for her future.*

As an adult, your child with Down syndrome will need to receive at least some federal benefits for help in paying her living expenses—unless she is likely to get a job that pays enough to cover all her costs for housing, utilities, groceries, clothing, and transportation, or unless you and your family are willing and able to support her financially her whole life. Qualifying for these government benefits is not always simple. You, your child, and other family members will need to cut through red tape and avoid pitfalls that could disqualify your child for benefits.

# Federal Government Income and Medical Benefits

While specific benefits available through the federal government do change, the basic underpinnings of the programs that will be discussed—Medicaid, Medicare, Supplemental Security Income, and Social Security Disability Income—do not regularly change. For instance, although income guidelines and some of what is covered may change, the basic eligibility for adults with disabilities with the kind of limitations that occur in Down syndrome has changed very little over the years.

In a nutshell, Social Security assumes that adults with nonmosaic Down syndrome have the kind of limitations that will qualify them for eligibility. They also understand that there is such variability in individuals with mosaic Down syndrome that they must individually consider the functioning and limitations of adults with mosaic Down syndrome to determine whether they qualify for benefits.

The rules for these government programs are very complex, and most people find them very confusing. With the exception of the right to a free and appropriate education, all other federal benefits that people with disabilities can qualify for are meant to assist those in financial need and act as a safety net. These government benefits almost always use income and resources to determine eligibility. They are often referred to as "means tested programs." As long as your child with Down syndrome is under 18, the government will almost always consider the resources of you, the parents, when determining eligibility, and your child will only qualify if you have limited income. There are some exceptions to this rule, so it is always best to do some of your own research. Once your child is an adult, you will need to make sure she remains "poor" so that she will meet the means test or income eligibility for many programs.

# Financial Eligibility and Keeping Good Records

Individuals qualify for the programs described in this chapter by meeting financial eligibility criteria. In some cases, they also have to meet specific disability criteria. The sections below that describe specific government programs will explain the qualifying criteria for those programs.

You will be required to present documentation to illustrate your child's financial need. Generally, you do not have to provide any financial information related to your spouse's and your own earnings and assets after your child turns 18. However, if the benefits are based on household income, and your adult child is still living in your home, has roommates, or is part of another household, you may have to provide additional information about the other members of the household.

The following is a list of the information your child *may* be requested to present:
- proof of identity—birth certificate or other proof;
- proof of residence;
- paystubs verifying earned income;
- most recent copy of Supplemental Security Income and/or Social Security Disability Income, if receiving benefits;
- bank account statements;
- documentation of nonreimbursed medical expenses (e.g., out-of-pocket medical expenses such as co-pays, doctor visits, or medications not paid for by insurance);
- utility bills and the name on the accounts;
- rental expenses.

Remember to keep the original documents and only send copies. This includes pay stubs, anything from Social Security, bank statements, and utility bills. Do not get upset if you have already discarded some or all of these items. You can always get copies of the original bills or documents; it is just a hassle if you have to request original documents and it slows down the process of determining financial eligibility. Some people like to keep a three-ring binder for each item, and other people use large manila envelopes. You do not have to keep your documents forever. Most of the time you only need to provide current information, so you can probably discard items safely after three years or so.

## Transportation Expenses

Remember to keep records of the cost of specialized transportation that your son or daughter may require. It is important to have her physician document her need for such transportation. This information may be used by agencies that determine her benefit level (Social Security Administration, housing authority, food stamp program, etc.) as consideration for an offset to her income. For example, she might earn $300 a month, but pays $250 month for specialized door-to-door transportation. You will want to request that her transportation costs be subtracted from her income to reflect the true availability of money available to her.

# Medicaid

The Medicaid program provides health benefits to eligible people. As a health insurance program, it covers physician and practitioner visits, medications, hospitalizations, hospice care, medical equipment, physical and other therapies, transportation, and institutional care. Specific services may vary by state. Those who qualify for Medicaid usually have low incomes. In most states, an individual also qualifies for Medicaid if she qualifies for Supplemental Security Income (SSI) (see below).

Although the general guidelines for Medicaid are established by the federal government, each state establishes its own eligibility requirements. Some of these state-specific guidelines address individuals with disabilities.

While your child is under 18, she will probably not qualify for Medicaid unless your family's annual income is below the cut-off established for your state. Once your child becomes an adult, she will most likely qualify for Medicaid coverage. Again, this is because once your child reaches adulthood, the federal government looks only at her income and assets, not your family's. Each state has some latitude in determining what income level qualifies an individual for coverage. This level is based on the federal poverty level (see www.cms.hhs.gov/medicaideligibility). In some states, individuals may qualify if they are earning up to 133% of the poverty level; in other states, the level is higher.

Medicaid is the primary payer of healthcare benefits for adults with Down syndrome in this country. If your child qualifies for Medicaid as an adult, she will receive a medical card that she can use at the doctor's office like you would an insurance card. Co-pay policies vary greatly by state.

Unfortunately, this important benefit has its flaws. Physicians, dentists, and other healthcare professionals can choose whether to participate in the program, which means they can decide whether to accept Medicaid as a form of payment. Since the Medicaid reimbursement rates are notoriously very low and payment is often delayed, many healthcare professionals have decided not to accept Medicaid patients. This creates a two-tier medical system. Individuals with private health insurance are free to go to anyone who accepts their health insurance, but those on Medicaid are limited to healthcare professionals who will accept the low and often late Medicaid payment. Almost all hospitals, however, accept Medicaid as a form of payment.

## Private Health Insurance

Your state's laws determine who qualifies as a dependent for coverage under a family's private health insurance plan. Some states allow an unmarried adult child up to the age of 30 to remain on a parent's policy. Other states cut off coverage for children at age 19 unless they are full-time students. Many states have different cut-off ages for dependents who are out of school and those who are full-time students. (See www.ncsl.org/programs/health/dependentstatus.htm for information on your state's current insurance laws.) Most private health insurance programs allow for coverage of children who are permanently disabled even after they are no longer full-time students. However, you must inform the health insurance company and apply for this exception according to the company's rules. You will have to provide documentation of the disability and you must notify the insurance company before your child turns a certain age. Failure to comply with the rules of the insurance company's plan may result in the loss of private health insurance for your child. Check with your human resources department at work and your health insurance company for specific information about your benefits.

There are also programs in all the states to assist families to obtain health insurance for children through the Medicaid program. This eligibility is based on the family's income, and each state has different eligibility criteria. The other way to get Medicaid eligibility is through the State Children's Health Insurance Program (SCHIP). This program provides health insurance to children whose families do not meet the low income levels required for Medicaid eligibility but who cannot afford traditional health insurance. Each state has different eligibility criteria, benefits, and requirements for co-payments. The federal government has centralized eligibility and application procedures at www.insurekidsnow.gov.

## ADULT SERVICES AND MEDICAID

At this stage, you are probably thinking of making sure your child has a meaningful life as an adult: a productive way to spend her day, a good place to live, people who provide support to her with respect and efficiency. However, you may not fully understand the relationship of Medicaid to these positive things. If you are like most people, you think of health benefits when you think of Medicaid. Although Medicaid is the primary health insurer for adults with Down syndrome, Medicaid is also an important piece of the funding for many adult services—day programs, personal assistance, residential services such as group homes or independent living, family support, transportation, etc. ***The importance of ensuring that your child is eligible for and receives Medicaid cannot be overstated.***

Because Medicaid will likely be vitally important in your child's life, you should consult with a competent attorney or certified financial planner if it appears your child may be able to earn a living wage without Medicaid. He or she can help you determine whether it would be to your child's advantage to earn a salary that would disqualify her from Medicaid and can also ensure that you understand the cutoff for assets and income to qualify.

Medicaid is actually a partnership between the states and the federal government. The state and the federal government share the costs of providing services under Medicaid. The state pays the costs for the services and the federal government reimburses the state for a portion or "match" at a rate that is determined through a complicated formula.

While the funding for these services and supports differs among states, every state uses the Medicaid program to pay for some—and, in many cases—all of these services for adults with disabilities such as Down syndrome. In some cases, if an individual is not eligible for Medicaid, she cannot receive the services. In other cases, you might be allowed to purchase the services. These services and supports can be quite expensive. Only the very wealthy would find paying out-of-pocket reasonable. This is why it is essential to make sure your child always remains eligible for Medicaid.

*About a year after my son's Bar Mitzvah, where he knew he had received a significant amount of money, he asked, "Where did my Bar Mitzvah money go?" It was a difficult question since the money had been "spent" so that it would not affect his eligibility for services in the future.*

States use the federal Medicaid program to pay for services for individuals with disabilities in two ways—either through the Medicaid State Plan or as part of the state's Medicaid Waiver. The Medicaid program is very complicated and entire books, sites, and educational institutes are dedicated to it. I want to give you enough information so you can be an informed consumer, but not so much that you feel overwhelmed.

### MEDICAID STATE PLANS

Health services such as doctor visits, hospitalization, and medications are mandatory under each state's Medicaid State Plan. There are also a number of optional Medicaid state plan services. Some of these state plan services are very important to adults with Down syndrome. Optional state plan services include:

- eyeglasses;
- hearing aids;
- physical therapy;
- occupational therapy;
- speech therapy;
- audiology;
- dental care;
- transportation to medical or Medicaid-approved programs.

The Henry Kaiser Family Foundation website lets you compare states and see what your state covers: http://medicaid/benefits/kff.org.

### MEDICAID HOME- AND COMMUNITY-BASED SERVICES (HCBS) WAIVER

All states provide home- and community-based services through the federal Medicaid Home- and Community-Based waiver program. Among the services that can be included are residential services, employment services, transportation, and family and individual supports. HCBS is often referred to as just the "Medicaid waiver." Prior to 1981, Medicaid funds were only allowed to be used for institutional programs such as state-run facilities for people with intellectual disabilities or hospital or nursing home services. Part of our country's reliance on institutions for people with cognitive disabilities was due to these outdated regulations, which reimbursed the states 50 percent of the costs of these institutions. As families decried institutionalization and the community movement gained political strength, the regulations were changed so that states could ask for waivers to allow these Medicaid funds to be spent on services outside of institutions.

Today, the HCBS Waiver allows states to use Medicaid funds in the community for a wide range of home- and community-based services—provided they are used for people who used to live in institutions or who were at risk of being placed in institutions. What this means in practice is that adults with Down syndrome usually qualify for these services since they are the kinds of individuals who often found themselves in institutional settings in the past.

The Medicaid waiver has become an important way for states to obtain federal reimbursement for services that they would otherwise have to fund alone or not fund at all. In many states, this federal reimbursement has led to important expansions in services. The size of each state's waiver is determined by the amount of state funding appropriated to your state developmental disability agency and the number of individuals covered by Medicaid. This, unfortunately, limits the number of individuals who can be covered by the waiver. This means that your child might qualify for waiver services, but be unable to obtain them from your state. For more information, visit cms.hhs.gov/medicaid/stateplans.

*I do not know where Jonathan would be without the benefits of Medicaid. To begin with, there is the health insurance benefit. Even though Jon has private health insurance, there are important gaps which Medicaid fills in. For example, Medicaid covers his hearing aids, batteries, and the repair of the hearing aids. It also pays for the CPAP machine and the services of a respiratory therapist that he needs for his sleep apnea. Jonathan lives an hour from the hospitals where he receives cardiac and other specialized services. Medicaid pays for door-to-door transportation to and from the medical center. Medicaid also pays for the Personal Care Attendant who provides Jonathan with the assistance he needs for some of his daily care. When he gets older and may not be able to work competitively, Medicaid also funds Day Habilitation programs and the transportation needed to get to them.*

# Social Security Benefits

There are two programs often referred to as "Social Security Benefits" that can provide financial assistance to children and adults with Down syndrome. These are the Supplemental Security Income (SSI) program and the Social Security Disability Income (SSDI) program.

**SUPPLEMENTAL SECURITY INCOME (SSI)**

Supplemental Security Income (SSI) provides monthly payments to people with low incomes who are aged 65 or older or to people with low income who are blind or have a disability. If your child is under 18, she *may* qualify based on your family income or as described below. For most individuals with Down syndrome, however, eligibility for SSI will begin when they are 18.

The Supplemental Security Income program, although administered by the Social Security Administration, is not a part of Social Security. Funds from the program come from U.S. Treasury funds and not from Social Security taxes.

### SSI PROGRAM FOR CHILDREN

For SSI purposes, a "child" is under 18 (or under 22 if still attending school). To be eligible, a child must have a disability that is expected to last throughout her life and that results in severe limitations. The parents' income and resources are almost always considered in determining a child's eligibility. This is called "deeming." This occurs because it is assumed that a parent's income and resources are available to the child. Generally, only families with low incomes are eligible, and income guidelines vary by state. There are several conditions when "deeming" does not apply, but they are not particularly relevant to most families. However, when your child reaches the age of 18, only your child's income and resources will be considered in determining eligibility. If your minor child received SSI, she will have to undergo a redetermination when she is 18.

## SSI PROGRAM FOR ADULTS

It is to your advantage to apply for SSI for your young adult child with Down syndrome as soon as possible since it will provide income for her current living expenses, provided she qualifies. In addition, Medicaid is provided to all SSI recipients, although in a minority of states a separate application is required. While the basic monthly amount paid by SSI is the same throughout the country, many states contribute additional money to the basic benefit.

**Meeting Disability Criteria.** For your child to qualify for SSI, she must first demonstrate that she has a disability. Social Security uses a manual called *Disability Evaluation under Social Security* (also known as the Blue Book) to define "disability." It includes both the adult and childhood listing of impairments.

Theoretically, the diagnosis of Down syndrome should automatically qualify your child as having a qualifying disability, unless she has mosaic Down syndrome. This is because Section 10.06 of the Social Security Blue Book states: "If you have confirmed non-mosaic Down syndrome, we consider you disabled from birth." It also states "Non-mosaic Down syndrome is an example of an impairment that commonly affects multiple body systems and that we consider significant enough to prevent you from doing any gainful activity." (See www.socialsecurity.gov/disability/professionals/bluebook under "Adult Listings," Section 10.00.) In practice, however, some employees of some Social Security offices may not be familiar with this section of the Blue Book and may insist on other proof of disability such as intelligence testing.

If your child has mosaic Down syndrome, the Social Security office will evaluate her on a case-by-case basis, since the Blue Book states that "the resulting functional limitations and the progression of those limitations also vary widely."

Your child will be asked to provide contact information for the professionals who treat her and who will be able to furnish Social Security the information on her disability they need to make an eligibility determination. You do not actually provide proof; instead, you provide access to the professionals who can substantiate the existence of a disability. If the information furnished on behalf of your child is inconclusive, Social Security will require your child to be examined by their own professionals. These professionals do not typically work for the Social Security Administration, but are under contract to conduct evaluations.

**Meeting Financial Criteria.** Your child will also have to qualify based on her income and her resources. She may not have more than $2000 in liquid assets such as bank accounts, savings bonds, or other investments. She also may not earn more than the "substantial gainful activity" level, which in 2009 was $980 month. SGA amounts change every year. Earnings or earned income is the money your daughter receives from working. It is the amount she receives in a paycheck and is further defined as "gross earnings" or "gross earned income"—that is, it is the amount she earns before taxes are deducted. Substantial gainful activity (SGA) is the cutoff point in dollars for eligibility for disability benefits.

In order to determine eligibility, your child should bring the following items when she applies:

- Social Security card or record of Social Security number;
- birth certificate or other proof of age;

- information about where she lives, including mortgage or lease information, if applicable;
- documents related to her income, including payroll slips, bank books and statements, check books, and insurance and burial policies;
- names, addresses, and phone numbers of all the physicians, hospitals, and clinics that have treated your daughter;
- proof of citizenship or eligible noncitizen status.

If your child is employed, the amount she receives in a monthly cash benefit will go down gradually as her earnings from work go up. This is not a bad thing. Her first $85 of earnings is not counted ($65 for those who receive both SSI and SSDI). Then the remaining amount she earns is divided by two. The resulting sum is called "countable income." The countable income is subtracted from the original SSI amount and the amount left over is the new SSI payment. For example, if your son earns $800 a month from his job, $85 is subtracted from that, leaving $715. Then $715 is divided by two, leaving $357.50—the countable income. If his original SSI amount was $600, then $357.50 would be subtracted from that, leaving $242.50. Every month he will receive a $242.50 SSI payment, plus the $800 he earns at work, for a total of $1042.50. The new SSI payment and your child's earnings are always significantly more than the SSI payment alone. Working always produces more income in the world of SSI.

Most people find the Social Security office and its programs very confusing. They are! For the most part, however, I have found the Social Security employees, while very busy, to be very helpful. Enter this system knowing that there will be times when you will be confused, but if you are patient, you will find someone who will be helpful. That being said, before I go on, let me answer some of the most common questions I have been asked:

### When should my child apply for SSI?

It is important to apply for benefits at your local Social Security office the day your child turns 18 or as close to her birthday as possible. Some people may wonder what

the rush is if their child is already covered by a private health plan. In the case of SSI benefits, I do not know too many families who are in a position to say that several hundred dollars a month would not help to cover the housing, food, and clothing expenses associated with their child. In addition, your child usually also receives Medicaid, as a result of her SSI eligibility. It can take a few weeks or a few months to be approved for benefits, but your child's eligibility is determined by the date that application was made. So, the earlier you apply, the more money your child will get in the long run. It is just good practice and common sense to apply for benefits once your child becomes eligible. It is a lot easier and much less stressful to do when there is not a crisis.

### How do we keep assets below the qualifying level?

The income limits vary by state but the asset limits are the same in all 50 states. An individual may not have more than $2000 in liquid assets to qualify. This amount has not changed in over 20 years. Some assets are excluded, including pre-paid burial policies, $1500 in burial funds, and a house and a car with certain value limits. I like to tell families to use a lower figure such as $1500 in assets when determining whether their child's meets the asset ceiling. This can help prevent your child from inadvertently winding up with too many assets. For example, this sometimes happens when Social Security sends additional money, perhaps because they are several months behind in calculating benefits and have to catch up with a larger-than-anticipated payment. In this situation, your child will have to spend-down the additional funds to remain within the asset limit. Some individuals use additional money to purchase needed furniture or equipment.

### My daughter lives at home and she is over 18. Why do they ask about our mortgage and other household expenses?

The SSI program is intended to help people meet housing and other living expenses. When your daughter lives in someone else's home, even your own home, those expenses have to be considered. The expectation is that your daughter's SSI payment will allow her to contribute her fair share of the household expenses. If your household expenses are large and the full SSI amount would not permit her to be an equal contributor to the household, SSI assumes that she is being subsidized by you, and her monthly benefit will be lowered as long as she is in your home. For example: if the maximum SSI payment in your state is $600 and there are 4 members of your household, your daughter will be eligible for the full amount if the total household expenses are $2400 or less ($600 x 4). One of the flaws in this reasoning is that an SSI payment would not even allow an individual to meet her monthly expenses if she were living in her own apartment without some additional forms of government assistance—like Section 8 and Food Stamps (see below).

If you are a typical middle class family or above, your daughter's SSI payment will be lower than for someone who lives in a family with lower household expenses. This inverse reasoning perplexes families who think that if you have more expenses, your child should receive more benefits. It seems to some families that SSI actually punishes the individual with Down syndrome for living in a household with higher expenses. It puts some families in the position of considering underreporting their household expenses.

If your child is enrolled in a postsecondary education program, even a residential one, she is still considered to be living at home, since the nature of school is temporary.

Your mortgage and household expenses only become irrelevant to determining your child's SSI payment if she moves out of the family home into another permanent setting such as a group home.

### Why do I have to provide the name of every doctor, hospital, and clinic we have visited?

I know what you are thinking: My child has Down syndrome and it is not going to go away and I am tired of having to demonstrate her disability. Many families have asked me why they can't just bring a picture. The answer is that the Social Security office must determine that your child has a disability, and mental retardation definitions are still often used, rather than the category "Down syndrome." Some Social Security offices still continue to use the mental retardation definitions rather than the newer "Multiple Body Systems" definition in the Blue Book, which assumes that adults with non-mosaic Down syndrome are automatically eligible.

### Why do they ask for a blank deposit slip?

It is very likely that Social Security will require that a Representative Payee be appointed because your daughter's disability prevents her from managing her money. (See the box below.) The deposit slip will enable Social Security to deposit her SSI payment directly into a bank account that you or another trustworthy person can access.

### Is it true that my child's payment will be reduced if she gets married?

There do seem to be financial penalties when two SSI recipients get married. These include a lower combined monthly benefit for a married couple as compared to two individual benefits and an asset limit of $3000 for a married couple (as compared to $4000 for two individuals). The rationale is that it is less expensive to operate a household of two than to run two households of one each.

## What Is a Representative Payee?

When your child begins to receive any Social Security benefits, whether through SSI or SSDI, a determination will be made whether she is capable of managing these funds. Most likely it will be determined that she cannot and that a Representative Payee (commonly referred to as a "rep payee") needs to be appointed. Generally, a parent, trusted relative, or a representative of an adult service agency is selected. Social Security regulations allow agencies to charge a small monthly fee to provide this service.

The representative payee is responsible for managing the money on behalf of the individual. This may include writing checks from the account that is specifically set up as a rep payee account. The funds cannot be mingled with any other person's funds. Annually, the representative payee files a simple report that details how the funds were spent—on housing, food, health care, etc., and how much is still available.

**SOCIAL SECURITY DISABILITY INCOME (SSDI)**

Social Security Disability Income (SSDI) is another federal program that provides monthly payments to qualified individuals. It is also sometimes simply referred to as "Social Security Benefits." This program is paid from the Social Security Tax that all workers contribute to. To qualify for these benefits, you have to have a disability and either: 1) have worked enough quarters to have paid into the Social Security system, or 2) have a parent who did and is deceased, retired, or disabled himself or herself and receiving Social Security benefits. When our adult children have worked and paid into the Social Security System long enough, they may receive SSDI benefits in addition to their SSI benefit if their earnings are below the SGA amount. SSDI recipients receive Medicare (in addition to Medicaid, if they are eligible for that). (See below for information on Medicare.)

Your child does not have to apply for SSDI if she works enough quarters to be eligible herself. Social Security will automatically make the adjustment. That is, they will determine whether your child is entitled to a monthly payment due to both SSI and SSDI eligibility. If there is a change in status of a parent (death, disability, or retirement), this must be reported to your local Social Security office.

## SOCIAL SECURITY CHILDHOOD DISABILITY BENEFIT

As previously noted, your child with Down syndrome may also be eligible for Social Security Childhood Disability Benefit (CDB) if her parents have worked enough to qualify for Social Security benefits. When a parent becomes disabled, retires, or dies, the adult child with a disability may receive this benefit based upon the parent's Social Security record. The child would receive 50 percent of her retired parent's benefit and 75 percent of the benefit if the parent is deceased. However, one special rule can complicate eligibility for this benefit: Since turning age 22, the adult child with a disability must never have earned money at or above the substantial gainful activity (SGA) level for more than three months.

On the face of it, this might not seem like such an important distinction. However, assuming that you will retire before you die, and begin collecting your own Social Security, if your child with Down syndrome has ever earned more than the SGA level, she may have forever forfeited her ability to receive SSDI benefits as an adult child with a disability. This is because if your daughter has demonstrated the ability to be gainfully employed, Social Security makes the assumption that once gainfully employed, she is capable of being gainfully employed indefinitely. Since your Social Security benefit is probably significantly more than the income your child receives from her current sources, it is something to consider when your child is in the workplace. Most families are not aware of these issues when their child with Down syndrome accepts full-time employment, but they are worth careful consideration, even though your own retirement or death is still, hopefully, years away.

### DIRECT DEPOSIT

It is likely that Social Security will require your child's benefit checks be directly deposited each month via an electronic transfer. It is not only easy and convenient but it is an important safeguard from check fraud and identity theft. Individuals with disabilities and the elderly are often targeted as victims of check fraud since it is common knowledge that they may be receiving paper checks at the beginning of each month. Simplify your life and protect your child by signing up for direct deposit any time you are given the opportunity.

## MEDICARE

Although Medicare is most often recognized as a health insurance program for people 65 years of age and older, some people with disabilities under the age of 65 are eligible, as are individuals with end-stage renal (kidney) disease. When people with Down syndrome become eligible to receive SSDI, they automatically become eligible to receive Medicare as well. This creates a group of individuals referred to as having "dual eligibility," meaning they receive Medicaid and Medicare. The Medicare benefit does not begin until 24 months after the beneficiary begins to receive SSDI.

Medicare is our national health program for the elderly and it is a social security program—not a need-based program. Since everyone over 65 is eligible, it is generally accepted by healthcare providers. Medicare does not have the far-reaching benefits of other services of Medicaid and is of less benefit for a person with Down syndrome living in the community. However, it may be easier to find doctors who are willing to accept Medicare than Medicaid.

Medicare has four parts:

- Part A is hospitalization insurance.
- Part B is medical insurance.
- Part C allows participants to enroll in alternative plans like Health Maintenance Organizations (HMOs), Preferred Provider Organizations (PPOs), and Point of Service Plans (POSs) at reduced rates.
- Part D is prescription drug insurance.

Unless your child also has Medicaid or private health insurance, there will be gaps in coverage that will require payments or co-payments as with typical health insurance.

## WORKING AND SOCIAL SECURITY BENEFITS

There are several programs within Social Security that reduce the impact that employment earnings would otherwise have on benefits paid to individuals with disabilities. They permit individuals to subtract certain work-related expenses from their income in order to maintain eligibility for SSI and SSDI and to reduce the amount taken out of their monthly benefit check.

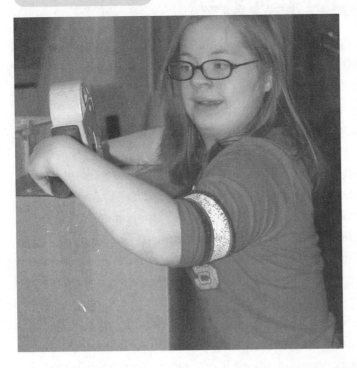

### IMPAIRMENT-RELATED WORK EXPENSES (IRWE)

IRWE's are expenses for items and services that a person with a disability needs in order to work. Social Security allows its recipients to exclude these employment-related costs from their gross earned income for SSI and SSDI purposes as an incentive to work. Some IRWE qualified expenses are transportation, job coaching, attendant care services, and equipment. Your local Social Security office will determine whether your child's expenses qualify. Note that the expense must be paid for by the individual. It cannot be paid for by insurance, a family member, a trust, or any other source. It must be an actual expense paid by your child. Since claims for impairment-related work expenses can be filed on an ongoing basis and you only need to make a phone call and provide written documentation such as invoices and receipts, it is a very accessible program.

*We have used an IRWE for several years. Caitlin is competitively employed and she does not receive transportation services from any adult service agency. She arranges for and pays for her transportation herself, and it is over $200 a month. There is no public transportation and she would not be capable of using it, even it was available. Our doctor provided documentation that Caitlin needed door-to-door transportation because of her cognitive limitations due to Down syndrome. It was pretty easy to work it out with our local Social Security office.*

## PLAN FOR ACHIEVING SELF-SUPPORT (PASS)

The PASS incentive allows a recipient of SSI to set aside money to achieve a vocational goal. The money that is set aside does not count as income and does not count toward the $2000 resource limit for SSI recipients. For an individual with Down syndrome, a PASS plan could be used to save and set aside money for postsecondary education, to start a business, or to purchase a car that will be used to drive to and from work. A PASS plan is time-limited and is approved in eighteen-month blocks of time. It requires a complex application and must be approved by the Social Security Administration. PASS plans are not easy to obtain.

## STUDENT EARNED INCOME EXCLUSION (SEIE)

The Student Earned Income Exclusion is of benefit to students with Down syndrome under the age of 22. This incentive allows Social Security to exclude up to $1510 of monthly earnings for purposes of calculating SSI benefits. To be eligible, the student must be in school for a certain number of hours per week, dependent on whether it is high school, college, or a training course which leads to employment.

## Tips for Managing Social Security Benefits

These tips are adapted from *Going to Work—A Guide to Social Security Benefits and Employment for Young People with Disabilities—2007 Edition*, by Linda Long-Bellil, Melanie Jordan, and Linda Landry, and published by the Institute for Community Inclusion (UMass Boston).

- Develop a good relationship with your local Social Security office.
- Arm yourself with information: Learn about the different programs and learn as much as you can about the impact of employment on benefits.
- Do not rely solely on what the Social Security representatives tell you verbally. Some representatives deal mainly with retiree benefits and only occasionally with disability benefits. Therefore, their knowledge may be limited. For example, most representatives are unaware that adults with Down syndrome can use Section 8 vouchers toward housing that their family owns. (See below.)
- To assist individuals and families with managing benefits, additional help is available locally, including from legal and advocacy organizations. The Social Security Administration sponsors a network of Work Incentives Planning and Assistance (WIPA) programs throughout the country.
- Discuss the best method for reporting earnings with the local Social Security office. This is particularly important if a recipient's earnings vary from month to month. SSI and SSDI beneficiaries should keep good records concerning work history, wages (pay stubs), and benefits received.
- *Be aware that the Social Security Administration (SSA) sometimes sends checks that should not have been issued.* The recipient will then get an "overpayment notice" and will be told to pay the money back. This may occur because the recipient neglected to report a wage increase, or because the SSA made a mistake. To avoid hardship, the recipient may want to set aside unexpected funds from the SSA in a separate bank account. If a recipient

### IF YOUR CHILD IS BLIND OR LEGALLY BLIND

If an adult is blind or legally blind, the amount of money they can earn before SSI or SSDI payments are reduced is more generous. Their SGA level is $1500 per month for SSDI as of 2007. In addition, if they receive SSI, they qualify for another special consideration, Blind Work Expenses. Under this incentive program, the recipient can deduct any expenses paid in order to work. They do not even have to be related to the person's disability. (Legally blind means that even with glasses or contacts, the person's vision is 20/200 or worse. If your child's vision cannot be corrected to 20/20, you may want to ask the eye doctor whether she qualifies as legally blind.)

# Government Housing Assistance

The availability of affordable housing is one of our country's challenges. Individuals and families should not have to spend more than 30 percent of their gross income on housing, yet many Americans spend 50 percent or more of their income on this

feels he or she should not have to return the funds, that person has 60 days to file an appeal or waiver form. If the person does not qualify for an appeal or waiver, it may be possible to work out a payment plan. ***Always appeal.***

- Make and keep copies of everything sent to the SSA. Send important letters (e.g., appeals) by certified letter, return receipt requested. Keep a separate three-ring binder of correspondence.
- Keep a written record of all phone calls to the SSA—whom you spoke to, date and time, information given and received. Always follow up any substantive phone conversations in writing. Put it in the binder.
- Respond quickly to all letters from the SSA.
- If the recipient goes into the hospital, and will be there for at least a month, the SSA should be notified immediately to help preserve benefits.
- An individual has the right to appeal any decision that the SSA makes. Up to 60 days are allowed to file an appeal. SSI recipients can keep getting their checks if they appeal within ten days of receiving the decision letter from the SSA. This is called the "ten-day rule." Under limited circumstances, SSDI beneficiaries may be able to keep their checks by appealing within ten days. Check with a local Social Security office, legal advocate, or benefits planner to find out whether the ten-day rule applies in individual situations.
- If an individual has more than $1200 in bank accounts, the SSA must verify the amounts, even though it is below the $2000 allowable limit. This includes the total of all bank accounts.

I have found it particularly useful to obtain the fax numbers of the local office of the Social Security Administration. As easy as this sounds, I have not found the fax number listed on any website or correspondence.

expense. If you spend more than 30 percent of your gross income on housing, then you are considered burdened by the cost of housing and can have trouble paying for other necessities such as food, clothing, and utilities.

Public housing was established in the U.S. to address some of the housing needs for low income families, the elderly, and people with disabilities. These housing units can be single-family houses or apartments. The U.S. Department of Housing provides

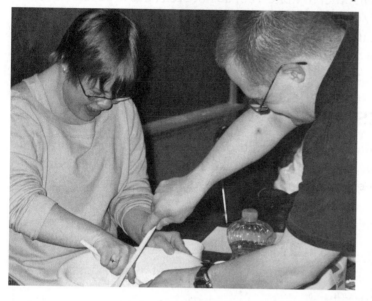

money to local housing authorities to administer the housing units, which are generically referred to as subsidized housing projects. Individuals who live in these low income housing developments pay according to their income.

In addition to government-funded, low income housing projects, your community may also have low income residences sponsored by religious organizations or units set aside, as low-income or affordable, in regular housing projects.

Housing authorities also administer federally funded housing choice vouchers (also known as Section 8 vouchers). The housing authority usually uses a lottery process to award the vouchers to people with low incomes who have applied for the program. The lottery system is necessary because there is not enough funding to subsidize housing for everyone who needs it. An individual or family who succeed in getting a voucher then locates a housing unit whose owner has agreed to rent it to someone with a housing voucher. The family or individual pays 30 percent of their income in rent and the owner receives a direct subsidy from the housing authority for the balance. (Generally, the amount the property owner receives from both the voucher and the tenant equals about 80 to 100 percent of the fair market rent established by the housing authority.) Participation by property owners in the program is voluntary, so you need to ask prospective landlords whether they accept housing vouchers.

Some families with low and moderate incomes who happen to have a child with Down syndrome use this housing voucher program. It is not because they have a child with Down syndrome, but rather because their family qualifies on the basis of income. However, many more adults with Down syndrome benefit from this valuable program. It allows people who are living on SSI or SSDI to rent or own their own home, while only paying 30 percent of their income for housing. Since there is a waiting list for Section 8 vouchers, you should investigate the approximate length of time it takes to get a voucher long before you actually want to use one. This can become part of your transition planning. Contact your local housing authority to find out local waiting times and procedures.

Once an individual receives a voucher, it must be used within a certain period of time. Usually it is a few months, which gives the recipient some time to locate an apartment. Housing authorities will often allow an extension if there are extenuating circumstances.

The amount of rent your child will pay will be determined when her financial situation is assessed during the certification process. Generally, she will be required to spend 30 percent of her income on rent. To prevent abuse, the housing authority establishes reasonable rates, depending on the size of the apartment.

Some landlords do not accept Section 8 vouchers and some families do not like the location of some apartments where Section 8 certificates are accepted. Since the process to receive Section 8 certificates is easy for property owners, you might be able to ask a family member or friend who owns an apartment to rent it to your daughter.

Generally, federal housing regulations prohibit relatives from accepting Section 8 vouchers. This is to prevent fraud. However, there is an exception, and that is when the person with the certificate has a disability. In this case, it is considered a "reasonable accommodation." This means that if you own a home, you can rent it to your daughter. Or, if you have a separate apartment in your house, your daughter can rent it from you. If you want to use your adult child's Section 8 certificate in this way, you may have to remind the housing authority that it is legal. They may not have had the experience before and there are many housing regulations for them to remember. If you take this route, your child is not considered to be living at home for purposes of figuring out SSI payments, as she will be in her own household.

Whatever housing you locate for your child, the local housing authority will inspect it initially and then annually thereafter to ensure that it meets safety and sanitation codes.

*My daughter wanted to live in her own apartment. We just weren't ready for her to really live away from us. We had an area of our house that we were able to convert into an apartment for her. When her name came up on the Section 8 list, she was able to use her voucher to rent the apartment we created for her.*

Since people who live in public or subsidized housing qualify on the basis of their income, they must be recertified biannually to continue to receive the subsidy. During the recertification process, the local housing authority will check whether your son or daughter still meets the financial requirements to receive the subsidy. You must report any change in her employment situation to the housing authority when it occurs and not wait for the recertification process. While it is unlikely that your adult child will earn enough money that she is no longer eligible for a Section 8 voucher, there are housing incentives that allow your daughter not to have her new earnings count for two years. Ask about "self-sufficiency" programs in this situation.

The Section 8 Housing Choice Program is an important pathway for adults with Down Syndrome to achieve housing independence. Unfortunately, since 2002, the federal government has not issued any additional funding, so vouchers only become available when someone leaves the program. Many local housing authorities have closed their waiting lists, although some states operate their own version of the Section 8 program using state funds.

# Food Stamps

The federal Supplemental Nutrition Assistance Program (formerly known as the Food Stamp Program) provides low income families with financial assistance in purchasing food. Using an Electronic Benefit Transfer card (EBT), qualified individuals and families can buy eligible food in authorized stores. The card is funded monthly with a predetermined amount and users draw down each time they use the debit-like card.

This assistance can be very helpful to families with low incomes and those who find themselves temporarily in a difficult financial position—for instance, due to the loss of employment. It can be a very important benefit for our adult children, as well. Most adults with Down syndrome will qualify for the SNAP program when they are no longer living in their family home.

Applications are taken at your local Supplemental Nutrition Assistance Program. Some states also allow online applications. To find your local office or to apply online go to ttp://www.fns.usda.gov/FSP/applicant_recipients/apply.htm. The asset limit is the same as for other programs: $2000. The income limits vary by state. As of 2009, the average monthly food stamp benefit is around $100 a month. If your child qualifies, she must report any change in income when it occurs so that the food stamp amount can be recalculated. Determinations are made semiannually.

## Food Pantries

Most communities operate food pantries, and they are usually open to anyone who receives any form of public assistance. Since food stamp (SNAP) benefits are inadequate to cover an individual's entire food needs, food pantries can be an important resource. They can be especially useful for people with Down syndrome who need to maintain a healthy diet. Often it is a good idea to apply the food stamp benefit to buying healthier foods, which can be more expensive than less healthy foods, and visit the food pantry for additional items. Some food pantries allow people to pick out what they need, while others provide predetermined groceries based upon availability.

# State Government Assistance

In addition to the federal benefit programs described above, there are some state-funded assistance programs. These are often programs provided by your state developmental disability agency and your state vocational rehabilitation agency. In some states, the disability agency is called the Department of Mental Retardation or Division of Developmental Disability or some variation of a similar name. The vocational rehabilitation agency often has the word "Rehabilitation" in it.

Eligibility for services and supports and the services provided vary widely by state. What is important is to find out is whether your state has a family support program that you might be eligible for. These valuable programs might provide you with a cash subsidy, access to respite care, or any of a number of other supports. Families can usually use funds in any way they want. A family might use them to purchase a health club membership so their teenaged or adult child can use the facilities. Or they could use the funds to pay for a companion to accompany their child on community outings to the mall or a sporting event. Some of these programs are Medicaid funded and therefore subject to the eligibility criteria discussed above, but many programs are funded with state dollars. If only state dollars are used, states are free to establish their own eligibility criteria. To find out about your state, contact the state agency that is responsible for individuals with mental retardation, developmental disabilities, or intellectual disabilities. You may also want to contact your local chapter of The Arc or your Down syndrome support group for more information.

If the lack of resources concerns you or you are offended by long waiting lists, remember this at election time. Vote for the politician who is brave enough to call for tax increases. The services and supports our children need and depend upon come from one primary source—state and federal taxes. If you vote for tax relief, you are doing it on the backs of your child and mine. If you are not registered to vote, put that on your list and take your child with Down syndrome with you to register.

*Jonathan registered to vote when he was 18 and he has voted ever since. At every election, he wants to know about each candidate's position on people with disabilities. Then he votes for the candidates who will be on his side. He is a one-agenda guy.*

Each state program can come with a confusing and complex maze of rules and regulations that sometimes appear to have no reason. Be a good investigator and know the limits of each funding program so you are not caught off-guard. Remember these three rules:

1. Keep excellent records.
2. Ask a friend or another family member to come to meetings with you.
3. You can appeal most decisions.

# Other Potential Resources

If you truly want your child's vision to become a reality, it is important not to overlook any potential sources of financial support. If your child is blind or legally blind, she may be entitled to additional benefits from your state agency that serves individuals with visual impairments. Historically, the lobbies for people with blindness have been very successful and as a group, they often receive special consideration. If your child qualifies for benefits for the blind, take advantage of them. These services can be coordinated with other benefits that she is entitled to through your developmental disability services agency. Some of the benefits may include financial assistance, access to adaptive equipment, employment, and important tax considerations.

It may also be worth checking into benefits for people with hearing losses. These benefits are not as extensive as for individuals with visual disabilities, but your child may qualify for adaptive equipment, such as phones, alarms, and doorbells, through your state agency that supports people who are deaf and hard of hearing.

If your child has a dual diagnosis of autism, she may qualify for special programs in your state. Some states have used the Medicaid waiver to establish programs for individuals with autism. Generally, these programs were established for individuals who did not otherwise qualify for state services for people with developmental disabilities. People with Down syndrome almost always categorically qualify for services, so you may not find these autism funds helpful.

Consider checking with family members, close friends, and civic and religious organizations to see if they are aware of sources of funding. Civic and religious organizations might be able to help your child with one-time expenses such as scholarships for postsecondary education or home adaptations.

*There was an opportunity to buy Jonathan his own home. It required a sizable down payment and we did not have the cash available, as our daughter was beginning college at the same time. We knew we could cover the mortgage, since Jon had a Section 8 certificate and would have a rent-paying roommate. I discussed the situation with my parents, who have always expressed a desire to see Jonathan settled in his adult life. They worried about him a lot and needed to know that he would be fine. Generously and happily, they provided the funds for the down payment.*

# Making It Work

The leap from knowing what options exist—which you learned about in earlier chapters—to making your vision a reality is often very difficult. David Lloyd George said, "Don't be afraid to take a big step if one is indicated; you can't cross a chasm in two small steps." Think about this for a moment. This advice is actually different from the kind of advice that has been guiding us throughout our lives. As families, we have been told to appreciate the small steps, the small achievements, and the small successes of our children. But the truth is that big things sometimes require big steps. They require risk.

Suppose you developed a vision for your child. You, your child, and your family know what you want. You may even have developed a Person Centered Plan. You know how to get there. But how do you pay for it? If you are among the most fortunate, money may not be a consideration. You can buy what you want. If what you want is not available, you probably have the means to create it. Others of you may have complete funding from your state for your vision. Or maybe part of your vision. Many states, using a combination of state and federal funds, can offer families some sort of day program for their son or daughter. In most cases, however, the demand for residential supports far exceeds the availability.

This is probably the most complicated part of transition—figuring out how to pay for what you want. You have to be creative, and a little luck won't hurt.

To get you started, you need to list your expected sources of resources or funding and your expected expenses. If your child is under 18 or still in school, you might have to estimate these resources and expenses. Here are blank charts:

## Annual Available Resources:

Wages _____

SSI _____

SSDI _____

State Agency Subsidy—cash benefit _____

State Agency Support—service benefit _____
*(for example, the state will provide your child a slot in an employment or day program)*

Section 8 or other housing subsidy _____

SNAP (Food Stamps) _____

Other _____
(health insurance, PCA, family or other contributions, etc.)

## Anticipated Expense:

Rent _____

Food _____

Utilities _____

Clothing _____

Phones _____

Program Services _____

Other Staffing _____

Cable TV/Internet _____

Transportation _____

Entertainment _____

Uninsured medical _____

Other _____

I often find blank charts intimidating, so I have provided a real-life example for someone who receives support from a state agency and sees staff 3-4 times a week for 1-2 hours:

| _**Available Annual Resources**_ | | _**Annual Expenses**_ | |
|---|---|---|---|
| Wages | $6,000 | Rent | $10,728 |
| SSI | $1,920 | Food | $4,200 |
| SSDI | $5,400 | Utilities | $3,200 |
| State Agency Subsidy | $6,000 | Phones | $460 |
| Service Benefit | $20,000 | Program Services | $20,000 |
| Section 8 | $8,760 | Other staffing | $11,856 |
| SNAP (Food stamps) | $1,200 | Cable/Internet | $400 |
| $10/week from grandpa | $520 | Transportation | $5,200 |
| Personal Care Assistance | $11,856 | Entertainment | $5,200 |
| **Total** | **$61,656** | **Total** | **$61,244** |

Other benefits could include staffing resources (e.g., services provided by salaried workers that your child receives at no cost) which cannot be easily quantified. For example, if your daughter receives services from a personal care attendant (PCA) or other similar supports, they are usually granted in hourly increments. I quantified this kind of assistance in the example above by using 19 hours of PCA services a week for 52 weeks, at the $12/hour rate that the PCA receives. Other benefits could include health insurance or family contributions. Remember that you must be very careful in providing family contributions. They can be counted as an asset and your child may lose her SSI, SSDI, or Medicaid benefit. You can still give small gifts (including gift cards to stores) and take your daughter shopping. Just be careful.

## Adults with Down Syndrome as Taxpayers

I have often been to conferences (and perhaps you have too) where speakers emphasize that our kids are taxpayers and as such are full citizens. Our children are full citizens, but we should be very careful in describing our children as taxpayers. Yes, my son pays taxes. However, he receives all his taxes back when he files his tax returns since he does not make a lot of money. Second, he receives so much in public benefits, from SSI, SSDI, and Medicaid to support from our Department of Disability Services, that I never try to make the argument that he can be self-supporting. However, my husband and I pay taxes and so do his grandparents and many other people who love him.

# CHAPTER 7

## It's a Jungle Out There—Creating a Meaningful and Purposeful Day

*Among dictionary definitions of a jungle is one that mentions intense competition. Another definition mentions confusion and a maze-like atmosphere. While many aspects of transition are confusing and maze-like, you may truly feel like there is a jungle out there when you are working to find the right job or a meaningful way to spend the day for your child with Down syndrome.*

*Mary Poppins taught us that "In every job that must be done, there is an element of fun, you find the fun and—SNAP—the job's a game." This chapter will help make the jungle a snap. There are teenage work rules to understand, and you may need help identifying the skills necessary for your child to succeed later in the workplace. We will share with you the work lives of students as young as 14. You will be invited to sit in with groups of young adults with Down syndrome as they discuss what the workplace means to them.*

*Competitive work is only one way to give a person's day meaning and dignity. Others may find meaning in supportive employment, an enclave, self-employment, volunteer work, or in an environment that does not include work.*

*This chapter outlines the types of support that individuals with Down syndrome need. They include employment supports (such as a job coach or employment specialist) and sometimes the use of fading and a follow-up specialist. We also examine the use of coworkers or natural supports in the workplace and explore workplace "rules."*

Having a good idea of what your child might do with his time after he leaves school is crucial to good transition planning. If I wanted this chapter to be politically correct, it would deal exclusively with employment options. Like me, you may have attended many workshops and heard many speakers extol the value and virtues of work. I even agree with them. Everyone should work. It is the goal. But, like inclusion, it is not always the right thing, every time, for every person with Down syndrome.

I have given up being politically correct. In this chapter, I share with you a variety of activities, including working, that might occupy your adult child's day. I also describe a continuum of supports for you to consider as you and your child decide how to create a meaningful day for him. I want to be helpful more than I want to be politically correct.

Work, for most people, is an economic necessity. Since most of us have to work, most of us try to do something we like and are good at doing. Most of us, also, love our free time and our vacations. We rest, we explore, and we replenish ourselves. We long for more vacation time so we can be with our families or ourselves. Although there are a few workaholics among us, most of our lottery-winning fantasies do not revolve around work. We want our lives to be busy, meaningful, and productive. I bet you can think of a dozen ways to accomplish this besides showing up to work and dealing with your boss.

In the typical world—that world that has been held up to us as the "ideal" since our children were born—not everyone actually works. My mother never worked during my lifetime. None of my friends' mothers worked, either. My mother and her nonworking friends did have meaningful lives. They were tireless volunteers for community organizations, drove endless carpools, played endless card games, and became good golfers. My husband's mother tended her garden and was a voracious reader. Even among my own friends, a generation later, there are many women who don't work. I noticed this phenomenon when I went back to work shortly after Jonathan was born. On most afternoons as I drove home from work, I saw women in work-out clothes or groups of mothers leisurely taking their babies for walks in their strollers.

These women and some men, too, felt their lives had meaning and they got their meaning without work. They each did it differently but they all shared some common elements. They were busy and they cared for their children or other family members. They volunteered for charitable organizations or in schools. Some took art classes, joined book clubs, became politically active or engaged in the arts. Some exercised a little and others became proficient athletes.

Although work is clearly not a necessity for a life to have meaning, somewhere along the way, we let the professionals decide for us that the only way for people with Down syndrome to have meaningful days is through paid, competitive work. For example, when Jonathan was eight years old, I went to a workshop by a famous leader in the field of employment for people with disabilities. He told us that our children had to work and that they should learn work skills in middle school.

The famous speaker also said that students with intellectual disabilities such as Down syndrome should be "tracked." By middle school, he said, academics should be sacrificed for vocational skill development. Our children should have lots of work experiences beginning in middle school, and the school should be doing more to accommodate work during the school day. They were heading to work and not college. I looked around and it didn't make complete sense.

If I had listened to his advice and the advice of the teachers at Jon's first high school, Jon would have been working during the school day. At first, he would have worked in the school's recycling center, and later he would have left school for work. I bristled at the suggestions. The only students who participated in recycling were the special education students, and I was not about to let my son pick up the other

students' paper and cans. Those students were supposed to be his peers and the school wanted him to pick up their trash! Jon did not even pick up his own trash at home.

The suggestion that Jon work during the school day also did not make sense to me. Students don't work during the school day. They are in school. If Jon worked during the school day, he would be out of the rhythm of teenage life. Furthermore, Jon loved school. He liked learning for learning's sake. He enjoyed science and history. I knew it was important for Jon to work, but I also knew he should work after school and on weekends, when teens work. That is what he did. He got a job as a bagger at the local supermarket where many of his classmates also worked.

# Work Opportunities for Adults with Down Syndrome

I will not dismiss the importance of work. It is very important. We define ourselves by what we do. Work provides us with a sense of accomplishment, contributes to our feelings of self-worth, and improves our self-esteem and self-confidence. It also provides structure and meaning to a day. Often it can lead to skill development, better physical fitness, and an expanded social life, as well. And, of course, it provides the economic benefits and rewards that come with receiving a paycheck.

Adults with Down syndrome can greatly benefit from all of these advantages of working. Let us remember, however, that working is not an economic necessity for most adults with Down syndrome. While I am sure that somewhere there are people with Down syndrome who are entirely self-sufficient from the wages they earn, I have never met such a person. I have, however, met many well-employed individuals with Down syndrome who still need Medicaid, affordable housing assistance, and other forms of support to make ends meet. Many individuals also value the money they earn, no matter how small the paycheck.

I have already mentioned that our children will not have to work in order to make a living, but to make a life. I have heard many people speak and write about the important contributions our children can make as taxpayers. I have done the math and it just is not true. Our children, in order to maintain eligibility for essential government benefits and programs (discussed fully in Chapter 6), rarely make enough to actually pay very much in taxes. If they do pay taxes, most if not all are refunded when they file their annual tax return.

I will spend a considerable amount of time addressing work in all its varieties. You will learn about:

1. Competitive Employment
2. Supported Employment
3. Enclave Work and Mobile Work Crews
4. Sheltered Work
5. Volunteer Work

## COMPETITIVE EMPLOYMENT

Competitive employment is one option, both during high school and beyond. Competitive employment is just that—competitive—and it is often a goal that individuals with Down syndrome can achieve with limited job supports. Broadly speaking, it is any job that pays at least minimum wage and that nondisabled members of the community might compete with one another to get.

*When he was a teenager, Jon got hired at the supermarket, which was pretty easy. The store hires many high school students and I knew a manager. We just filled out an application and got working papers (which are required for students aged 14-15 to work). Lots of people knew Jon from youth sports and the community. He attended orientation with the other employees and they watched a video on bagging techniques. Jon borrowed the video so he could watch it again at home.*

*Things went well for a few months and then I noticed that he was not working as many shifts as the other students were. Nobody wanted to tell me why. Finally, I learned that he did not know how to "bag and walk" or bring in carriages effectively form the parking lot. "Bag and walk" is a supermarket term that refers to a bagger being able to finish the groceries he is bagging and look around to see what other cashier needs help and "walk" to that check-out area. I strongly believed that Jon could learn these concepts. So, I hired a job coach, using our own funds, to job coach him for a few hours. He learned to "bag and walk" and return carriages efficiently. Shifts were added to his schedule.*

The idea of "job carving" can be very helpful to people with Down syndrome. It occurs when there are aspects of a job that the individual cannot perform, but the employer is willing to carve those tasks out of the position so the resulting job can be performed successfully. For example, "job carving" might occur for a supermarket bagger who lacked traffic safety skills if there were concerns about his ability to retrieve carriages in a busy parking lot. The supermarket might be willing to eliminate this from the job. On the other hand, it may be possible to teach the person to safely do this task. As another example, a golf course attendant might ordinarily be expected to have a driver's license and operate a golf cart and other small vehicles. The employer may be willing to put together a job that does not require driving.

### FULL-TIME VS. PART-TIME EMPLOYMENT

The issue of part-time vs. full-time employment can be a sensitive one for families during transition. When my son was young, I assumed he would someday have a full-time job. It seemed both reasonable and attainable. He had great work skills and many job experiences. He was a good worker and he had a good resume and great references.

What I failed to consider was that working full time is time consuming. It takes 40 hours plus commuting time. It leaves little time for anything else such as going to medical appointments and learning other new skills. In addition, while I do not want to discourage anyone from accepting a full-time job, you need to be mindful that full-time employment could affect Medicaid benefits, even if it pays the minimum wage. However, if your child is working full time, it is likely that he is receiving health insurance and does not need Medicaid benefits. If his employment situation changes

## What Is a Job Coach?

"Job coaching" often is the bridge to competitive employment. Most individuals with Down syndrome will need at least some support from a job coach. A job coach may work for the adult service agency or might be hired by the family to help the person with Down syndrome learn his job at the work site. The job coach typically begins assisting the individual during the orientation process to help him learn the rules of employment, and ideally continues until the new employee is comfortable with all aspects of his job. If your child is still not independent on the job after receiving coaching for several months, the agency or employer may conclude that it is not the right job for him. A decision might be made to pull the job coach, which would lead to your child losing that job.

Among the things that a job coach might help an employee with are:

- clocking in or using an other method to record his time at work;
- understanding the dress code;
- learning about breaks and lunch routines;
- understanding personnel policies such as sexual harassment policies (this is important for our children to understand because their disability may not protect them if they make coworkers uncomfortable. For example, unwanted attention is sexual harassment, so being "too friendly" can be interpreted as sexual harassment);
- most important, learning how to perform the job.

or he no longer has health insurance, he can apply or re-apply for Medicaid. You will want to ensure that any future benefits will not be affected by his salary level.

*Martha has been working full time in a position with good benefits. She actually makes more money than the staff who periodically check on her progress and address any work-related problems. She has a retirement plan and health insurance. She does not need Medicaid. When she retires, she will be eligible for a pension and health insurance like all other retirees.*

As of 2005, the average number of hours worked by people with developmental disabilities who were employed was 23 hours a week, according to the National Survey of Community Rehabilitation Providers conducted by The Institute of Community Inclusion of the University of Massachusetts, Boston. Although only 29 percent had access to an employer's health insurance, almost 60 percent had paid time off. Individuals were most likely to work in food services and in maintenance jobs.

My observations are the same as the Institute's. I believe that while adults with Down syndrome may be able to work full time, this may not be a desirable aspiration.

Even to work part-time, your child (and you, if you are providing transportation) often need to be able to deal with working hours that are at night and/or on weekends. If your child is trying to get his foot in the door, he has to be flexible, and that includes a willingness to work weekends and evenings. There are fewer and fewer part-time jobs that do not include some nontraditional hours.

*One summer, Jon worked full time. He was living at home and I made it possible for him to hold a full-time position. I made his breakfast and packed his lunch. I drove him to and from his job. I did his laundry, shopped, and cooked his meals. I flexed my own work schedule so he could accept the job. Sure, Jon could have done his own cooking and laundry, but at the speed he accomplishes things, he would have had to get up really early and go to bed really late. It wasn't reasonable. He needs a large amount of sleep.*

*That was when I realized that Jon could not work full time if he were to live in his own apartment. Jon does not multi-task. He doesn't talk on the phone while he is unloading the dishwasher. He would also need time for staff to assist him with budgeting and taking care of his house. He would need time for friends and leisure time. Most importantly, he would need "down time."*

*Full employment for Jonathan is between 20-30 hours a week.*

## SUPPORTED EMPLOYMENT

Supported employment is closely related to competitive employment. It is competitive employment that pays the individual at least minimum wage. The main difference is that the worker has a job coach. In fact, supported employment is almost always the path to competitive employment for adults with Down syndrome. It is rare for a person with Down syndrome to become immediately employed without a period of some kind of support. This is where the name "supported employment" came from.

When a "typical" worker is hired, there is usually some orientation and job training. The job training period is usually brief and the employee is usually expected to learn "on the job." For people with Down syndrome, the job training often takes more time. It can be quite extensive, depending on the individual and the skills required for the job. It can best be described as a long orientation to the job.

Adult service agencies provide staff to help the employee on the actual job site. In the human service or disability world, these staff people have various titles such as "job coach" or "employment specialist" or something similar. The job coach accompanies the employee to work for several hours, weeks, months, or until the person is successful in the work place.

Ideally, the staff person should be able to provide support to the person with Down syndrome for as long as necessary. Job coaching or supports can begin as full-time support and then should fade over time until the individual is independent. "Fading" is a technique where the support person slowly reduces his or her help. The coach stays involved just enough to ensure the person continues to be successful, gradually decreasing support until it is finally eliminated.

After the job supports are removed, a staff person needs to be continually available to the employer in a "follow-along" role. In this role, the same staff person, or someone from the agency who may be referred to as a "Follow-Up Specialist," regularly checks in with the employer. He or she makes sure the employee with Down syndrome continues to meet workplace expectations and helps identify and brainstorm solutions to any problems. Too often, this important component is overlooked. As a result, people sometimes lose their jobs, even though they could have succeeded with a little bit of intervention.

The concept of supported employment *should* permit anybody, regardless of their level of disability, to be employed in the community. Individuals with Down syndrome or other disabilities *should* be able to depend on job supports for as long as necessary, even if it is forever. This "should" happen. It rarely does.

The reality is that financial constraints and reimbursement rates of funding for employment services determine how long supports will be available. There are great differences among states and even among agencies within states as to how long supports are made available. Many agencies and government entities have imposed time limits to how much support they will provide because of the expense it incurs. Agencies may not be able to afford coaches, even when they are needed.

Generally, the adult service agencies locate potential supported work for individuals with disabilities. Sometimes it is the job coach's responsibility to locate jobs for the people on their caseload. Other times, a separate individual called a "job developer" or similar title is responsible for locating jobs. Whoever does this task is usually grateful for good job leads from family members. Otherwise, they will typically read the help wanted sections of the newspapers and online sources, make cold calls, either by telephone or in-person, and use whatever contacts the agency has in the community.

My experience is that families make great job developers, but should leave the job coaching to other people. If you are able to locate employment for your child, there is an excellent chance that the agency will put him at the top of the list for a job coach, since you have already done the job developing for them. However, you must make sure that it is a job that your child can do and that he can get to.

> Rick was hired by the YMCA to operate a coffee and pastry cart in their lobby. In the beginning, he couldn't even pull a coffee cup from the stack of paper cups. To make it easier for him to make change, all items were priced at $1.00. Over time, he learned all the skills he needed to be independent. Years went by, and Rick still had a full-time job coach provided by my agency. Staff assured me that the coach was necessary. However, it became a matter of equity. There were many individuals who were waiting for job coaching services and yet Rick had had a job coach for three years. At some point, wouldn't it be fair for someone else to have a job coach and for us to consider whether Rick could ever be independent?
>
> Eventually, there were new staff supporting Rick on the job and I told them that they needed to fade their supports within three months or Rick would have to be replaced by someone who could be independent. Not long after, staff faded and Rick has been successful ever since. What was the trick? Finding new staff. The old staff liked Rick and hanging out at the Y so much that they never tried to fade. Rick has earned his 5-year pin at the YMCA and continues to operate his coffee cart by himself and greets all his customers by name.

## NATURAL SUPPORTS

The most overlooked opportunity in employment is the use of "natural supports" in the workplace. Natural supports refers to the guidance that coworkers give to a worker with disabilities by assisting, prompting, and providing general help to him—just as they would to any other employee. If you think about it, many of us use natural supports in our work.

Coworkers do not always offer natural supports, but when they do, it allows our children to succeed in the workplace without having an outsider (the job coach) at the workplace for assistance. Sometimes, natural supports just develop; hence the word "natural." For example, your daughter has a job packaging small items and she does well except that she can't use the tape dispenser to seal the packages. Her job coach performs the function for her and she is able to complete her assignments. Eventually, another packager notices that your daughter is unable to use the tape dispenser and offers to do that job for her. The supervisor agrees and makes a minor modification of the workload, so the job coach is no longer needed.

## THE FAMILY'S ROLE IN SUPPORTED EMPLOYMENT

As mentioned above, families can play an important role in providing good job leads or even convincing friends or other family members to hire your son or daughter with Down syndrome. Another important role is to communicate with the adult service agency during the job development and job coaching process about potential problems. For example, if your daughter has significant mood swings while she is menstruating, you should mention this before any job development is begun. This shouldn't become a barrier to employment, but could be useful in ensuring that her work schedule is modified at appropriate times of the month.

In the workplace, your child will be considered an adult. Generally, families shouldn't be dropping in to "check up" or meeting with supervisors. If your child works somewhere that you frequent, like the supermarket, florist, or health club, you might want to consider asking him if it is okay for you to go there while he is working. Some of our kids can handle the distraction, but for others, it may interfere with them doing their job.

*Jon's first job was at the local supermarket. I wanted to shop there to demonstrate my support for the store. It was more convenient to shop when I dropped Jon off or picked him up, so I asked him if he was comfortable with me shopping while he was working. He was, but I tried not to distract him when I was there. Now, almost 16 years later, he works in the off-season at a wholesale club store, BJ's. His attitude has changed. He doesn't want anybody who he thinks might be checking up on him to come to the store. It is his place of employment, he is a successfully employed adult, and he wants respect. Jon's poor job coach has had to buy lots of paper towels as an excuse for coming in monthly to check with his supervisor to see how things are going.*

Best Buddies Jobs, a program of Best Buddies International, provides individualized employment services to persons with Down syndrome and other intellectual disabilities in several states. You may want to check their website at www.bestbuddies. org to see if they can be of assistance to your son or daughter.

## Natural Supports in Action

- Robin was a well-liked employee at the supermarket where she bagged groceries. However, Robin could not manage her own time and she always returned late from breaks. This problem was easily addressed by having another worker remind her when the 15 minutes were up.

- Jon had a habit of chewing his index finger. Shoppers really did not like to have their bags packed by someone who had just taken his finger out of his mouth. The cashier he worked with therefore began sending Jon to wash his hands each time he chewed his finger. It didn't take long for Jon to get tired of going all the way to the back of the store and up a flight of stairs to wash his hands. He learned not to chew his finger, at least while he was working at the supermarket.

- Sarah's job in a law office is not accessible via public transportation. With a little guidance, she found her own solution. A lawyer in the firm drives her to and from work.

**ENCLAVE WORK AND MOBILE WORK CREWS**

An enclave refers to a small group of individuals with disabilities who work together in a business or industry under the supervision of staff from an adult service agency. The employer has a contract with the adult service agency to perform specific duties and pays the agency for the completed work. The agency provides the onsite supervision and pays the workers, who generally receive minimum wage. Jobs that adults with disabilities may perform in an enclave or mobile work crew include maintenance, cleaning, landscaping, or production and assembly work.

The benefit to employers is clear. Employers do not need to provide unemployment, workman's compensation, or other benefits to the workers, because the individuals with disabilities are not the company's employees. Rather, they are employees of the adult service agency. The relationship between the employer and the workers continues for as long as there is work.

The enclave also has benefits to the individual. It provides a step toward competitive employment, offering community-based work experience under the supervision of someone who understands the needs of adults with disabilities. Although the individuals with disabilities may work in a setting with nondisabled workers, there is little interaction between the groups in an enclave.

A mobile work crew is formed by an adult service agency to meet some identified need in the community such as custodial work or lawn care. The agency assembles a group of workers who have been trained to perform the needed work. The agency operates like an independent contractor and is paid by the person or company receiving the service. The agency in turn pays the workers.

Both enclaves and mobile work crews can accommodate a more diverse group of workers whose work skills and behaviors still need much development. Especially in a mobile work crew, where there may be no contact with other workers, allowances can be made for behaviors that might not be tolerated in a crowded work setting. These options are also more cost effective to the adult service agency than providing 1:1 job coaching, as in a supported employment.

Most communities have an agency that includes enclaves and mobile work crews among its service options. You will have to inquire with each agency to determine whether they currently have enclaves or mobile work crews. Their availability will depend on local market needs. Some agencies may operate these crews seasonally or on an as-needed basis.

**SHELTERED WORK**

Sheltered work is a softer term for sheltered workshops (also known as day activity centers). These are separate settings for people with disabilities that provide the opportunity to do subcontract work. Subcontract work usually consists of mailings, packaging, or assembly. Some workshops have developed "prime products" such as tie racks or holiday wreaths that they manufacture, distribute, and sell. However, the variety and types of work are limited in these settings.

Workers with Down syndrome and other disabilities are paid "piece rate" and the workshops have a special license to be able to pay below minimum rate. Rates are established based on the prevailing wage for the job being performed and time studies of typical workers. Workers with disabilities are paid depending on how their productivity compares to the standard for typical workers. For example, the prevailing wage for the job in a mail house might be $12.00 per hour and a worker might be expected to assemble 100 mailings in an hour. If your daughter can only assemble 10 mailings per hour, she will be paid 10 percent of the prevailing wage, or $1.20 per hour.

Since much of the work is completed while sitting, workers with Down syndrome do not have the opportunity to develop work skills that are necessary in many competitive work settings, such as being able to stand for over three hours or regularly lift more than ten pounds. After spending several years in a sheltered setting, many adults with disabilities fail at competitive jobs because they do not have the stamina to complete the tasks.

Most workshops struggle to come up with enough of the kinds of work that everyone can do. Since different jobs require a different set of skills, not every worker in the workshop can do every job. The most versatile workers are busiest. Other workers may have a great deal of "down time" to contend with. Many of the jobs that workshops formerly depended upon are now done either in states with cheap labor or overseas. Technology has eliminated others.

Some workshops have the staff resources to teach individuals new skills, while others have only a limited ability to teach. Although the expectation is that adults in a sheltered work setting will learn skills needed for employment, the staffing ratios are often so high that it precludes most teaching.

If your adult child attends a workshop, be sure to ask what happens when there is little or no work. Since it is a work setting, you should expect that nonpaid work time will be used to develop work skills. Some workshops use this time to develop resumes, practice interview skills, go on job tours, or offer work-related classes. Others offer enrichment classes in voting rights, first aid, or art. Still others provide training work. Training work is one of my least favorite alternatives for "down time." An example of training work would be giving workers nuts and bolts to place in a plastic bag. When the work is completed, the staff person empties the nuts and bolts from the plastic bags (often in front of the person who has just completed the task) and hands the materials back to the worker to do over and over again. It seems a little dehumanizing to me.

*My daughter's special education teacher and the transition coordinator in our district had limited information about the main employment agency in our community. They continually talked about "sheltered employment" even though that wasn't our goal. This created lots of anxiety for me. Turns out the sheltered employment services were a small, small part of the agency and they had such a wide range of other services including a social/recreation program, a job club, a self-advocacy group. School staff had no clue. Be sure the people who give you information are closely connected to these agencies. Things change and evolve over time.*

Some workshops have become so commercially successful that they have to hire workers without disabilities, sometimes called "pacers," to ensure high quality, timely completion of work. Agencies may point to these settings as being inclusive because of the presence of typical workers. However, these typical workers are usually immigrants. In my experience, these workers eat, work, and socialize separately from the workers with disabilities. They are not there to provide an inclusive environment, but to do the work that the workers with disabilities are unable to do or are unable to do fast enough and well enough.

So, why do we have workshops at all? The answer is three-fold: resources, friendship, and need for day care. To begin, the staffing at sheltered workshops can be as high as 16 to 1 or more. It is economical to support people in large groups. When workshops first began in the 1960s, they were initially staffed by volunteers or staff who were paid by local fundraising efforts. In order to support as many people as possible, staffing was lean. When government began funding these settings, they continued with the same staffing ratios.

Another reason workshops thrive is that they are often very nice, welcoming settings for adults with Down syndrome. In fact, staff members are required to speak in respectful ways to the individuals with Down syndrome and other disabilities. Nobody is allowed to raise their voice. There are few consequences if someone doesn't feel like working since there is always someone else who is willing. There are regularly scheduled breaks and lunch. Contrast that to a real workplace. You are entitled to breaks and lunch according to rules established by the Department of Labor. Your boss tells you when to take these breaks according to the work flow. Supervisors and bosses tell you what to do and you are expected to do it—when they tell you to do it.

Since workshops are community based, students who formerly attended school together are often able to remain together in the workshops. On the one hand, this helps to maintain strong and often important friendships. On the other hand, these friendships can act as strong barriers to getting a competitive job. Many people don't want to leave the workshop and their friends, favorite staff, and the parties and other social celebrations that occur in workshops

*Sam had lots of skills and had always been successful in community jobs. That is, until Kathy came to the workshop. The two of them struck up a friendship that eventually turned into an unhealthy relationship. Kathy was so possessive of Sam that she convinced him to quit his competitive job and refuse any others so that they could be together at the workshop.*

Perhaps the most compelling reason that workshops have enjoyed such a long run is that they offer a safe and supervised place for adults with Down syndrome to spend their days. Competitive jobs usually offer 5 to 20 hours a week of work for individuals with Down syndrome. These hours are not always during the typical Monday through Friday, 9 a.m.- 5 p.m., work week. That leaves families with a considerable amount of time that needs to be filled if both parents work or the family is headed by a single parent. Many adults with Down syndrome cannot be left alone, and even if they are able to be left alone, most families prefer that they be actively engaged in some activity or with other people. Enter the sheltered workshop. There are plenty of people to interact with, and, although the setting may not be continually stimulating, workshops are generally safe and secure places.

If you are considering a workshop setting for your child, find out about all of the programs within a reasonable commuting distance. Get suggestions from other families and teachers. The local office of your state developmental disability agency can provide a list of all the providers in your area. Visit every one of them, make a list of the ones that interest you, and return with your child to observe them.

The eligibility process for sheltered work will differ depending on where you live. Generally, the agency will want to see assessments, testing, and the most recent IEP. The agency may have its own assessment process, which may include some formal and informal testing, as well as a meeting with your child.

## Change Comes Slowly

Most state and federal funding goes toward supporting segregated work settings such as workshops because these settings are often considered to be less expensive than individualized supported employment. Also, considerable expenses are involved in converting from segregated settings to more integrated settings. There never seems to be a period of time when there is enough revenue for long-term, sustainable innovation. Even though many people with Down syndrome are successful working in integrated, community employment, more people end up in segregated settings. Families of transition-aged students are fighting this trend.

# The Ticket to Work and Work Incentives Improvement Act

In 1999, President Bill Clinton signed the Ticket to Work and Work Incentives Improvement Act of 1999 (TWWIIA). The Act was designed to help people with disabilities go to work and address their concerns over their potential loss of benefits. In 2002, when the program began phasing in, SSI and SSDI recipients over the age of 18 began receiving official documents that looked like large tickets. They actually said "Ticket to Work and Self-Sufficiency," and got many individuals with Down syndrome and other disabilities very excited. They started bringing the tickets to their support staff, thinking that they had jobs. It wasn't a farfetched thought. You usually get something

with a ticket. You have a ticket for a movie, you get to see a movie. You have a ticket to a baseball game, you get to see the baseball game.

Unfortunately, the ticket was not actually a ticket to work, as so many hoped. It is a voluntary program that allows individuals who receive Social Security benefits to get help in finding employment using public agencies or private organizations that have agreed to participate in this program. These organizations and agencies have agreed to join "Employment Networks." Employment Networks coordinate and provide vocational rehabilitation or other supports needed to help the person find and keep a job. A potential employee can choose among any Employment Network in his local area. The individual and the Employment Network must agree to work with each other.

There lies the rub for most individuals with Down syndrome. These Employment Networks pick and choose employees from those requesting services. That is because the Employment Network is paid based on the success of each individual. They get a little money in the beginning, during the person's so-called Trial Work Period. But they don't really get enough money to make their services worth their while unless the worker becomes a full-fledged, successful employee earning a certain amount of money every month. People with Down syndrome do not usually have the kind of job success that makes them attractive employees to Employment Networks.

I do not think that the program has much applicability to our children. It may be something to consider if your child has excellent work skills, a good work history, and is likely to be successful at a job placement. Even so, it will be up to the agency to accept your child, and that decision will be made if it is a good business decision for the agency to do so. For more information, see www.ssa.gov/work.

# Alternatives to Traditional Employment or Work Programs

For a variety of reasons, most adults with Down syndrome need to come up with at least some nonwork activities to fill their days. Even if they have a good part-time job, or even two part-time jobs, each job is unlikely to take up more than about 10 to 15 hours a week. Some adults may not be satisfied with a traditional job at all, may not be able to find suitable work in their community, or may not be capable of working to others' expectations. Others may have medical or behavioral issues that make it difficult for them to handle the structure required in traditional work settings.

Most adults with Down syndrome will spend at least some of their time involved in one or more of these activities:

- volunteer work;
- nontraditional careers;
- microenterprises;

- day habilitation programs;
- Job Corps;
- Community-based leisure programs.

## VOLUNTEER WORK

Volunteer work is a great option if earning a pay check is not essential, if your child needs to gain additional work experience, or if the pressure of employment is a challenge. Some families prefer volunteer work to a sheltered workshop since volunteering has all of the benefits of competitive work with the exception of being paid.

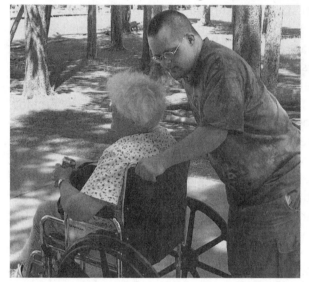

It is important to realize that people may not volunteer for jobs that others are paid to do. For example, you may volunteer at the public library or at a food pantry to perform specific roles that are only done by volunteers. But you may not volunteer at McDonald's, Toys R Us, or any other establishment that does not rely on volunteers for specific programs. The Department of Labor does not permit this. It is considered exploitive to have individuals perform unpaid labor for work if others are doing the same work and receiving compensation.

There is an exception to this rule. Under the auspices of an educational program, students can have unpaid internships. So, while a person with Down syndrome is in school, there are many more options available to gain some work experience. See Chapter 2.

## NONTRADITIONAL CAREERS

We have seen a little explosion of nontraditional careers, beginning with Chris Burke's successful television debut in the 1980s. He paved the way for other actors such as Andrea Friedman, Ashley Wolfe, and Eddie Barbanel. From that beginning sprang a group of individuals with Down syndrome who are motivational speakers. Among them are Carrie Bergeron-Desai, who is an active volunteer when she is not on the road doing motivational speaking. Karen Gaffney, the first person with Down syndrome to swim the English Channel, heads up her own foundation when she is not speaking, and Ann Forts has an active volunteer life in addition to her community job when she is not motivating audiences. My own son, Jon, does some speaking during the months he is not working on the golf course.

Some of these self-advocates are paid an honorarium for their public speaking or get their travel expenses covered. Others receive no reimbursement and do it to help educate the community and change attitudes and expectations. The recognition they receive is often more motivating than a payment. In other cases, their foundation may receive payment. Since any payment has to be reported as self-employment income, it is sometimes easier not to get paid.

In addition, we have seen some of our self-advocates develop their excellence in art and music into careers. Sujeet Desai dazzles audience around the world with his ability to play several musical instruments, and there are hundreds of gifted artists such as Michael Johnson who paint, draw, sculpt, and design jewelry. Just attend a Down syndrome convention and see these talents on display and for sale. While artistic pursuits may or may not be economically viable, they enrich lives, demonstrate talent, and add meaning to the artists' lives.

If your child is interested in pursuing a nontraditional career, talk to people you know who have pursued a similar interest and see if you can identify either a mentor or support person. In many cases, family members fill these roles and help the teen or adult with Down syndrome succeed.

**MICRO-ENTERPRISES**

A microenterprise is a small business that requires minimal funding to start up and has five or fewer employees. It may also be referred to simply as "owning your own business" or an entrepreneurial opportunity. Microenterprises can offer opportunities for individuals with Down syndrome to be self-employed. Especially in place where jobs are scarce and transportation difficult, developing a home-based business might be worth considering.

Some individuals with Down syndrome have developed small businesses involving making and selling greeting cards or other items they personally produce. Others act as a middle person and sell and distribute goods manufactured by others. Some individuals use the Internet to sell their products in addition to using local outlets. Dusty Dutton, of California, is a self-supporting puppeteer. With support from a local agency, she delights young audiences at local schools, private parties, farmer's markets, and at other venues.

The *Down Syndrome News* featured an article about Ryan Banning's successful vending machine business, "Ryan's Vending Services," which he owns and manages with active support from a job coach and his family. With a small business grant and lots of research, a marketing plan, an operating plan, and financial forecasting, Ryan's business got off the ground and is very successful. Ryan is a happy and contributing member of his community.

Other examples of microenterprises include a company called Simply Adorable Blankets that specializes in personalized baby blankets made by several young women with disabilities, and an online company that packages and sells buckwheat hulls (used as nonallergenic stuffing for pillows). Tracey Newhart of Massachusetts began her own bakery after a successful start-up out of her home, and then moved into her own space—utilizing the donation of a store front for her store. She receives support from her family.

There may be financial support available from your state vocational rehabilitation agency or through groups that assist small businesses. Otherwise, you and other family members will probably need to finance the start-up costs. In addition to monetary costs, there are also usually considerable investments in your own time if you start a small business for your child. (An alternative is to hire someone to help run the business.) As for any small business owner, there are great sacrifices and the failure rates are high. Make sure you begin with a good business plan. For assistance, you might want to contact the business department of a local college.

*In addition to working at the supermarket, Jared is also a small business owner. Capitalizing on his passion for karate (he is the 2001 Krane Ratings World Champion in a challenge division), he is the owner of a small company that sells sports headbands. With the support of his Circle of Friends and lots of help from his father, he gets plenty of satisfaction and a boost to his self-esteem as an entrepreneur. Since he does not yet make money with his company, he has no plans to quit his day job.*

*Several years ago, in our remote village of southeast Alaska, the cruise ship industry began visiting four days a week from May to September, bringing hundreds of tourists to our community. Our family and school had begun thinking of a life skill project that our son, Casey Bitz, could be involved in and sell in the local gift shops. We came up with the idea*

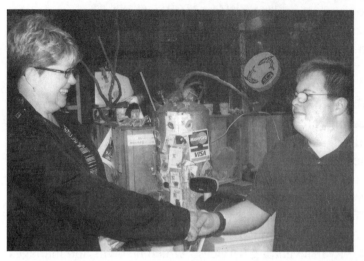

*of beach glass. For years, Casey and I had been collecting beach glass while my husband scuba dived off the beach. We used some available funding as start-up money to purchase a good quality rock tumbler, grit, gift bags, jars, paper for personalized tags, and printer ink. A few gift shops agreed to give Casey space for a display and we named the project "Bitz of the Beach."*

*Casey is involved in every step of the beach glass process. He collects, cleans, sorts, tumbles, tags, bags, and delivers the glass. He understands that by collecting and processing the beach glass, he earns money to buy things he wants. He is motivated to do this and feels successful.*

*Casey wears a specially designed T-shirt when he delivers his glass and it is not uncommon for tourists to stop him and tell him they bought his glass. He has received email and mail orders from all over the country.*

*In Casey's words: "I have a beach glass business. I pick up glass off the beach and put the glass into a tumbler. When the glass is done I put it into the red box. I then fill my bags with the glass, I tie them closed and place a tag on them. I put the bags of glass in the green box. I take my bags of glass to shops to sell. At the end of the month I get a pay check. I keep $20 and put the rest in the bank."*

## DAY HABILITATION PROGRAMS

Day Habilitation programs are Medicaid-funded, nonresidential programs for adults with developmental disabilities who are receiving Medicaid. Since Medicaid is a medical program, these programs offer instruction in functional skills such as food shopping, meal preparation, and personal hygiene and provide physical, occupational, and speech therapy along with nursing services. They are not allowed to offer job-related services.

Day Habilitation programs vary greatly among states and even among communities within a state. Some may offer community activities such as using the local YMCA's fitness centers and others may offer school-like field trips. Some may encourage volunteer work. Individuals may attend full or part time. Part-time participants can use their other time any way they want or for any other program that they have the funding for. This includes paid work, sheltered work, or any of the other alternatives we have described, including staying at home.

The advantages of day habilitation programs are that the reimbursement rates are usually better than state-funded programs so that the staff-to-individual ratios average 1 to 4. As a result, these programs can provide services to adults with Down syndrome who have greater needs. Additionally, because they are federally funded programs, they are not at the mercy of the state legislators and there is not usually a waiting list for these programs. An annual plan is required so progress can be measured and tracked. Generally, any adult with developmental disabilities who receives Medicaid is eligible for these programs.

There is wide variability among day habilitation programs in an area, with some having an institutional feel. It is therefore wise to visit several if you are considering this option. Some of the questions to consider when you observe are:

- Are individuals grouped with people of similar ages or are 22-year-olds with 50-year-olds?
- Are the activities and classes of interest to your child?
- Is there variety to the day or will your child spend most of his time in one room?
- Are the classes and activities dynamic? For example, is the latest technology used and current pop culture integrated into activities?
- How is the concept of health and wellness made a part of each day?

*We looked at a dozen day habilitation programs for my son, who has some behavioral challenges in addition to Down syndrome. We were very disappointed in what we saw—groups of people sitting around doing table-top activities and going into the community once a week and that was often to a fast food place. Finally, we found a program that was designed around community activities and that grouped four or five individuals of similar ages together.*

*In this program, my son gets to explore his community. He works out at the YMCA, buys ingredients for a healthy lunch, and can get assistance preparing it. He learned to create jewelry, which taught him sequencing and let him work on his fine motor skills at the same time. Technology is big at this program and he uses the Wii system and Dance Dance Revolution, as well as the computer for all sorts of things. There is also a big community service component to the program and he gets to give back to his community through volunteer work. It took months to find the right program, but it was worth it.*

**COMMUNITY-BASED LEISURE PROGRAMS**

These mostly state-funded programs provide supervision and activities for adults with disabilities, but no work options. There are few expectations or demands placed on the individuals and the day revolves around leisure activities. These activities may include community trips, board games, and center-based classes. The difference between these programs and day habilitation programs is that they do not offer the health-related services of nursing or occupational, physical, and speech therapy and they are not Medicaid funded. While is possible to combine a community-based leisure program with a work program, these programs are often considered for individuals who do not have employment as a goal.

**JOB CORPS**

Job Corps is a no-cost education and vocational training program administered by the U.S. Department of Labor that helps young people ages 16 through 24 get better jobs, make more money, and take control of their lives.

At Job Corps, students enroll to learn a trade in areas such as business technology, health occupations, hospitality, culinary arts, construction, and auto mechanics. Students also take academic classes in subjects such as basic reading and math and Limited English Proficiency courses, and can work toward earning a GED or high school diploma. Courses in independent living, employability skills, and social skills are offered in order to help students transition into the workplace.

Participants are paid a monthly allowance. The longer they stay with the program, the more their allowance is. Job Corps provides career counseling and transition support to its students for up to 12 months after they graduate from the program.

To qualify for Job Corps, a young person must:

- be 16 through 24;
- be a U.S. citizen or legal resident;
- meet income requirements (generally speaking, a student's income must fall below federal poverty income guidelines, but students with disabilities may qualify without meeting income requirements);
- be ready, willing, and able to participate fully in an educational environment.

Students with disabilities have been successful participants and graduates of Job Corps and there are both residential and nonresidential positions available. More information is available at www.jobcorps.gov.

There are other government programs such as AmeriCorps, Vista, and City Year that might be worth checking out. They all have different requirements and may not be suited for all individuals with Down syndrome. AmeriCorps is covered in Chapter 3.

# Barriers to Employment

There is no right to employment for individuals with Down syndrome or other disabilities. Your child has neither a right to employment nor to the services and supports that would help him find, train for, and maintain employment (except while he is still in high school and has the right to transition services). Although state vocational rehabilitation agencies exist, your child does not have an absolute right to their services. There is no entitlement for any adult services. Families can find this confusing, because even though their child may be "eligible" for services, he is not entitled to them. Receiving adult services is dependent upon the availability of funds to pay for the services.

The lack of appropriate services for adults with disabilities in general leads to three major barriers to employment:

- lack of skills;
- lack of readiness; and
- lack of formal support.

These barriers result in a very high unemployment rate for people with intellectual disabilities in the United States. Estimates vary, but it is close to 70 percent.

**VOCATIONAL REHABILITATION AGENCIES**

Vocational rehabilitation is a federally and state-funded program that provides funds and other support for employment-related services and training to help people with disabilities prepare for, find, or keep a job. Your state vocational rehabilitation agency *may* be able to help your adult child overcome the barriers of limited job skills, readiness, and support—*if* he qualifies for services from the agency and *if* there is enough funding for services.

Each state has its own eligibility requirements and application process. In general, however, qualified applicants:

- must have a documented disability that has a significant impact on their ability to get or keep a job;
- must need VR services to locate, get, or keep a job; and
- must be able to get or keep a job after receiving VR services.

If your child is found to be eligible, he will work with a counselor to develop an Individualized Plan for Employment. This plan will cover: 1) your child's job goals; 2) the services needed to meet those goals; and 3) how progress toward the job goals will be measured.

Examples of vocational rehabilitation services that can be provided if there is sufficient funding include:

- counseling and guidance to plan vocational goals;
- vocational aptitude testing;
- funding for some costs of job-related education (tuition, books, transportation);
- medical treatment or therapy to lessen the impact of disability on the person's employability;
- assistive technology needed to perform a job (TTY, adapted keyboard);
- training in work behaviors;
- assistance in writing a resume or practicing job interview skills;
- job placement assistance.

In general, people who qualify for assistance need to contribute to the cost of most services unless their income is low enough to qualify for free assistance.

# Concerns That Should Not Become Barriers to Employment

Sometimes parents of adults with Down syndrome inadvertently put up barriers to their own children's employment. These are the three most common reasons families give when they turn down employment opportunities for their child:

- concerns about loss of benefits if their child works;
- worries about possible mistreatment in the workplace; and
- concerns about their child's safety.

There is no denying that benefits such as SSI and Medicaid are important and you need to be careful not to do anything that will jeopardize your child's eligibility. Concern about loss of benefits, however, is not a reason for our children not to work at all. It may be a reason not to work full-time in a well-compensated position. Someone just has to be on top of the issues and manage wages so your child does not lose benefits. Preserving eligibility for benefits is discussed in detail in Chapter 6.

Worrying about possible mistreatment on the job is also understandable. Many of us have had to become "helicopter parents"—hovering and managing our children's lives. Probably none of our children with Down syndrome would be where they are today if it were not for our constant advocacy. In the past, you may have bristled every time your child was insulted or stared at. Once your child is no longer at school, where he is supervised and protected, it is natural to wonder how he will manage in the workplace. Will he be shunned at lunch? Will people play jokes on him or call him names? Will customers be mean and hurtful? Probably not. You will probably worry anyway, but you can check in frequently with your child or the staff responsible for the support your child gets. You will be on top of it.

If your child is nonverbal or you have concerns about him being abused, you will want to make sure that he works in an environment where people are willing to take the time to understand him. Additionally, you will want to ensure that he is working in a setting where opportunities for abuse are minimized—for example, by avoiding jobs where he works alone or in an isolated location or has to wait for transportation alone or be transported alone.

Safety issues are most often addressed during the job search. It may be logical to eliminate a particular job from consideration if it poses too much risk. Often, however, whatever risk is identified can be addressed either by additional training or by modifying the job. For example, if the job requires using a weed whacker to trim the lawn, your child might need to be taught to wear long pants and wear safety glasses, assuming he knows how to actually use the machine.

*Jon had a maintenance job he enjoyed at a YMCA camp. The camp was in a remote location and his supervisor was often off-site. The only other people in the same location were not close or visible. Jon would often have to wait for his ride alone. In the winter months, with shorter days, he would have to wait alone in the dark, at the end of a long and empty road. It took Jon several months to tell anyone that he was nervous about this situation. When I found out, his transportation arrangement was changed. That was too much risk for me to take.*

# Figuring Out the Right Job

If your child is still in high school, there are people at school who may be able to help you figure out what jobs your child might enjoy and be good at. They may also be able to arrange opportunities for him to begin to learn some job skills. (This might have to be deferred to after high school if your child is totally included in an academic program.) In addition, if he qualifies for Vocational Rehab services (see above), staff can theoretically help him with his job search. In reality, though, parents often end up playing the major role in finding the right job for their teen or adult child with Down syndrome.

It should be our goal to help our children find the right job. It may be easier if your child has particular interests. Many people think that the interests must be job related, but I think you need to think about other likes and dislikes that factor into whether someone enjoys a job. For example:

1.  What kinds of settings does your child like to be in?
    *My son likes to be outdoors.*

2. What does he like to wear?
   *We also know that he dislikes dressing up.*
3. How active does he like to be? (How active should he be?)
   *We think that it is desirable for our son to have a job where he can be active and burn calories without going to the gym.*
4. How important is social interaction to him?
   *There should be at least some social interaction, like at lunchtime.*
5. Is he a morning person or a night owl?
   *He loves to stay up late and sleep in.*
6. Are there other considerations that may affect when and where he can work?
   *He can't miss Special Olympic bowling on Saturday.*

When we began job exploration for our son, we considered all the above factors and the fact that he is an excellent golfer. We began with where he might like to work rather than what he might like to do.

I am sure that you and your child can easily put together a list of similar likes and dislikes. This will help you to identify possible job sites.

*Since Jon likes to golf and be outdoors, he thought he might enjoy working at a country club. He could dress casually and have something in common with the golfers. We were also sure that he would be more likely to move around than sit in one place. We brainstormed about what kind of job he could do there and we came up with several possibilities: setting up banquet facilities, kitchen and dining room responsibilities, golf course maintenance, work in the pro shop, taking care of the driving range, and helping in the bag room. Then we identified a country club and a member we knew who set up an interview with the manager of the club. Country clubs like to keep their members happy, and in this case, giving Jon a job opportunity was keeping a member happy.*

I think there are several questions parents should address when narrowing down job possibilities for their child. In my experience, asking "Where should my child work?" in addition to "What should my child do?" has been extremely helpful. Finding a welcoming and supportive environment is very important for our children's success. It is how I have directed Jon's job searches. I find someone who wants to hire him and then I figure out what kind of job he could do.

You might want to begin by focusing on what your child wants to do and then find a welcoming employer. There is no one right way to conduct a job search.

Sometimes the path to the right job includes taking a less than ideal job. We encourage our other children "to get their foot in the door" and this same mantra might be helpful to our child with Down syndrome.

I am not sure who the first person was to start using the phrase, "food, filth, and flowers," but there is a good chance you might someday hear it and I want you to know how it came to be developed and widely used. In the not-too-distant past, students with Down syndrome and other disabilities received little in their education that would prepare them for meaningful jobs. Their potential was unrecognized. If they were able to get jobs, it seemed to be in very limited areas and someone had the bright idea of calling these areas "food, filth, and flowers." In other words, adults with disabilities often ended up working with *food*—as in supermarkets and the fast food industry, *filth*—as in janitorial work, and *flowers*—as in the florist world.

Soon many people were talking about the "3 F's." I heard many parents of children with Down syndrome fall into step with the professionals and say that their children would not work in food, filth, and flowers. I believe in the rights of our children as much as the next parent, but I also live in a real world. In my world, and, I'll bet in your world, most teenagers find their first jobs in food or filth. Actually, I have always wondered about the flowers in the 3 F's, as only once in my personal and professional life have I come across someone with intellectual disabilities working with flowers. I am not saying that these workers don't exist. I just don't believe that there were ever enough people working with flowers to get a mention. I think it was just catchy.

Professionals sometimes responded to my retort that most typical teens work in food and filth by saying that typical teens have many more options available and do not have to look forward to a lifetime working in these very limited fields. That is true. People with Down syndrome should have options and choices available. Today they do. People with Down syndrome work in hundreds of different environments—law offices, schools, all levels of government, and even for a Major League Baseball team!

Still, I believe that every job has value. If we value all jobs, that brings value to the people who perform them. I appreciate both the person with Down syndrome and the retired man who bag my groceries because it gives me a chance to catch my breath as I finish my shopping. I usually do not see who cleans the many public restrooms I use, but there is nothing I appreciate more than finding one that is clean and well-stocked.

*Jonathan's job at the YMCA included cleaning toilets that the campers used. He didn't complain and we made sure that he was taught to wear gloves and practice personal safety. My husband and my parents hated the fact that he cleaned toilets. My parents were on my case to find him another job. However, Jon lives on Cape Cod and year-round jobs are not plentiful. There were other aspects of his job that were positive. He liked his coworkers and his boss. When I asked Jon whether he liked cleaning toilets—a pretty dumb question, as I am sure nobody "likes" cleaning toilets—he had great responses. He told me "they don't clean themselves" and "someone has to do it." Jon happily worked there for four years, until he found a job he liked more. He is still nostalgic when he thinks about his coworkers and the fun they had. Now, he volunteers at the YMCA when he has spare time so he can be connected to something that he remembers fondly.*

Our children are all different and they should not be forced into careers that they are not suited for. However, neither should they be kept from jobs that they might find satisfying.

HELPING YOUR CHILD EXPLORE EMPLOYMENT POSSIBILITIES

If you, your child, or someone else has identified that he may be interested in a particular job, there are several ways to explore these jobs in advance to see if they might be a good fit.

First, you can ask an employer for an *informational interview*. You are not asking the employer to interview your child for the job, but to let your child interview someone there about what the job entails. This has no risk to the employer. It gives them an opportunity to meet your son and for your son to find out about possible job opportunities there, the company, and the environment. You will have to judge for yourself whether your child can do the interview alone or whether you or another support person should accompany him. Try to set up the interview with someone who is

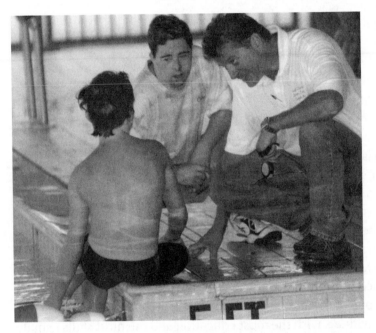

doing the kind of work that your son wants to do. He should come prepared with a list of questions to ask the employee—does she like her job, what does she dislike about the job, what does she do in a typical day, etc. Not every employer will consent to an informational interview, but it can be an easy way for them to appear civic minded.

Another strategy is for your child to *job shadow* people who are doing jobs that interest him. This means that your son would spend a few hours to a couple of days following someone who is doing the job he is interested in. This would give you, your son, and/or a support person an opportunity to see if the skills required for the job are in line with your child's skills.

If your child is a strong visual learner who does not require actual live demonstrations, there are short videos on different jobs that can give him an idea of what a job is really like. For example, a number of videos are available on www.careeronestop.org. Click "Explore Careers." Then, under Occupations, click "Browse." In the bottom left, you can choose "Videos." This website also has some interest tests your child can take, either on his own or with assistance.

MAKING A DREAM A REALITY

I had the pleasure of filling in, at the last minute, for a facilitator who was stuck in traffic at the Down Syndrome Society of Rhode Island's Conference. My assignment was to speak with the young adults about employment. I asked them where they have worked or what they did, and here are their answers:

- Supermarket
- Hair salon
- Restaurant—waiting tables, trash, dishes
- Car dealership
- Custodian
- Adult care

- Black Box Theater—teaching children with disabilities
- Antique store
- Kaleidoscope Theater—working with an integrated theater troupe
- Computer stuff
- Elementary school

Then I asked them what jobs they *wanted* to have. Here they had big dreams:
- Work with transition students
- Work in a movie theater
- Carpenter
- Blacksmith
- Engineer
- Lawyer
- Be in a music video with Hillary Duff
- Voiceover artist
- Dance teacher
- Radio person
- Weatherman
- Television Actor
- Lifeguard on "Baywatch"

Clearly, some of the above jobs are more realistic than others. Our job is to make a dream job a reality by breaking it down a little bit. Here is what I mean. If your child with Down syndrome wants to be a carpenter, for example, you have to dig a bit more to find out what parts of the job appeal to him. Does he like working with his hands? being creative? building things? Perhaps you are a carpenter and he wants to be like you. Does he like to dress like a carpenter? Perhaps he is also good at filing. Maybe if he got a job in the office of a contractor where he could spend time around carpenters he will feel like one of them.

Individuals with the most education and the most skills usually have the most employment choices. People without a college or trade education have more limited job prospects. It is definitely more challenging to find a job with fewer skills, but parents of children with Down syndrome are used to challenges.

Even if your child can't read and has trouble communicating his preferences, you can still determine the likes and dislikes he has that might lead to a successful job. It may be helpful to use the strategy of pinpointing the environments where he expresses pleasure. Maybe listening to music lights up his life and the joy is evident in his face. What are some places where music is part of the environment? I can think of:
- concert halls;
- music stores;
- the music or band room at school;
- department stores that play music continually;
- medical offices where music is played in the background;
- any place where workers can privately listen to music

Next, consider whether you know someone who knows anybody at these locations. Say, a friend of a friend knows a trustee of your local symphony. You might be able to meet or talk with the director of the symphony and find out what kind of tasks are done there. You might discover that ticket takers and ushers get to listen to the concerts for free and that your son might be able to pass out programs or take tickets. Or he might be able to fill napkin dispensers at the café and stay for the concert.

What about our kids who want to be on TV? Not all of our kids have the talent of Chris Burke (of *Life Goes On* fame), but every community has cable TV stations and local access programming. There are also many jobs our children could do in television and radio besides performing. For example, lots of actors began their careers working as secretaries for agents.

In talking with young adults with Down syndrome, I have discovered that they more often define themselves by where they work than by what they do. Their self-esteem, I believe is more related to the status of the workplace rather than by the status of the job itself.

## Work Rules for Self-Advocates by Self-Advocates

Here are some (unedited) rules for succeeding at your job, from self-advocates at a National Down Syndrome Congress Convention and the one from Rhode Island referred to above. As so often happens, they taught me much and I could not have said it better.

Rules for Work

- Be on time at exactly the right time.
- Don't stay up too late.
- Behave and be on your best behavior.
- Stay on track.
- Stay focused.
- Come prepared for work.
- Always listen to the weather report and dress accordingly.
- Wear uniform if they have one.
- Work hard.
- Try your best.
- Make sure you are clean. Take a shower and shave.
- Lay out your clothes the night before.
- Wear clean clothes.
- Pay attention to your boss.
- Take your job seriously.
- Clean your workspace before you go home.
- Return from breaks on time.
- Speak nicely.
- Don't argue with the boss.

Don't we all wish that everyone we met in the work world had these rules?

**YOU DON'T HAVE TO GET IT RIGHT THE FIRST TIME**

More than likely, your child will have many different jobs over the course of his life. The first job he gets doesn't have to be the job he keeps for life. Like anybody else, he should have the opportunity to grow and change and try new things. He should also be allowed to leave jobs that are not a good fit, for one reason or another.

To illustrate this principle, let's take some time to explore our own experiences with employment. Get a piece of paper and something to write with. At the top of the page, write:

*Jobs I Have Had* ........................ *Age*

Now, make a list of all the jobs you have had and the age you got them. Include volunteer assignments, too. Don't forget all those summer jobs. Number each job. This is what the beginning of my list looks like:

1. Babysitter.............................................12
2. Swim instructor...................................14
3. Camp counselor ..................................15
4. Lifeguard...............................................17
5. Summer program director..................20
6. Substitute teacher ..............................23
7. United Way intern ..............................23
8. Community planner ...........................24
9. Sold watches at Macy's........................24
10. Health systems planner .......................24
11. Disability planner................................25
12. Disability policy analyst......................26
13. Advocacy director...............................28

Your list will look different. Your first job may have been mowing lawns, delivering newspapers, or selling lemonade. The point I am trying to make is that we have had lots of jobs. It was part of the experience of growing up. Trying different things. Exploring new environments. Learning about the expectations of different bosses and the responsibilities of different jobs. Finally, most of us find a job that we like. And we stick with it—at least for a few years, but maybe not forever. Very few of us are still working at the first job we got, the second, or maybe even the tenth or twentieth. Expect the same for people with Down syndrome.

Here is my son's list:

1. Volunteer at community center............ 14
2. Supermarket bagger........................... 15-22
3. Classroom assistant............................ 17-19
4. Office assistant.................................... 17-19
5. Summer mail room ............................ 18-22
6. Golf bag room assistant ...................... 21
7. Summer camp maintenance ................ 22
8. YMCA maintenance............................ 23-26
9. Golf course assistant............................ 26 -28
10. Maintenance on Air Force base ............ 26
11. YMCA volunteer................................. 26

    12. Pro shop assistant...............................28 and continuing
    13. General maintenance .........................29 and continuing

On another piece of paper, list the reasons you left each job. Even if they were just summer jobs, indicate why you didn't go back. Here is my list:

    1. I didn't like babysitting. The children were brats.
    2. I was a volunteer and could get a paying job.
    3. I could make more money at lifeguarding.
    4. I decided to stay on campus and not come home for the summer.
    5. It was only for college students. I graduated.
    6. I quit. I hated substitute teaching. The schools were dangerous.
    7. The internship ended.
    8. It was a temporary job.
    9. It was a seasonal job.
    10. I moved to another state
    11. It was a temporary job.
    12. I resigned and found another job. I didn't like being a bureaucrat.

Here is Jon's list of reasons for leaving jobs:

    1. It was a resume builder and he was old enough to get a paying job.
    2. He finished his education.
    3. He moved from the area to pursue postsecondary studies.
    4. He moved from the area to pursue postsecondary studies.
    5. Summer job associated with camp.
    6. Summer job and they didn't hire those without driver's licenses.
    7. Moved out of the area.
    8. Got tired of cleaning toilets.
    9. Got my dream job.
    10. Something to fill in when the golf course is not open.
    11. Something to fill in when the golf course is not open.
    12. Seasonal.

We all have the freedom to leave or quit, and sometimes we get fired or we are "downsized." Job loss is a fact of life, especially for adults with disabilities. Supervisors change, corporate expectations rise, and underperforming workers are often the first to go.

    *Haley worked in a bagel shop that was part of a national chain. She had been there for over a year and her evaluations were all good. Then a new manager was assigned and he fired Haley. When we tried to find out why, we learned that the new manager had been sent by the corporate headquarters to "straighten out the store." We learned that the store had been performing badly and the new manager was told to clean house.*

You need to expect the same job turnover for your child with Down syndrome. Too many professionals and some families fall into the "employment trap." When our child finally gets a job, we want him to keep it at all cost—even it is the wrong job, the wrong fit, or the wrong boss. We make the mistake of not checking in often enough with our child about the job. We forget to teach him how to quit a job, a freedom we had as we were going about our business of finding ourselves.

But people with Down syndrome are smart. If we don't teach them how to quit or when it is time to move on and try something else, they will figure it out themselves in less than productive ways. They will find a way to get fired. I have seen it over and over. They will sabotage the job to get out of doing something they find unpleasant or dislike for other reasons. I have seen young people smash grocery carts into cars because they do not like pushing them around the parking lot in the rain.

*Janice worked at a fabric store and her job was to wind the ribbons around the spools and organize different sections of the store. The manager began complaining that she was working very slowly. This had not been a problem previously. Eventually, she was fired. Her mother was disappointed, but Janice was happy not to be doing a job she didn't enjoy.*

Here is the last time you have to use a piece of paper—in this chapter, at least. For every job you have listed, write down how you got the job. Did anyone help you? Did someone in your family know someone? Did you reply to an ad? Did you network?

I won't bore you with how I got each of my jobs. My father did help me once, and being a competitive swimmer in an era when few women were in athletics helped me get all my aquatic-related jobs. Having a college and graduate degree got me started professionally. From there on, it was all me, using what I like to call my "social capital."

In contrast, I helped Jon get almost every single job that he has had. I did not rely on "job developers" or other professionals with many individuals on their caseload. I used my connections, the people I knew, and the people those people knew to network and get Jon a job offer. My view is that you can sit back and hope that somebody finds a job for your child or you can do something about it. I feel that getting and keeping Jon employed is way too important a task to leave solely in the hands of other people.

*We were very grateful to the YMCA for hiring Ethan. The Executive Director of our local YMCA, a friend and previous employer of Ethan's, called the Executive Director in the area where Ethan now lived. That call got him hired. They carved out a job for him. When they conducted their annual fund appeal, we gave generously. Some people might have viewed this as paying for some of Ethan's salary. We preferred to see it as supporting a valuable community organization that supports individuals with disabilities. Wealthy families have been contributing to colleges to get their kids admitted for years. We can play the same game.*

*Sarah works in a law office. Neither of her parents are attorneys. But, her godfather knew someone in the firm and that helped Sarah get her foot in the door. However, it is Sarah's ability to type and do other office tasks, fix the jams in the copy machines, attend hearings, and respect the clients' confidentiality that makes her a valuable employee.*

At the same time that we are helping our children, we want to make sure that they are building their own social capital so they do not have to continually depend on yours. They will develop their own social capital the same way that we do, through social contacts and their work and volunteer experiences.

# Why Hire People with Down Syndrome?

People with Down syndrome are dependable. Perhaps because they like routines, work offers predictability for them. Once their job becomes a routine, they are rarely absent and are diligent in completing their tasks. People with Down syndrome are loyal to their employers and often have strong social skills that make them likeable partners in the workplace.

*Mr. Rubin, the owner of a family-owned supermarket, enjoys being greeted every morning by Amy, a cheerful employee with Down syndrome. He also appreciates that she is a good worker who is dependable. "She makes everyone at the store happy," he says.*

In the United States, there are tax incentives for businesses to hire individuals with disabilities. They are:

1. **Disabled Access Credit:** This is a tax credit available to eligible small businesses to make their business accessible to customers or employers. A business may receive 50 percent of "eligible access expenditures," up to a maximum of $5000 per year to remove barriers that make their business inaccessible to individuals with disabilities or to make modifications, acquire equipment, or provide services that enable employees with disabilities to do their job. For example, your child may be deaf and need strobe lights on a fire alarm.
2. **Architectural/Transportation Tax Deduction:** This deduction is available to businesses of any size that remove physical, structural, and transportation barriers. This deduction can be used in combination with the Disabled Access Credit, above.
3. **Work Opportunity Credit:** This credit is the one that is most often referred to when encouraging employers to hire persons with disabilities. For-profit companies are allowed to take a tax credit when they hire employees from nine different groups of potential employees, including people who are referred by a Vocational Rehabilitation agency, and people who are receiving SSI.

Despite the opportunities to earn tax credits, employers do not usually hire people with Down syndrome for the tax incentive. In practice and reality, people with Down syndrome get hired because there is an open-minded employer. Often you will discover that the employers themselves have been touched by someone with an intellectual disability. This has actually happened at the country club where Jon works, as I discovered when I read an article that his boss, Keith Gagnon, wrote about him over the summer. In the article, Mr. Gagnon states that Jon "is someone whom I respect and admire. If I wasn't lucky enough to meet him through the wonderful game of golf, I feel that the loss would have been mine without question." Another excerpt:

> *Jon works with us in Outside Operations here at The Club at New Seabury. This is his second year in this department. In fact, you may have seen him cleaning golf clubs behind the eighteenth green of the Ocean Course. You also may have been greeted by him at the Cart Barn. As I mentioned earlier, Jon has special needs and while the rest of the world might call this developmentally disabled, I would say that Jon is extraordinarily able. Jon comes to work each day with a smile on his face that is just an extension of the happiness that resonates from his heart. He is one of the happiest and most positive young men I have ever met. Jon could put a positive touch on anything. Jon also loves people with a purity that can only come as a special gift.*

Quite possibly, you will know someone who will give your child a chance. More and more often, it is our children themselves who are opening their own doors to employment. Being active members of their communities introduces them to many people who are in a position to hire them. These people may work at the place where they bowl, the supermarket where they shop, the gym they belong to, and their mother's office.

Our children, as adults, should have rich and meaningful lives. There are endless ways to achieve that.

# Conclusion

I want to end this chapter by sharing with you a thought from one of the most likeable sages of our time, Charlie Brown (aka Charles Shultz). There is a *Peanuts* cartoon that always comes to mind when I am discussing employment issues for adults with disabilities. It is the one where Charlie Brown and Sally are watching people drive past the school bus stop. Sally wants to know where all the people are going. Charlie tells her that these people used to be just like them, waiting for a school bus. Now, he tells her, they are going to work, every day for the rest of their lives. Sally responds with, "Good Grief! Whose idea was that?"

Indeed, whose idea was it?

# CHAPTER 8

## Feels Like Home to Me

*In our culture, there is a lot of emphasis on young adults moving on and into their own "home." When the young adult has Down syndrome, the uncertainly around what level of independence the child will develop and the possibility that she may outlive her parents often begin to haunt families during the transition period. This makes it advisable to investigate residential options and plan carefully for your child's transition out of your family home before that transition actually needs to take place.*

*There are many types of "homes" and finding the right one is important. Apartments, condominiums, group homes, shared living, foster care, and family homes are among the options that individuals with Down syndrome call "home." There are many important factors to consider in choosing a home that may contribute to enjoying a rich and satisfying home life.*

*In the U.S., there is a growing affordable housing crisis, and its effect on individuals with Down syndrome and other disabilities cannot be overstated. People with Down syndrome usually cannot afford to pay market rates for housing. They need access to affordable housing. The lack of affordable housing units limits the opportunities for individuals with Down syndrome.*

In our culture, there is an expectation that young adults will move out of the family home and into their own home or living arrangement. This was not always the case. In the past, young people (especially women) moved out only when they got married. Today many young adults establish residences outside of their family home when they go off to college or achieve financial independence through full employment. People with Down syndrome may also take these paths, but there are different paths as well.

The transition period is a time of uncertainty for parents of children with Down syndrome, since it is hard to predict the level of independence their children may achieve and how that may affect their ability to have a full and rich life. Parents must also begin to consider the possibility that their child will outlive them and wonder how she will live without her family's continued active presence.

Until the early 1970s, people with Down syndrome lived in only two settings. They either lived with their families or other relatives or they lived in large, mostly state-run institutions. Families did not worry about their child with Down syndrome outliving them, as the life expectancy was very low.

Institutions often housed thousands of individuals in crowded and filthy conditions. Institutionalized babies with Down syndrome spent most of their day in neat rows of cribs. Education for children was largely nonexistent and the neglect continued through their adulthood. There were always courageous families who believed that their children with Down syndrome belonged with their families and worked to develop services in the community for their children. Fortunately, many of these families worked together with advocacy organizations such as The Arc of the United States, governmental agencies, and the courts to begin to dismantle the institutional system.

Many states have eliminated their institutions. Sadly, however, other states still operate what we call a "dual system" of both institutions and community services—decades after it has been well established that all people with Down syndrome and other disabilities can live successfully in the community with the right supports. The danger of keeping even one institution open is that they could once again be used to serve people with Down syndrome. There is an enormous taxpayer cost to fund two systems. As long as state-run institutions exist, there will not be adequate funds for community-based services. We must all commit ourselves to doing away with the dual system where it still exists.

Today, adults with Down syndrome live in a variety of settings or places. Most actually live with their own families. Some live with other families. Still others live with various kinds of roommates or in group homes. Some live in their own home or apartment. Some live in special communities. Each setting has its advantages and disadvantages, and like everything else in this journey of transition, there is no one "right" choice. We all have different values, and different things are important to us. Each adult with Down syndrome has different needs and those needs will help you determine what may be best for your child. In addition, financial considerations will probably play a major role in your decision making.

Always remember that whatever decisions you make initially, they can always be changed. You have probably lived in many different settings since you graduated from high school; your child with Down syndrome may also live in several different environments in her adult life.

# Time to Move Out?

There is no one "right" time for an adult with Down syndrome to move to a new setting. Maybe you are reading this when your child is 14 and you are thinking that 23 is a good age to move out. Or your child may be 55 and you now realize that this is the right time. While we generally talk about the transition period lasting from about age 14 to somewhere in the early 20s, I think that the residential piece is one that may have a much longer timeframe. Some families of transition aged students don't even address moving out during transition. They concentrate on creating a meaningful day or postsecondary education options. Other families begin planning for their child to move into a new home during the transition process. There is no specific time when most families of children with Down syndrome begin thinking of having their children move out.

In my experience, most families fall into one of two categories when it comes to deciding when their child should move out. The first group believes that it is best for their child to move into her own home at some point. Although these families may not agree on when the right time is, they still have an understanding that moving out is part of the process of life. They also usually agree that they want to be around to help facilitate the move and to make the transition as smooth as possible. They recognize that moving may be traumatic for their child and want to make it easier by being there to train caregivers, reassure their child, and make sure that as many traditions and family customs as possible continue in the new setting.

The families in the other category simply don't want their child to move out. They prefer for their home life to continue in their regular routines. Sometimes parents in these families outlive their child and she never needs to move into a place outside of the family home. Other times, however, there is a crisis and a placement that may or may not be appropriate has to be quickly found for the adult with Down syndrome.

## A Word about Waiting Lists

In the U.S. today, families who need residential care for their adult children with Down syndrome are facing a waiting list crisis. This crisis has been well documented in the media and in scholarly articles. There simply are not enough places for adults with developmental disabilities to live. In some states, the wait for a residential placement may be decades, or parents or other caregivers have to die before a placement is made available. In other states, the wait may be more reasonable. It may be to your child's advantage to put her on the waiting list as soon as she is 21 or 22, whether or not she's ready to move out. Depending on your state, however, if she reaches the top of the list before you're ready for the placement, and you decline the placement, your child could end up on the bottom of the list.

# Prioritizing Your Child's Needs

As you begin to think about finding the right housing situation for your child as an adult, it may be helpful to think in general about the types of housing arrangements that might appeal to her, as well as the features that would be necessary or important to her. It can be helpful to prioritize your child's wants and needs before you need to determine whether a given residential option is or is not acceptable. Some things to think about are:

- If a private bedroom in a shared apartment or house is available, how many roommates are acceptable?
- Is a shared bedroom in an apartment or house acceptable?
- Is it important to be able to decide on roommates? Or OK if they are chosen for you?
- What types of public transportation must be accessible? How far away?

- Is a walking friendly neighborhood important?
- What stores and recreational facilities should be within walking distance?
- Is air conditioning a necessity?
- How accessible does the building need to be?
- What level of noise in the house and community is acceptable?
- How much personal space in areas besides the bedroom is needed?
- What is the pet policy?
- Is outdoor space for garden, basketball hoop, etc. needed?
- Any obvious allergens in the house or yard?
- Is a housing subsidy available?
- Is it preferable to own or lease a housing unit versus live in an agency-controlled unit?
- Is there Internet access?
- What leisure activities are available?
- Is there staff availability to meet needs—are they in the home 24/7, on call 24 hours a day, scheduled to make visits several times a week or once a day?

What your child *needs* is not always the same as what is important to her and your family. Obviously, if your child has allergies, finding a location and environment that will not trigger her allergies is nonnegotiable.

Likewise, if your child has difficulty walking up stairs, living on the third floor would not be recommended. It has been my experience that service providers do not make recommendations that are unsafe or inappropriate based on these kinds of situations. However, in an otherwise desirable location, if something that is important to your child is not currently present, you may be able to figure out how to make adaptations. For example, if the residence has no air conditioning, you may be able to buy a window air conditioner for your daughter's bedroom. Or, if there is no Internet access, you might show her how to get to the public library where there is free Internet access.

# Residential Options

Once you've thought about the issues above, you should become familiar with the kinds of residential options that exist in your community. Some families restrict themselves to what is available and affordable. Other families decide what is best for their child and devote energy to creating it. In most communities in the U.S., the options for residential living for adults with disabilities include:

- living with your own family;
- living with other family members;

- adult foster care/specialized home care;
- group living/supervised living;
- shared living;
- supported living;
- intentional communities;
- apartment without a roommate

## LIVING WITH FAMILIES

The greatest numbers of adults with Down syndrome continue to live with their families as adults. There are many advantages to this arrangement. Your child gets to stay in a familiar home with people who love her. Your child's routines and needs are well known and established. There is no disruption to her routine and no transition to worry about. There are no staffing issues to handle and you do not have to worry about other people making decisions that you might not agree with. You might have respite workers or other caregivers coming into your house, but it is generally easy to establish boundaries and working relationships with employees who work in your home. In addition, there are no "waiting lists" to think about.

You will be the primary person to support your child. You will be responsible for making sure her needs are met, such as by coordinating medical care and transportation. This does not mean that you always have to do everything for your child.

Many states develop partnerships with families who have adult children living with them to help support them. For example, you may be familiar with "family support." Many states provide stipends, cash subsidies, or staff support to families through these programs. Families can use the money to purchase staff support, transportation, recreation activities, or whatever has been agreed upon. This assistance is provided in recognition of the fact that when an adult with Down syndrome lives at home, the family is saving the state money. States also value the work families do and want to strengthen them by providing assistance. Since families are often in the best position to determine what they need, state agencies and service providers work closely with families to determine funding levels. Family support funding is not available once your child moves into a residential setting.

*Carolyn will need residential placement sometime in the future, as I am now 90 years old. But for now we are both happy just the way we are.*

There are also social and financial reasons that many families choose for their adult child with Down syndrome to continue to live with them. Our children generally make good company. Single or widowed parents in particular may find that having their child with Down syndrome in the house eases their loneliness. There is always someone to watch television or go out to dinner with.

*I remember the summer that both my children were away at residential summer camps and I was separated from my husband. I was very lonely. I had one of those "ah-ha" moments. I knew why some of those older mothers never encourage their children with Down syndrome to move into other settings. They never want to feel like I did. They do not have to figure out what to do with their lives. They do not have to face the "empty nest." Nobody would look down upon them either if they cared for their child*

*forever. They would be considered a martyr and they would never have to feel the loneliness I felt that summer. I vowed then not to let my needs ever interfere with Kyle's needs for growth and independence.*

The financial issue is also a practical one. Once they turn 18, our children are usually eligible to collect monthly payments, in the form of Social Security Disability Income or Supplemental Security Income, without their family's income being considered. They also may be eligible for food stamps (SNAP). This can have considerable impact on a family, as your child could receive hundreds of dollars each month, or, rarely, even more. While you might have lived very nicely for many years without this income, the guaranteed additional income may be very important to your family. In some cases, it may be so important that a family might not permit their child to move to a different setting because of the loss of her income. This money, which is for your child's benefit, will travel with your child to help pay for her housing and other costs. So, if your child moves to another setting, this monthly income will go with her to pay her fair share of housing, food, and staffing costs.

You might never intend to become dependent on your child's contribution to the household expenses, but it happens to some families. Your family may not be able to withstand the loss of the income and your child with Down syndrome may not get the opportunity to discover just how independent she could have become. A full discussion of all the financial benefits that your child with Down syndrome is entitled to is discussed in Chapter 6.

*Janet moved into the group home where I was the manager. She had lived with her widowed mother in a home in a nearby town. She loved her new home. One day, without any warning, her mother came and announced that Janet was moving back home. Janet was very disappointed that she had to leave "her" home and friends. My guess is that her mother had become too lonely or needed Janet's monthly income.*

As some parents age, they may not be able to provide the level of care that their adult child needs. Your inability to drive at night, for instance, might restrict the kinds of social activities your child can participate in. In fact, the number one barrier that families report in accessing recreation opportunities is the lack of transportation and/or the high cost of transportation. Although most adults with Down syndrome are eligible for transportation to day programs and maybe to other locations such as a competitive employment site or even to a medical appointment, this assistance will probably not be available at other times.

Another drawback for aging parents is that you will have to actively and continually parent your child. You will probably continue to provide much assistance to your son or daughter and you may inadvertently fail to provide her the opportunities to learn new skills. Your child may never know all that she might have been capable of becoming.

> *I never meant not to teach Adam how to do the laundry or how to cook more than microwave dinners. It was just as easy to throw his clothes in with the rest of ours and not take the time to teach him to sort and do small loads. I guess I rationalized that I was saving water and energy costs, too. Same with cooking. If I was already making a meal, why take the time to show him how to cook?*

## Reasons to Consider Having Your Adult Child Continue to Live at Home:

- She has recently finished school and the goal is for her to get accustomed to a job/day program before you make any other major changes in her life.
- She is on the waiting list for another type of housing.
- She is on the waiting list for funding for supports needed to live elsewhere.
- She is not receiving enough money through a job or disability benefits to live anywhere else.
- She has a serious health issue and appropriate support/care is not available elsewhere.
- You don't want anybody else caring for her.
- She doesn't want to move.
- You have concerns about community living options.

**LIVING WITH OTHER FAMILY MEMBERS**

Some families believe strongly in "looking after their own." This means that the parents care for their child with Down syndrome as long as they are able, then formal or informal arrangements are made so that other family members will assume the caregiving responsibilities. In many cases, this means a brother or a sister, and sometimes a niece, nephew, or other family members.

If you plan on having another family member care for your child, it is crucial to discuss this well in advance. Some parents assume that one of their other children will care for their child with Down syndrome, while the sibling may not feel the same way. In other situations, a sibling has made it clear that he or she will always provide a home for their sibling with Down syndrome.

I have seen every situation you can imagine when it comes to siblings and caregiving responsibilities. I have seen siblings who made deathbed promises to their parents to never place their sister in a group home honor their promise, and others who went back on their promise. I have seen a brother who had nothing to do with his sister while his mother and father were alive become an active part of his sister's life after his parents' deaths. You *must* have the talk with your other children. If they have a spouse, partner, or significant person in their life, include those people in your discussions as well. Also make sure that the potential caregivers have a complete grasp of the benefits and financial issues explained in Chapter 6 and that you have done your utmost to ensure that your own estate plan will provide for your child with Down syndrome after your death and not create a financial burden on your other children.

If you want another family member to care for your child after your death, it may a good idea to make that transition before you die, while you still can help ease the transition for your child with Down syndrome. If your child is going to move to another community, it is important to consider whether this should happen before or after your death. Much will depend on your child's reaction to change, disruption, and stress. Some people with Down syndrome seem to expect change and go with the flow, but others find changes difficult and rocky.

One thing to remember is that your other children have no legal responsibility to take care of their sibling with Down syndrome. They may feel some pressure to do so, and the funding authority may play into this feeling if you die suddenly. While the state can't compel your other children to care for your child with Down syndrome, once they take your child with Down syndrome into their home, the state may presume that your child is safe and being well cared for and make less of an effort to find a suitable placement. The state may take a very long time to find a suitable residential placement in this situation. Instead, the state will focus on more pressing emergencies, such as the adult with Down syndrome who has no place to go.

## Reasons to Consider Having Your Adult Child Live with Family Members:

- It may be a comfortable situation for your child and the family members, if everyone involved in the family agrees to the placement.
- Your child's needs are well known and will be attended to.
- You can avoid waiting lists.
- You don't have to deal with bureaucratic rules.
- Your child is able to keep her monthly government benefits.
- There may be good access to transportation, and therefore more opportunities for social and recreation activities.

## ADULT FOSTER CARE

Some people with Down syndrome may not be able to continue to live with their families, but thrive in the rhythm of family life. Adult Foster Care—also referred to by other names such as Specialized Home Care—may be a good option for them. This is a residential model first developed in the 1970s that celebrates family life. In this situation, an adult with Down syndrome typically lives in another family's home. Occasionally, the home of the person with Down syndrome is used instead. This might happen if the parents die, leaving the home in trust for the adult child. This arrangement is always set up while the family is still living and the appropriate state agency and provider of services must agree to it in advance.

The adult foster care model recognizes that a family unit can often be the best environment for an individual with Down syndrome. It may be the best place for an adult with Down syndrome to receive individualized supports such as assistance with personal care and medication. Generally speaking, the person can also receive more attention than in group settings. This program type can successfully meet the needs of a wide range of individuals, including those who have autism and complex medical conditions in addition to Down syndrome.

A foster family may be more likely than the adult's own family to teach her the skills she needs for independence. One reason is that parents are accustomed to doing things for their children such as washing clothes and scheduling medical appointments. They may also do these things because it is easier than taking the time to teach the skills. While you might see teaching your child with Down syndrome to do laundry as redundant because you are still doing it for the household, a foster family may see it as an opportunity to teach a skill, and, in the long run, make less work for the foster family.

If you are considering adult foster care for your child, there should be an extensive matching process by either the responsible state agency or the contacted provider. This matching process should ensure that the family is equipped to meet your child's developmental, medical, and behavioral needs. As part of the process, your child should visit the family, and, if the visits go well, have dinner with the family and then an overnight visit. At each step, it is essential for your child's preferences to be considered.

> Matt lived in a very nice group home. He had his own room and bathroom and shared beautiful common areas. He was well cared for and the staff was nice enough, but I always felt that Matt could do so much more than he was being allowed to do. He had four other housemates and everyone's needs had to be balanced. Matt grew increasingly unhappy, so our service coordinator for the Department of Developmental Disabilities suggested Adult Foster Care. It has been wonderful. Matt is part of a great family and his needs do not have to be balanced with four other people's needs. He still goes to his job, but when he comes home, he is now much happier.

Potential foster families are usually recruited by a licensed agency to provide for the physical, social, health, and emotional needs of an adult with a developmental or intellectual disability. In addition to being paid a monthly stipend by the state, the families also receive a majority of the person's SSI funding. These families should be well screened. While it is common practice, you should make sure that screening includes background checks for criminal activities and that references are thoroughly examined. Background checks should be done for anyone over the age of 18 who will be living in the house. Additionally, families should receive ongoing training in CPR, first aid, and medication administration and behavior management, if necessary. Their homes should be licensed and inspected annually. Do not be afraid to ask to see the results of the annual licensing report and to inquire about what kind of training and supervision is given.

You do not have the legal right to examine the results of criminal background checks or references. This information is the property of the agency, which must protect the individuals' confidentiality. You can, however, ask the agency what its policy is in hiring people with criminal records. If they do hire people with criminal records, ask what the process is for determining who should be hired. For example, I don't know of any agency that would hire a sex offender. On the other hand, if an individual is otherwise qualified, most agencies would hire her if she had received a single conviction for driving while intoxicated fifteen years ago when she was eighteen.

If you are considering adult foster care for your child, find out how many other adults with disabilities are being cared for by the family and make sure that your child is comfortable with everyone who will be living in the house. Ask if she can decorate and personalize her room and if you are free to visit without prior notification.

Caring for an adult with disabilities in your own home can be very rewarding. Many former human service staff actually like this arrangement, as it provides them the opportunity to do something they love while working at home.

## Reasons to Consider Adult Foster Care for Your Child:

- It is a family unit, so your child can be involved in the natural rhythms of a family.
- May be a good choice if your child does best in a family setting, but you and/or other family members need a break from care giving, or if you are slowing down with age and your child needs to be with younger, more active people.
- There may be fewer individuals with disabilities who need care in the home.
- The caregivers are not "staff."
- There is less turnover of caregivers.
- There is consistency.
- Your child can keep her government benefits

**GROUP LIVING/ SUPERVISED LIVING**

Different names may be used to describe residential settings where several people with Down syndrome or a related disability live and receive the supports they need to do daily living tasks. They may be referred to as group homes, community residences, supervised living arrangements, and care homes, to name a few.

The supports typically available include case management, assistance with bathing and toileting, shopping and meal preparation, laundry and house cleaning, banking and money management, medication administration, medical management of appointments, transportation, and leisure activities. The support is available 24 hours a day. However, the residents typically leave the home to go to work or a day program, so even though staff are considered to provide 24-hour support, they are usually only onsite when the residents are home.

While the community living movement has done much to promote the rights of adults with Down syndrome and other disabilities to live in small homes *in* the community, these homes are not always *of* the community. This is not meant to be a criticism, but rather to state one obvious consequence of having a group of adults with disabilities live together. The individuals in the setting are considered as a group and it is harder for a group to become assimilated into the general community. You may have already experienced this phenomenon with your child in the school environment. It can be easier for our children to be part of their school community on a one-to-one basis instead than in a group of special education students.

Usually four to six individuals live in a home, and they are often lovely houses or apartments in nice neighborhoods. The agency that owns or leases the property controls the house, and a governmental agency establishes regulations that the agency must follow, such as how many staff people must be present at every hour. (To me, tell tale signs that a house may be a group home include seeing three or more cars of varying makes and models in the driveway or parking lot , as well as a ramp.) The regulations also address water temperature, fire safety, food safety, and other issues.

The people who live in the home are often referred to as "residents." Ideally, there should be an emphasis on helping them develop new skills, such as in meal prepara-

tion, budgeting, cleaning, laundry, and shopping. Too often, however, staff do much of the shopping, cooking, and other tasks, and don't provide enough opportunities for residents to practice or learn these skills. In all situations, the individual should be given opportunities to make her own decisions and express her preferences. Of course, adults with Down syndrome should be given these opportunities wherever they live. It can be harder, however, to provide choices when there are limited staff resources and several individuals whose needs and preferences have to be balanced.

Staffing levels vary and are determined by the needs of the individuals. Typically, these homes begin their staffing in a 1 to 4 ratio—one staff person for every four residents. If residents have additional medical or behavioral needs, there will be more staff people per resident. Many homes have additional staff during what may be called "peak hours"—times when medical appointments are scheduled or when residents need personal care or opportunities to participate in community activities.

Evening and overnight ratios are usually established to ensure safe and timely evacuations in the event of a fire or other emergency or to ensure that any significant medical needs are addressed (for example, suctioning needs or respirator use). In my experience, overnight staffing levels are not increased for residents who use a CPAP machine for sleep apnea.

Rarely, a family may pay privately for a group home. Ordinarily, however, the agency receives a contract from a state agency to operate the home. In this case, each individual may be required to contribute a significant part (75 percent) of her personal income from wages and government benefits. Individuals are permitted to keep a small amount to purchase clothes and personal items. Some families may be surprised by this requirement, but if you put on your taxpayer hat, it makes sense. Almost all of us must contribute the majority of our income for housing, food, and personal items.

Since there are many regulations to follow in a group residence, you might see large "EXIT" or other safety signs and fire extinguishers visible and marked. There is usually an area designated for staff which the residents may or may not be permitted to enter. In this area there will be mandated staff notices such as those required by the Department of Labor. There will be a sleeping area for staff or even a separate apartment for staff. These regulations vary from state to state. In progressive states, families and advocates have been able to lobby successfully for regulations that allow the house to appear more like a home. For example, in some states a group home may not have more stringent regulations than any other single family home. In these states, you will not see" EXIT" signs.

Although each resident should ideally have his or her own room, some adults are required to share bedrooms. Private bathrooms are a rarity. Dinner is always a group activity, and, while special diets are accommodated, personal choices are not always permitted. Medicine is kept securely locked and there is sometimes a chair near the locked area where individuals receive their medication. If your child is able to take her medications by herself, accommodations will typically be made for her to keep her medications in a secure place in her room.

> *Gail was one of the very first people to move into a group home thirty years ago. We were pioneers. After fifteen years or so, she just couldn't stand living with seven other women. Some she liked; some she didn't. There was too much noise. Someone always had the TV on and every meal was a circus of ten people. Can you imagine a lifetime of that? Sharing your life with people you didn't choose to be with? I started requesting that she move into her own apartment. The agency supporting her found a place for her to live and Gail finally got her own apartment. She and her best friend moved into it and they have never looked back. The apartment is paid for with the money that was supporting Gail and her friend in the group home, plus income from their jobs. Another woman lives in the spare bedroom and provides some supervision in return for free rent.*

Everyone in the house often participates together in recreational activities. Although efforts are made to consider everyone's personal interests, it is often difficult to balance the needs of the individual against the needs of the group. Often, the staff's interests play a considerable role in planning leisure time activities.

People who live in group homes do not get to choose who they live with. It's like freshman year of college—only it lasts forever. There is little recourse for getting "rid" of a roommate unless there are compelling health and safety reasons. Remember, this environment is home not only to your son or daughter but to each resident. Although the residents are not related, the group functions in ways similar to families. Sometimes, individuals are offered opportunities to learn to get along with others through individual or group counseling.

> *We got a new housemate. Her name is Sharon. She is younger than most of us and has lots of energy. She never stops talking and gets right up close to you when she talks. I hate her and I wish she didn't live here. Nobody asked me if I wanted her to live in our house.*

> *A new resident named Tony moved into my brother's group home. He is having a hard time adjusting and it has been over two years. Tony is brighter than the rest of the guys in the house and he can be very mean*

*and vindictive to them. They are afraid of him. He is emotionally abusive to the guys and the staff. There is nothing that any of the families or the agency can do since the state really decides who will move into a house when there is a vacancy. Everyone talks about choice but nobody ever asks the residents if they want a particular person to move into their home.*

You might be getting the idea that I do not like group homes. While they are not my personal preference, I am a realist. It is more cost-effective to provide housing and support services to a group of people than it is to provide those same supports on an individualized basis. The present funding structure of services for adults with intellectual disabilities does not allow for individualized and self-directed services for everyone.

There are many wonderful group homes that do a great job in meeting individualized needs as much as possible. If you are looking at group homes, then you need to make sure that you discover both the culture of the group home and the agency that supports it. For example, does the group home you are considering promote growth and individuality by not treating everyone the same? Your child might be more independent than her housemates and there should be a process to determine whether she is capable of going out into the community alone or being left alone in the group home. Also be sure to find out how the group home helps new residents make the transition. Any good transitioning plan should include at least several visits and overnight stays. These visits should be conducted at various times of the day and week.

Also find out whether the agency values families and their input. Be sure to inquire about how families are involved in decision making. Most agencies are required to conduct annual satisfaction surveys from families, residents, and staff. Find out how this process works and how feedback gained from the surveys is used. You might want to inquire about who will conduct the satisfaction survey that your child will be participating in to make sure that she will have a valued way to provide her opinions.

## Reasons to Consider a Group Home for Your Adult Child:

- Staff supervision and assistance is always available.
- There is a built-in social network of friends.
- Social and recreational activities are available.
- Transportation to work, day programs, and community activities is provided.
- Staff can provide medical management.

**SHARED LIVING**
In shared living, an adult with a disability lives with, and is provided support by, an adult without a disability. The specifics of the arrangement vary, but often include free housing for the support person and some financial compensation. For example, the support person may get free rent in exchange for being there at night and payment for providing assistance with specific skills such as personal care or food preparation.

Shared living may take place in an agency-controlled apartment or one that is controlled by either the parents, caregiver, or the person with Down syndrome. Although there are similarities between shared living and adult foster care, there is a basic distinction made in some states. Generally speaking, the person with a disability and the person without a disability are the only people who make up the household in a shared living arrangement. For example, the person without a disability might be a college student with an interest in special education or a younger person who is looking for assistance with her own rent. In contrast, in adult foster care the individual with a disability becomes part of a household. Another distinction is usually in the method of reimbursement. In shared living, free rent may be considered part of the reimbursement. In adult foster care, the care provider receives payment for serving as a foster parent and also part of the income of the individual with disabilities. A more complete description of funding is provided in Chapter 6.

If shared living is being provided under the auspices of a provider agency, that agency is ultimately responsible for hiring and firing the person. If your family member is not offered an opportunity to participate in the hiring and evaluating of the individual, you will want to make sure there are other ways for your child to express her preferences. However, if you are hiring someone for your child, you can determine what qualifications and qualities you are looking for. You will also need to check references. You can ask the individual to obtain his or her own criminal background check, and, in this situation, you are permitted to review it.

> *Our son had been living on his own for over five years when he decided that it was not working out with his roommate. Since he controlled his home (we owned it), Ron decided to live by himself until we could find another, more suitable roommate. I found myself calling Ron each night, just to make sure he was OK. After about a month of my daily calls, Ron said, "I know that you love me and that you worry about me. I know I am your first born. You call every day, right? Can you call me every other day instead?"*

## Reasons to Consider Shared Living for Your Adult Child:

- It is easier for your child's preferences to be honored since there are fewer people in the household.
- Assistance and supports can be more individualized.
- Your child may receive more attention.
- Your child can keep her government benefits.
- For adults who want to live on their own with a roommate like other adults do, it can be an attractive arrangement.

**SUPPORTED LIVING**

Supported living is sometimes referred to as independent living. In supported living, staff come in at scheduled times to work with the adult with disabilities. The schedule often changes weekly according to the adult's work and leisure schedule.

The relationship with staff people is usually more of a mentoring one, where the staff comes to understand the needs and opinions of the person with Down syndrome.

There are two problems with using the term "independent living" to describe this arrangement. The first problem is that it creates the expectation that the individual actually lives independently. To begin with, almost nobody lives independently. We all receive support. Some of it is paid support, such as the support I receive from the people who maintain my garden or who get me into my house when I have locked  myself out. Some of it is unpaid support, such as from my husband, who takes care of the bills and maintains our house, or from a coworker who drives me to the airport

The second problem with calling supported living "independent living" is that it makes it sound as if it is only for people who have the skills necessary to live with minimal supports. Supported living, however, is a living situation that anyone, with the right amount of supports, could benefit from. Naturally, since supported living is individualized, it costs much more for individuals with greater support needs than for individuals with minimal needs. As a result, the vast majority of adults with Down syndrome in supported living are those who require few supports. In fact, some states limit the opportunity for supported living to adults who require the least amount of support.

The kinds of support that an individual might receive are case management, and assistance with budgeting, time management, and transportation. The person might need help getting to the supermarket but be able to shop and cook independently.

In contrast to group homes, where services are "bundled" together, in supported living, services are usually "unbundled." This means that housing and the support services that are provided are often separate. The housing can be owned by the person with Down syndrome, the family, a landlord, or even the agency that provides the supports. An important consideration is whether your child's name will be on the lease, regardless of whoever actually owns the property. If your child's name is not on the lease, someone else controls the housing. Control of housing is one element that may distinguish supported living from other models of housing. See the section on "Home Ownership and Control" at the end of the chapter.

*We own Dan's house and that means we wrote the lease. We included some obvious restrictions like forbidding the use of candles and establishing "quiet hours." We also stipulated that we had to approve of any overnight guests and that each tenant was financially responsible for weekly housekeeping services.*

### ROOMMATES

If your child is going to live with another person in supported living, she should have the opportunity to choose her own roommate. While you might be inclined to consider a "best friend" as your daughter's roommate, you might want to think this through carefully. It is not necessary to be best friends with your roommate. In my experience, you may be better off resisting the urge to have your child and her best friend share a house or apartment.

Best friends are really hard to come by and if your child has one, it is possibly her most important relationship aside from family relationships. You do not want to jeopardize it. There are inevitable roommate problems that will have to be addressed and they can lead to some uncomfortable moments. In fact, roommates often request to move out. Most roommate situations end up being relatively short-lived and I do not think it is a good idea to risk an important friendship.

I think that it is also important to consider the compatibility of the families involved. Although the roommate's family does not have to share your culture, for example, it is important to know that you will resolve challenges in a similar fashion. You might want to consider each of your family's lifestyles or the amount of independence your two families expect the adults with Down syndrome to have. You and your child are getting more than a roommate; you are getting another whole family in the mix. This can be more intense than acquiring in laws.

I have observed that after several years of supported living, some individuals with Down syndrome become more confident and express the desire to live alone—if they can afford to do so. For them, the daily annoyances of having a roommate may begin to overshadow the advantages. Looked at from a developmental perspective, wanting your own place is perfectly normal and expected. Most young people eventually grow tired of roommates and may only put up with them until they can afford to live on their own.

On the other hand, many adults with Down syndrome live happily for long periods of time with roommates.

*When Jon had a roommate, they never did much together, but just knowing he had a roommate and was not alone at night provided me with some sense of security. Now that Jon lives alone in his house, I have had to grow a lot in order to let Jon grow. He occasionally goes over to a friend's place next door to watch wrestling. He doesn't always bring his cell phone and I get nervous when I call him after 11 p.m. and he is still not home. I am a worrier and I begin to imagine all sorts of scenarios except the one that is real. Jon is close to 30, he has a life, and he doesn't want me to know everything he is doing every minute. It was so much easier when he was a baby in the bedroom next to mine.*

When deciding upon a roommate, you might want to consider the following:
- Noise: Does your child need quiet to sleep? Does she blast music or would she be bothered if someone else did?
- Media Habits: Does your child like to control the television or need her own TV for viewing? What are her habits in terms of video games, computers, and phones?
- Friends: What kind of friends does your child like? Do certain types of people make her anxious?
- Medication: What kind of medication does a potential roommate take? Are the effects of the medication or the condition it is treating a consideration?
- Level of support: What are the needs of the potential roommate and are they compatible with your child's needs and abilities?

- Family values: Do you share the same values as the roommate's family?
- Problem solving: Can you agree on a strategy to solve differences within the household? How will conflicts be addressed?
- Cleanliness: What are your expectations as to how the living areas are to be maintained? Can the roommates be reasonably expected to clean the area or does cleaning help need to be hired? Is one a "neat freak" and one a "slob"?
- Compatibility: Will your child enjoy living with this person?
- Personal Hygiene: Do you expect that housemates will shower or shave every day? If there is a shared bathroom, are there likely to be conflicts during morning routines or at other times?
- Rules: What kind of rules, if any, do you want in the home? Some areas to consider: visitors, candles, security, borrowing, pets. Will both roommates be able to abide by them?

It will not be easy to gather some of the information suggested above, as it will require openness by the roommate, her family, and the service provider. Since some of the information is considered confidential, people will have to give permission and whatever releases are necessary to share information freely.

*Our daughter Cara had a roommate named Alex. Alex was a nice young woman, but she had a temper that often startled Cara. She also destroyed some property when she was angry— nothing too major. Since Cara has Down syndrome, her disability is obvious, but we were never told about Alex's disabilities. We often saw medication bottles and pills around and Alex told us she has bipolar disorder, ADD, learning disabilities, and celiac disease. I think if the agency had been forthcoming about Alex, we would have understood her needs better and we might have been more understanding. After a couple of years, Cara couldn't take Alex's unpredictable temper any more, so she requested that Alex move out of her house.*

## Reasons to Consider Supported/Independent Living for Your Child:

- Overnight staff are not required.
- The adult gains ultimate control of the daily rhythm of life.
- The arrangement can work well if your child has a good support system and is able to make good decisions and use spare time wisely.
- It can be a good option for someone who prefers to choose her own roommate or not to have one at all.
- Your child can keep her monthly government benefits.

*I live in my own home and right now I do not have a roommate. It is OK. At night it can get boring with nobody to talk to. I was really sick last month with a stomach thing and I called a friend to help. But, my parents would come in a heartbeat if I needed them.*

## INTENTIONAL COMMUNITIES

There are many examples of intentional communities in which individuals with a shared vision live together. Some of these communities are organized like a commune, where everyone contributes to the running of the community. Others are part of the "green" movement, where the community is established to be environmentally friendly.

In the late 1960s, a European model came to the United States that included people with Down syndrome and other disabilities living together. These communities were called L'Arche and Camp Hill and they had strong Christian roots. In some cases, the communities were agricultural in nature, and everyone worked together; in others, individuals held different jobs in the community. In 1972, a small group of wealthy families, all worried about the lack of residential options for their children with intellectual disabilities, founded New England Villages in Massachusetts.

Since then, many different kinds of intentional communities have been developed. They may go by other names, including coops and co-housing. The founders of these communities are often committed to celebrating diversity in all its forms, including diversity of social and economic levels, disability, race, and lifestyle. There is a strong sense of community in these settings, and members often share meals and maintenance chores. In these communities, people with Down syndrome may live as individual residents, with their families, or in small groups of other people with disabilities.

More recently, groups of families of children with Down syndrome and other disabilities have developed their own versions of intentional communities, including LIFE, Inc., on Cape Cod, and Specialized Housing, Inc. These families are either not interested in the housing options traditionally available or are discouraged by the lack of availability and have come together to address housing issues. Working by themselves, with housing consultants, or with established disability agencies, they are creating new intentional communities. In some instances, families have purchased a house where each resident owns his or her own bedroom and a share of the common area. In another community, land was purchased and houses built, then families purchased houses to rent to their children. Each community also has to decide how supports will be delivered. For example, will the individuals or their families pay an annual fee for a certain level of services, or will they be charged on an a la carte basis for services they use?

What makes these new intentional communities unique is that they are made up of individuals who have spent their entire lives included in regular community life. They take these values with them to their new communities. In these new intentional communities, there is a larger pool of peers from which the adults with disabilities can choose friends than in a community residence. The communities operate much like assisted living communities that are popular for older adults in general. The residents work in the community or attend other community-based day or employment programs. A few may be employed by the community. They shop, pray, and play in their local communities.

## Reasons to Consider an Intentional Community for Your Child:

- There are more people to socialize with than in a community residence.
- Built-in activities are available in the community.
- Adults have the freedom to be part of a local community. On some level, we are all seeking a "community."
- There is a sense of permanency.
- Your child can keep her government benefits.

# Support for Adults with Down Syndrome Living in the Community

The greatest single challenge to community living for people with Down syndrome, in my opinion, is ensuring that there is a qualified work force to support them. When our children leave the public school system, where teachers have competency requirements, testing standards to achieve, and are fairly compensated, they depend on human service workers to assist them in many areas of their life. Direct Support Professionals (DSP) are poorly paid, but do very difficult work. They administer medication and are often certified to do so, they stay up all night with our sick children, and they take them to medical appointments and hospital procedures. They ensure that healthy and nutritious meals are provided and encourage healthy lifestyles. They teach our sons and daughters to clean, shop, and do laundry, or, if necessary, do it for them.

Agencies must compete for adult service employees with fast food restaurants, which can often pay more than human service agencies. Although the work can be very rewarding, there is much turnover because the pay is so low. It is a sad fact that many of the staff who support our sons and daughters are eligible for housing subsidies and food stamps themselves. Often they must work overtime or take a second or third job to make ends meet.

Outside of family-funded agencies, staff salaries are established by the state through a contract with the agency. Individual agencies have little control over the salary level and must depend on state funding for increases in staff salaries. Agencies can try providing good working environments, supervision, job training, and advancement opportunities to attempt to retain staff. However, these measures are often not enough to convince people to stay on their jobs when they need higher salaries to pay off college loans or to save for a home of their own.

For the past 28 years, I have advocated for our state and federal elected officials to adequately compensate our direct care professional work force. I have always known that if my son was to be well cared for as an adult, there needed to be a well-educated and well-compensated work force. It's not the 1960s anymore. Without better pay, most people are not willing to do the kind of emotionally draining and often backbreaking work necessary to help our children live in the community. It is up to us to help secure fair wages for them.

> *We started recruiting overseas staff over a decade ago and it has been an important method for finding qualified and dedicated staff. All of our overseas employees have degrees and many have advanced degrees in teaching or social work. We have staff from over fifteen different countries. They bring a richness of diversity that makes us a better agency. They are hard working and have been very well received by the individuals we support and their families.*

This workforce crisis is projected to get worse in the coming decades. As the baby boomers begin to face age-related disabilities and require the support of direct support professionals, they will compete directly with our children for services. There simply will not be enough workers to meet the needs.

## ENSURING YOUR CHILD'S SUPPORT NEEDS ARE MET

Given that you may very well encounter a lack of well-trained staff and high turnover rates among staff, how can you ensure that your child's support needs are being met?

First, when your adult child receives state-funded services and supports, there will be an annual plan developed. This may be called an Individualized Support Plan or Individualized Service Plan or a similar name. It is like an IEP, but for adults. This is where the strengths and needs of your child are documented. You and the service providers and your child jointly come up with goals for her to achieve, such as learning to take a city bus to her job or learning to schedule her own medical appointments.

Then it is determined who will provide and pay for the services to help your child achieve those goals. Finally, there is an annual review where progress is noted and new goals are set.

At any point during the year, your child's support team can be convened if there are issues or concerns that cannot wait until the annual review date. For example, if you want to change the day program or setting for your child, it will usually require a team meeting and a revision to the plan.

Another way you can help ensure your child receives needed supports is to volunteer to serve on governing and advisory boards of local adult service or governmental agencies. As a board member, you can have input on setting policy and help to raise awareness and funding to ensure the program's viability.

> *I am on the Board of Directors of the agency that supports Emily. As I have my own job, I feel this is one way that I can contribute to the strength of the organization. I believe that all families have an obligation to contribute in some way. Maybe you can raise needed funds or your family can do the spring lawn clean up. Sadly, the majority of families do nothing but complain.*

Informally, you will want to continue to be as much a part of your child's life as possible. Look for opportunities to be involved in productive ways. For example, you can invite her and her friends from the group home to your house for a summer cookout or holiday celebration or accept an invitation from the group. You might also suggest that your child's residence organize an open house for the neighbors.

Sometimes you will probably want to drop in unannounced, as long as you can do it without making a nuisance of yourself. While you shouldn't need permission to visit your child, it is courteous to ask the staff if there are times that may be better for you to visit. If 7:00–8:00 p.m. is the time that the staff are assisting in showering routines, it may be hard for them to spend time answering your questions.

> *I rarely hear our staff complaining about the people we support, and they have to do some tough work. Imagine when the stomach flu hits a whole house and the staff has to be nurse and maid and then go home to their own families. I do hear staff complaining about some of the residents' families. It is only a couple of families who seem to never be satisfied. Then there is the family that calls staff at home or on their cell phone for non-emergencies. Our staff do have lives outside of work and some families do not respect that.*

# Adjusting to a New Home

Change is stressful. Even good change can produce stress—ask any bride. When your child with Down syndrome moves out of her family home, there will definitely be lots of emotions to handle. Everyone might not even think it is a good idea. In addition to the parents, siblings and even grandparents will weigh in on the decision. Other parents of children with Down syndrome may offer their opinions. At times, you might wish you only had to worry about your child with Down syndrome and about what others are thinking or saying about your decision.

> *We hoped that someday Beth would have her own apartment. It was a matter of when and how. While we figured it all out, we helped her to become as independent as possible. If we went away for the night, she stayed in the house. We figured it was a great way for her to learn some in-dependence. She knew that she could go to the neighbors for help. We also used holidays and birthdays as opportunities to buy her items for her future apartment. It was years before she got an apartment, but I think these steps made it that much easier for her when she finally did move out of our house.*

This can be a difficult time for families. You are not in total control any longer. Your child does not live under your roof. If you have other children, you know the feeling I am talking about. If not, you might want to remember your own experiences when you left your family home. Your child will make decisions that you might not have allowed her to make if she were living with you—just like you did when you left your family home. She might just eat in front of the television, fall asleep in the living room, or stay up later than you'd like.

When your child moves from your home into another setting, your world changes and you had better be prepared to experience some new and sometimes uncomfortable feelings. To begin with, the individuals who are assisting your child are paid staff. Although assisting your child is their job, they are usually not paid a fair and living wage, as discussed above. In addition, they have their own lives and your child is probably not their highest priority. Understanding that will help you become a better partner. I suggest that you don't tell the staff how to do their job and that you also learn the difference between dropping in to say hello and dropping in to check up. Find constructive ways to make suggestions. If the house seems dirty and the staff busy with the residents, rather than complaining, you might say, "My church/synagogue/mosque is looking for a community service project. Would you mind if they came in and did a deep cleaning?"

My biggest piece of advice is simple. "Don't sweat the small stuff and most of the stuff is small." Much easier said than done and I have the mistakes to prove it.

Of course, your child will have her own adjustment to go through. If you are committed to having your child move out and you have a timeframe for this to occur, you should develop a plan, as far in advance as possible, to make your daughter as comfortable as possible. Here are some suggestions:

- Show your child the living situations you are considering.
- If she is not used to spending nights away from you, find family members or friends who are willing to invite her to spend the night with them so she can practice sleeping away from home.
- Find peers who are living away from their families who can invite your daughter to watch a movie with them or even have a sleepover, if possible.
- If you have older children who have moved out, use them as role models.
- If your child has favorite TV programs (*Friends*) or movies (*Wedding Crashers*) where characters live in apartments, watch the shows together and use them as a basis for discussions about living arrangements for adults.
- Encourage family members who are looking for birthday and holiday gift suggestions to give your child presents that will be useful in her new place—linens, towels, utensils, potholders, etc.
- If your child has been asking for a cell phone or iPod or another "adult" device, use it to help motivate her to want to move out. For example, you might say, "You will need one when you move out, so let's go and see what kind you will get when you move out."

In the end, you might have done everything possible to make your child comfortable with the move, but she simply does not want to do it. If it is nonnegotiable to you, you will simply have to make the decision for her. She may not initially like the move, but I bet there have been dozens of situations in your daughter's life that she initially didn't like, but over time came to accept and even love.

*Jon's learning to be independent is continual. When he first moved into his own home, he used to call home for all sorts of permissions. He would call to ask if he could use his credit card or his debit card. He would call from the mall and ask permission to buy a CD. He would call and ask if he could have a beer. Since Jon manages money well and can be trusted with credit and debit cards, and has always made reasonably good decisions, we would tell him that he didn't need to call for permission. After all, we would reinforce, he was an adult and living in his own home and we trusted him to make good decisions. Still, the calls persisted. Eventually, they became less frequent and finally disappeared.*

*Last summer, on a visit to Jon's home, I found a trash bag filled with empty beer bottles and cans. It was evident to me that he had learned to make his own decisions. His sister took him aside and told him that next time he should get rid of the empty cans and bottles before we visit.*

# Home Ownership and Control

*The ache for home lives in all of us, the safe place where we can go as we are and not be questioned.*
*— Maya Angelou*

In the early 1990s, a grassroots initiative developed to help individuals with disabilities, including Down syndrome, own or control their own housing. It was commonly referred to as "The Home of Your Own "Initiative. In the early days, there was some federal funding for a demonstration project which provided technical assistance and even some financing assistance. The project was successful and demonstrated that people with intellectual disabilities could be successful home owners. There is now a National Home of Your Own Alliance which disseminates information, suggests policy, and is working on systems changes.

The Home of Your Own Alliance has looked at the opportunities and challenges of home ownership and has learned that people would rather have control of their homes in spite of the challenges. The challenges include financial responsibility, lack of support services, and the physical upkeep of the property.

Everyone wishes to have a place they can call their own and individuals with Down syndrome are no different. Home ownership or control promotes independence and positive self-esteem. The feeling that comes with being able to control your living space is important to adults.

*I love having my own home. I have my own bedroom and bathroom and a room for my computer. There is a place for my family to stay when they come to visit. I go to bed when I want and I eat when I want. Sometimes, I eat after I work out at 8 p.m. If I don't have to work, I can sleep until noon. I think I will try to go to bed earlier.*

As the idea of home ownership began to catch on, the concept of "home control" also gathered momentum. This concept includes situations where families purchase property and their child with Down syndrome occupies it and may have her name on the lease. For example, in 1983, David Wizansky organized a group of families to purchase and renovate a building in Brookline, Massachusetts, which was converted into condominiums. Since then, families have continued to play a large role in the development of housing options for their children.

> *I think we found the perfect balance for our son. We were in a position to buy a house for him. We looked into home ownership, but Jon would have had to take a homeownership preparation class and we knew he would find it boring. There were no tax advantages for him to own the house. At the end of the day, we would be responsible for making or arranging repairs and budgeting for replacement of large items.*
>
> *While we actually "own" the house in every legal way, it is Jon's house. He pays all the bills he is capable of—rent, utilities, phone, cable, and the weekly housekeeper. We pay the mortgage and taxes and cover all the maintenance costs. He feels he is a "homeowner." His personality is reflected all over the house. You wouldn't see my bedroom, living room, and dining room adorned with pictures of Tom Brady, Arnold Schwarzenegger, WWE personalities, and championship flags of the Boston Red Sox, New England Patriots, and the Boston Celtics. There would be a lot more water and less beer in my refrigerator, too.*

Most people dream of having a place they can call their own. Somewhere that is a refuge from the day and a place that reflects their interests and personalities. It is a place they can freely invite friends and celebrate special occasions. It is a place to dream about the future. This is in contrast to the majority of housing situations for persons with Down syndrome, where an agency owns and controls the home or apartment. The differences are significant.

> *I love my house. I am going to ask my dad to finish the basement and have a bar down there and a big flat screen TV and the guys will come over to watch football and drink beer.*

It is important to point out that the home ownership and control movement is not limited to those adults with Down syndrome who are considered "high functioning." The level of assistance and support for the individual can be adjusted according to her needs. Bear in mind, though, that unlike renting, where the landlord is responsible for the repair and maintenance of the unit, the homeowner is responsible for taking care of everything. An adult with Down syndrome must be able to make her own repairs, rely on responsible people to make them, or be taught how to obtain help.

> *Last month Jon called to say that the light did not go on inside his freezer, which is in his basement. He said everything else was working. Three days later, his support person emailed me and said the freezer and some of the lights in his basement were not working. I asked him to check*

*the electrical panel, and the staff person reported that the problem was not with the panel. It was late in the day and an electrician could not be reached. My husband was concerned that Jon might be in a dangerous situation with an undetected electrical problem. Could there be a short somewhere and a fire brewing in his walls? Chet made the two-hour trip only to find that several of the breakers had indeed been tripped. Apparently, even the staff didn't know how to recognize a tripped breaker.*

*The next day, I called the director of the program and suggested that an in-service training on electrical panels be held for staff and residents.*

The biggest barriers to home ownership are obtaining a mortgage, coming up with the cash required for closing, and obtaining support services from individuals or agencies that value decision making by the person with Down syndrome. These are some of the same barriers that other adults with low incomes experience. They often rely on government support and have limited opportunities to develop a credit rating.

Nonprofit organizations and local or state agencies may offer grants, gifts, and down payment assistance programs to help first-time home buyers afford a home. Adults with Down syndrome usually need someone to cosign their loan since they don't earn enough per month to qualify for a loan by themselves. Note that owning a home does not jeopardize government benefits such as SSI or Medicaid, as a home is not considered when calculating the person's assets.

*Our kids with Down syndrome are different from even a decade ago. They all live in families and in neighborhoods. They might have to share a room with their siblings growing up, but I don't see Scott living in a group home with several other individuals just because his needs are greater and he is not one of those Down syndrome superstars. He should have his own home and he should direct the people who will assist him.*

# CHAPTER 9

# An Apple a Day

*If only it took an apple a day to maintain health and wellness, we would all invest in apples. Finding access to quality adult medical and dental care for individuals with Down syndrome takes more than apples. Paying for health care is different for adults with Down syndrome than it is for children. Some of us will find obtaining quality care challenging and may have to educate health care professionals and those who care for our child. However, it takes more than physicians and doctor visits to maintain your child's health and wellness. It actually requires a lifetime commitment from you, your child, support staff, service providers, and everyone in your child's life. Individuals with Down syndrome have some special considerations related to healthcare to consider during the transition years. It is also important to introduce the importance of a lifetime of sustainable fitness goals during the transition years.*

Among the more difficult transitions that you will have to make is leaving your child's pediatrician. Pediatricians are trained to care for the medical needs of children up to the age of 21. While some pediatricians are willing, and even happy, to continue to see children with Down syndrome after they turn 21, it is important for you to consider a physician whose training includes adults. Adults have very different medical problems than children. Your child also deserves the dignity of not having to wait in a room with a bunch of two-year-olds. Generally, that means finding a family practitioner or an internist.

Our children usually have several physicians. Among them could be pediatric cardiologists, gastroenterologists, otolaryngologists, or other specialists. Some of them may be certified in the adult specialty in addition to the pediatric specialty.

If your child was a patient of a pediatric hospital before his twenty-first birthday, the hospital will usually permit him to continue to be seen by any specialist that he had previously seen. If your child develops a new condition as an adult, the pediatric hospital will generally not permit him to begin a new relationship with a physician in a new specialty.

# Finding Adult Medical Care

Adults with Down syndrome often have complex medical needs, from ongoing issues related to congenital heart disease to adult issues including new physical and mental health concerns. Our children can be expected to live longer lives and, as a result, face aging issues, including Alzheimer disease. It is important to find a physician who specializes in either family practice or internal medicine and is comfortable with the adult issues associated with Down syndrome.

Finding the right adult doctor for your child may take some time, so you might want to begin thinking about it in advance of your child's twenty-first birthday. This is something to discuss with your pediatrician and other families of teens or adults. Your pediatrician probably has a list of local physicians who are accepting new patients. You can ask around, get some recommendations, and then make some telephone calls and discuss your child with the office staff. Once you find someone who seems to be able to meet your expectations for a physician, make an appointment and bring your child and see if it is a good match.

Information that you might want to find out includes:

- the doctor's experience with Down syndrome;
- whether the doctor is committed to the highest quality of life for your child;
- office hours;
- availability for extra time at appointments;
- your child's comfort level with the physician;
- whether the doctor respects your child and communicates with him directly rather than talking to you;
- coverage when the doctor is away;
- medical insurance accepted;
- hospital affiliations;
- availability of same-day appointments;
- ease of referral to specialists;
- willingness to partner with caregivers in addition to family members;
- office location and accessibility via public transportation.

I do not suggest that individuals with Down syndrome go to any medical appointments alone. Having someone else there to hear the information being provided helps improve healthcare outcomes—for everyone, not just those with Down syndrome.

During the transition years, it may be important to begin to work with your child on knowing when he needs to see a doctor, scheduling his own appointments, and refilling prescriptions. While guardianship, medical power of attorney, or healthcare proxies may have some impact on your child's ability to manage these issues, in the day-to-day application of these legal instruments, there is usually much leeway for adults with Down syndrome to develop independence. These legal instruments usually come into play when considering surgery, testing, and invasive treatments. They are usually not used to deny an individual the ability to call in his own prescription refill.

*When Jonathan was 22, he moved to Cape Cod, about two hours from our home. At first I was reluctant to find a physician there. His pediatrician, who had followed him his entire life, was a trusted anchor in our lives. I knew that some families with children with Down syndrome stayed with their pediatricians long after their children became adults. I knew that this was not in Jonathan's best health interest, however, as he was really an adult and would develop adult health issues that were not in the realm of the pediatrician. So, I started the difficult task of finding a primary care physician for Jon. I asked around, got some recommendations, and found that many practices were full. I didn't give up and I finally found a physician, accepting patients, who came recommended from a family friend.*

*I accompanied Jon to his first visit. While we were waiting, a patient with an obvious cognitive disability was having a very difficult time when exiting the exam area. In fact, she sat down on the floor of the receptionist's office. Her staff was attempting to assist her. But, what I witnessed next convinced me that Jon was in the right place. The staff in the physician's office treated this patient with dignity and respect, even though she was very disruptive and loud. I knew that Jon would get what he needed, and I have been right. This office talks to me, works well with Jon and his staff, and responds quickly to health needs.*

## A SPECIAL NOTE FOR CARDIOLOGY PATIENTS

The following information should be very important to those of you whose children are living with either corrected or uncorrected heart defects. Until just a few decades ago, children with heart defects rarely became adults, so they could safely receive their follow-up care from the pediatric cardiologist who was familiar with them. Now that our children and other patients with congenital heart disease are living well into adulthood, new issues sometimes emerge relative to their heart disease. Pediatric cardiologists are often not equipped to address some of these adult issues or issues related to the original corrections. Recognizing this, a new specialty has been developed—the cardiologist who specializes in adult congenital heart disease. These cardiologists have training in both pediatric and adult cardiology.

Patients with Down syndrome, especially those with Tetrology of Fallot, should make sure that they are seen by one of these specialists. There are over 60 adult congenital heart disease programs in North America. You can locate the one closest to you at the website of the Adult Congenital Heart Disease Association: www.achaheart.org.

## HEALTH INSURANCE

Most of our children are eligible for private health insurance as dependents of working parents. This important benefit can be maintained for your child as long as you are working and you are covered by your employer's health insurance program. You must notify your health insurance company that your child is permanently disabled before your child's eighteenth birthday or at regular intervals thereafter, at the request of the insurance company.

If your child is still a student at 18, you may not have to notify the insurance company that he has a disability until he stops being a student, but you will have to provide documentation that he is a full-time student. To continue his eligibility once he is no longer a student, you will be required to provide medical documentation of your child's disability. This is usually a simple form that must be completed by your child's physician.

Some of our children will have access to their own private health insurance through their employers. Eligibility for employer-sponsored insurance is generally based on the number of hours worked in a week. Employers cannot discriminate against our children by not offering them health insurance or any other company benefit, provided it is offered to other members of the same class of workers. However, if your child works seasonally or part-time, and no part-time or seasonal workers receive benefits, then it is not discrimination. If your child is eligible for health insurance, you will need to consider the expenses related to that insurance (employee contribution toward costs, deductibles, etc.) compared to his other health insurance coverage and decide whether the expense is worth it.

If you retire before age 65 and your company provides its pensioners and its dependents with health insurance, your child with Down syndrome will still be eligible for this insurance as well. At age 65, you will qualify for Medicare if you are a U.S. citizen or permanent resident, and your private insurance may cease unless you keep working beyond age 65. At this point, your child with Down syndrome will most likely rely on Medicaid and/or Medicare (see Chapter 6).

Having private health insurance in addition to Medicare and/or Medicaid means that the private health insurance is "primary" and is used first, followed by Medicare and Medicaid. For example, if the private health insurance covers all the costs of a doctor's visit except for a $20 or $30 dollar co-pay, your child will only have to pay the co-pay from his Medicaid benefits.

During the transition years, you may want to help your child learn how to hand over his insurance and Medicaid cards at a doctor's office and identify where his identification number is on the card. Or you may want to make sure that all this information is provided prior to any medical visit.

## MEDICAL CARE IN GROUP HOMES

As if understanding the adult service system wasn't confusing enough, there are many new rules and regulations to familiarize yourself with. Most of these are intended to protect and safeguard the health and safety of individuals with disabilities, while others are supposed to increase the efficiency and effectiveness of the system. To many families, some of them make no sense.

*Megan moved into a beautiful residence less than a mile from our home. I expected that living with four other young women would mean there would be compromises. I didn't expect they would serve Megan's favorite food at every meal, like I did. I was not prepared for all the regulations about medications, however. We take Megan to an out-of-state homeopathic doctor and he prescribed several herbal remedies that we thought were helpful. Now that she is living in a group home, though, every medication, whether prescription or over-the-counter, must be prescribed by a physician in the state—it has to be a prescription and filled by a pharmacy. If she has a headache or cuts her finger, there must be a prescription for ibuprofen or an antibacterial ointment. It is very frustrating to have to give up on common sense to ensure safety.*

Situations like those described above make the already daunting access to healthcare for adults with disabilities even more challenging. In addition to having prescribing regulations, most states require that special forms be filled out for every medical appointment for adults living in group homes or for adults who receive financial support for their living arrangements. Clearly, it is important that caregivers be given exact instructions about medical care. It reduces medication errors and helps to ensure quality medical care. However, these types of rules can result in doctors refusing to accept our children as patients. Considering the poor reimbursement rates of Medicaid plus the additional administrative burdens placed upon doctors, it is not surprising that so many doctors close their doors to our children.

Whenever families get frustrated by administrative burdens of state agencies, I gently remind them that "when you give the money, you can make the rules." State and federal governments spend billions of dollars on individuals with Down syndrome and related disabilities, so taxpayers and legislators demand accountability for that money.

Before your child moves into a residential setting outside of your home, you might want to learn what the medical expectations are for your child in that residence. At a minimum, you want to make sure that yearly physicals, blood work, gynecology exam (if appropriate), twice yearly dental exams, and biannual eye exams are required and documented.

**DENTAL CARE**

Typically, only pediatric dentists receive training in working with individuals with disabilities. While attempts are underway to include training for adult dentists, many individuals with Down syndrome continue to see their pediatric dentists into adulthood. Another reason for this is that the Medicaid reimbursement rates for dentists are so low that few adult dentists accept Medicaid. Since many people with Down syndrome do not have dental insurance, they rely on Medicaid to pay for dental care (if they are lucky enough to live in a state that covers dental care for Medicaid recipients).

Too often, however, adults with Down syndrome go without proper dental care because access and affordability are limited. Your adult child may be able to get treatment at a special dental clinic for adults with Down syndrome and related disabilities run by some states. At some Special Olympics venues, you may also encounter Special Smile dental clinics, where oral hygiene is taught and treatment for some concerns may be provided.

Many adults with Down syndrome will have to pay for dental care out of their own pockets. This is one reason adults with disabilities receive Social Security or Supplemental Security benefits—to pay for necessary expenses. Parents or other family members might also want to "treat" the person with Down syndrome to a dental visit as a birthday present or for another special occasion.

# Emotional Well Being

Most transition planning emphasizes developing employment goals, with some consideration to the various other issues I have covered in this book—housing, postsecondary education, government benefits, and financial planning. Missing from most discussions is perhaps the most important subject of them all and the one where the family is central. That is providing emotional support as the child becomes an adult. This is a period that dredges up old conflicts between our desire to protect our child, yet foster independence—between the fear of risks and the desire to provide opportunity. How do we begin to turn over the advocacy role to our children with Down syndrome? These and other issues are central in the development of an emotionally healthy adult who happens to have Down syndrome.

The National 4-H Council has identified eight "Keys for Kids"—experiences that are essential for healthy youth development. I found them in an article by Kris Peterson that appeared in the Fall 2007 *Advocate* of The Arc of Massachusetts. They are:

- **Security:** Youth feel physically and emotionally safe ("I feel safe").
- **Belonging:** Youth experiences belonging and ownership ("I'm in").
- **Acceptance:** Youth develop self-worth ("What I say and do counts").
- **Independence:** Youth discover self ("I like to try new things").
- **Relationships:** Youth discover quality relationships with peers and adults ("I care about others").
- **Values:** Youth discuss conflicting values and form their own ("I believe…").
- **Achievement:** Youth feel the pride and accountability that comes with mastery ("I can do it").
- **Recognition:** Youth expand their capacity to enjoy life and know that success is possible ("I feel special").

For young people with Down syndrome, having opportunities to develop these key elements of a healthy life is essential for their well being. It is important for families and those who work with transition age students to work on helping the young adult achieve these goals. Below are some real-life examples of how people with Down syndrome and their families were able to work on these key elements of emotional well being.

### SECURITY

*For several years, Megan had a roommate with some learning disabilities and emotional problems. After a couple of years, Megan began to feel emotionally unsafe around her roommate. While she didn't actually come out and say it, her family picked up on her uneasiness and asked her if she wanted a new roommate or to live alone. Megan's answers suggested that she needed a change. This observation was supported by staff who knew Megan best, although it was really her family who sensed her uneasiness and acted upon it. Staff alone would not have rocked the boat, which resulted in her roommate having to find a new place to live, as Megan owed the condominium where they lived.*

To ensure that your child's own feelings of uncertainly are addressed during the transition process, it may help if he is able to get together with a group of other transitioning students and a teacher or counselor to discuss concerns. If there are several students in your child's class transitioning in a similar period of time, you may want to suggest this to the teacher or make this part of the IEP.

> *Melissa was the only person in her school with Down syndrome and she found herself facing the whole transition process without a peer. The local Down syndrome clinic realized that there were other girls like Melissa who were totally included in their local schools, who also could benefit from some peer support. They formed a "girls' group" to enable these students to discuss transitioning issues as well as being the only female in their class with Down syndrome.*

**BELONGING**

During Jonathan's journey of inclusion, which I once called, "the isolation of inclusion," he has certainly been included in his community, but belonging has been another story. When you belong, you are "in" or a part of the group because of who you are. For someone with Down syndrome, it can be hard to be allowed to belong as you are, rather than contingent upon how close you can get to being typical.

As your child moves out into the adult world, you have a great role to play in helping him to feel like he belongs. Prepare him for this change before he separates from his high school friends by helping him identify and join other social networks. For example, you might find scrap booking clubs, bowling leagues, or book clubs with members from his new place of residence or employment.

**ACCEPTANCE**

After a visit to a new physician in a hospital that Jonathan had not previously been in, Jonathan told me, "I do not feel safe in this hospital." The doctor had addressed his questions to me instead of Jonathan, and had suggested some invasive tests that I wasn't sure were needed. When I probed Jonathan about his feelings, he said, "This hospital is not like Children's Hospital" (where he had been a patient many times). Indeed, it wasn't. He had not been treated like he had anything of value to contribute. While I did not share Jonathan's feelings of not being safe, I did not like the experience, either. However, the medical issue that brought us there was serious and did need to be addressed.

After thinking about it for a few days, I began making telephone calls in hopes of identifying another specialist. I was given a name within the same hospital department and when I called to make the appointment, I explained what had happened and that we were looking for someone who would speak to Jonathan and treat him with respect. The new physician was as respectful as any we had ever seen. He agreed with me about the invasiveness of the required tests and was able to identify a new blood screen that might eliminate the necessity of the other tests. Just as importantly, Jonathan felt that what he says and feels matters.

During the transition years, when your child is gaining the emotional maturity that leads to more independence, you can help him feel accepted by making sure he knows that what he says matters. You may need to seek out professionals who will actually listen to what your child has to communicate, whether he communicates verbally or not. Or you may need to brainstorm ways to enable him to better participate in discussions—perhaps by slowing down the rate of a conversation so he can participate or by stopping to deliberately ask your child for his input.

## INDEPENDENCE

Nothing is more exhilarating and more frightening to families than contemplating the independence of their child with Down syndrome. I once worked with a family whose son lived in his own apartment, had a job, and traveled by himself in the community. In spite of all these accomplishments, the family requested that we never use the works "independent" or "independence." Although this family allowed their son quite a bit of independence, his family was not ready to embrace what it means.

Although I can sympathize with families who are wary of letting their adult child be independent, I cannot support them. That is not to say that I don't have my own struggles. For example, I have previously mentioned needing to let go of my control of what Jonathan drinks. Jonathan loves to have a beer or two—watching Sunday football or after a long day's work. He is not unlike a lot of other young men—except that he has support staff who report his consumption to me. Sometimes, that results in my having a conversation with him where I talk about moderation and weight gain. Jon listens carefully, tells me that he values my opinion, but lets me know that this is his life.

If you are having trouble "letting go" in a specific area, you might want to have someone else help you. For example, you might not be comfortable with having your daughter cross a busy street to get to the video store, but perhaps a sibling or a staff person can teach her.

## RELATIONSHIPS

As our children venture forth into the adult world, they will have more opportunities to develop relationships that you are not a part of, just like your other children will. You will probably not know your son's coworkers, or even his boss. I think it is very important that you not be the person to meet with the boss or a supervisor to get input on his job performance, unless you have a previously established relationship.

Bosses are not like teachers or other staff people in your son's life. They do not come to yearly planning meetings. They are operating a business and usually do not have the time to attend meetings. However, as discussed in Chapter 7, during the annual meeting, the work supervisor and the family might both be invited to discuss annual goals and progress. More commonly, though, someone from the vocational agency will speak to the work supervisor and represent the work supervisor's concerns at the meeting. Most work supervisors do not have the time for the additional burden of attending a meeting. This meeting should not be held at a work site in the community, but at another location so that your child is treated like other employees. Since typical employees do not have meetings where all aspects of their lives are discussed, I believe strongly that they should be held away from the workplace and in a place where your child feels comfortable—like his home.

The only time a boss is typically involved in a meeting, and it would be at the place of employment, is when there is a problem. My experience is that when it reaches the level for a meeting, there is a major problem and, often, the meeting is a courtesy before a termination.

Outside of work, your child will find friends and even lovers and have the opportunity to explore adult relationships. Carrie Bergeron and Sujeet Desei, two young adults with Down syndrome from different cultures and different religions, found love with each other. While most would agree that Carrie had a full and rich life, she shares that her life was lonely before she met Sujeet. Now married, they do not live near either family. Instead, they were able to establish their own home.

If your child has limited or no verbal skills, he will require assistance in developing relationships in a safe environment. You will have to help determine whom he would like to have relationships with—peers, caregivers, or both. You may also have to help identify the leisure time activities he enjoys that will help him expand his relationships and ensure that those opportunities are available.

## VALUES

While most family members share some of the same core values, during the transition to adulthood, we find out that our children don't share all of our values. This may create conflicts, but having conflicts with your parents is part of the process of becoming an autonomous individual. For example, I do not drink alcohol. Jon enjoys beer. Likewise, although many American thought that President Bill Clinton had brought a degree of shame into the White House in his affair with an intern, Jon steadfastly argued that it was a personal situation and should not be part of the public discourse.

As a parent, you must allow your children to demonstrate his own values even when they might clash with your own values—unless your child's values will put him at risk. Many teenagers, for example, develop their own taste in music. Some of the music may contain lyrics that you might not like. If your family has a rule that nobody can listen to those kind of lyrics, then applying that standard to your child with Down syndrome is fair. However, if your other children are permitted to listen to whatever music they want, then that same standard should be applied to your child with Down syndrome.

As your child becomes an adult, and you become aware that he has different values than you do—whether they be in music, style of dress, or political views—you should be proud of his ability to know himself.

## ACHIEVEMENT

Becoming an adult means having the opportunity to achieve and accomplish. The pride of going to the Senior Prom, of walking across the stage at graduation, of getting a driver's license or staying alone—these all contribute to feelings of achievement. Sometimes even failure can contribute to feelings of achievement. For example, Jon failed the test to receive a learner's permit. But, the sense of accomplishing something he had never tried dulled the disappointment. He had taken a timed test, unassisted, in an unfamiliar environment, and, for the first time, used a computer to take a test. (Jon did eventually pass the test, on his third attempt.)

Families can use the transition period to make sure that the opportunities for achievement continue. While your child is still in public school, make the IEP goals meaningful—learning to take the bus, to manage a bank account, to order and pay for lunch at a restaurant, or to figure out whether a tip is necessary and the amount. Once your child is beyond IEPs, you can still set goals for him and provide the opportunities to reach them, such as learning to order a pay-for-view television program, trying a new activity or sport, or interacting with people outside of the family. And as for most adults, the best recognition may come from performing your job well enough to earn a promotion or salary increase.

*Jon had been working for several years at a country club maintaining the golf courses as part of the grounds crew. He liked the job, but really wanted to work in the pro shop or golf operations. At the end of his third summer, he was told he was being promoted to the pro shop for the next season. He was elated, as it was his "dream job." The job with the grounds crew required much physical activity and it was sometimes "boring." He now washes members' clubs after their golf rounds and he receives tips. All the guys pool the tips, and my husband suspects that Jon is a "tip magnet" and thus a highly valued member of the team.*

**RECOGNITION**

Our children often receive recognition. It is important to differentiate the recognition that comes too easily, as when everyone on the bowling team gets a trophy at the year-end banquet, from the real feeling of recognition that comes with individual success. For example, when an adult with Down syndrome uses his communication device for the first time to ask for a preferred activity, the recognition he receives should be significant.

In the real world, adults receive far less recognition than children do and it may be harder to ensure that your child receives the kind of formal recognition he might have received as a child. However, the adult service system understands the importance of recognition, and your child will continue to receive positive reinforcement for his work performance and athletic skills.

# Peer Pressure

Peer pressure is not just an adolescent behavior. It exists at every stage of life, but the desire to conform and fit in is felt very strongly by teenagers. For our children, that adolescent mindset can extend well into their twenties. In addition to dealing with pressure from peers in their community, our children are also susceptible to the peer pressure that comes from advertising and popular culture. It may be more difficult for our children to differentiate between what is real and imaginary. For example, some individuals with Down syndrome who enjoy watching wrestling on television have difficulty understanding that it is entertainment and not a competitive sport.

Even though people with Down syndrome are apt to feel the same pressures as other young people do, they are less likely to be able to rely on their peers for accurate information (about sex, for example) during this difficult time. They may need more active assistance from family and professionals.

When adults with Down syndrome move into their own places, they are likely to be living with individuals with similar skill levels to their own. This may diminish the chances that someone with more skills could take advantage of your child—for example, by tricking him out of his money. However, it does not eliminate the possibility that other pressures may occur—such as the pressure to order large amounts of take-out food or to stay up late watching TV.

Helping your child develop good self-advocacy skills is an important step in making sure he has the skills to stand up for himself. If your child does not have adequate skills, it is likely he will require more supervision in his daily life so that he is safe. See Chapter 2 for more information on self-advocacy.

## A Seventeen-Year-Old's Views on Peer Pressure

Peer pressure is tough for teenagers and their families and their parents. Peer pressure is when some of your friends can force you to do things and make bad choices. If you don't do what they want you can get in trouble with your friends. They won't be your friend anymore or hang out together. It is hard to think. You have confusion in your mind. Your friends are like the bad devil telling you to do something that you don't want to do. You are the good angel. Now you have a choice of what to do.

At parties you don't know what they're going to serve for drinks. A friend has an ID and wants to buy you something to drink. You don't want to drink or make your friend mad. Sometimes kids might have cigarettes. They might tell you to have one to be popular. You might not want to smoke. At the party a guy might look at a girl he thinks she is cute. He might be ready to do it with a girl. Maybe the girl isn't ready for it yet. She might do it anyway because her friend thinks it is cool. Maybe the guy is popular and she wants to be his girlfriend. Friends might also try to make you skinny dip. Maybe you don't want to do it. Some friends might do drugs at the party. They could try to make you do them too. After the party some kids might drive home after they got drunk. You should tell them to stop. They yell and get mad. You don't want them to get hurt. You also don't want them to be mad at you.

There are a lot of choices at a party. Pick the easy choices first. These lead the way to help you with the bigger ones. Stay calm and try to figure out what the problem is.

You should believe in your self to stand up and tell them not to do drugs or have sex. Maybe have two sets of friends. Trust the good ones to help you. Maybe you can talk to a guidance counselor, therapist or your parents. Maybe your parents can do some things to help you out. You can also talk to your friends.

I learned that I have to trust myself and believe in myself that I can make decisions. It can get hard. A tip for the hard ones is to go to an adult for help if you can't handle it.

—Jon Derr, Age 17 (Health Class)

I return again to the self-advocates from Rhode Island I first introduced in Chapter 7. They had this advice about peer pressure:

- If someone asks you to drink beer, walk away.
- Listen to your inner voice.

The most poignant observation was this one from a young adult: "My inner voice doesn't sound exactly like me—it sounds like my mother."

# Sexuality

There is an entire book devoted to the subject of sexuality: *Teaching Children with Down Syndrome about Their Bodies, Boundaries, and Sexuality: A Guide for Parents and Professionals,* by Terri Couwenhoven. I am not going to try to summarize the important issues to consider during transition. I just want to remind you that our children are fully sexualized beings.

Individuals with Down syndrome are primarily heterosexual, as is the majority of the population. They can also be homosexual, bisexual, and transgendered. Having a child whose sexual orientation is not heterosexual can be very difficult for families of typical children to come to terms with, and can be even more difficult for parents when it is their child with Down syndrome who will be facing this challenge.

I think it is very important for our children to receive the same health and sex education as other students throughout their education. In high school, sex education is usually part of a health class. Child development and psychology classes might also expose your child to some important information in these areas. Some students may receive sexual education in a special education classroom.

Although sexuality training is available for adults with Down syndrome, it usually is presented in the context of a current need. For example, if a woman indicates she has decided to become sexually active, education about birth control and related issues may be explored. Sometimes this kind of education occurs within the context of couples counseling. Other times, if it appears that an individual is participating in high risk behavior, sexuality counseling is essential.

You can ignore the sexuality of our children, as one mother I know does. Upon learning that her son might be sexually active, she forbade him from having his girlfriend in his bedroom. The result? The sexual activity occurred in the living room where there were no adequate shades on the windows. Although studies have shown that both men and women with Down syndrome have reduced fertility, it is important to consider protection from pregnancy and disease if there is even the slightest chance that your child will have the opportunity for sexual intercourse.

# Food and Diet

More Americans are overweight than ever before and the number of Americans who are obese grows yearly. It is a national epidemic that has huge implications for people's health and our healthcare system. The problem is particularly serious for people with Down syndrome. You can consult data from research studies or you can just look at any group of adults with Down syndrome and you will see what I have known for many years: Most adults with Down syndrome are overweight, and, in many cases, grossly overweight.

There are several reasons for excessive weight among people with Down syndrome. To begin with, people with Down syndrome are shorter than typical people and the number of calories people need is partially based on their height. Talk to any short person who is of normal weight and you will find a person who eats fewer calories than someone who is taller. Right off the bat, our children need fewer calories than most other people their age, based on their smaller stature. Unknowingly, many

families are over feeding their child with Down syndrome when they give everyone at the dinner table the same food portions.

Another variable working against people with Down syndrome is that their bodies are not very efficient at burning calories. A person with Down syndrome burns fewer calories than a typical person when they are both at rest. Most of our children eat too much relative to the number of calories they burn. Finally, there is some speculation that people with Down syndrome may not experience the same feeling of fullness that other people experience.

This means that our children need to learn or re-learn good eating habits. Obesity is a complex issue with no easy fixes. The best strategy for families with children with Down syndrome is to prevent excess weight gain. Preventing it is hard work. Our children, however, do not have to become or remain obese. They do not have to be "couch potatoes." Here is where you have lots of control while your child is living with you. It is not up to educators, physicians, or therapists. You have the ability to influence your child to change his behavior, and the sooner you start, the better off your child, and even you, will probably become. You owe your child the healthiest life possible.

As we get older, we have to work harder to stay active and to remain healthy. It will be even harder for our children with Down syndrome. Today is the first day of the rest of your son's life. If you want him to be healthy, you better be prepared to be a positive role model. Having a healthier life is not rocket science. It is really very simple. It is about diet and exercise.

*Jonathan always seemed to love diet soda. I tried to keep it away from him as a baby by drinking mine from a coffee mug. As he got older, however, we encouraged diet soda over high-calorie, sugar-sweetened soda or even fruit juices.*

*Then some studies came out suggesting that artificial sweeteners may be harmful. I went to his pediatrician, who has always been very wise, and asked for his opinion. He said that there was no conclusive evidence that artificial sweeteners were harmful. However, he did share with me conclusive and convincing evidence that there was great harm in Jonathan becoming overweight. In addition to the social stigma he would encounter as an overweight person with Down syndrome (which could affect his social life and employment), his health would be in jeopardy. People who are overweight are at increased risk for cardiovascular disease, diabetes, and stroke, he told me. He advised me to go with what was real, which were the health risks of obesity, and ignore the unfounded risks of artificial sweeteners. If the diet soda kept Jonathan from consuming other calories from beverages, I should not worry about it. I don't.*

## SETTING THE EXAMPLE WITH EXERCISE

By now, you are probably well aware that exercise is something that must be part of everyone's daily life—every single day of every single week, all year long. It is not something I have made up. The current recommendation is that we all need cardio and weight bearing exercise at least thirty minutes a day.

This recommendation is particularly useful for our children with Down syndrome, since they like predictability and routines in their daily life. Here is where being the parent is so important. You are going to have to establish those routines and, if necessary, participate in them with your son or daughter.

If you are reading this book when your child is in his early teen years or younger, you have the luxury of more time to establish a good attitude toward exercise. If your child is already leading a sedentary life and has an unhealthy attitude toward exercise, it will require a big commitment on your part and by all the other people in his life to support you and him.

When our children are in school, there are more opportunities for both formal and informal exercise to be part of their daily life. In high school, many of our children participate in physical education classes. Hopefully, our kids have access to regular gym classes and can use weights, circuit training machines, and cardio equipment and are not participating in "watered-down" classes. While many schools have faced cut-backs in funding, physical education is still a requirement in some places. Even if it is not a requirement at your school, it can still be an elective that you may want to consider. Classes that introduce a variety of sports and activities will give you and your child an opportunity to discover new interests, and, perhaps, find an activity to follow throughout his life.

In high school there are typically many varsity and intramural sports and club teams where you may find a welcoming and appropriate place for your child. There are literally thousands of examples of students with Down syndrome participating at all levels and in every sport of high school athletics.

*Jonathan was on the junior varsity golf team. He played in the sixth position out of a field of ten. The team practiced three or four times a week and there were unforeseen benefits. Jon got the opportunity to be a member of a team and the rigorous practice schedule gave him a real advantage when he competed in Special Olympics. He got rides home from other guys on the team.*

*But, the best part? He had to carry his clubs during every high school practice and competition. Those were the rules established by the state high school athletic association. I considered, ever so briefly, requesting "reasonable accommodation" under the Americans with Disability Act to allow him to at least pull his clubs on wheels. But, I had fought all his life so he could have these opportunities for inclusion. Carrying his clubs gave him lots of exercise and built his stamina. Most of all, Jon was really proud of himself. He came home many days tired and exhausted, but very happy. He was like the rest of the guys on the team.*

Many of you are probably thinking that your child hates sports. You are not alone. Unfortunately, however, there is no way around the need for your child to be active. It is like brushing his teeth. It has to be done. It does not mean that it can't be fun.

You have to introduce your child to lots of different activities and experiences so he can discover what he likes. As long as calories get burned and muscle mass is being developed, it doesn't matter how it gets done. Walking, hiking, dancing, and biking are all activities that can be enjoyed by everyone in the family and may not seem as much like "exercise" as an aerobics or a spinning class.

Sometimes it is the idea of "exercise" that people dislike. So, make it fun and enjoyable and don't call it "exercise." Some people are able to stick with an exercise routine by having a workout partner or participating in activities with people with whom they enjoy spending time. For me, the type of exercise is secondary to the people who join me in exercise. I have always exercised, but my exercise has varied over the years—walking, aerobics, kickboxing, swimming, weight training, dancing, and biking. It all depended on the individuals who were interested in exercising with me.

Maybe the truth is that you dislike exercise and it is not important to you. You might be out of shape or overweight. You might not even care. I know, however, that you care about your child with Down syndrome and you might just have to make a commitment yourself to get in shape.

Here are some ideas to get you started:

- Have your child walk to and from school. If he does not have the safety skills for this, make it an IEP objective or find a neighborhood kid to walk with him. Or walk with him yourself.
- Take the stairs everywhere. Ban elevators from your routines.
- Do not circle the parking lot looking for the closest parking space. Instead, park as far away as possible and walk.
- If your child is addicted to video games, get games that require your child to get up and off the couch. The Wii system and *Dance Dance Revolution* are two examples.
- Ride a bike to do errands.
- Do not use handicapped license plates unless your child has a bona fide reason to have one (and Down syndrome alone is not a reason).

Here is another list. It contains some activities that most teens and adults with Down syndrome can participate in, that are fairly easy to master, and that are accessible to most people:

- Billiards
- Tennis
- Golf
- Bicycling
- Swimming
- Running
- Cheerleading
- Badminton
- Dancing
- Skating
- Basketball
- Bowling
- Walking
- Weight training
- Bocce ball

Our children thrive on predictability, schedules, and routines. They can even get stuck in them. Dennis McGuire, at the Adult Down Syndrome Clinic at Advocate General Hospital, calls them "grooves." As your child is transitioning out of the home or is already out of the home, you can ensure that exercise will become part of his adult routine by making sure it is on the schedule. There should be a daily written schedule for your child. Get your child used to a written schedule if he is not already using one and include exercise on it. You don't have to call it exercise. You can call it "take the dog for a walk," "dance class," or "swimming." If he is not motivated to move, but has someone in his life who can be motivating, use that person. For example, if there is someone who takes him to a movie, change the activity to one that includes movement.

## REDUCED CALORIE NEEDS

As discussed at the beginning of this section, people with Down syndrome need fewer calories because they are shorter and burn fewer calories. They just have to get accustomed to eating fewer calories than everyone else. During the teen years, typically developing children begin to consume additional calories, as these are years of rapid physical growth, and, usually, additional physical activity. If you are the parent of a typical teenage boy, you have probably been amazed to discover how much he can eat and not gain weight. However, if teens with Down syndrome eat as much as their peers or siblings, they will become morbidly obese.

Jonathan really relates to the fact that if he were Michael Jordan he could eat more. He knows about the metabolic rate issue, but comparing his size to various athletes has really helped him understand. When he was first beginning to understand this concept, he would say, "I can eat one hamburger, but if I were Michael Jordon, I would need to eat four."

After years of inclusion, our kids want to be like everyone else. Only in the food area, they can't. So, I have worked with families to devise strategies to help with what I call the "volume problem." If your child wants to go to the Fourth of July cookout and have both a cheeseburger and a hot dog, and maybe even some chicken, if you are creative, he can have it. It means a veggie burger (80 calories) and a veggie or turkey dog (45 calories), and low-fat wheat rolls. The chicken must be grilled and served without bread. It means fat-free dips and vegetables and shrimp cocktail. I have found that our kids crave volume, and with some ingenuity and maybe some suggestions from Weight Watchers, you can help your child succeed—at least while he is still living at home.

It is not fun being what I refer to as "The Food Police." It is similar to "The Homework Police," but rather than enforcing homework guidelines, you are encouraging healthy food guidelines.

Parents and other family members need to be supportive of good food choices all the time. You cannot expect teachers or staff to promote healthy food choices and practices if you are not going to support the effort 100 percent.

*Sarah was obese and so was her mother. Her mother worried about Sarah's weight, and it was often a source of contention between the staff at her group home and her mother, Mary. Mary didn't think the staff was doing enough to help Sarah. Sarah was pretty independent and until her money was curtailed, she would use it around town to buy large quantities of food. After she was given less money, she still found ways to get money or steal food. The staff at the group home were frustrated that whenever Sarah went home, her mother gave her complete access to food. Mary even sent large trays of unhealthy leftovers "for the kids" from family gatherings. The staff, who were working very hard to provide healthy food to the residents, felt compelled to accept and serve the food since they didn't want to hurt Mary's feelings. After bringing their concerns to the administration of their agency, the staff was told to say thank you and were given permission to discard the food.*

It is very hard to get everyone around our children to support healthy eating, but it is important to try. It must start with the family. Our kids have too many forces working against them—including television commercials peddling food and their favorite athletes or stars promoting restaurants. I tell families that our kids can't have a day off from good eating habits because it seems that every day brings another opportunity for a day off. Count up all the holidays, celebrations, birthdays, and special occasions in a year and you will begin to get a sense of what I mean. Some of us have willpower and can turn down the extras on these occasions. Others of us will eat more than we should and then diet rigorously the next week or take double workouts. When our children overindulge at a special event, it is unlikely they will have the willpower to cut back their intake in the days following the event.

*Janet has always been relatively thin. When I asked her how she handled food and living by herself, she shared a couple of secrets. Many years ago, her doctor told her to eat only half of what was on her plate. Always. So, to this day, Janet only eats half of what is on her plate, and if she is eating out, she has the rest packed away and takes it home for another meal. She also walks everywhere, in all kinds of weather. She just makes sure she is dressed properly.*

Even the most informed and well-intentioned people can unwittingly contribute to unhealthy eating and weight gain. I used to have a candy dish on my desk. It was a way for me to encourage staff to drop by and say "hello." Staff would indeed come to visit me and to take some candy. So did Joe, a personable young man the Arc served. He made a habit of coming in every day to chat with me as well as to take a piece of candy. I enjoyed his visits and our exchanges. One day one of our managers told me that someone from Joe's group home had called. He had gained weight recently and his cholesterol had gone up. It seems that I was not the only one on Joe's daily route. He was getting candy and baked goods from a few staff members. We were all asked not to provide food to Joe, so I put the candy dish away. After that, Joe still came to visit me every day—for our conversation and not the candy.

## EDUCATING FAMILIES ABOUT FOOD

So many of our own food decisions are guided by our experiences, and if we didn't learn healthy habits, some of us do not realize that our habits actually may be unhealthy. In my previous position as Executive Director of the Arc of East Middlesex, I once sent a letter to all the families that the Arc supported to announce our initiative to encourage healthy lifestyles. The purpose of the letter was to inform the families of what we were doing and to ask for their support. One of our suggestions was that families send healthy lunches and snacks with their sons and daughters in our employment and day programs.

I was surprised when Michelle's mother called to ask me for some help. She wanted to know exactly what a healthy lunch or snack was. She did not know, even though she was a wonderful cook and baker. As a stay-at-home mother, born in another

country, she loved preparing wonderful meals for her family. I gave her some suggestions about fresh fruit and vegetables, whole grains, popcorn, and other things. She was able to incorporate my suggestions into her daughter's food plan, and Michelle has now enjoyed some weight loss success.

If you are unsure of what healthy eating and a healthy lifestyle is about, seek some help. Registered nutritionists or dietitians are a good source of information, and your physician will probably be able to give you a recommendation. Local hospitals often hold free workshops on these subjects. Weight Watchers is a well-regarded program that promotes weight loss through the use of readily available foods. Any program that supports weight loss is built around eating healthy, well-balanced foods, limiting portions, and keeping track of the food you eat and keeping within an established daily calorie count. (Weight Watchers uses a "point" system to keep track of food.) Weight control programs can be very successful when there are appointments or other sources of support outside of the meetings.

Your child may not have a problem with excessive weight gain. Your child might be one of the few individuals with Down syndrome with a normal appetite for his height or a commitment to exercise. You are probably also committed to eating small portions and to exercise. You are the kind of role model our children need.

*Steven is obese. By any standard, he needs to shed about 150 pounds. He has tried many popular diet programs and has had some success at all of them. He has been on Weight Watchers for over a year and he has lost almost 50 pounds. He has had lots of slip-ups, but we take the long view, and 50 pounds is a lot of weight. He has managed to lose this weight while living in a group home where some of his housemates are quite thin and can eat whatever they want.*

## THE FRESHMAN FIFTEEN AND THE DOWN SYNDROME FIFTY

You may be familiar with the term "the freshman fifteen." It is used to describe the typical weight gain (in pounds) of a college freshman. There are many factors involved in this weight gain and some of them include access to college dining services twenty-four hours a day, less time to exercise, alcohol consumption, poor sleep habits, and the loss of parental influence. With our children, even those who do not go on to postsecondary education, there is a great likelihood that they will experience these same phenomena.

Only it is not fifteen pounds.

Our children seem to gain considerably more weight once they leave high school. I have observed weight gains in excess of 100 pounds. Often this weight gain seems to be linked to the increased independence and access to food choices that individuals with Down syndrome enjoy in residential settings outside of their own home. However, I have seen some of the greatest weight gains by individuals who continue to live with their families.

The challenge for families is to continue to provide strong and positive input to your child and to his or her caregivers—and that may be you! A large weight gain is not inevitable—no more inevitable than "the freshman fifteen," but it takes a willingness to be ever-diligent of the potential. Bad habits, like an extra piece of pizza, begin innocently, but they inevitably lead down the path of increased eating that is hard to reverse.

You can provide assistance to your child by shopping together, making sure there is ample time for physical activity, and educating yourself on the decreasing caloric needs of everybody as they age. By the time our children finish high school, their growing has long ended, and they need to adjust their caloric intake for their new roles as adults.

## THE ROLE OF SERVICE PROVIDERS IN REINFORCING HEALTHY EATING HABITS

While there is much that families must do to ensure the wellness of our children, we cannot be the only players on the road to healthy eating. As our children spend more time under the support or supervision of agencies, it is essential that the agencies and their staff support your goal of wellness for your child. In fact, it should be an agency goal as well.

Progressive agencies are ensuring that their snack and beverage machines are loaded with only good choices. It is very hard for our children to face a snack machine filled with tempting food and perhaps one lonely box of raisins as a healthy choice. It is much easier for our children to make a good choice when the machine contains only good choices such as dried fruit, fat-free yogurt, popcorn, rice cakes, and sugar-free gum and mints. Beverage machines that only contain water and non-calorie drinks also make picking a drink so much easier for our children. When the Arc of East Middlesex embarked down the healthy lifestyle path, we completely eliminated the snack machine and replaced the beverages containing sugar with sugar-free beverages. Not one single individual the agency served complained, and an added benefit was that there were no longer any worries about adults with diabetes purchasing a product with sugar.

Another decision the Arc made was to rethink lunch. There was a longstanding tradition of a lunch or canteen truck coming daily. Dennis, who owned and operated the truck, was as much a part of the agency as any employee. He knew everyone by name and he contributed products to the Arc's events. He extended credit to individuals when they told him they didn't have money (even if they didn't have money because they had brought their lunch that day because their family did not want them buying from Dennis) and was especially generous to the folks with Down syndrome. All they had to do was ask for an extra scoop of macaroni and cheese or for more French fries. Dennis liked seeing them happy, and the extra food did make them happy.

I met with Dennis about offering more healthy choices, but, while he carried some healthy items, it was the smell of the cheeseburgers frying on his grill and the French fries deep frying that were big hits. Despite how much the Arc staff all liked Dennis, they eventually asked him not to stop at their sites any longer. It was a difficult decision. He had established nice relationships and was an important part of some people's days. We gave sufficient notice and provided an opportunity for everyone to say goodbye. This one step, eliminating the canteen truck, resulted in much weight loss. People now eat the lunch they made at home without supplementing it with items from the truck, which is helping them make good decisions.

If you are in the process of considering adult programs for your child, ask about their role in promoting good health and how their strategies are implemented. If your child is already in a program and you are not satisfied with its commitment to health and wellness, you may want to consider raising your concerns. If you are not successful, see if there is another local program that will better address your concerns.

### A WORD ABOUT FOOD AT CELEBRATIONS

There is always a reason to celebrate. Just a quick count of holidays, family occasions, birthdays, and work festivities probably gets the number to between twenty and fifty a year for most of us. Then there is the calorie-laden period between Thanksgiving and the holiday season. Most of us are aware of how quickly the pounds can add up. We might even have a plan to get through the season by skipping some of the food or doubling up on our exercise.

Adults with Down syndrome are often in environments that celebrate even more occasions, and often food is the centerpiece of those celebrations. If they are in any kind of group housing, employment, or recreation, the food opportunities multiply quickly. Your child might be following a healthy and reasonable food program at home only to have it sabotaged by well-meaning, but misguided people.

*As parents, we have the responsibility to always set examples. I couldn't ask staff to help Jon with his diet and then celebrate his birthday or other occasions with unhealthy food. His last birthday did not have much food. We took everyone on a four-hour boat ride and the only food was diet soda and a small brownie-sized piece of birthday cake. Whenever we have cookouts, I use veggie burgers, 40-50 calorie hot dogs, light rolls, and plenty of fruit and vegetables. It is being together that really matters, not the food.*

It is very important for your child with Down syndrome to be surrounded by people who understand the importance of consistency in his life, especially when it comes to the messages around food. All it takes is 150 extra calories a day—the calories in a large apple—to gain 15 pounds a year.

*In addition to Jon's salary, the benefits of his job at the golf course include free golf and free lunch prepared in the country club's kitchen. Jon recognized that sometimes the food is not healthy, as it might contain fried food or pasta dishes. The lunches might be appropriate for the other guys, guys who burn more calories than Jon, but a summer of those lunches would quickly get Jon into trouble with maintaining his weight. He spoke to his boss about his problem and decided to bring in some healthy frozen meals to keep at work on the days that the meals are unhealthy. On other days, he eats the food but takes smaller portions and then works out after work. One summer the spigot that controlled the diet soda broke and Jon slipped into the habit of drinking regular soda. Eight additional pounds showed up very quickly.*

# Conclusion

Maintaining good health is essential for individuals with Down syndrome during the transition period and beyond. Whether you are trying to ensure your child gets proper medical care or support to make good lifestyle decisions, it is a balancing act between allowing him to exercise his independence and self-advocacy skills and keeping him safe and healthy. Each family will navigate these waters differently and their values will guide them. The one thing you have to remember is that you don't have to do it alone. There is help from physicians, human service agencies, trainers, dieticians, and other families.

## Jonathan's Grocery List

When Jonathan began living on his own and went grocery shopping with staff assistance, I developed the following shopping list to help guide everyone to make healthy choices. This list still provided Jonathan ample opportunity to exercise choice and decision making within the various food categories:

- Egg substitutes
- Low calorie whole grain bread or pita
- Light bagels with a calorie count between 110-120
- Whole grain pasta
- Brown rice
- Diet soda
- Water
- Non-fat cheeses
- Turkey bacon
- 94 percent fat-free popcorn
- Veggie burgers
- Meat substitute for ground beef
- Fat free or 97 percent fat-free hot dogs
- Light hot dog/hamburger rolls
- Single serve and individually packaged low-fat ice cream treats
- Low calorie frozen meals
- Frozen vegetables
- Pre-washed and packaged salads
- Fat-free salad dressings
- Boneless chicken breast

This is not an exhaustive list, but an example of Jon's preferred foods.

# CHAPTER 10

## I Get By with a Little Help from My Family and Friends

Families often develop dreams and goals for their child with Down syndrome and forget to include other stakeholders on the journey. For example, school and state officials are often not included in the planning process, yet are expected to assist with funding. Other family members may be excluded from discussions when parents start formulating transition plans for their child with Down syndrome. Yet, these very same family members, whether they be siblings, grandparents, or other extended family members, are important to include. They may be expected to make significant future contributions, in the form of resources or time, yet if they are not included in the decisions, they are not likely to buy into them.

It is important to include all important stakeholders in transition planning so that everyone feels committed and valued. Furthermore, your dreams are more likely to be achieved when everyone has been involved in an open and inclusive process.

Having something to do and someone to do it with makes it a "wonderful world." Finding friendships and leisure activities as an adult is challenging, but finding friends is critical, as they can make life every day seem like a party. However, preparing your child for the real and undeniable loss of the rhythm of school life is important. There is more to life for individuals with Down syndrome than TV, video games, WWE, and show tunes, and this is the time to continue introducing new opportunities. This encourages flexibility, which may lead to a more balanced life.

# Grandparents and Older Relatives

If your child has grandparents or other older relatives in his life, she is very lucky. While I will use the word grandparents, I intend it to mean any older relative or involved friend. Notwithstanding those grandparents who are actually raising their grandchild, there are many ways that grandparents can play important roles during the transition years.

Some grandparents are in a position to contribute financially to college costs. If your parents are in this situation, you may want to have a frank conversation about making a similar contribution to the postsecondary or other goals you have for your child.

If your parents are not able to make a financial contribution, they may still be healthy enough to help you by supervising your son or daughter, if this would help with your work or vacation needs. Many older adults are looking for ways to actively contribute to their communities and your parents may want to volunteer or fundraise for the agencies that support your child.

As your child enters adulthood, it will become apparent to older relatives that you truly have a lifetime of responsibility. If your parents were emotionally available to you when your child was a baby, they may be able to again help you through these new waters.

*Recently I have been assisting my parents as they move into an independent living community for active seniors. It has given me many opportunities to reflect on their lives and my life. While walking out of a Red Sox game one evening with my husband, there was an elderly couple also leaving the game. The gentleman was assisting his wife, who was walking slowly. I was admiring their love of baseball and each other when I whispered to my husband, "That will be us one day." He replied, "Except for one thing. Someone else will be with us."*

# Brothers and Sisters

The role of brothers and sisters is a dynamic and complex issue. Entire books have been devoted to the subject of siblings and disability. In this section, I would therefore just like to discuss what is unique about the relationship during the transition years. Other than the time when parents die and the siblings are often left to assume much of the role that parents played, the transition period can be the most difficult.

It is likely that your other children may be having their own transitions—perhaps obtaining a driver's license, graduating from high school or college, leaving home, beginning military service, finding a first home or job, or having a baby. Each one of these milestones is reason for celebration for your family. Never far from the surface, however, is the reminder that these are milestones that might not be celebrated for your child with Down syndrome. These differences can result in a change in dynamics among your children. For example, when your younger child without a disability gets a driver's license, it will be important to address the emotions your child with Down syndrome might be feeling. It might be a good time to talk about the advantages of not having a license—such as avoiding some of the responsibility and costs. Or if one of your children is getting married, your daughter with Down syndrome may need to mourn her own loss of this dream.

Each family dynamic is different and each individual with Down syndrome is different. For one family, having a sibling get a driver's license can bring anger and frustration to the child with Down syndrome. In another family, the sibling may go out of her way to minimize the loss by driving her sister everywhere and letting her "ride shotgun."

As siblings begin to achieve milestones that may not be attainable for the child with Down syndrome, parents need to be very honest but also very sensitive. The truth may be difficult to deliver if we suspect it may hurt the feelings of our child with Down syndrome. Sadness, anger, frustration, and disappointment are as important to address as joy, happiness, and acceptance.

If your child has difficulty with communication, take care to communicate complicated situations as clearly as possible. Make your explanation simple, repeat it regularly, and try to make a visual representation.

*My family may have been unusual. Jon, the child with Down syndrome, never complained about the opportunities his sister had. She, on the other hand, regularly complained about how little homework he had and that he got to sit in the front more often than she did.*

# Developing Community Connections

Numerous studies tell us that people who have friends and good social networks are happier and healthier than people without these connections. When our children were younger, it may have been fairly easy to ensure that they were involved with their typically developing peers in community activities such as baseball, swimming, theater, art, etc. There were the kids in the neighborhood and the kids at school. Your other children and their friends might have included your child with Down syndrome in their lives and activities.

Maybe these community opportunities are still available for your teen or young adult. Often, however, they decrease as the typical kids develop more independence. They leave the neighborhood by foot or by bike and you might be uncomfortable with your child with Down syndrome following. She might not even be invited to join the other kids. The typically developing kids acquire even more freedom as they go on to get their driver's licenses. While some of our children may also eventually receive their license, a driver's license for the typical kids is often a gateway to less parental supervision. A driver's license for our children often means increased concern.

Although high school activities still offer the promise of inclusion in activities with typical students, at this point many of us recognize our child's need for mean-

ingful friendships with other kids with disabilities. We want them to have real friends who are traveling the same journey and have points of commonality. Not that I do not advocate for our children to have friends from school and the neighborhood. I am just trying to let you know that most of these friendships are hard to sustain.

If we look at our own lives, we may be able to identify various subgroups of friends, neighbors, associates, and acquaintances in our lives. Our subgroups also change over time. Here are my present subgroups and my current involvement:

- Work out/gym friends (see daily)
- Mah jong group—a Chinese game played with tiles (see weekly)
- Work friends (rarely see outside of work)
- School and child friends (occasionally see)
- Neighbors (run into in nice weather, not planned)

What is not obvious is that in all these groups, all the members are fairly homogenous. They have similar education levels, share many of my values and most of my politics, come from a similar socioeconomic grouping, and are in the same general age bracket. If you do this exercise, you may add a religious group to your list. When I look at my connections like this, I realize I do not have a rich and diverse group of friends. None of my friends have obvious disabilities.

Jonathan's present subgroups as he would identify them and how often he sees them would be:

- Friends with disabilities (daily)
- High school friends (rarely)
- Work friends (sometimes outside of work)
- Special Olympic bowling league (weekly)
- Drama, fitness, swimming, nutrition, fishing clubs (weekly as scheduled; all are with peers)
- Social and recreation club (weekly, with peers)
- Staff (when scheduled)

This is not how I imagined his social life would be when we began this journey, but, as they say, "it is what it is." It is sometimes a difficult transition for us and for our children with Down syndrome because we may have put a lot of importance on friendships with typical children. We may have believed that the friends our children made in school and in the community would always be there. If we think of our own experiences, however, we might not be so disappointed. How many of your present friends were your friends in elementary school or high school?

We might have also realized the risks involved in our teenager with Down syndrome being part of the fabric of life outside of high school with her peers. Typical teens may be exposed to peer pressure to experiment with alcohol, illegal drugs, and unsafe sexual behaviors. These are situations that are more difficult for teens and young adults with Down syndrome.

*As the only student in his grade with an intellectual disability, Jon had many opportunities to be part of school activities. He played on the golf team and managed other sports teams. He was part of the class shows and coached the girls' powder puff football team. Lots of these activities included group dinners and other supervised events that were often followed by unsupervised parties. As much as I wanted Jon to be part of the group, I was actually grateful that someone always drove him home after the supervised portion of the evening. I always wondered if they did that for his safety or if they didn't want him around. Either way, I didn't have to worry about him being in a car with drinking teens.*

## LOOKING FOR NEW FRIENDS

This brings us to the point in our lives where we begin to recognize and value the importance of our children having true peer relationships—friendships with people who share similar interests and abilities. Let's say we understand the importance of our child with Down syndrome having relationships with others with disabilities. We face two challenges:

1. How do we change the paradigm we might have created?
2. Where do we start?

Intentionally or unintentionally, we may have created an environment where our children prefer being around people without Down syndrome or other disabilities. This may have happened as a byproduct of inclusion in school and other activities. Maybe we inadvertently encouraged it. Whatever the reason, many families report that their children with Down syndrome do not want to be with other people with disabilities. So, when the time comes—and it comes for everyone—that our children need real peers, our first hurdle is often our child's attitude toward people with disabilities. He or she might not be open to it.

*In 1989, Chris Burke, an actor with Down syndrome, burst into history as the star of the popular TV show, Life Goes On. I was very excited to share this news with Jonathan. When I told him about the show, he asked, "Did he play someone with a disability?" To Jon, it seemed like a perfectly obvious question, Did he play a person with a disability or did he portray someone unlike himself? Jon understand that actors "act" and, in doing so, portray someone else. Adam Sandler is Jewish, but he doesn't portray Jews in his movies.*

It is our responsibility to change the paradigm, and we can do that by creating a welcoming environment for people with disabilities in our psyche and in our lives. If our children only think that they are valued for how close they come to being typical, they will never value themselves for who they are—individuals with Down syndrome. If you think about it, many of us celebrate people with Down syndrome by noting how close they come to being typical: He walked at 18 months, she read at 5, she got her driver's license, he graduated with a real diploma, etc. Our national conventions feature the best and the brightest, and we read about the accomplishments that, in reality, only a few are able to obtain.

Some of our kids inadvertently get the message that their value comes from how much they are able to diminish their "Down syndrome-ness," so to speak. They may not get the message that they have intrinsic value, just for being who they are.

> We were very proud that Jon was able to go off to an overnight camp for boys and be the third generation of our family to attend this camp. He was only 10, but we were confident that he could spend a month without seeing us or even getting a phone call. We were surprised that when he returned he told his therapist, "You try and you try, and you are still not good enough." Even so, Jon wanted to return to camp for six more summers, but we realized that he also needed to have places to go were he was good enough.

It should not come as any great shock if our children seem to shy away from other people with disabilities. They may not recognize themselves. Or they don't want to. It is up to us to begin to create an environment where they can appreciate their ordinary gifts so that they can appreciate them in others.

> I remember the exact moment when Jon "got it." There was an end-of-year pizza party for the bowling league for adults with developmental disabilities my agency sponsored and I didn't have a babysitter to watch Jon, 14, and Emily, 10. I put them at a table away from the festivities. When I came over to check on them, Jon said, "You do this kind of work because of me, don't you?" I realized then that he understood that he was like those adults. He was a person with a disability, in spite of years of inclusion, regular sports teams, and wanting to be "good enough." He was good enough—It was just that this "good enough" included Down syndrome.

Teens who go to school with other students with disabilities have many more opportunities to develop natural relationships since they are with each other every day. It is more difficult to sustain these relationships after graduation. To prepare for the transition from school, families need to consider community-based activities that support individuals with disabilities such Special Olympics and those sponsored by the local Arc and Special Olympics.

> Like most people with Down syndrome, Jon has a great memory and he remembers the many positive experiences he has had in his life. He remembers his "friends" in high school very fondly. He seems OK that the typical kids don't keep up with him. He recently received an email from the most popular guy in the class and Jon responded (spelling corrected) with: You are right about one thing. It has been a long time. I work at a golf course doing maintenance. It is hard work but fun because I get free lunch and free golf. It is a lot of fun. The Celtics may get a first round draft pick in the NBA draft. I cannot wait until next year for our 10th high school reunion. A great response from Jon, but it did not get a reply.

# The Use of Leisure Time

To begin with, leisure time is the time we have when we are not working or don't have other obligations such as appointments and chores. Many people find leisure time difficult. For example, workaholics know how to work, but don't know what to do with themselves outside of the work environment. Other people use their leisure time productively to enjoy areas of interest or discover new ones.

Leisure is important because it can bring balance into our lives, connect us to other people, expand our interests and competencies, and give us opportunities for growth and expression. Most of all, it plays a large part in our feelings of well-being.

To use leisure time you need:

- activities that interest you;
- someone, if necessary, to share the activities with you;
- money to pay for your activities;
- a plan to enjoy the activity;
- transportation to get to the activity.

All of these are difficult for adults with Down syndrome. Also, since teaching young people how to use leisure time does not get the attention that employment or residential supports do, young people with Down syndrome often do not have the skills to plan and use their leisure time successfully.

If you are lucky, developing the ability to use leisure time might be or has been a priority in high school, but with all that we expect our child to master in school, leisure skills sometimes do not make it to the top of the list. That's OK, because you can develop leisure skills anytime.

**FINDING ACTIVITIES THAT INTEREST YOUR CHILD**

One thing most of our children are great at is watching television, managing the DVD player, and handling the remote control. While these are leisure time activities, they are not highly desirable ones. That being said, my son and a few of his buddies watch wrestling or football on TV two or three times a week.

Ideally, every adult with Down syndrome should have several leisure activities that require both physical activity and social interaction. Here is a broad list of some leisure activities that can fit the bill:

- Sports—bowling, swimming, golf, tennis, horseback riding
- Games—mah jong, Scrabble, cards, checkers, etc.
- Physical activities—kite flying, dancing, roller blading, etc.
- Exercise—Tae Bo, aerobics, weight training, yoga, Pilates, etc.
- Religious activities
- Groups—self-advocacy organizations, book club
- Hobbies—stamp, coin, or doll collecting, gardening, photography
- Creative expressions—art, drama, music
- Caring for a pet (if this includes walking the pet, shopping for its food, taking it to the vet, or some other kind of interaction)

- Spending time with friends (not watching TV)
- Going to the movies or concerts

I have purposely left off most activities that people do in isolation from other people and where contact with other people is not necessary—like using a computer. I am a big fan of technology, but I want to focus on activities that help our children make connections with other people in our communities.

So, what if your daughter is now finished with school, has more unscheduled time, and is watching too much TV and talking on the phone with old school friends? How do you begin to get her involved in more physical, social activities? You start off with thinking about what she likes, what she is interested in, and what she might enjoy and be good at. Get a piece of paper and develop a list of "Leisure Interests" (activities she already does at least occasionally and enjoys doing) and "Leisure Possibilities" (activities you think might appeal to her). Here is an example:

*Leisure Interests*
- Spending time with friends (not watching TV)
- Swimming
- Bowling
- Watching basketball on television
- Computers
- Traveling
- Eating out
- Going to the movies

*Leisure Possibilities*
- Attending religious services
- Joining a gym

By far the easiest way for your daughter to have a life filled with a variety of leisure activities is for you to organize, plan, and arrange all aspects of each activity. You can even participate with your daughter. Although this is the easiest way, it does not mean it is preferred and even desirable. Instead, it is better if you can ensure that a plan is devised to make sure that the activity occurs. This way, your child can become more independent in pursuing the activity and will take some ownership in it.

Let's go through the above list, taking one activity to show you what I mean:

**Swimming:** If your daughter enjoys recreational swimming and has enjoyed swimming with the family, you have your first leisure activity. Now you need to help your daughter identify a peer or a buddy to enjoy the activity with. This is the most crucial ingredient to ensuring that your child will want to do the activity without your presence or reminders. You might have to help her think of friends to invite. The next step would be to help your daughter locate a pool and to learn the days and times that adult recreational swim is offered. She may be able to call or look up this information on the Internet. She will need to find out how much the activity costs and decide how often she can afford to participate. Next she needs to find out where the pool is located and how she will get there. She may need assistance in deciding what clothes and other items she needs and how to navigate the pool if it is unfamiliar to her.

*Jonathan has a computer and I think he uses it more for checking up on the NBA, NFL, and NBL rankings than as a way to communicate. I have been encouraging him to use it more and he has an EBuddy he was connected with through Best Buddies.*™ *Occasionally, I will send him an email that I know will be of interest to him. Recently, I ordered some wrest-ing DVD's for him and in return I was rewarded with the following:*
*"thanks for oding thos dvds there is no other moms*
*in the wolewourl like mine and siple the best."*
*For the very few of you who could not translate that, it goes:* **"Thanks for ordering those DVD's. There are no other moms in the whole world like mine. You are simply the best."** *Some days I get the most unexpected gifts.*

## COMMUNITY ACTIVITIES AND ACTIVITIES IN THE COMMUNITY

We might be splitting hairs here, but to me there is a difference between community activities and activities "in the community." Let me clarify what I mean.

Many organizations, including Park and Recreation Departments, local Arcs, and special programs, offer activities in the community specifically designed for people with disabilities. There are even dozens of companies that offer trips to far-off destinations for individuals with Down syndrome and related disabilities. Your child, like mine, has probably participated in many of these activities. She may have enjoyed

trips to sporting events or special events or any number of wonderful activities with her peers. These events are typically run by paid staff and there may also be volunteers to provide additional supervision. Although these activities occur in the community, they rarely include participants without cognitive disabilities.

"Community activities," on the other hand, are activities that occur naturally in the community. People with Down syndrome or other disabilities participate in them on an individual basis with the necessary support.

A balance between these two kinds of activities can provide variety and opportunity for our children. In some activities, our children have the opportunity to be seen as individuals and, in other activities, they are seen as a member of a group—a group of individuals with disabilities.

*On Friday night, Jon and Alex walked down to the Commons to have dinner. On Saturday, a group of about twelve individuals from the agency that supports Jon traveled together in a van to a large mall. Jon spent the day with a friend wandering the vast array of stores. On Sunday, Jon went with his Spe-cial Olympics coach and teammates to practice. On Sunday night, Jon and two friends took a cab to attend a Passover Seder at his synagogue.*

## SPECIAL OLYMPICS

No program has done more to change the opportunities for and attitudes about people with Down syndrome and other intellectual disabilities throughout the world than Special Olympics. The actual birth of Special Olympics is identified as July 20, 1968, when

the First International Special Olympics Games were held at Soldier Field in Chicago, Illinois. City officials were so sure that athletes with intellectual disabilities were not capable of swimming that they required lifeguards to surround the pool, five feet apart from one another. Chicago Mayor Richard Daley, who attended the First International Special Olympics Games that day, said to Eunice Kennedy Shriver, "You know, Eunice, the world will never be the same after this." And it isn't. Today athletes with intellectual disabilities participate in Special Olympics and on regular teams and in regular competition throughout the world.

However, the concept of Special Olympics was actually born much earlier, when Eunice Kennedy Shriver started a day camp for people with intellectual disabilities at her home, "Camp Shriver." Recently, "Camp Shriver" has begun again at both the Shriver home and at sites throughout the world. I had the privilege of volunteering at the Shriver home one summer and was able to witness firsthand the indomitable strength of Mrs. Shriver, well into her 80s, as she got right into the pool and taught swimming to a group of campers.

Today, 2.5 million athletes from more than 180 countries around the world are involved in Special Olympics.

*I am perfectly aware and awed that the opportunities that my son has had in sports and competition exist because Special Olympics changed the possibilities for him. He would not have been on his high school golf team, stolen home on a wild pitch in Little League, or won three youth basketball championships if the world had not seen the Special Olympics movement. Neither would he have been third at the 1995 World Special Olympics in 18-hole golf or have discovered his current favorite activity, his Special Olympics bowling team.*

The following individual and team sports are offered by Special Olympics (although not every chapter of SO offers every sport):

- alpine skiing
- athletics
- basketball
- bowling
- cross country skiing
- equestrian
- floor hockey
- golf
- judo

- aquatics
- badminton
- bocce
- cricket
- cycling
- figure skating
- football (soccer)
- gymnastics
- kayaking

- netball
- roller skating
- snowboarding
- softball
- table tennis
- tennis

- power lifting
- sailing
- snowshoeing
- speed skating
- team handball
- volleyball

**Special Olympics Unified Sports** brings together athletes with and without intellectual disabilities to train and compete together. Unified Sports includes virtually all Special Olympics sports. If your family enjoys sports together or wants to try something new, you may want to consider joining a team together.

In addition, Special Olympics now offers age-appropriate activities and activities for athletes with lower abilities. For individuals with severe limitations who do not yet possess the physical and/or behavioral skills necessary to participate in sports, Special Olympics offers the **Motor Activities Training Program (MATP).**

Adults who have never participated in Special Olympics or who have never participated in sports and athletic competition are welcome to join at any time. To get involved, look for the nearest local program at www.specialolympics.org. Special Olympics can provide wonderful opportunities to just your child with Down syndrome or your entire family. Your child will get to train and compete and may even have the opportunity to experience an overnight away from you during a competition

Family members are welcome in Special Olympics as unified partners, coaches, volunteers, and officials. Families are often the initiators of local teams. This happens when a family member has someone in the family who wants to participate in a sport. Rather than waiting for someone else to be the coach, they volunteer and step up to the plate themselves.

> *I had a bias against bowling from my own early experiences. When I first started in the disability field, it seemed as if the only activity for people with Down syndrome and similar disabilities was bowling. So, you can imagine that I never put much emphasis on bowling. We exposed Jonathan to lots of other sports and he only bowled occasionally, like at family outings or birthday parties.*
>
> *When Jonathan became an adult and began living in his own home, he joined not one, but two Special Olympic bowling leagues—candlepin and ten pin. He and a couple of friends take the bus to the bowling alley and sometimes proceed from there to do other activities such as shopping or dining out. He loves to bowl. Thankfully, my desire to be "politically correct" did not cost him this opportunity to direct his own life.*

## ATHLETE LEADERSHIP PROGRAM (ALPS) OF SPECIAL OLYMPICS

Adults with Down syndrome who participate in Special Olympics can take part in the organization as self-advocates. The Athlete Leadership Programs (ALPs) of the Special Olympics allow athletes with disabilities to receive training and support to serve on Boards of Directors at all levels of Special Olympics organizations or on local organizing committees. Athletes are also given training to become spokespersons, team captains, coaches, and officials.

# Establishing Effective Networks

Anetwork is a connection. Thinking of a computer network, information is shared between or among two or more computers. It connects computers. It makes work easier, more efficient, and more productive. A personal network does the same things. It just depends on people sharing information.

You can never have too many connections or contacts. You need to use your address book to the benefit of your child with Down syndrome. To do so, you first need to identify who your connections are. One good way is to get two pieces of paper; one for yourself and one for your child. Title it "Building a Network" and make the following columns:

1. Family Members
2. Friends and Neighbors
3. Past and Present Employment connections
4. Organizations and Groups (that you or others belong to)
5. Businesses and Professionals (places you frequent or where you are known)
6. Teachers and coaches

These people don't necessarily have to be people who are close to, or even know your child with Down syndrome. They could be your other children's coaches or friends.

The important thing to consider is whether they have something to contribute.

Under each column, list as many individuals and their phone numbers as you can. Remember, you are doing this for both you and your child, so it might be an excellent idea to have your child participate. She will probably have suggestions that you might not have considered. Involving other family members or friends can help turn this into a brainstorming activity and perhaps make it more productive and fun. Your two lists are now the beginning of your daughter's network. Don't forget to update it regularly as you both make new connections.

Once you have listed everyone in your network, you have to be prepared to work the network. You have to ask these people for suggestions, ideas, and assistance when you are building a life for your child. For instance, she might need a job, transportation, a roommate, or the name of a good physician. Or maybe she needs someone to show her how to use email or load songs onto her iPod. You will not know how to do everything, but someone in your network either does or knows someone who does and may be willing to ask for you.

*I noticed something very interesting with our Unified Softball team. It was a nice group of mostly men—half of them members of the local Rotary Club and the other half Special Olympics athletes. When the team was first formed, most of the Special Olympics athletes didn't have jobs and spent their days in a sheltered workshop. As time went on, more and more of the athletes found competitive jobs. What I learned was that most of them got their jobs through the network of fellow softball players—Rotarians with a vast community network they were willing to access on their teammates' behalf.*

To be part of an effective network for your child, you have to be prepared to give assistance as well as get it. I use my network to assist Jonathan all the time. I have used it to find jobs, medical specialists, and staff for him. Personally, I use my own network to check references, find jobs, locate good restaurants, and even pick paint colors. In a good network, information and assistance is shared both ways. Using my computer example, the network is not effective if the information only goes one way—received but never given. You need to be willing to assist people in your network for the network to thrive and be successful. Expect to pick up the phone or make an introduction or suggestion

Most of our children are going to need assistance throughout their adult lives with everything from sports to housing, and employment to transportation. Make it easier on yourself and your child by putting together and relying on a network.

# Paid Support

The single biggest issue that will affect our children at every point in their life is the availability of a well-trained and fairly compensated workforce. Our children need staff to teach, model, train, and support them. The adult service system is not like the educational system, with college-trained and certified teachers who are fairly compensated and receive excellent benefits, as well as planning time during their week and generous vacation time.

How successful our children are in employment, community living, and virtually everything they do that requires support is directly related to the quality of the direct support professional workforce. Unfortunately, this workforce is in crisis. This crisis in linked to low wages and compensation and poor benefits. These pose enormous challenges in recruiting, retaining, and providing adequate training for direct support professionals. It is not a new problem, nor is it likely to go away soon. It is important for you to understand the problem so you can be a better partner with the agencies and individuals who will be providing services and supports to your child with Down syndrome.

The vast majority of adult service agencies receive reimbursement either directly from the state or from Medicaid. Some may fundraise in order to cover expenses or to offer innovative programs. These companies do not operate in the open market. Their rates are set by the state or federal government and can go decades without any increases; often they experience deficit budgets. Some agencies have not had rate adjustments in twenty-five years. This means they have not received any additional funding to adjust for the normal increases in operating an agency, such as rent, utilities, and fuel. As a result, there is little money for the kind of training that motivates staff or for salary increases. Many staff members have gone years without salary increases; if they are fortunate, they may have received modest cost-of-living increases.

Add to this mix the lack of long-term career opportunities and you have a broken system with problems in the recruitment, retention, and quality of trained staff. Turnover in some positions can be over 100 percent. That means that the position becomes vacant, a new staff person is recruited, hired, and trained, and a few months later, the individual resigns and the process starts all over again. As a consequence, our children are denied the reliable and consistent staff they need for success.

When an agency hires employees, there are often state-mandated trainings which must occur. They are generally related to safety and agency procedures. The safety trainings may include the following:

- first aid and CPR
- fire safety
- human rights
- medication
- behavior intervention
- incident and abuse reporting
- health standards

In addition, the agency may require the following types of training during the orientation period:

- record keeping and documentation
- use and maintenance of vehicles
- Individual Service Plan (ISP)
- budgeting and money management

However, the bulk of the training is actually on the job and conducted by either coworkers or by supervisors who sometimes do not have much more experience than the newcomer. So great is the need to fill vacant positions that comprehensive training is just not possible.

I am not including this information about the crisis in direct care services to scare you. I just believe that families have the right to know the facts. Most people who work in direct care are wonderful and caring. They do not all have a college education, but I have found them to be willing to do the hard work that is expected of them.

Given the lack of incentive for good workers to stay in direct support positions and the possibility that your child's support people may lack adequate training, what can you do? Here are my suggestions:

1. First, try to give lots of praise to staff people.
2. Advocate for their wages and benefits to be increased.
3. Make tactful suggestions—not commands—about ways to work with your child more effectively.
4. If anyone who comes in contact with your child makes you or your child feel uncomfortable, find out what is going on and report your concerns to the supervisor.

Be advised that this is not usually a situation where the "squeaky wheel gets the grease," but where you get labeled as difficult if you are too abrasive and demanding. Work in partnership with staff to address your concerns.

# CHAPTER 11

## Technology, Transportation, Recreation, Risk, and What's Left Over

*Over the years, I have experienced and observed lots of situations related to transition that do not fit neatly into any of the previous chapters. They are still important and worthy of inclusion in a comprehensive look at all the issues that individuals with Down syndrome face as they make the transition to their adult lives. This chapter will bring together some issues you may expect and some issues that are new and emerging.*

*I believe that the biggest barrier to accessing community activities and building a meaningful day is the lack of appropriate transportation (although others may say it is the lack of appropriate social skills or attitudes of people in the community). Families, buses, trains, cabs, cars, boats, and feet can all be part of the transportation continuum for adults with Down syndrome, and your child needs to be able to use the appropriate conveyance to get where he needs to be.*

*Other important issues to address during transition include using technology to enhance your child's safety and success, disaster planning, legal requirements such as jury duty and registering for the Selective Service, and safeguarding your child from identity theft.*

# Technology

Technology is part of all of our lives. We can either bemoan its intrusion into our lives as we battle with every new gadget or we can embrace it when it makes our life easier. My father-in-law, a very intelligent man, calls computers "confusers" and refuses to use them, while my father is on his third laptop. Everyone is different, but it is important for you to at least consider whether technology can assist your child with Down syndrome during and after transition. Also remember that just because something confuses you doesn't mean that it won't come easily to your child.

While your child is still covered by IDEA, it is important to remember that he has a right to whatever assistive technology is necessary to help him meet his IEP goals. This is the right time to take a careful inventory of the barriers that may exist for your child

and insist on assistive technology evaluations if they might help. Types of technology to consider include augmentative communication devices, adaptive keyboards, talking watches, and devices that remind someone when medication should be taken.

If you are unsure about what devices might help your child, I have found an Internet search helpful. For example, if your child is deaf or hard of hearing, try typing in "devices deaf or hard of hearing" into a search engine (Google, Yahoo, etc). You may discover some items that you might not have thought of such as extra loud alarm clocks or other alert systems. Or, if your child has trouble with time, there are watches that can be used to schedule reminders for such things as getting ready for the bus.

For individuals with speech difficulties, there are a variety of assistive devices that can help with communication. These devices can be low tech, such as a wallet-sized notebook with pictures the user can point to, or they can be high-tech, such as a portable electronic device that contains pre-recoded responses.

Although it is possible to have an assistive technology evaluation after your child ages out of IDEA eligibility, it is much simpler to ask for your child's technology needs to be assessed while he is still in school. Additionally, if a piece of technology is necessary to meet your child's IEP goals, the school system must cover the costs under IDEA.

## TECHNOLOGY AS TOOLS FOR SAFETY

Technology is making it easier and safer to let our children take risks that we might not have considered without the technology. Some of them you may already have thought of and others may be new to you.

### CELL PHONES

A number of years ago, I remember meeting a teenager with Down syndrome who used a cell phone and thinking that was something that my son could never learn to manage. How wrong I was! Cell phones have become almost standard tools for all teens and that includes many teens with Down syndrome.

Cell phone technology is changing rapidly and there are several styles of

phones that may provide some independence for your child and peace of mind for you. There are cell phones with big buttons, bright screens, and extra-loud sounds. There are phones that are easy to use and others that only allow the user to place calls to a few people. There are also phones that have a tracking system that allows parents to know where their child is.

If your child has limited oral communication skills, finding the right cell phone may be a challenge. If this is the case, think about adding a goal related to the use of phones to his IEP. Phones and automated attendants (voice mail) can be very discouraging for our children.

If your child does not yet have the ability to keep track of how many minutes he uses his cell phone or how many text messages he sends and receives, you can set up a cell phone with limits. The phone is loaded with a certain dollar amount and when that is used, more minutes must be purchased and applied. This might be a better option than receiving an unexpected surprise when the phone bill arrives.

> When Jon was in high school, I was late picking him up after a basketball game and I went inside the school to find him. He was on the pay phone, politely trying to explain to an automated message, "I told you, I already deposited 25 cents." It was an appropriate response to the request, "Please deposit 25 cents." He had no idea he was not talking to an actual person. I realized again the barriers to his world and that I was not ever going to be able to get the world to adapt to him. It is just a truth. While Jon is now comfortable with his cell phone, there may be some barriers that will never be overcome.

## LIGHTING

As your child begins to live more independently in the community, you may want to investigate lighting options that can enhance his safety. For example, there are light systems that can automatically illuminate baseboards and can be helpful to someone who is afraid of the dark. There are sensors that automatically turn on lights when someone enters a bathroom or approaches a dark area. Whether an area is inside or outside, it can be illuminated automatically if necessary.

## SAFETY SYSTEMS

There are products marketed to the elderly that use wireless sensors to monitor daily activities such as meal preparation, sleep and bathroom habits, wake-up time, medication usage, and household temperatures. The sensors are placed around the home and transfer information to a central monitoring system. Caregivers are notified if, for example, someone has been in the bathroom for two hours and their normal routine is to spend thirty minutes there. Other products enable the user to summon help using either a device worn around the neck or on the wrist like a watch. They work on the principle that if someone needs help, they press a button. The person requiring assistance needs to be within hearing range to be able to speak into a device and let the attendant know that help is required.

Other products, designed for Alzheimer's patients or young children, can track people either through GPS or other technology. These tracking services typically cost between $1 and $3 per day. You have to weigh safety against privacy issues when using any kind of measure or device to monitor an individual. If your son is his own guardian, you also need to make sure he agrees to anything that might violate his rights to privacy. For example, while I have imagined having web cams placed all over Jon's house to ally my worries, I realize that his right to privacy is far greater than my anxiety. I have to be satisfied with telephone calls.

Other types of technology that can increase safety include:

- smoke alarms designed for those with hearing impairments;
- showerheads designed to prevent burns from hot water;
- grab bars to prevent falls in the bathroom;
- a "stove guard" that will turn off the stove burner if no motion is detected near the stove after a certain amount of time;
- door alarms.

### REMINDER SYSTEMS

There are various technological solutions that can be used to remind someone to take his medicine, prepare a meal, or do another important task. For example, there are services that will make automatic telephone calls as reminders. Reminders, either visual or auditory, can also be set on cell phones, watches, and computers. There are medication reminder wristwatches that note the pills to be taken, as well as vibrating pocket pill boxes.

*Jon is quite dependent on technology. I am not sure he recognizes this, though. His cell phone provides both him and me with a measure of security. When he misses a call from me, he will see that I am on caller ID and return the call. He also wears hearing aids to assist him and has bed shakers to wake him in case of a fire if he happens not to hear the smoke detectors. Jonathan uses a CPAP machine nightly to address his sleep apnea. He has learned to set the machine and its humidifier. He has an internal defibrillator and needs to check its battery every day with a magnet. He has also been taught that the device will make a ringing noise at a preset time, to let him know that it is not working properly. Shortly after his operation to insert the device, he was on a treadmill and someone's cell phone began ringing. He looked at me and wondered, "Is that me going off?"*

# Technology and Risk

Just as technology can be helpful, it can also put our children at risk. One case in point: Jeremy, a young man with Down syndrome who lived in his own apartment, often found himself alone and longing for a girlfriend. One evening, he responded to a television commercial that targeted "lonely" people. Using his credit card, he dialed the "900" number and soon afterwards, a young woman and her "Uncle Jerry" visited him and robbed him. When they called back to visit him again, Jeremy was lucky that a staff person was present and notified his family. He got the sexual experience he thought he desired and, fortunately for him, a negative result on tests for HIV and STDs.

Besides falling for ads that ask you to call 900 numbers (for a steep price), there are other risks to watching television. For example, you might send text messages in response to a TV appeal to vote for something and then find out there is a charge for every message you send. Even voting by text message for your favorite American Idol can cost money.

There are also many risks of using the Internet—for all of us, not just teens and adults with Down syndrome. Everyone needs to beware of divulging personal information to the wrong person in a chat room or clicking on something on a webpage or popup ad that results in the purchase of some unneeded, expensive product.

Teens and adults with Down syndrome can be taught about the risks of technology. The transition years are a good place to begin reinforcing these potential problems. However, these are actually lessons that should have begun in preschool when your child first started learning about strangers. Hopefully, your child has already learned to distinguish strangers from friends, and never to tell a stranger his name, address, or phone number. As your child gets older, these conversations need to be broadened to make sure he understands these same rules apply to strangers they may meet on-line. Many public school systems present these types of lessons and often include presentations by local law enforcement officials. It is important that your child be part of these presentations, that the lessons be reinforced at home, and, if necessary, that safety issues be addressed through IEP goals.

> *When Jon was attending a residential postsecondary program, he had a computer in his room. Since he was over 18, we decided he should be permitted to be able to access the Internet without any parental controls. After a female staff person came into his room and found a group of guys around Jon's computer viewing a pornographic site, staff taught Jon that viewing that kind of material was not a group activity. Later that year, his AOL account suddenly was suspended. Someone had obtained Jon's screen name and password and set up a pornographic site with it. AOL closed down the site and Jon's access to AOL. Although we were able to restore Jon's AOL account, Jon learned a valuable lesson about the danger in giving out your password.*

# Transportation

One of the biggest barriers to employment and leisure activities for teens and young adults with Down syndrome is the lack of transportation. The transportation issue becomes a major barrier when public education ends. While your student is in school, transportation to school and to any jobs that the school has arranged for is generally provided. In addition, your child's social network revolves primarily around school and school functions and getting your child to these events is not usually difficult.

Parents expect to provide the majority of transportation for their young children, but many look forward to emancipation from that task. They celebrate their freedom from having to be their child's primary form of transportation as he becomes able to safely walk, ride a bike, take public transportation, or drive to his friends' houses, school activities, or soccer practice.

This kind of freedom does not usually come easily if your child has Down syndrome. Many families report that they still provide the majority of transportation

for their adult children so they can get to work, their day programs, or be involved in community activities. States and agencies vary as to how much transportation they provide for adults with disabilities. Some states make arrangements for transportation related to employment, but few provide any assistance for transportation to leisure activities.

*I had a wonderful experience this summer with a program called "Lose the Training Wheels"—a nonprofit organization based in Kansas that teaches kids with disabilities aged 8 to 18 how to ride a bike. They travel around the country holding clinics called "bike camps."*

*The organization is pretty flexible and accepted Jon, who is now 30 and has never learned to ride a bike. We had repeatedly tried to teach him over the years and had given up and settled for him riding on the back on a tandem. Jon agreed to try the bike school as long as it didn't interfere with his work schedule and various social activities. Fortunately, it didn't. To my utter shock and with much pride, Jonathan actually learned to ride a bike over the course of the five-day program. He didn't notice that the other students were younger than he was, and I could have cared less, because how often do you get to see your kid, especially as an adult, acquire a skill he never thought possible?*

*Jon is not yet ready for riding on the street in traffic, but enjoys riding around the grounds where he lives and on bike paths. Who knows? He might even be able to ride his bike to work next summer.*

## DRIVING

While some individuals with Down syndrome are successful in getting their driver's license, this may not be a realistic goal for many people with Down syndrome. Even those individuals with Down syndrome who are successful in driving are often limited as to where and when they can drive.

That being said, the independence that comes with having a driver's license is important and most families ought to consider the possibility that their child could learn to drive. Driving can definitely increase an individual's independence if he has access to a car. There is a high cost to car ownership or rental, however. Although you can use the PASS program of Social Security to save for a car (described in Chapter 6), the ongoing expenses of a car may not make this a realistic option even if your child is able to drive.

The first time I heard of a person with Down syndrome driving, I was amazed. It also opened my eyes to possibilities that I hadn't considered. It took the young woman an entire year of on-the-road driving lessons after she had taken the classroom course, used a simulator, and took a practice course to earn her license. More recently, Nathan, an 18-year-old I know, just took the regular course offered in his community and practiced driving with his family and passed his driving test on the first attempt. Nathan lives in a suburban community with busy streets and some highway access.

I had a very different experience with my own son. When Jonathan was a junior in high school, he did what all the other juniors did—he took the driver's education course offered by our high school. For most of the students, the almost daily videos on the hazards of driving, including graphic car crashes, were just a time to sleep. Not so for Jonathan. He watched those videos so intently that he came to the conclusion that driving was too dangerous and he lost interest in driving. His decision came as a great disappointment to the driving instructor, who believed that Jon was more than capable of driving. Neither of us was able to convince Jonathan to sit for his learner's permit, which would have allowed him to drive with the instructor.

Over ten years later, Jon was willing to study for his learner's permit, as he could not progress at his job on the golf course without a driver's license.

The decision as to whether your child should drive depends on many factors—including your child's reaction time, judgment, reading skills, sense of direction, financial ability to maintain a car, and place of residence. There's a big difference in the reaction times and judgment needed for driving safely in a quiet town where everyone drives courteously and there are wide streets with low speed limits, and, say, a congested, suburban area where many people drive aggressively and exceed the speed limit, there are numerous one-way streets and narrow roads with cars parked on both sides, drivers are often impatient and may rear-end you unless you go through the yellow light, and there are few breaks in traffic as you are flying down the highway at 70 miles an hour trying to merge. Fortunately, in larger cities, public transportation is usually readily available.

If you are not sure about your child's readiness to drive, there are driving assessments that may be available through your state Vocational Rehabilitation agency. Some agencies have driving simulators that can be used to determine whether a potential driver has the skills, and some of the video gaming systems also have very realistic simulated driving games. There are also commercially available adaptive driving schools. Some driving programs even have private driving courses that provide a bridge between a simulator and public streets and roads.

## PUBLIC TRANSPORTATION

Goals related to using public transportation can be excellent additions to your child's IEP during the transition years. He can learn to read schedules for buses, trains, and subways, to understand and pay fares, or to call for a cab and tip the driver. There may be opportunities for your child to practice these skills to get to and from places within the school day or to get to and from school.

If your child is on a more academic track in high school, you may want these skills to be addressed in a postsecondary program or when he is being served by an adult service agency. Travel training is often part of adult employment programs to teach an individual to get to his job. Some residential programs might also teach adults the travel skills for shopping and leisure activities. If travel training is important to you, make sure it is part of either your child's IEP in high school or in his annual adult planning document.

Under the Americans with Disabilities Act, individuals with disabilities cannot be denied access to public transportation. As a consequence, your child may be eligible for specialized transportation. For example, some communities offer door-to-door van, taxi, or bus service for people with disabilities (and may offer the same service to seniors). Some communities only provide this transportation for essential travel such as medical appointments, while others also provide it for shopping or other leisure-related transportation needs.

Your child might also be eligible for reduced fares when using public transportation. If so, he will need to obtain special transportation identification to receive the reduced fare, generally from your local or regional transportation authority.

Some teens and adults with Down syndrome feel bad if they are not able to drive when their siblings and peers can, and they are not eager to use public transportation as a replacement. While this is not usually a problem in larger cities such as New York City where everyone uses public transportation, it might be more of an issue in a suburban car-dependent community. There is no one way to address this, but being open, honest, and frank is a good place to start.

It may also help to point out some of the advantages of taking public transportation instead of driving. Below are some of the advantages of not driving, as shared by the Rhode Island self-advocates that I have quoted from in previous chapters:

- You can relax.
- You can sleep while someone else drives.
- You don't have to worry about repairs.
- You can read books.
- You can watch TV.
- You can talk on your cell phone.
- You can enjoy the scenery.
- You can take photographs.

The Rhode Island self-advocates used a variety of ways to get to work. They were:

- bike
- Job coach
- regular public transportation
- agency staff
- walk
- special public transportation
- parents
- sister

Each of these are viable options involving different risks and expenses.

# Self-Advocacy

Self-advocacy is all about people with disabilities taking charge of their own lives. People can accomplish this individually, as in when they speak up for themselves, but it is also a worldwide movement.

The group originally called the "Mohawks and Squaws" and now known as the "Massachusetts Advocates Standing Strong" was the first self-advocacy group for individuals with intellectual disabilities in the U.S. (according to the late Gunnar Dybwad, who was considered one of the founders of the parent advocacy, inclusion, and self-advocacy movements, and related to me by David Wizansky). The group began in 1959 when a group of male students with special needs at Brookline (MA) High School came together with a leader for a traditional afterschool activities program. David became connected with them in 1967 and developed a speakers' bureau and a self-advocacy format. The next change was to incorporate the "Squaws" and become coed.

Most references to the self-advocacy movement begin with a meeting in Sweden in 1968 of people with developmental disabilities, followed by similar meetings in England and Canada. In 1974, a few individuals from Oregon attended one of these meetings and returned to plan their own conference. Success came quickly, and today the self-advocacy movement has a strong international component. There are nearly 1000 self-advocacy groups in the United States.

Many self-advocacy groups are named "People First" in recognition that people should not be labeled. While many of us family members think we came up with this phrase, it was actually an adult with an intellectual disability who inspired the phrase

in 1974. The United States national self-advocacy organization is called "Self Advocates Becoming Empowered" (SABE).

If our children are to become effective as self-advocates, they need to know that their voices are important and are heard and respected. Parents have a large role to play in giving our children opportunities to be valued and listened to within our families and in modeling this behavior in the community.

As our children become teens and begin to form their own opinions and values, we need to respect and celebrate their words and actions unless they are violating societal or family norms. For example, how they choose to express themselves in clothing and music choices should be respected. Choices in food should also be respected. You should not require your child to taste any food that is presented to him, because he has probably already developed his food tastes and preferences. "Requiring" him to taste food, unless the specific food is medically necessary, is not being respectful and not teaching him self-advocacy skills. He needs to learn that his opinions matter and that he should, and, in fact, must question adults and other authority figures, if his safety or self-worth is in danger.

The Down syndrome community values, respects, and encourages the self-advocacy movement among people with Down syndrome. They accomplish this through meetings, workshops, and participation in governing bodies. Both the National Down Syndrome Congress and National Down Syndrome Society have active Self-Advocacy Boards in addition to self-advocate representation on their governing Boards. Most state and local Down syndrome organizations have adopted this practice as well.

## Self-Advocacy in Action

This was an email sent by Leia, a young adult living in an in-law apartment in her family's home, to her mother, who works for the Department of Disability Services (DDS):

Hi mom, it's me. You do lots of hard work with DDS and you really do lots of hard work with people who are like me. I want to say you are the best of everything you do. I think you will like my email because I really think you do lots of things to help me out. I want to say thank you for trying to help me. I really love you. You are the best of all. You are my favorite mother that I have in the whole wide world. I just want to say I am lucky to have you as a good mother and a good friend, too. I want to say that I am proud that you have worked with me my whole life.

Now I am getting older and I want to thank you for that. I am getting bored being at home for nine years and I think I need a change like everyone else. All my friends are moved away from their parents and that is what I really want. I would like to bring it up at my ISP at DDS because it really is about me and what I want to do in my life. Because I would like to be more independent and I will really work hard with you and my staff.

I will always be your baby girl and I will call you in my new place. I will let you call me too and I will let you in my new place if I get it. Maybe next year if my name comes up.

Okay. I love you, mom. Signed your daughter, Leia.

## Disaster Planning

Most of us have some idea of how to take precautions in case of extreme weather such as blizzards, tornados, or hurricanes, and are prepared for power failures. We must also be prepared for other situations such as acts of terrorism and epidemics of bird flu or other illnesses.

If your child with Down syndrome lives at home, then you just need to include him in your own family disaster plan. The American Red Cross can provide you with information to assist you in developing your plan. If your child with Down syndrome does not live at home, you need to make sure you are aware of the plans for him during an emergency. What happens in a simple emergency, such as when the power is lost for several hours? What happens during a larger scale natural disaster? What is the agency's plan to make sure that staff members continue to report to work? What happens if they do not?

*After the country became aware of the potential consequences of a bird flu epidemic, I set aside space in my home for a disaster kit. It contains an ample supply of nonperishable food and water. I also followed the Red Cross suggested list and included lots of over-the-counter medicines that could help relieve symptoms of flu- or stomach-like illnesses. In addition, I included items that would be helpful in a power outage, such as battery-operated and hand-cranked flashlights, radios, and a television. My first aid kit includes all the usual items and I added a package of latex gloves, masks, and protective glasses in case we had to care for a contagious person at home. I also put aside some cash in case the ATM machines were not working or had run out of cash. Finally, I spoke to my son's physician about obtaining anti-viral medications in advance of any pandemic flu. I feel so strongly about being prepared that I gave other members of my family battery-operated and hand-cranked items for gifts.*

Recently, the Arc I worked for developed a pandemic flu plan. It was required by the state. The core of the plan is that we hoped that families would care for their family member. We also asked each staff person what they would do in case of a major event. We wanted to know whether they would come to work or would stay home to reduce the likelihood of infection themselves. Many staff members had their own families to protect and care for.

If an evacuation was necessary, where would your child go and who would be caring for him? It might be to another site the agency operates or it could be to the evacuation site that everyone in the community reports to.

Agencies that provide services to adults with Down syndrome are required to have emergency plans, and you can ask to see them. Agencies should conduct drills so they can practice their emergency plans and so our children are familiar with them. My son recently received an unannounced call to report to a central location with his sleeping bag and emergency supply kit of food and water. He was told to prepare for a hurricane. He was happy to learn it was only a drill, and I was pleased to know that he responded appropriately to the drill.

It is impossible to plan for every contingency or emergency. We have all had to learn to accept an element of risk. How much risk you are willing to allow your child to be exposed to will be an individual decision. There are some simple instructions you can teach your child in the event that his plan goes wrong. They are:

- Stay with someone.
- Go to a public place.
- Call 911.

*My plan is simple. At the first sign of a deadly flu virus or a natural disaster that comes with warning, Jonathan comes home or I go to be with him. I rarely travel any great distance unless there is another family member who could assist Jon in an emergency. He has great paid supporters, but who knows where they might be in a disaster.*

Personal networks are really critical in a disaster. Having caring neighbors and friends is often more helpful than the "official" response, especially if it is a long time in coming. We all saw how long it took local, state, and federal governments to respond to Hurricane Katrina in 2005. Make sure that you know your neighbors, and, a bit more importantly, make sure your son knows his.

# Voting Rights

People with Down syndrome have the right to vote. In fact, they can be some of the most informed voters I have met. Some of our children are "news junkies" and are exposed to the same information as any other voter. As a result, they enter the voting booth armed with the knowledge to vote intelligently. Others participate in discussions with family and friends. They watch TV or read newspapers. Their self-advocacy activities likely include voter and candidate information. Not too many years ago, a voter with Down syndrome gave a speech at the Republican National Convention on primetime television.

Your child's right to vote is protected by both the Voting Rights Act and The Americans with Disabilities Act. Under certain situations, however, when an individual has been determined by a court to be incompetent in all areas of his life, as in a complete guardianship petition, voting may not be allowed. Guardianship, as previously discussed, is a very serious consideration and has consequences, both negative and positive, to explore.

During the transition years, you can help ensure your child learns what voting is about by making sure he takes classes that cover government and voting at school, attending voter information nights in your community, and discussing elections at home. Get Out the Vote, an initiative directed at young voters, has special events that may be exciting to your child. During a presidential election cycle, it is hard to escape the barrage of media attention, and most of our children will get exposure through television. There is strong research that shows that voters are influenced by where they live, their family, and how those around them are voting. Our children will be similarly influenced. When your adult child no longer lives with you, it will be important to ensure that she has a way to get to the polls or receives an absentee ballot and the support to complete it. If you cannot make other arrangements, there are voter advocacy groups that often provide transportation to the polls.

*Jon is highly influenced by what he perceives as a candidate's attitudes toward people with disabilities. He liked the first George Bush because he appeared in a public service announcement with Chris Burke. He has since voted for Democratic candidates. He probably watches too much television, and, like most Americans, that's where he gets his candidate information. The last time around he joined with a majority of Americans to vote for change.*

# Selective Service

Almost all young men who are living in the United States, whether or not they are citizens, must register for the Selective Service at age 18. This includes men with disabilities, provided "they can reasonably leave their homes and move about independently."

The Selective Service System is an independent agency within the Executive Branch of the Federal Government. The mission of the Selective Service System is to provide the numbers of men needed by the armed forces, within the time required, should Congress and the president decide to return to a draft, in the event of a national emergency. Selective Service would also be responsible for administering a program of alternative service for conscientious objectors.

Your son can register at a post office or online at www.sss.gov. Men who do not register can face fines of up to $250,000 or prison time, and also are not eligible for federal student loans or grants, federal job training, or federal jobs. For young men with Down syndrome, I think registering for the draft is a great opportunity to stand up and be counted. A friend or relative may help your son fill out the registration form if he can't do it himself. Even if you think your son would not qualify for military service or if he is a conscientious objector, he must still register with Selective Service. If in a time of war his number was called, the draft board would then determine whether or not he is qualified to serve.

I have not yet heard of a man with Down syndrome serving in any branch of our military. In Israel, where most citizens serve in the army, individuals with Down syndrome have chosen to serve and have worked in noncombat roles, away from danger, such as kitchen or landscaping assistants. I think there are many safe assignments in the United States that individuals with Down syndrome could perform safely and honorably.

# People with Disabilities Targeted for Identity Theft

You have seen them and so have I. I am talking about those clever television commercials that warn us about identity theft. I admit I thought they were cute but I brushed the worry of identity theft aside because I have been shredding my identifying documents for years and I request and receive my free credit report yearly. I felt safe.

But, I never thought that Jonathan, my adult son with Down syndrome, could ever be at risk for identity theft. He doesn't have credit. Doesn't need credit. He wasn't going to be getting a home mortgage or car loan. How wrong and uninformed I was.

I have learned that individuals with intellectual disabilities are, in fact, perfect victims for identity theft. They have credit, since most of our children have small savings and/or checking accounts. Some of them may even have credit cards, and even if they are only an "additional cardholder," they are establishing a credit history. If their name appears on an electric, phone, gas, or cable bill, more credit history is being made.

Sometime last summer, as Jonathan's representative payee, I received his wage report from Social Security. In reviewing it, I noticed something unusual. Earnings were reported, under Jonathan's social security number, from an Irish pub in a midwestern state, although he lives in a state in the northeast. I called Social Security to tell them there had been a mistake and they sent me an affidavit to complete, but that's another story for another column. Coincidentaly, or so it seemed, the month before, a bank from the same mid-western state had called our home looking for Jonathan because he owed over $8000 in credit card changes. At the time, my husband simply told the caller that they had the wrong Jonathan, since our Jonathan lived in Massachusetts.

I thought these two incidents were strangely related and spent a few days doing some of my own investigative work using the telephone and Internet. I decided to see if Jonathan had a credit report. He did, but I couldn't get it since I was not able to answer the security questions because they were based on the "other" Jonathan. With the information I was able to get from some helpful financial institutions and reverse look-up on the Internet, I was eventually able to answer the security questions and see Jonathan's credit report. First of all, I was wrong. He has had a credit report for years built on his own checking and saving accounts and some other accounts. However, he did not have the dozens of fraudulent accounts that were established, beginning in 2006, by the "other" Jonathan. The "other" Jonathan, using our son's birth date and social security number, had numerous credit cards, a car loan, satellite dish, and mobile phones, to name just a few of the accounts that he established. During a weekend, I was able to find his phone number, address, and apartment number in the mid-western city where he was living. Now, what was I going to do?

Eventually, I knew I was going to have to clear up Jonathan's credit, which now also included some issues with collection companies that were more regularly calling our home and the whole issue with Social Security. But, I was angry and worried. Who was this other guy?

I called the local office of the Secret Service. The Secret Service returned my call immediately and transferred the information to their office in the city where the activity was originating. The agent, Jack Leskovar, collected all the information I had and began his own investigation. He was committed to finding out who had perpetrated this crime. Some days, it looked like the "other" Jonathan was going to get away. But, Jack persevered, an arrest was made, and the individual was indicted on seven federal counts and is awaiting trail. Under other aliases he had previously used, he was also wanted in other states.

The question remained. How did this thief obtain Jonathan's information and why was he targeted? This is the most important part. Jonathan was targeted because he has a cognitive disability. This criminal had learned in prison that if you want to successfully commit identity theft, pick a person with a disability or someone with a chronic illness because they are most likely not to have a job or a work history. How am I so sure? The criminal told the Secret Service agent that that's why he chose Jonathan.

But, the how? I was scammed. During the summer of 2006, a young man posing as a freelance reporter for the British Broadcasting Corporation contacted a state Down syndrome organization and asked to be put in contact with the family of a young adult. He wanted to do a story on inclusion in the United States. I have talked with many reporters during my career, so I readily agreed to meet with him. He was bright, charming, and personable, and during the course of the interview, I told him where Jonathan was born and his approximate date of birth. That was all he needed. With $25 and a visit to vital records in the city of our son's birth, he got a birth certificate. With the birth certificate, he got a replacement social security card. With both, he got employment, loans, credit cards, and a life as "Jonathan." I was simply scammed by a con artist.

*Katie's story is different and this is how her mother tells it: We had an incident with Katie's debit/credit card a couple of years ago where somebody got their hands on the number and actually cleaned out her checking account. I felt so violated for Kate. Now I feel like I am always looking over my shoulder in certain situations.*

PREVENTING IDENTITY THEFT

There are steps we can take for ourselves and for our children to prevent a thief from stealing their identity. Some of them are:

- Register all land, cell, and fax telephone numbers with state and federal "Do Not Call Lists."
- Reduce unsolicited junk mail, especially credit card solicitations by returning each solicitation, using the postage-paid business reply envelope and attaching a label (you can make a sheet of them at a time by buying mailing labels and using the mailing label function in your word processing program) that contains this statement: Remove my name from this mailing list. I forbid the use or sale of my name on any mailing list whatsoever.
- Teach your child not to give any personal information out over the phone or the Internet or to anybody, unless she knows who she is talking to or is accompanied by another responsible person. If a social security number is required for a transaction, request that only the last four digits be used or revealed. Ask whether a random number can be assigned.
- Order your free credit reports annually form the three national credit reporting bureaus by visiting: www.annualcreditreport.com. You must use this site and spell it correctly. Otherwise, you may be directed to a site where you will be charged for the reports.
- Be wary of everyone. Resist the temptation to be open and forthright with strangers—even reporters. Instead of telling someone where or when you or your child was born, you can say in the 1980s and provide a general region such as the southwest.
- Never share ATM pin numbers or security codes. If your child cannot remember banking pin numbers or security codes, have him use the services of a teller instead. He might even prefer the social interaction.
- Shred all identifying documents.
- Change the locks of your child's home regularly, especially after staff leaves employment.
- Do not give out bank account numbers or your mother's maiden name.
- Make sure your child's phone numbers are unlisted. That way you and your child can control who calls.
- Make sure your child keeps all credit card and ATM receipts so they can be matched against monthly statements. Follow up on any unusual activity immediately.
- Review wage reports by Social Security carefully and report any errors.
- Use direct deposit or other electronic deposits for wages, social security benefits, food stamps, etc. This decreases the possibility of mail theft and the misplacement of the documents.

If you believe it is important for your child to learn and practice some or all of these steps, you might want to include them as IEP goals if your child is still in school, or as adult service goals, if he is out of school.

# CHAPTER 12

# It's a Brand New World

*There are new roles and new opportunities for parents as their child with Down syndrome makes the transition to adulthood. Families may need to look again at their advocacy roles and develop new roles for siblings as well. Some of the same emotions that we experienced when our children with Down syndrome were born may return as we mourn what might have been. In this chapter, you will hear from other families and self-advocates as they discuss these new challenges.*

## The Family as Caregiver

You may be surprised to learn that families are the largest group of caregivers of residential services for adults with Down syndrome and related intellectual disabilities in both the United States and the world. While many of us operate with the understanding that children grow up and move out of the family home, it is simply not the case with most people with intellectual disabilities. In spite of all the residential options that exist, most adults live with their families.

There are many reasons for this. Practically speaking, there can be long waiting lists of individuals who have requested residential services. The waitlists can vary from years to decades, depending on where you live. Since residential supports can be very costly and taxpayers are not excited about paying more in taxes, you can understand the waiting list. Some families simply give up and adapt to having their adult son or daughter with Down syndrome live with them.

Many families *choose* to have their adult child remain with them. Not too many years ago, it was typical for several generations of a family to live together, even in the United States. Our children make great family members. It works very well for many families for their child with Down syndrome to live with them.

*Amy enjoyed an inclusive education, studying Shakespeare, singing in the chorus, and acting in many plays. Her family had big expectations for her and even had an "in-law" apartment in their home so that she could live more independently in the future. Recently, her father gently suggested that she try living in the apartment. She thought about it and asked, "What are you trying to do—get rid of me?" Her father told her he just wanted her to have more independence. Amy quickly responded, "Don't you use that 'I' word with me." Amy has a vision and because she is comfortable expressing her preferences (formally called self-determination), she was able to explain that "I am not interested in independence. I much prefer being pampered at home."*

Sometimes, after one parent dies, the child with Down syndrome can be company for the remaining parent. In the case of illness, the child may even help with the cooking and housekeeping chores.

## When You Have an Only Child

I have written this book and this chapter for families, not for parents, in the recognition that families are all different. There are large families, single parent families, single child families, and families with two moms or dads, as well as children with Down syndrome who are being raised by grandparents, siblings, or other family members or even family friends. Each family, in celebrating its uniqueness, is special. However, when a family only has a child with Down syndrome, they often feel very different. They have only had the opportunity to see the world through this unique prism. They do not have the option to consider the roles of other children in planning for the future. Families in this situation do, however, have opportunities to consider bringing extended family members and close family friends into the circle of support they create for their child.

# Families as Case Managers

In many ways you have already been acting as a case manager for your child with Down syndrome. You schedule medical appointments and procedures, organize out-of-school activities, file taxes as necessary, and keep benefits current—to name just a few of the many ways you assist your child. Because of the love and commitment you have for your child, you don't see her as a "case," but you provide endless hours of organization to ensure the highest quality of life for her.

In the adult service system, there are people assigned to these roles who are typically called "case managers" or "service coordinators." States vary in their practices, but these individuals are either employees of the state developmental disability agency or private agency employees subcontracted by the state agency. Your child will typically be assigned a case manager who will assist in the coordination of services. Sometimes there may be an additional person in the agency that supports your child who acts as a service coordinator or case manager. Titles may vary.

In reality, case management is actually a shared responsibility. Caseloads are typically high and if you expect that there is a person who will take over all the

responsibilities for your child, you will be disappointed. Working together, collaboratively and in partnership, families and case managers can better ensure opportunities and success for your child.

Developing collaboration is an art. Yearly meetings to develop an annual service plan are usually mandated by the state agency that has responsibility for your daughter. In most cases, this may be the only time you actually meet or speak with your daughter's case manager. It is helpful if you email or call the case manager one or two other times a year to provide medical or other updates. You can accomplish the same thing by including the case manager on the list of individuals to receive health and medical reports. And don't forget to periodically send a holiday greeting or some other "thank you" to acknowledge the work the case manager does for your child.

## Especially for Siblings

As a sibling, you may already be involved in activities relating to the transition to adult life for your brother or sister with Down syndrome. Chances are you are aware of the financial planning decisions your parents have made, and they may have discussed with you what their wishes are for the future care of your sibling. You may have been involved in discussions with their financial and tax advisors and attorney. You may have accompanied your sibling to medical appointments and you may have been a partner in decisions about her employment, day and living situations.

Or you may know nothing at all. If you are aged 18 or older and you have never had a frank discussion with your parents about these issues, now is the time to have one. It is possible that your parents have planned for your sibling's independence without the need to involve you in any way, but it is more likely that your parents envision at least some ongoing role for you in your sibling's life. You need to find out what the arrangements and expectations are now before an emergency or crisis situation arises and you need to step in without any preparation.

# Families as Employers

As explained in Chapter 1, consumer-directed supports give individuals and their families control over a specific sum of money to be used to purchase goods and services to support an adult with disabilities. Families and individuals have lobbied long to have the opportunity to be free from some of the bureaucratic constraints that assigned individuals to programs. As these opportunities become more widespread and more flexible, more individuals and families are participating.

Families who use these funds to hire people to support their child find themselves in a new role—employers. Often with assistance from the state, parents must do everything an employer does—from criminal screening to dealing with payroll issues such as filing taxes, unemployment, and worker's compensation.

Although they provide the most flexibility, consumer-directed supports also give families the most responsibility. Families recruit, train, set wage scales, evaluate, and, when necessary, fire employees. While this may seem a great burden to some families, others enthusiastically support the opportunity to control the process. You may also hire an agency to provide these duties. Since you will have to compensate the agency for its work, that will reduce the amount of money available to purchase supports for your child, however.

Since there is a critical shortage of direct support professionals, some families see consumer-directed supports as an innovative way to address the recruitment, retention, and reimbursement issues that agencies face in trying to maintain a quality workforce. As a family, you only have to provide staffing for your family member.

In recruiting support people, families have the opportunity to tap their vast network of friends, family, and community members as potential staff. You don't have to limit yourself to hiring individuals with previous experience or a college degree, which prevents many agencies from considering some potential staff. You can consider former classmates, teachers, and aides of your child. You can also consider siblings and other family members. You can use traditional recruitment methods such as placing newspaper and Internet ads, or you can use word of mouth.

If you go beyond your own personal network, you will have to acquire some ability to read a resume and some good interviewing techniques. You should decide, in advance, what role your child will play in the process. You may both want to participate in the interviews, taking turns asking questions. It helps to ask the same questions, in the same order, to every applicant. Record the answers to the questions. Typically, you would ask about past jobs and describe some real-life situations and ask the applicant how he or she would handle them. It is very important, from the beginning, to be clear about what the job expectations will be.

There are some questions that are illegal to ask. These include questions about age, religion, sexual orientation, and marital status. Avoid questions that ask for this type of information in a roundabout way, such as "What year did you graduate from high school?" or "How many children do you have?" These appear to be an attempt to get the applicant to answer questions that are illegal. You do want a good match for your child, however, so if the job requires the applicant to take your child to religious activities, you can share that as a job requirement. Someone who is not comfortable will probably decline the offer.

When you are hiring someone to support your child, you can individualize the training. While you may find training in your community that you might want to send staff to, such as classes on first aid and CPR, you will actually be training the staff yourself about the unique and special needs of your daughter. For example, you might provide training on self-talking, which most people with Down syndrome use as a healthy way of working through issues and is not typically seen as a mental health problem. Or you might want to emphasize healthy eating and daily exercise.

You will want to familiarize anyone who is working with your child with the best ways to motivate her and interact with her, the elements of a good learning environment for her, etc. You might also want to establish a clear procedure to ensure that staff will notify you about any problems that come up so that they can be addressed immediately. You don't have a chain of command that staff has to respect, so concerns can be immediately solved.

The biggest challenge that agencies have in maintaining a quality workforce is wages and benefits. As the employer, you can set the salary and determine time-off benefits, as long as you stay within your allocated budget. You should be realistic about your budget and ensure there is enough money to provide salary increases. After you hire staff, you want to make sure that you keep them. Remember that while wages are important, they are not the only reason people stay at a job. It is also essential that staff feel respected and as if they can make positive contributions. Most support people also appreciate flexibility and being part of the decision making.

*Jacob is a valued member of his community. Although he attended a postsecondary program away from home after high school, he and his family knew that the best place for Jake to live and work would be in the community where he was wellknown and had many connections. So, when there was an opening in a nearby group home, they eagerly accepted the placement. Jake found himself living in an unsafe neighborhood, with older men and staff who did not respect his religious customs. Attempts to improve the situation were not successful and after a series of mishaps (including one where the evening staff left before the overnight staff showed up and the overnight staff ultimately never arrived), Jake's family took him home to explore a family-directed model.*

*Using the funds that were previously being used in the group home, they rented a two-bedroom apartment with amenities that Jacob loved, including a tennis court and swimming pool. His family used their social network and found a social worker to be his roommate and to provide the supervision that Jake requires when he is not working. His parents are full partners in this arrangement. They have Jake home some weekends so his roommate can have a break, provide transportation to some of his activities, and fill in when necessary.*

*They worry about the day when they will not be able to find staff or will not be around to provide physical and emotional support, so they have spoken to an agency that assists families in consumer-directed projects. For the time being, they are comfortable in being the case managers. This lets them save the 14 percent an agency would require to provide payroll services, training, and supervision of the caregivers. Instead, the family pays 4 percent of the funds that Jake receives to an agency that acts as a fiscal intermediary and processes the payroll. (Something like this is required in most states, since families are not legally able to receive this disbursement directly.)*

# Family Members as Mentors

In every family there is a shift in authority as children become adults, whether they live in the family home or in their own home. This is something that all families experience, and it continues throughout adulthood. You can probably remember the shift yourself as you became more autonomous from your parents. First your parents made decisions for you, then you shared decision making, then you asked for your parents' advice, and finally you made your own decisions. For most parents and children, this path is long and sometimes bumpy. In decisions about curfews and cocktails, friends and spouses, your parents probably played an important role in your life. They probably still do so if they are still alive. Hopefully, they are a source of advice and guidance and of stability and consistency.

When your child has Down syndrome or a similar disability, the journey can be different because we never actually stop what I call "active parenting." Still, in recognition that our children do become adults, we need to make a shift in our relationship with our children and assist them as mentors. Mentors guide, teach, and lead. Parenting is more instructive and direct. The distinction may be subtle, but it is important.

In many families, parents demand that any adult children living with them abide by their rules. I call it the "this is my house and while you are living in it, you are going to live by my rules" way of exerting control. It may work in some areas of life, such as

getting your child to pick up dirty clothes or not co-habitating under your roof. While this kind of absolute authority may not stifle your "typical" child, it can have devastating effects on the emotional well-being and development of your child with Down syndrome.

Usually our typical children will find their own mentors. Our kids with Down syndrome, however, are unlikely to find mentors, although there will be many people who are paid to be in their lives (like staff) or who volunteer (like Special Olympics coaches). Mentors are different and family members can often fill that void.

As your child becomes an adult, I am suggesting that you create an environment in your home where you are not simply the parent who makes all the rules and your child is the one who obeys them. Instead, your child will benefit from a home environment where she is guided, respected, and brought along to establish her own rules and boundaries. It may be helpful to discuss the idea of mentors with your child, and point out any mentors in your life. You might also point out how you receive and give advice to friends and family members.

In a typical mentoring relationship, mentors need to have time to mentor and are matched for interest and experience. This is an ideal new role for families. They work together on goals for the individual being mentored. Using their own social networks, the mentor helps build relationships, networks, and identify both immediate and long-term needs.

Becoming a mentor does not mean abdicating your responsibility as a parent to keep your child healthy, safe, and a responsible member of her community. If your child lives at home, it is reasonable to have "house rules" such as that it is quiet time from 11 p.m. to 6 a.m. or that you expect your daughter to maintain a job and get adequate sleep time to ensure that she is able to perform her job. Sometimes you will have to be a parent, make rules, and enforce them.

Ideally, other adults with Down syndrome would become mentors to transition-aged students. While some formal mentoring programs have developed that match adults with disabilities to teens with the same disabilities, most of these programs have not focused on individuals with intellectual disabilities. You might, however, be able to facilitate a mentoring relationship between your child and an adult with Down syndrome.

# Family Members as Advocates

When our children were born, we became more than family. As we grappled with our children's health and developmental delays in those early weeks and months, we learned that we had another title: advocate. We became educational advocates, health care advocates, and inclusion advocates, and became committed to protecting our child and ensuring her a full life wherever we were needed. We were in the classroom, the ball field, the gym, the playground, the lunchroom, and in places of worship. We may have been called overinvolved, overprotective, too invested, and unrealistic. We might have been told that we didn't accept our child's limitations and we didn't get the whole picture.

Then came the helicopter parents, and we look pretty good compared to them. These parents of "typical kids" call college professors to complain about their child's grades, human resources departments to find out why their child didn't get the job, and supervisors to object to performance reviews. They also might think they are advocating. They are not. They are not allowing their children to develop into independent adults. Our responsibilities are different. They are essential to our children's successful inclusion into a world that is not fully welcoming.

I have seen suggestions that parents of children with Down syndrome read some of the literature written for families who are sending their kids to college. I don't find this material particularly helpful. It tells parents how to help their children become their own advocate. I think it is important for our children to become their own advocates and to find their own voices, but to supplement the voices of other advocates, not to replace them. We must nurture our child's self-advocacy and self-determination, but we, or our representatives, will be lifelong advocates in partnership with the individual with Down syndrome.

> *Recently we saw "Happy Feet," a delightful animated movie about a penguin, Mumbles, who can dance but not sing like the other penguins. He is ostracized, he has few friends, he is not allowed to go to school with the other penguins, and his father does not accept him. His parents do little but stand by and wring their hands in worry and disgust. After the movie, Jonathan told us, "I am like Mumbles. Except I always had your support." Unlike the penguin, we have been Jon's advocates, ensuring his acceptance by our schools and by our community.*

**LIFETIME ADVOCACY SERVICES**

Some organizations provide lifetime advocacy services for individuals with Down syndrome and related disabilities. These services provide the kind of oversight that families do, when families are not available or no longer able to do so. There are many circumstances when contracting for this kind of service may be important—when parents die or live too far away to provide the oversight needed. In other cases, families who are quite healthy and active benefit from the additional support that an advocate can bring to discussions and negotiations with service providers.

Generally, these organizations provide trained and supervised advocates. Some lawyers who specialize in serving people with disabilities are hiring social workers and adding this as an additional service to their clients. These advocacy services are also available through some local Arcs or independent agencies. The advocacy services differ from agency, so be careful that you get the services you need.

If you are going to use advocacy services while you are still alive, you should interview the person who will be the advocate to make sure you are both on the same page. You will also want to make sure that you leave detailed instructions for future advocates.

# The Family's Role in Ensuring Quality

One of the most important tasks you will have as a family member or as a professional guiding families is deciding on the "right" services or supports for your child. Hopefully, you live in an enlightened state where families and individuals with Down syndrome get to decide where and from whom they will receive adult supports. It is not usually like a school district, where the location of your home determines what school you attend.

Whether you are choosing a postsecondary program, residential supports, or a place for your child to spend her day, there are many ways to get information so you can make a good decision. Remember, whatever decision you make, you can always change it if circumstances or needs change.

Some of the elements that make up a quality life are:

- adequate resources—enough money to have what you need, and, occasionally, what you want;
- physical health;
- emotional health;
- positive relationships, including some with people who are not family members or paid to be with you;
- the opportunity to do what you want, when you want, and with individuals of your choosing;
- the opportunity to grow and learn new things;
- the freedom to make your own decisions;
- participating in social activities in your community;
- access to transportation.

Peter Lynch, perhaps among the most successful stock pickers of our time (and the brother of a person with an intellectual disability), often picked stocks by "looking around." He would notice what people were buying when he went to the mall or notice the latest trends his children were excited about. He said, "If you spend more than thirteen minutes analyzing economic and market forecasts, you've wasted ten minutes." I am not suggesting that you only spend ten minutes in picking the "right" program for your child, but I am suggesting that you take a somewhat relaxed approach to transition planning.

# More Perspectives on Quality

Families have different definitions of quality. Over the past couple of years, I have often asked families with transition-aged children a simple question, "What does quality look like for you?" If you don't know what it is, you certainly won't know it if you see it. What is remarkable is how varied the responses are. Each of us will have a different measurement. Here are their responses:

- Collaboration between individual, provider, family, and government
- Individuals are engaged in their programs
- Successful and positive outcomes
- Professional and informed staff
- Inclusive setting
- More money
- Smiles
- Happiness
- An agency that values families
- Emotional well being is a priority
- Quality is being tuned into who my son is and what he needs
- Competence
- Follow through
- I look for staff who are happy and like what they do
- Consumer centered
- Individuals feel competent and satisfied
- Loving and caring providers
- Appropriate friends
- Continuity
- Qualified and caring staff
- Total acceptance
- Safety
- Structure
- Setting that promotes positive self-esteem and self-worth
- Music and movement
- My daughter enjoys attending
- Flexibility
- Staff who are responsive to my son's needs
- Clear, plain talk
- Progression of exploration of new experiences
- Successful employment
- Meaningful activities
- Trust
- Making continued progress towards independence
- Supported job opportunities

Quality really is different for different people. Your measures of quality may be different and will most likely change over time. That is a good thing. Because as your child grows and matures, so will you, and your measures of quality will as well.

Below are Peter Lynch's eight fundamental principles to his stock selection process. In parenthesis, I have put some changes that make them relevant to picking programs or supports:

1. Know what you (want) *own.*
2. It's futile to predict the future and (what your child may need) *and interest rates.*
3. You have plenty of time to identify and recognize exceptional (agencies) *companies.*
4. Avoid long shots.
5. Good management is very important.
6. Be flexible and humble. And learn from mistakes.
7. Before you make a (decision) *purchase,* you should be able to explain why you're (picking it) *buying.*
8. There is always something to worry about.

The important concept to remember from Peter Lynch's list is that you already know the principles of picking quality services and supports. You have been doing it for years. You have chosen excellent schools, qualified doctors, and good recreational programs. You also knew when those same doctors, schools, or programs let your child down and you moved on. You will get to that same point with selecting new physicians, programs, and supports with and for your adult child.

There are some things you might want to pay particular attention to when choosing adult services and providers. Here is my own list of things to consider:

1. Are there bathrooms that are designated "Staff Only"? That tells me that the staff bathrooms are probably cleaner than the ones used by our children. All the bathrooms should be of the same quality and cleanliness and there should not be a special designation for any group of people. It reminds me of segregation.
2. Now this might seem pretty insignificant, but I like to observe lunch room behaviors and candy dish etiquette. Generally, people in different groups eat together. It happens in high school and it will happen in adult programs. Staff members eat together and the people they support eat in other areas. But, are the separations voluntary or forced? What happens if an adult with Down syndrome wants to eat with the people who provide her with support? Now, for the candy dish. If a staff person keeps a filled candy dish on her desk, who is allowed to take from it? Anyone? Or is it somehow implied that it is only for other staff?

*One day, Dave, one of the young men supported by the Arc I worked for, passed a candy dish that was on a filing cabinet near the human resources office. He asked me if he could take some. I was stunned that he thought he needed permission and then it occurred to me that he had somehow internalized a nonverbal message that the candy was just for staff.*

3. Observe the interactions between staff and the individuals they are paid to serve. Are they respectful and genuine? Would you want to be spoken to in this manner? What are the nonverbal interactions like? In this world where physical contact is frowned upon or forbidden, is there any physical contact that is appropriate and warm? How is feedback given?

4. Interview a direct support professional. The Executive Director, CEO, or whatever hotshot you met is going to be polished and tell you what they think you want to hear. Ask to meet some staff people and ask them what matters most to them. Do they like their jobs? Do they feel supported?

5. Notice if there are any individuals with Down syndrome employed by the agency besides as contract workers in the sheltered workshop. Does the agency ask other companies to employ people with disabilities, but they do not have any in their company? Who is answering the phones, doing the filing, cleaning the offices, washing the vans, or performing yard work? Does the agency "walk the walk," as they say?

6. Would you want to spend the day here or live here? Would you want your other children to be served by this agency?

*One afternoon, a staff person came to me with concerns about a support person who stayed overnight in a community residence operated by the Arc. After hearing the concerns, we both were unsure of whether that staff person should continue to work in that position. We were in a tough position. We really did not have the documentation required to terminate the staff person, yet we felt uncomfortable with him working alone with residents who were not able to speak. He was also in a very difficult-to-fill position—an awake overnight staff person. Finally, I said, "If this were Jonathan, I would not want him to be there, and if the house is not good enough for Jon, then it is not good enough for anyone else's child, either." We terminated him that afternoon and we just had to deal with finding someone to cover his shift.*

# Quality in Group Residential Settings

Community residences or group homes are where several people with disabilities live together and share staff. If you are considering this environment for your son or daughter, make sure that you are comfortable with the agency that operates it, the staff who run it, and the other individuals that your son or daughter will live with. In many cases, families are not given a choice; they are simply offered a program. In some states, you may be given an opportunity to pick from several options, and in other situations you may actually be able to participate in developing a program.

Assuming that you will not be developing your own program, what are some of the things that you should be considering when you are in the market for a residential setting for your daughter? I believe that it is most important to think about the physical environment and the people who will be providing supports to your child.

*Katie lived in a beautiful home that was in a wonderful location. She was the first of four women to move in, and her family was very happy because the home was modern, large, and airy, and Katie had a big room. After the other three women moved in, it became obvious that their needs were much greater than Katie's. They had a lot of behavioral issues and the house could not have pictures on the walls or curtains on the windows. There were lots of rules. The women had to earn the right to cook, and when food was purchased, it was immediately repackaged into single servings. It seemed to Katie's family that there was new staff every three weeks. Katie found it boring and came home every weekend. Finally her family requested a new residence for Katie.*

*There were no options until a woman who lived in a home run by another agency passed away. The agency had a good reputation, but this house was older and worn and had seven other residents. The house had a natural feeling, though, and the staff people were warm and friendly and had been working there for many years. It was a happy and busy house. Katie's family and Katie herself immediately picked up on the differences and what was important to them. She moved into her new house and called her parents before her first weekend and told them, "I am staying here this weekend." She happily baked with staff and she discovered that it was her right, not a privilege. A house does not make a home. People make a home.*

In the end, you need to pick a program or an agency to provide supports to your child that you and your child are comfortable with. There are two areas to consider—the big picture and the little picture.

## THE BIG PICTURE ISSUES

Big picture issues include:

- The agency's mission and values: These ought to be readily accessible and you should be able to understand them.
- The agency's internal monitoring: The agency ought to be able to tell you how they ensure quality.
- State monitoring and oversight: You should be able to find out what state agency oversees the agency and view past reports.
- National Accreditation: There are several national accreditation bodies.
- Family Participation: You want to ask how families are represented in the organization and how they participate in ensuring quality. You might want to ask what percentage of the governing board are family members and in what other ways families are able to influence policy. Are there satisfaction surveys? If so, who reads them and how are they interpreted?

## THE SMALL PICTURE ISSUES

Small picture issues include:

- Hiring practices: Are family members or residents involved in personnel decisions?
- Family visits: Can family members drop by or do they need to call first?

- Family meetings: Are there regular family meetings or any other forum for families to get together and share mutual issues, outside of parties?
- Staffing patterns: Are there enough staff working during the evening and weekend hours to encourage community activities and some individual activities?
- House patterns: Who does the shopping and cooking? Are these opportunities for learning or do staff members do these tasks? Some agencies buy in bulk or use food pantries to save money, but this limits opportunities for adults with Down syndrome to shop. If this is the case, do individuals get to express their food preferences?
- Leisure and community events: How are these opportunities planned? Do the individuals plan them or do staff? How are individual preferences taken into consideration? Since the residents are usually expected to pay for these costs with their own money, are there funds available to pay the admission fees or meals for staff during events outside of the house?

*When the Arc's residential agency was smaller, I used to review the receipts. One receipt really angered me. The group home had gone to a popular ice cream stand for dessert, ant the staff members were requesting reimbursement for their banana splits. I might not have thought this was excessive until I noticed that they purchased single scoop ice cream cones for the residents. Then I began to look at other receipts and noticed that in restaurants, the staff lavished nice meals upon themselves and expected reimbursement, while the residents purchased simple and less costly meals. That led to an agency policy which limits the amounts that can be spent on meals. It was the inequality of it all that concerned me.*

# Communication

It is very important for you to develop and maintain positive communication with everyone who provides services or supports to your child. Whether it is a physician, the direct support professional, or the Executive Director of the agency who has the contract to support your child, having a mutually respectful and productive relationship is essential.

**COMMUNICATION STYLES**

The trouble is that we all have different styles of communication and even preferred modes of communication. I think that most of us fall into one of the following categories:

**Walk Softly But Carry a Big Stick.** This person tends to be respectful and collaborative, but knows when to bring in the big guns—like an attorney. These individuals are also usually very knowledgeable themselves.

**The Squeaky Wheel Gets the Grease.** These people can be very persistent and border on heavy handed. They have usually learned that they have to ask often to get what they need and sometimes have to be demanding.

**You Get More with Sugar Than Spice.** These are the people everyone likes. They are not pushovers; they have just learned that being nice and understanding can have great benefits in the long run.

While there are other styles of communication, you might want to consider adopting one of the styles above, as they tend to be effective. If you have a passive style, are reluctant to initiate communication, or have found that people sometimes walk all over you, you might want to ask a friend or other family member to help you advocate. On the other hand, if you generally assume that everyone else is incompetent or have a habit of yelling at people first and asking questions later, you might want to consider finding someone else to advocate on your child's behalf. These are entirely ineffective ways to communicate!

*When I was in my mid-twenties, just starting out in this field, I met Tommy B and his mother. Tommy was a young man with some very challenging behaviors, including spitting great distances and with great accuracy. Given his behavior, you would think it would have been difficult to find respite care providers for him. His mother, however, practiced the communication style of "you get more with sugar than spice." She was just lovely and appreciative of anyone who came into her home and was willing to work with Tommy. Because she treated staff so respectfully and overlooked their occasional mistakes, people were excited to work with Tommy.*

## COMMUNICATION METHODS

We also all have different ways we like to communicate. These days, most of us usually rely on either the telephone or email. Important communication regarding your child with Down syndrome should always be written (either email or letter) and copies should be kept of all communication.

Face-to-face meetings are often the most effective at moving issues along or making decisions. Since meetings require effort and resources to arrange and to take place, people tend to want to make them productive. However, you need to have the right people in the room. Having a meeting when nobody there is authorized to make a decision is a waste of time.

Whatever style and methods of communication you use, you want to make sure that they are useful—which is not always the same as effective. If you scream at someone, it may be effective, but rarely is it useful. I define "useful" as communication that results in the desired outcome. That means that your child is able to obtain the benefit you set out to achieve.

### A SPECIAL NOTE ABOUT EMAIL

Unless it is absolutely necessary, never send an immediate response to an email that regards your child. If you feel the urge to answer immediately, write the email and then "save" it to read later. (The exception is if an immediate response is medically necessary.) Read your email again before you send it and make sure it conveys your intentions. Remove your emotions from the email. Keep to the facts and remember that your email is now part of a trail you are leaving. It is now public information.

Unlike with a phone call, once you hit that "send" button, you cannot take an email back. You can rarely even clarify a misunderstanding. You have to assume that your email will likely be forwarded to people you might not have chosen to read it. While an email might be marked "confidential," it may not stay that way.

*Technology has made our lives easier, but it has also made our lives run faster. I sometimes wish for the "old days" before email, cell phones, voice messaging, computers, faxes, and personal handheld devices. In the days before these so-called conveniences, we wrote more letters, waited several days for responses, and we had more time to be thoughtful. We would not expect people to get back to us immediately. We enjoyed our time away from work and our vacations. What we have gained in convenience, we have lost in kindnesses. Many family and professional relationships have been unnecessarily strained or damaged by our technology gains. We expect instant responses, instant feedback, and instant solutions. Sometimes, we just need time.*

# A Word about Helicopter Parents

As mentioned earlier in this chapter, the term "helicopter parent" is usually applied disparagingly to a parent who hovers over his or her typically developing older child, perhaps stifling the child's development and successful entry into adulthood.

In my opinion, having a child with Down syndrome calls for a healthy amount of hovering. It is perfectly reasonable for our adult children to have cell phones and for us to expect them to check in with us periodically. Once a day seems reasonable to me. Checking your child's email for any unusual conversations or transactions may even be warranted, if you think this is necessary for her safety. It is also important for you to have a key to your child's house or apartment, but it is just as important for you to know when not to use it. Installing web cams so you can conduct surveillance is probably not warranted, but even so, there may be medical or safety reasons that might require it.

While you are hovering, you need to be able to distinguish between what is truly important and has to be addressed immediately by phone and what you can handle more leisurely, such as by email. You want your child's staff to take you seriously when matters are important, so don't make everything important.

# Volunteers

Chances are that many of you are volunteers for organizations and agencies that support individuals with Down syndrome. Some of you may help in raising funds to sustain those groups. Others of you may be active in the PTO/PTA or other groups at the school your child attends. These are very important roles for you both during your child's transition, and after she has completely transitioned (although I think we are always in some kind of transition). Some of you may have even more time to volunteer once your child leaves school, if she is not living with you or is spending a longer part of her day at work or out of the house. If so, consider dedicating some of your most valuable resources—your time and your money—to your child's future.

Agencies are not naturally innovative, but families are. If you do not like the opportunities you see for your child, you might have to take action. You can change existing agencies by becoming agents for change within the organizations. You might have to gather a group of like-minded families together and begin your own agency. Other families have done it.

You have an opportunity to contribute to the community that sustains your child. Your child is going to have Down syndrome for the rest of her life and she will be depending on service agencies. The overwhelming majority of these agencies are locally governed and not-for-profit agencies that rely on a combination of government contracts and the contributions of corporate and individual donors. These agencies depend on volunteers in many capacities—as board members, program volunteers, quality monitors, and human rights committee members, to name just a few. As importantly, these agencies need individuals who are able to make donations, or connect the agency to donors, to ensure that the gap between what the government funds and what is truly needed is filled.

*There are lots of worthy charities who ask for my money and I wish I could support them all. Jonathan has lots of needs besides Down syndrome and I should be giving to all of them. The truth is, though, that Jon's biggest challenge is not his heart or that he is hard of hearing. His biggest challenge is that he has an intellectual disability caused by Down syndrome. I decided a long time ago that the vast majority of my volunteer time and charitable dollars would go to agencies and organizations that either support him personally or work to support people like him. If we do not do it, who will?*

*Intellectual disabilities is not sexy enough to attract many people with "deep pockets," so each and every one of us has an obligation to do what we can. If you can't give money, you could do lots of other things. You could even plant a garden at a group home.*

# Will There Be an Empty Nest?

The "empty nest" is a condition that is ironically sometimes referred to as a "syndrome." It is the time when children leave the home for college, work, or marriage. The nest is the metaphor for the home, and, like the little bird chicks that grow strong enough to fly by themselves, children, the theory goes, also leave their homes to go on and fly by themselves. For parents who have finished their active childrearing years, there is probably no term more exhilarating or frightening than the "empty nest."

Many parents, especially mothers, experience great loneliness, and sometimes strains on a marriage become more obvious. Without children as a reason to stay together, some marriages fail during this time. Some couples just drift apart. Other individuals and couples find that this is the time they have been waiting for—to be able once again to devote time to themselves and each other. Some women return to careers they long ago abandoned or find new hobbies. Couples rediscover themselves. Some people travel. Some people "downsize" or "right size" their home for convenience or to make their lives easier.

If your child has Down syndrome, you might never know the feeling of the empty nest. In spite of everything we have learned about residential options, most adult children with Down syndrome will live the majority of their lives, if not their entire lives, with their parents. In this case, there will be no "empty nest" syndrome. That may even be the reason why so many adults with Down syndrome live at home. Consciously or unconsciously, many parents, especially single mothers, do not want an "empty nest." There is a nice rhythm to their day that their child with Down syndrome is part of, or they might need the monthly income their child represents. They might not want to be lonely or to have to look at their life with diminished daily responsibilities.

The truth is that even if your child lives in another setting, the "empty nest" is not quite empty In addition to coming home for holidays and other visits, your adult child may always vacation with you, she may not have a spouse or in-laws to enjoy family celebrations with, and you may want or need to continue to coordinate her healthcare needs.

*For the past six years, Jon has lived in his own home about 80 miles away. It is his permanent home. We still have his bedroom set up for him, however, with the only change being a full-size bed instead of his old twin bed. His closet is still filled with clothes.*

# The Sandwich Generation

I have often read about the "sandwich generation," as I am sure you have. The term refers to parents who find themselves taking care of aging parents while they still have the responsibilities of raising their own children. To be truthful, until recently, I just read the articles and moved on.

I felt very lucky. My parents, now 82 and 86, were vibrant and relatively healthy and living a stress-free life that included many friends, golf, and bridge. They divided their year between Florida and Massachusetts. I spoke to them daily and visited often. Although my father has survived open heart surgery, he still found time to work a few hours a day. I barely took note of his forgetfulness and I was not convinced when he began taking Aricept last summer for the beginning of Alzheimer's disease.

Recently, my mother had a TIA or "mini-stroke." Two months later, she fell and broke her shoulder. While I was at the Special Olympics Winter Games, my father called me from her hospital room and told me they were confused and didn't know what to do. I flew to Florida to arrange home care and therapies and speak to my mother's doctors. I left confident that my parents were being well cared for. A week later, some additional medical concerns developed and I arranged for my parents to come home and see local doctors. I had home care and nursing services started and made home modifications for them. Hospitalization, surgery, and a transfer to a nursing home for my mother to receive rehab followed.

At each hospital and doctor visit, I was asked if I had siblings who could share some of the growing challenges. But although I have a brother who lives out of town, this has become my singular responsibility.

I did not feel like the inside of a sandwich. I was beginning to feel like a passenger on a runaway train. I also felt honored. I have been able to witness the devotion of my father to my mother and it is more beautiful than any "young love." His genuine acts of affection have left me speechless, like when he went, one more time, after ten one evening, to kiss her good night at the hospital. It is a gift to have your parents with you for as long as I have had them in my life, and these new responsibilities are a reminder that nothing good comes without great effort.

As I look ahead, I have begun to realize that we are more than the "sandwich generation." We are "super-sized." As we begin to care for our aging parents, we will probably never be able to end our constant care giving for or oversight of our children with disabilities, no matter how old they become. Even though my son lives 80 miles away from me, I still feel like his case manager in many respects. We are forever parents—not in the poetic sense, but in the active sense.

*Last week, I was having dinner with my parents in the dining room of the independent living community where they live. Next to us was a couple I recognized. Peg and Dick, both 80, were also residents and they were also dining with their visiting daughter, Cheryl, 58, who has Down syndrome and lives independently in a nearby town. In that moment, I saw both my lives—my caregiver responsibilities to my parents and to my son. I wondered if my parents saw what I saw when I introduced them to the family next to us. Because I saw a glimpse into my future.*

# Letting Go

Most of us have been preparing our children for independence since they were small. We let them go to school and participate on sports teams and clubs, and left them in the care of others. We have encouraged independent decision making, brushed off small injuries, let them cross the street.

They will make mistakes, they should take risks, and we will learn to let go. Here is what my son Jon has to say about letting go:

*I want to tell you my side because she is not so good sometimes at letting go.*
*She thinks she is.*
*But, she could be doing a better job.*
*I try to tell her that she needs to let go.*
*I understand.*
*She can't help it.*
*I tell her it is in her genes.*
*She got the mother gene.*
*I have the Down syndrome gene.*
*Let me tell you a few things before she takes over.*
*She thinks she needs to call me every day. She doesn't.*
*She wants me to call her when I get back to my house after I am out.*
*I don't.*
*She thinks I should bring my cell phone when I am just going to a friend's.*
*Sometimes I do. Sometimes I don't.*
*She thinks I should not take the shortcut to the supermarket.*
*She thinks I walk the long way.*
*She thinks I should take a cab when it rains.*
*I do not melt.*
*She thinks she should be able to visit me more often.*
*I tell her if I have other plans.*
*She goes shopping with just my sister. I understand. It's a mother/daughter thing.*
*She has a hard time understanding I like to watch football with just my dad.*
> *It is a guy thing.*
*Sometimes I think my mother wants to know where I am every second of the day.*
*Does her mother know where she is every second of the day?*
*I don't think so—do you?*
*My mother tries very hard to teach me about making good decisions around*
> *food and alcohol. Sometimes, I have to learn things for myself.*
*I like to eat but, I know it is bad for my heart and for looking my best. My 10ᵗʰ*
> *high school reunion is next year and I want to show them that I am still in*
> *shape. So, I work out several times a week. And try to eat right.*
*I love beer and I limit it to one a week or special occasions. If I have beer in the*
> *house, sometimes I have to hide it because it is too tempting.*
*I told my mother recently.*
*When I was little and I fell down.*
*She was there to pick me up.*
*Now, I am an adult and I live farther away.*
*If I fall down, I have to pick myself up.*
*I am not her little boy anymore.*
*She's getting used to it.*

# Some Final Words of Advice

Finally, I have some advice to dispense to you. Like the hit song several graduation seasons ago, I'll start off by telling you to use sunscreen because it is the only advice that has been scientifically proven. The rest is based on my observations over the past twenty years of being both a parent and someone who is responsible for providing services to individuals with developmental disabilities.

*1. Teach your children how to use a bathroom.* This might seem really obvious, but good bathroom skills are essential. A lot of our children get "lost" in their thoughts and in their "self-talk" in the bathroom. This might be okay in the family home if nobody is waiting to use the facilities or if your child has her own bathroom. It might have even been overlooked as a problem in school. In the adult world, whether at a competitive job, day program, or in a residential setting, there are lots of people who have to use the bathrooms. I know the problem. My office used to back up to the bathroom and I could often hear singing and talking and sometimes even water play. Those are not valued habits in the real world.

*2. Resist the temptation to assist your child in the bathroom at an age when she should be doing it herself.* I know this advice is really important because I almost learned it too late. I wanted my son to be so clean that I supervised and participated in his bathroom rituals longer than needed. Invest in moist tissue wipes, make picture schedules, consult an occupational therapist for accommodations that might work instead.

*3. Make sure your child knows how to shower—ALONE. It is not a group activity.* Family showers can be fun and we certainly had our share of them, but for adults, it really is an activity that needs to be done alone, with rare exceptions that are beyond the scope of this book.

*4. Make sure your child knows that showering is a DAILY activity. It's also a rule. Make no exceptions to this rule. If in doubt, shower twice a day.* This is really important because our children will be spending their days among other people—people they work with, hang out with, or live with. Good hygiene is essential in the workplace and in friendship circles. If you are worried that water is a scarce resource, reduce it in other ways, such as by getting a low water use toilet, shower, or washing machine.

*5. Wearing clean clothes is essential. Changing them every day is important.* I know this makes more laundry, but having our children look good doesn't end with childhood. Teaching them that they should wear clean clothes every day takes the guesswork out of deciding whether the clothes are dirty.

*6. Teach your child to do her laundry. Show her stains on clothing so she knows what to look for and teach her not to wear clothes with stains.* You may already be familiar with someone who does not recognize stains. I remember when my grandmother did not seem to notice stains on her clothes, and even my fashion conscious mother, who is now in her 80s, is having the same problem. For them it is about eyesight, but

I see the same problem with my son. For him, it is just a matter of indifference. On a regular basis, I help him check his clothes and discard those with permanent stains. If I am buying him a shirt, I skip over the white shirts and buy one with a little color that is less likely to show every stain.

**7. While I am on the subject of clothes, if there is a choice, buy the next larger size.** If someone hasn't told you this yet, let me be the first: people do not look good in clothes that are too tight. I know what you are thinking—she is certainly loaded with opinions about clothes. I know that clothes do not "make the man," but they really help shape (no pun intended) public opinions. Fact: too many of our children are obese. If you have not been successful in modeling healthy eating and a healthy lifestyle, you need to be especially mindful of clothes. Although lately there seems to be more public acceptance of large people wearing very tight clothes, it is not an attractive look for our children—whether they are kids or adults. Allow for shrinkage when buying new clothes. While I am still on the subject of clothes, try to help your child balance individual preferences and good taste. If your child likes dark tee shirts with wrestling logos, you might want to suggest that she wear them at home or out in the community and wear more appropriate clothes to work. Consider yourself lucky and your work easier if there is a dress code or uniform at your child's workplace.

**8. Food is fuel. The wrong types slow you down and the right types give you energy.** This should be apparent, but, in a country with obesity rates as high as ours, it needs to be reiterated time and time again. Food is not love and food does not have to be the centerpiece of celebrations. Our children were born with the odds stacked against them in many ways. Obesity is one that can be avoided, and making sure that you and your child have a healthy relationship with food is important. We spend our lives trying to make our children as independent as possible, but the health problems associated with obesity—heart disease, diabetes, and stroke, to name just a few—will diminish and perhaps eliminate their independence.

**9. Do not let anyone tell you that your child cannot learn to read, or read better, or learn more than she does today. Learning never ends.** The concept of lifelong learning should apply to everyone, including individuals with Down syndrome and related disabilities. Learning takes many forms. It can be learning a new sport or a new card game. It can be learning to use a cell phone to send a text message or learning to use the computer to follow the weather.

**10. Respect. We all want it. Many of us want our children to receive it, but, truth be told, you and your child must be willing to give it. Then it will come.** Respect all the people in your child's life; respect is one of those concepts that just contributes to a better world. It starts in families with all members respecting each other, and then it builds outwards. It includes the people who teach your children, the bureaucrats who make the seemingly ridiculous rules, and the people who clean up after your child. It does not mean that you cannot question those people when their rules or strategies do not enhance your goals. It means that you need to respect the differences, hold steady to your beliefs, and compromise when needed.

*11. Make sure your child knows he needs to do what the boss tells him, whoever the boss may be.* Stated another way—the boss is the boss is the boss. This is a situation where our children may be confused. You may have taught your daughter that she is the boss of herself, and in almost all cases that is true. You have also probably taught her that there are some people who override that rule—firefighters, police officers, and, hopefully, teachers. If you have not added "bosses" to that list, do that right away. Your child will never be successful in the workplace if she doesn't get this rule.

*12. Remember daytime is for being awake and nighttime is for sleeping.* It is a good habit for almost everyone, with the exception of third shift workers, to sleep at night and be awake during the day. While this seems simple, if a reasonable bedtime routine is not practiced, it is hard to stay awake during the day. We have all stayed up too late and then suffered through the next day. We might have even called in sick. This luxury is rarely accorded to people with Down syndrome, who are always expected to go to work or attend whatever day activity they participate in, but that is a topic for another book. Also remember that our children generally need more rest than others. If they are indeed regularly falling asleep during the day and they spend 8 to 10 hours a night in bed, consider testing for sleep apnea. People with Down syndrome are at a much greater risk for sleep apnea. The only way to diagnose and prescribe treatment is by conducting a sleep study.

*13. Adults work. Many teenagers work, too. Your child should work. Somewhere.* The operative word here is "should." Our children are all different, and, while the goal should be work, some of our children may not actually achieve that goal because of the lack of resources or the choice to engage in activities besides work. It should still be recognized that work is the fabric of our economic society and it brings purpose and meaning to most of us.

*14. SSI guarantees a monthly income. It does not guarantee self-respect.* Government cash benefits are designed to meet the needs of the poor. Since disability often interferes with the ability to work, our children are often poor and as such qualify to receive cash from the government. Poverty is not a state that should be celebrated for anyone. Even if working reduces your daughter's monthly government benefit, the amount of money available to her is always greater when there are earned wages. Want to see joy? Watch a person with Down syndrome get a paycheck.

*15. Don't blame someone else for mistakes. You set a bad example. Mistakes are inevitable. Learn from them and move on.* As family members and professionals, we always seem to play "the blame game." Somebody did something to somebody. Somebody said something to somebody. Somebody did not do something. It is partially cultural and it partially comes with the territory of being family. We cannot fix the disability and we sometimes cannot get what we want. We all make mistakes. I have made them and so have you. Hopefully, we learn from them. One of the most important things we can do is to recognize our mistakes, acknowledge them, right any wrongs we made, and move on. Make sure your children see your mistakes, how you correct them, and how you continue to move forward. Our children will make mistakes, and they need to see examples of humility. Let them see it with you.

**16. *Don't expect siblings to be the parents.*** Brothers and sisters want information—lots of information. That is not the same thing as wanting responsibility. Responsibility is a choice. The cornerstone of what we want for our children with Down syndrome is that they are valued and have choices. Those same principles need to be applied to all our children. You may *want* your other child or children to have a relationship that you direct with their sibling with Down syndrome, but you cannot really control their relationship. We are all different and we all have different types of relationships with our siblings, and so will our children with Down syndrome.

**17. *Hit the ground listening.*** Now that you have read the book, you might want to "hit the ground running." Control the urge and instead think of "hitting the ground listening." There are lots of people in your daily life who can help you and be there for you as you help your child make the transition to adulthood. If we all listen more, we might all learn more.

*Finally, if you don't teach your child to cross the street, she will never know what's on the other side.*
*Neither will you.*

# CHAPTER 13

## Footprints for the future

*Now that you have an idea of what life can look like for your adult child with Down syndrome, it is critical to convey that vision in a personal planning document. Unlike footprints we leave in the sand, which get washed away with the tide, we must leave special footprints so others can follow where we have been.*

*A specially designed form that can be downloaded from the Internet can be used to record your plan. Once downloaded, it can be saved as a Word document. This will enable you to easily make changes to the document in the future, and, more importantly, to share it with those who provide support to your child with Down syndrome or related disability.*

I have learned that parents never really stop worrying about their children. Certainly, cultural differences and behavioral traits affect the extent of the worrying, but ask any adult child, and he will share with you some examples of worrying from his family. I must call my parents, who are well into their eighties, to report on every landing of every plane that I or my children board—regardless of the time of the arrival. I used to think that this kind of monitoring is somewhat ridiculous, but the apple must not fall far from the tree, as I worry about my adult children, too.

The kind of worrying I do about Jonathan has a different quality. I used to worry about everything a typical parent worries about, but I also worried about everything I know about Jon that other people might not know. Sure, current people in his life knew the important information, but what if I were not around to convey other essential details? How would people in the future know what was important to Jon if he could not adequately share the information?

Here are just a few of the things that I worried about:

- Jon's implantable defibrillator needs daily and monthly monitoring.
- Jon doesn't tell people if his hearing aid is broken. He will just keep changing the battery in an attempt to get it working again.

- Jon is afraid of the dark and sleeps with lots of lights and the TV on (without volume), and I don't want someone telling him to turn them off to save electricity.
- Jon has to have flashlights in every room in case of a power failure.
- Jon chews his fingers sometimes and he often chews a plastic straw instead. I don't want anyone trying to change this behavior. He knows what situations this is appropriate in and when the straw needs to be put away.
- Jon drinks an excessive amount of diet soda and we don't care. The effects of artificial sweetener are not clear; the effects of obesity are.
- Most of all, Jon's opinions need to be valued.

(If you get a piece of paper, I'm sure you can write down at least one or two things that only you know about your child. Add to it when you think of more.)

While my husband and I could not control future decisions made on Jon's behalf after we were no long around, I wanted some way to present important information to future support people in Jon's life.

My worries kept me up at night. I jotted down all my concerns and soon I had lots of pieces of paper filled with important facts about Jon. When the papers got out of control, I turned them into lists. Finally, I knew I had to organize them.

I was aware of the concept of a "Letter of Intent" or "Special Letter of Intent." It is a document that conveys important personal, medical, and educational information about an individual. It goes far beyond the kind of information contained in a will. Although a Letter of Intent is a nonbinding document, courts do consider its contents. I found many forms for Letters of Intent from many places—lawyers, financial planners, organizations, and government agencies. Many of these are very useful, and if you are already using one that provides a place to convey all the information you want, then continue to use it.

I was not completely satisfied with the forms I found, however. I wanted something simple to use and simple to change and update. I also wanted it to be free for families. It became a project of The Arc of East Middlesex, Inc., and we developed what became *Footprints for the Future*. It is a lengthy, fill-in-the-blank document. The form can be downloaded free of charge in either English or Spanish at: www.theemarc.org (click on "Resources").

You may want to fill out the form yourself, or you can grab a group of other families and make it fun by filling out your forms together. Be sure to update the form whenever there are important changes of information.

# References and Suggested Reading

**INTRODUCTION**

Glidden, L. M., & Jobe, B. M. (2007). Measuring parental daily rewards and worries in the transition to adulthood. *American Journal on Mental Retardation, 112*(4), 275-88.

Kraemer, B. R., McIntyre, L. L., & Blacher, J. (2003). Quality of life for young adults with mental retardation during transition. *Mental Retardation, 41*(4), 250-62.

**CHAPTER 1**

American Association on Intellectual and Developmental Disabilities. (2009). *Fact sheet: Person-centered planning*. (Available from www.aamr.org/content_191.cfm)

The Arc of Massachusetts. (n.d.). *Tools for Tomorrow: Pocket Guide*. Waltham, MA: Author.

Employment and Disability Institute. (2008). *The person-centered planning education site*. ILR School, Cornell University (Available from www.ilr.cornell.edu/edi/pcp/course01.html)

Falvey, Mary, Forest, Marsha, Pearpoint, Jack, and Rosenberg, Richard. *All My Life's a Circle: Using the Tools: Circles, MAPS, and PATHS*. Toronto, Ontario: Inclusion Press, 1997.

Families Organizing for Change. (1995). *Building a Home Conference*. Raynham, MA: Massachusetts Families Organizing for Change.

Forest, Marsha and Lusthaus, Evelyn. (1990). Everyone belongs with MAPS action planning system. *Teaching Exceptional Children, 22,* 32-35.

Mount, Beth. *Person-Centered Planning: Finding Directions for Change Using Personal Futures Planning*. Armenia, NY: Capacity Works, 1990.

Pearpoint, Jack, O'Brien, John, & Forest, Marsha. *PATH: A Workbook for Planning Positive Possible Futures and Planning Alternative Tomorrows with Hope for Schools, Organizations, Businesses, and Families*. 2nd ed. Toronto, Ontario: Inclusion Press, 1993.

Smull, Michael. *Listen, Learn, Act: Selected Writings by Michael W. Smull on Essential Lifestyle Planning, Self-Determination, and Organizational Change.* Annapolis, MD: Support Development Associates, 2000. (Available from http://learningcommunity.us/documents/listenlearnact.pdf)

Stancliffe, R. J., Lakin, K. C., Doljanac, R., Byun, S.-Y., Taub, S., & Chiri, G. (2007). Loneliness and living arrangements. *Intellectual and Developmental Disabilities, 45*(6), 380-90.

**CHAPTER 2**

Anderson, W., Chitwood, S., Hayden, D., and Takemoto, C. *Negotiating the Special Education Maze: A Guide for Parents & Teachers.* 4th ed. Bethesda, MD: Woodbine House, 2008.

The Arc of the United States. (1994). *Child care settings and the Americans with Disabilities Act.* Silver Spring, MD: Author.

The Arc of the United States. (2006). *The Individuals with Disabilities Education Act (IDEA): Eligibility, IEPs and placement.* Silver Spring, MD: Author.

The Arc of the United States. (2006). *The Individuals with Disabilities Education Act (IDEA) procedural safeguards and due process.* Silver Spring, MD: Author.

Couwenhoven, Terri. (2007). *Teaching Children with Down Syndrome about Their Bodies, Boundaries, and Sexuality: A Guide for Parents and Professionals.* Bethesda, MD: Woodbine House.

The Individuals with Disabilities Act (IDEA) H.R. 1350 (2004). *Section 602: Definitions.* (Available from http://idea.ed.gov/explore/view/p/,root,statute,I,A,602,)

Jewish Family Children's Service. (2006). *Family Education Workbook: A Step-by-Step Guide for Families of People with Disabilities.* Waltham, MA: Author.

Stinson, P. (1997). *Extended school year services for special children.* Philadelphia: Special Child, The Resource Foundation for Children with Challenges, and Stinson Law Associates, P.C. (Available from www.specialchild.com/archives/lf-003.html)

U. S. Department of Education, Office of Special Education Programs. (2004). *Secondary transition. Individuals with Disabilities Education Act (IDEA).* Available from http://IDEA.ed.gov)

U. S. Department of Education, Office of Special Education Programs. (n.d.). *Individualized Education Program (IEP) team meetings and changes to the IEP.* IDEA - Reauthorized Statute.

U. S. Department of Education, Office of Special Education Programs. (2006). *Procedural safeguards: Mediation.* (Available from http://IDEA.ed.gov)

U. S. Department of Education, Office of Special Education Programs. (2006). *Procedural safeguards: Resolution meetings and due process hearings.* (Available from http://IDEA.ed.gov)

U. S. Department of Education, Office of Special Education Programs. (2006). *State complaint procedures.* (Available from http://IDEA.ed.gov)

U.S. Department of Education. (n.d.). *Building the legacy: IDEA 2004.* (Available from http://idea.ed.gov)

University of Minnesota. National Center on Secondary Education and Transition. (2004). *Key provisions on transition: IDEA 1997 compared to H.R. 1350 (IDEA 2004).* (Available from http://ncset.org/publications/related/ideatransition.asp)

Zuckerbrod, N. (2007). *AP: NCLB and students with disabilities.* The Arc of the United States.

**CHAPTER 3**

Hart, D., Grigal, M., Sax, C., Martinez, D., & Will, M. (2006). Postsecondary education options for students with intellectual disabilities. *Research to Practice, 45*.
(Available from www.communityinclusion.org/article.php?article_id=178)

Heath Resource Center. (1991). *Young adults with learning disabilities and other special needs.* Washington, DC: American Council on Education. (Available from www.heath.gwu.edu)

Katovich, Diana M. *The Power to Spring Up: Postsecondary Education Opportunities for Students with Significant Disabilities.* Bethesda, MD: Woodbine House, 2009.

Kaufman, L. (2006, November 5). A dream not denied: "Just a normal girl." *The New York Times*, p.24(L).

LaConte, J. (2008, February 15). Tierney, NSCC president help take on autism. *The Salem News Online.*
(Available from www.salemnews.com/punews/local_story_046065356.html/resources_printstory)

Leuchovius, D. (1994). *ADA Q & A: Section 504 & postsecondary education.* Bloomington, MN: PACER Center. (Available from www.pacer.org/pride/504.htm)

Richards, L. & M. (2003, Fall). *An overview of 504.* Austin, TX: Author.

Schworm, P. (2007, December 10). Campuses widen the mainstream: Program welcomes some with cognitive disabilities. *The Boston Globe,* pp. B1, B8.

Tyre, P. (2006, April 13). Another barrier broken: For intellectually disabled kids, college has finally become an option. *Newsweek.* (Available from www.newsweek.com/id/46537)

U. S. Department of Education, Office for Civil Rights. (2007, March). *Students with disabilities preparing for postsecondary education: Know your rights and responsibilities.* Washington, DC: Author.
(Available from www.ed.gov/print/about/offices/list/ocr/transition.html)

U.S. Department of Education, Office for Civil Rights. Auxiliary aids and services for postsecondary students with disabilities. (1998). (Available from www.ed.gov/about/offices/list/ocr/docs/auxaids.html)

**CHAPTER 4**

American Association for Individuals with Developmental Disabilities. (2008). SIS and transition planning for students with intellectual disability. (Available from http://www.siswebsite.org/cs/transition).

Benson, E. (2003, February). Intelligent intelligence testing. *APA Monitor on Psychology, 34*(2). (Available from www.apa.org/monitor/feb03/intelligent.html)

Biasini, F. J., Grupe, L., Huffman, L., & Bray, N. W. (1999). Mental retardation: A symptom and syndrome. In S. Netherton, D. Holmes, & C. E. Walker (Eds.), *Child and Adolescent Disorders: A Comprehensive Textbook.* New York: Oxford University Press.

Bruininks, R. H., Hill, B. K., Weatherman, R. F., & Woodcock, R. W. (1986). *Inventory for client and agency planning.* Allen, TX: DLM Teaching Resources.

Department of Mental Retardation Central Middlesex Office (2007, May). *The road forward: A resource guide.* Arlington, MA.

IDEA, Transition planning, and the statement of performance: A new use for the supports intensity scale. (2007, April). *SIS Vantage: Perspective on the Supports Intensity Scale, 2*(2).(Available from www.siswebsite.org/cs/newsletter/SISandtransitionplanning)

Jurlando, A. (n.d.). *The role of intelligence tests in qualifying students as mentally retarded: Are intelligence tests biased?* Fredericksburg, VA: Fredericksburg City Public Schools.

Lang, S. S. (2003, December 2). The year in which an IQ test is given can make the difference between life or death, Cornell researchers find. *Cornell News.*
(Available from www.news.cornell.edu/releases/Dec03/IQ.retardation.ssl.html)

*Mental retardation.* (n.d.) Psyweb.com. http://psyweb.com/Mdisord/jsp/menret.jsp.

Office of Developmental Programs. (2007). *Policy for determining eligibility for mental retardation services and supports.* (Available from www.dpw.state.pa.ua/servicesprograms/mentalretardation/003670129.htm)

Office of Health and Human Services (EOHHS). (2007). *Massachusetts comprehensive assessment process FAQs.* (Available from http://mass.gov)

**CHAPTER 5**

ADA-Americans with Disabilities Act Fact Sheet. (n.d.). *Kids Together, Inc. Legislation.*
(Available from www.kidstogether.org/leg_ada.htm)

The Arc of Massachusetts. (n.d.). *Transition from school to adult life fact sheet.* Waltham, MA: Author.

Chatzky, J. (2006, December). Your money & your life: Lending a hand to kids with special needs. *Money, 35*(12), 42-44.

Combined Jewish Philanthropies and Jewish Family Children's Service. (n.d.) *The CJP Community Trust: A pooled trust for people with disabilities.* 1-11.

Council of Better Business Bureaus' Foundation. (1992). *Access equal opportunity: Fun & fitness centers.* (Publication Number 24-282).

Council of Better Business Bureaus' Foundation. (1992). *Access equals opportunity: Restaurants & bars.* (Publication Number 24-279).

*Dual eligibility.* (2005). Centers for Medicare & Medicaid Services, U.S. Department of Health & Human Services. (Available from www.cms.hhs.gov/dualeligible)

*Federation for Children with Special Needs Newsline* [Entire issue]. (2008, Winter). *28*(3).

Guardianship for your children. (n.d.). *Nolo's Lawyer Directory.* (Available from www.nolo.com)

Hadi, M. (2007, February 4). *Financing the care of a disabled child.* The Arc of the United States.

Henry J. Kaiser Family Foundation. (2007, March). *Medicare: A primer.* (Publication Number 7615). Menlo Park, CA: Author. (Available from http://kff.org)

Hoyle, D., & Harris, K. (n.d.). *Re-thinking guardianship.* The Arc of Colorado. (Available from www.self-determination.com/articles/printrethinkguard.htm)

Kaiser Commission on Medicaid and the Uninsured. (2007). *State Children's Health Insurance Program (SCHIP) at a glance.* (Available from www.kff.org/medicaid/7610.cfm)

Kenney, E. L. (2008, April 3). Early Start gives special-needs pupils smooth transition to working world. *The News Journal,* pp. A1, A5.

Knipper, S. (2004, September). *EPSDT: Supporting children with disabilities.* Tualatin, OR: Human Services Research Institute.

Ludwig, P. (2007, summer). *Family circle*. Jewish Family & Children's Services News.

*Medicare eligibility tool*. (2007). Centers for Medicare & Medicaid Services, U.S. Department of Health and Human Services. (Available from www.medicare.gov/MedicareEligibility/home.asp)

Misilo, G. (2007). *Coming of age: A legal guide for individuals with developmental disabilities and their families on transitioning to adult services*. Worcester, MA: author. (Available from http://www.ftwlaw.com/legal_resources.php)

*Position statement on health care insurance reform*. (1995). National Down Syndrome Congress. (Available from www.ndsccenter.org/resources/position6.php)

*Term or whole life?* (2008). SmartMoney.com. (Available from www.smartmoney.com/insurance/life/index.cfm?story=lifeterm)

U.S. Department of Labor Employee Benefits Security Administration. (2004). *The Health Insurance Portability and Accountability Act (HIPPA): Section 602: Definitions*. (Available from www.dol.gov/ebsa/newsroom/fshipaa.html)

Wasik, J. F. (2007, June 14). Titles for "certified," "accredited" financial advisors can be misleading. *The Boston Globe,* p. D4.

Wikimedia Foundation. (1993). *Family and Medical Leave Act of 1993*. (Available from http://en.wikipedia.org/wiki/family_and_medical_leave_act)

**CHAPTER 6**

Department of Health and Human Services, Centers for Medicare & Medicaid Services. (2005). *Medicaid at-a-glance 2005: A Medicaid information source*. (Publication No. CMS-11024-05) Baltimore, MD: Author. (Available from www.cms.hhs.gov/MedicaidGenInfo/Downloads/MedicaidAtAGlance2005.pdf)

Department of Mental Retardation, Central Middlesex Office. (2007, May). *The road forward: A resource guide*. Arlington, MA.

Henry J. Kaiser Family Foundation. (2007, March). *Medicaid: A primer*. (Publication Number 7334-02). Menlo Park, CA: Author. (Available from http://kff.org)

Long-Bellill, L., Jordan, M., & and Landry, L. (2007). *Going to work: A guide to Social Security benefits and employment for young people with disabilities*. Boston, MA: Executive Office of Health and Human Services, Center for Human Policy and Research.

A qualitative study of the experiences of transition-age youth on disabilities in relation to SSI redetermination [Entire issue]. (2007). *Policy Research Brief, 18*(1).

Social Security Administration. (2008, Sept.). Disability evaluation under Social Security: Impairments that affect multiple body systems. (Available from www.socialsecurity.gov/disability/professionals/bluebook/10.00-MultipleBody-Adult.htm)

Social Security Administration. (2007, June). *Supplemental Security Income (SSI)*. (SSA Publication No. 05-11000, ICN 480200). (Available from www.socialsecurity.gov/pubs/11000.html)

**CHAPTER 7**

Blue-Banning, Martha. (2007). Making business ownership a reality. *Down Syndrome News, 30*(6), pp. 85-87.

Brevetti, F. (2007, August 20). Disabled entrepreneurs face uphill battle. *Contra Costa Times* (Available from www.microbiz.org/html/disabled_entrepreneurs_news.htm)

Ciulla Timmons, J., Hamner, D., & Bose, J. (2003, May). Four strategies to find a good job: Advice from job seekers with disabilities. *Tools for Inclusion, 11*(2).

*Exceptional Parent.* (2008, March). [Entire issue], *38*(3).

Fleming, A., & Loud, D. (2007, July). Increasing placement through professional networking. *The Institute Brief.*

Jordan, M., Sawires Yager, A., Enein-Donovan, L., Fike, J., Gilmore, M., & Tautkas, L. (2002, July). Starting with me: A guide to person-centered planning for job seekers. *Tools for Inclusion, 10*(1). (Available from www.communityinclusion.org/publications/pub.php?page=to14)

*The Road to Work: An Introduction to Vocational Rehabilitation.* (2009). Bloomington, MN: Pacer Center.

U. S. Equal Employment Opportunity Commission. (n.d.). *Questions & answers about persons with intellectual disabilities in the workplace and the Americans with Disabilities Act.* (Available from www.eeoc.gov/facts/intellectual_disabilities.html)

**CHAPTER 8**

*Housing: Where Will Our Children Live When They Grow Up?* (2007). Bloomington, MN: Pacer Center.

New report underscores growing housing crisis for low income persons with disabilities; The Arc responds. (2007). *inSight, 1*(2), 21.

O'Hara, A., Cooper, E., Zovistoski, A., & Buttrick, J. (2007, July). Priced out in 2006: People with disabilities left behind and left out of national housing policy. *Opening Doors* (30), 12. (Available from www.tacinc.org/pubs/pricedout.htm)

U.S. Department of Housing and Urban Development Homes & Communities. (2006). *HUD's Public housing program.* (Available from www.hud.gov/renting/phprog.cfm)

**CHAPTER 9**

The Adult Congenital Heart Association and the International Society for Adult Congenital Cardiac Disease. (2007). *ACHD Clinic Directory.* (Available from www.achaheart.org)

The Adult Congenital Heart Association. (n.d.). *Personal Health Passport.* Philadelphia, PA. (Available from www.achaheart.org)

Chicoine, Brian, & McGuire, Dennis. (2006). *Mental Wellness in Adults with Down Syndrome: A Guide to Emotional and Behavioral Strengths and Challenges.* Bethesda, MD: Woodbine House.

Cohen, William I., ed. (1999, September). Health care guidelines for individuals with Down syndrome. *Down Syndrome Quarterly, 4*(3). (Available from www.ds-health.com/health99.htm)

Horrell, S. C. V., MacLean, W. E., & Conley, V. M. (2006). Patient and parent/guardian perspective on the health care of adults with mental retardation. *Mental Retardation, 44*(4), 239-48.

*Transition to Adult Health Care: A Training Guide in Two Parts.* (2005). Madison, WI: Waisman Center. (Available from www.waisman.wisc.edu/hrtw/Publications.html)

**CHAPTER 10**

Blacher, J., & Baker, B. L. (2007). Positive impact of intellectual disability on families. *American Journal on Mental Retardation, 112*(5), 330-48.

Peterson, K. (2007). Supporting healthy adolescent development for youth with disabilities. *Advocate* (Fall), 20.

**CHAPTER 11**

Moseley, C., Salmi, P., & Johnstone, C. (Eds.). (2007, Spring/Summer). Feature issue on disaster preparedness and people with disabilities. *Impact, 20,* pp. 1-36.

National Resource Center on Supported Living and Choice, Center on Human Policy. (n.d.). *What is self-advocacy?* Syracuse, NY: Syracuse University. (Available from http://soeweb.syr.edu/thechp)

**CHAPTER 12**

Bonham, G. S., Basehart, S., Schalock, R. L., Marchand, C. B., Kirchner, N., & Rumenap, J. M. (2004). Consumer-based quality of life assessment: The Maryland Ask Me! Project. *Mental Retardation, 42*(5), pp. 338-55.

Disabled and Alone/Life Services for the Handicapped, Inc. (2005, Summer). *Lifelines.* [Entire issue].

Hall-Lande, J., & Hewitt, A. (2007). Individual and family directed services: Implications for the DSP workforce. *Impact, 20*(2), pp. 4-5.

Investopedia. *The greatest investors: Peter Lynch.* (2007). (Available from www.investopedia.com/university/greatest/peterlynch.asp)

McCulloh, N. (2007). Five things families can do to find and keep great DSPs. *Impact, 20*(2), pp. 8-9.

National Center on Secondary Education and Transition and PACER Center. (2002, March). *Parent Brief.*

Robison, R. (2007). From the president. *Down Syndrome News, 30*(3), p. 34.

# Resource Guide

ADVOCACY AND
SELF-ADVOCACY

**Advocating Change Together (ACT)**
1821 University Ave., Ste. 306-S
St. Paul, MN 55104
800-641-0059; 651-641-0297
www.selfadvocacy.org

**Best Buddies**
100 SE Second St., Ste. 2200
Miami, FL 33131
800-89-BUDDY (892-8339)
www.bestbuddies.org

**Kids As Self Advocates**
Family Voices, Inc.
2340 Alamo SE, Ste. 102
Albuquerque, NM 87106
785-273-3398
www.fvkasa.org

**Pacer Center**
8161 Normandale Blvd.
Bloomington, MN 55437
888-248-0822; 800-537-2237 (MN only)
www.pacer.org

**Self Advocates Becoming Empowered**
P.O. Box 30142
Kansas City, MO 64112
www.sabeusa.org

**CANADIAN RESOURCES**

**Best Buddies Canada**
907-1243 Islington Ave.
Toronto, Ontario M8X 1Y9
Canada
888-779-0061
www.bestbuddies.ca

**Canada Benefits**
800-O-CANADA (800-622-6232)
www.canadabenefits.gc.ca

**Canada Business**
Services for Entrepreneurs
888-576-4444
www.canadabusiness.ca/eng

**Canadian Association for Community Living**
Kinsmen Bldg., York University
4700 Keele St.
Toronto, Ontario M3J 1P3
Canada
416-661-9611
www.cacl.ca

**Canadian Association of Independent Living Centres**
402-214 Montreal Rd.
Ottawa, Ontario K1L 8L8
Canada
613-563-2581

**Canadian Down Syndrome Society**
5005 Dalhousie Dr., NW, # 283
Calgary, AL T3A 5R8
Canada
800-883-5608
www.cdss.ca

**Canadian Human Rights Commission**
344 Slater Street, 8th Floor
Ottawa, Ontario K1A 1E1
Canada
613-995-1151; 888-214-1090
www.chrc-ccdp.ca

**Special Olympics Canada**
60 St. Clair Avenue East, Suite 700
Toronto, Ontario M4T 1N5
Canada
416-927-9050
www.specialolympics.ca

**COMMUNITY LIVING AND INCLUSION**

**Independent Living Research Utilization**
2323 S. Shepherd, Ste. 1000
Houston, TX 77019
713-520-0232
www.bcm.edu/ilru

**Institute for Community Inclusion**
UMass Boston
100 Morrissey Blvd.
Boston, MA 02125
617-287-4300; 617-287-4352 (fax)
www.communityinclusion.org

**National Council on Independent Living**
1710 Rhode Island Ave., NW
Washington, DC 20036
202-207-2334
www.ncil.org

**National Home of Your Own Alliance**
Institute on Disability/UCED
University of New Hampshire
10 West Edge Dr., Ste. 101
Durham, NH 03824
603-862-4320
http://alliance.unh.edu/nhoyo.html

**U.S. Dept. of Housing and Urban Development**
451 7th St., SW
Washington, DC 20410
202-708-1112
www.hud.gov
    (Find information on the housing rights of people with disabilities under "Fair Housing.")

**DISABILITY ISSUES**

**The Arc of the United States**
1010 Wayne Ave., Ste. 650
Silver Spring, MD 20910
301-565-3842; 800-433-5255
www.thearc.org

**Disability.Gov**
"Connecting the Disability Community to Information and Opportunities"
www.disability.gov

**National Association of State Directors of Developmental Disabilities Services** (NASDDDS)
113 Oronoco St.
Alexandria, VA 22314
703-683-4202
www.nasddds.org

**National Dissemination Center for Children with Disabilities (NICHCY)**
1825 Connecticut Ave., NW, Ste. 700
Washington, DC 20009
800-695-0285; 202-884-8441 (fax)
www.nichcy.org
    (Clicking on "Educate Children 3-22" and then "Transition to Adulthood" takes you to parent-friendly, online publications on transition issues.)

## DOWN SYNDROME

**National Down Syndrome Congress**
1370 Center Dr., Ste. 102
Atlanta, GA 30338
800-232-6372; 770-604-9898 (fax)
www.ndsccenter.org

**National Down Syndrome Society**
666 Broadway
8th Floor
New York, NY 10012
800-221-4602
www.ndss.org

## EDUCATION

**Going to College**
www.going-to-college.org
    (Website for college-bound students with disabilities with online videos that teach about exploring interests, requesting accommodations, choosing a college, what to expect in college, etc.)

**IDEA 2004**
U.S. Dept. of Education
http://idea.ed.gov

**Kids Together, Inc.**
Information & Resources for Children & Adults with Disabilities
1111 18th St., NW, Suite 501
Washington, DC 20036
800-1-USA-ABLE
www.kidstogether.org

**National Center on Secondary Education and Transition (NCSET)**
Institute on Community Integration
University of Minnesota
6 Pattee Hall
Minneapolis, MN 55455
612-624-2097; 612-624-9344 (fax)
www.ncset.org

**Online Clearinghouse on Post-Secondary Education for Individuals with Disabilities**
HEATH Resource Center
George Washington University
2134 G St., NW
Washington, DC 20052
202-973-0904; 202-994-3365 (fax)
askHEATH@gwu.edu
www.heath.gwu.edu

**Think College**
College Options for People with Intellectual Disabilities
www.thinkcollege.net

**Transition Coalition**
University of Kansas
Dept. of Special Education
1122 W. Campus Rd., Rm. 521
Lawrence, KS 66045
785-0864-0686
www.transitioncoalition.org
 (The website has a searchable database of 18-21 programs—community-based transition programs in age-appropriate settings for students with disabilities aged 18-21.)

**EMPLOYMENT**

**Cornell University**
Employment and Disability Institute
www.passplan.org
 (Has an online tutorial called "Introduction to PASS" to help individuals learn about the Plan for Achieving Self Support and decide whether it is a good option for them.)

**Job Accommodation Network**
Office of Disability Employment Policy
P.O. Box 6080
Morgantown, WV 26506-6080
800-526-7234
www.jan.wvu.edu

**National Collaborative on Workforce and Disability for Youth**
4455 Connecticut Ave., NW, Ste. 310
Washington, DC 20008
877-871-0744; 877-871-0665 (fax)
http://ncwd-youth.info

**Rehabilitation Research and Training Center on Workplace Supports and Job Retention**
Virginia Commonwealth University
1314 W. Main St.
Richmond, VA 23284
www.worksupport.com

**U.S. Department of Labor**
200 Constitution Avenue NW
Washington, DC 20210
866-4-USA-DOL (866-487-2365)
www.dol.gov

**U.S. Equal Opportunity Employment Commission**
131 M St., NE
Washington, DC 20507
800-669-4000
www.eeoc.gov

**U.S. Small Business Administration**
409 Third Street SW
Washington, DC 20416
800-U-ASK-SBA (800-827-5722)
www.sba.gov

## HEALTH AND FITNESS

**Adult Congenital Heart Disease Association**
6757 Greene St., Ste. 335
Philadelphia, PA 19119
888-921-ACHA;
www.achaheart.org

**Down Syndrome: Health Issues**
www.ds-health.com

**Special Olympics**
113319th St., NW
Washington, DC 20036
202-628-3630; 800-700-8585
www.specialolympics.org

## LEGAL AND FINANCIAL RIGHTS AND BENEFITS

**ADA Document Portal**
National Network of ADA Centers
www.adata.org/adaportal

**Americans with Disabilities Act Home Page**
U.S. Dept. of Justice
950 Pennsylvania Ave., NW
Washington, DC 20530
800-514-0301
www.ada.gov

**Centers for Medicare and Medicaid Services**
7500 Security Blvd.
Baltimore, MD 21244
877-267-2323
www.cms.hhs.gov

**GovBenefits.gov**
800-333-4636
www.govbenefits.gov

**Social Security Administration**
Office of Public Inquiries
6401 Security Blvd.
Baltimore, MD 21235
800-772-1213
www.socialsecurity.gov

**State Coverage Initiatives**
Robert Wood Johnson Foundation
www.statecoverage.net
  (Gives state-specific information on who qualifies for Medicaid based on how their earnings compare to the federal poverty level (FPL). For example, in Maryland, working adults with disabilities can earn 300% of FPL and still qualify; nonworking adults with disabilities can only earn 74% of FPL.)

## TRANSITION

**FYI: Transition**
www.fyitransition.org

**Person Centered Planning Education Site**
Cornell University
Employment and Disability Institute
Ithaca, NY 14853
607-255-7727
www.ilr.cornell.edu/edi/pcp/index.html

**Post-ITT**
Postsecondary Innovative Transition Technology
postitt@postitt.org
www.postitt.org

**Youthhood.org**
www.youthhood.org
  (Website for young adults with disabilities to use in exploring transition issues.)

# Index

Jo Ann Simons, MSW, is well known in the area of intellectual disability and her commitment has enriched the lives of countless individuals. Jo Ann received her BA from Wheaton College in Norton, MA, in 1975 and received their Alumnae Achievement Award in 1990. She received her MSW from the University of Connecticut in 1977. Currently the President/CEO of The Cardinal Cushing Centers, Inc., in Massachusetts, she was formerly the Executive Director of the Arc of East Middlesex (1993-2008). She holds positions on the Boards of the National Down Syndrome Society and LIFE, Inc. of Cape Cod. Jo Ann has also served as a consultant to Special Olympics, Inc. and lectures throughout the world on issues on transition and future planning. Previously, she was the Deputy Superintendent of the Walter E. Fernald State School (1989-1993), the Director of Policy for the Massachusetts Department of Mental Retardation (1988-1989), President of the National Down Syndrome Congress (1983-1991), and on the Board of Directors of Special Olympics International (1989-1995). She has been recognized by the Arc of Massachusetts with the Distinguished Service Award in 2005, Massachusetts Department of Mental Retardation Human Rights award in 1988, the Dr. Allen Crocker Award of Excellence from the Massachusetts Down Syndrome Congress in 2006, and the National Down Syndrome Society in 2004 for Vision, National Leadership and Advocacy. As a parent, professional, and leader, Jo Ann has challenged herself and those around her to turn problems into answers and challenges into opportunities.

Jo Ann and her husband, Chet Derr, have two adult children, Jonathan and Emily. Jonathan, who has Down syndrome, is a graduate of Swampscott, MA, High School and Cape Cod Community College. Currently, Jon lives independently in his own home on Cape Cod and has a life filled with meaningful paid work, important volunteer activities, many leisure pursuits and close friends. Emily, who reminds her that being "typical" is also special, is an attorney.